Major-General Sir C. E. Pereira, K.C.B., C.M.G.,
commanded the 2nd Division from 27th December 1916 until the break up of the Division on the Rhine, March 1919.

THE HISTORY OF THE SECOND DIVISION

Vol. II. 1916 – 1918

By
EVERARD WYRALL

PUBLISHED BY
THE NAVAL & MILITARY PRESS

PRINTED & BOUND BY ANTONY ROWE LTD, EASTBOURNE

PREFACE.

In writing this *History of the Second Division*, I have been extremely fortunate in having access, not only to the official War Diaries, but also to private diaries kept by officers of the Division. I willingly, therefore, acknowledge the great assistance afforded me by the private diaries kept (from 1914 to 1918) by Major-General Sir C. E. Pereira, K.C.B., C.M.G., and for the loan of maps and documents which have enabled me to follow accurately the operations of the Division; also the valuable help given me by Colonel C. P. Deedes, C.B., C.M.G., D.S.O., who (with General Pereira) has read the MS. of the *History*, and has supplemented this assistance by the loan of maps and documents. To other officers also of the Division who were kind enough to lend me their private diaries I extend my grateful thanks. And lastly, but not least, I wish to acknowledge the courtesy and help afforded me at all times by the Director and Staff of the Historical Section (Military Branch) of the Committee of Imperial Defence, without whose assistance it would at times have been almost impossible to unravel many of the intricacies which frequently confront an author of military histories.

EVERARD WYRALL.

AUTHORS' CLUB.

CONTENTS.

IV. THE ADVANCE TO THE HINDENBURG LINE.

OPERATIONS ON THE ANCRE.

TRENCH WARFARE, 13TH JANUARY TO 16TH FEBRUARY 1917	357
THE ACTIONS OF MIRAUMONT, 17TH AND 18TH FEBRUARY 1917	365
THE CAPTURE OF IRLES, 10TH MARCH 1917	377
THE GERMAN RETREAT TO THE HINDENBURG LINE, 14TH MARCH TO 5TH APRIL 1917	390

V. THE ALLIED OFFENSIVES, 1917.

THE BATTLES OF ARRAS, 1917.

THE BATTLE OF VIMY RIDGE, 9TH TO 14TH APRIL	405
TRENCH WARFARE, 15TH TO 27TH APRIL	414
THE BATTLE OF ARLEUX, 28TH TO 29TH APRIL	418
THE THIRD BATTLE OF THE SCARPE:	
Capture of Fresnoy, 3rd to 4th May	437
A NOTE ON THE SITUATION IN THE SPRING OF 1917	445
THE SECOND DIVISION MOVES BACK TO ITS OLD SECTOR, NORTH AND SOUTH OF THE LA BASSÉE CANAL	448
TRENCH WARFARE, 20TH JUNE TO 4TH OCTOBER 1917	454

THE CAMBRAI OPERATIONS, 20TH NOVEMBER TO 7TH DECEMBER 1917.

THE BATTLE OF CAMBRAI:	
The Tank Attack and the Capture of Bourlon Wood	475
THE GERMAN COUNTER-ATTACKS, 30TH NOVEMBER TO 3RD DECEMBER:	
I. 30th November	484
II. 1st to 3rd December	500
The Withdrawal from the Bourlon Salient	508
TRENCH WARFARE, 7TH DECEMBER 1917 TO 20TH MARCH 1918	515

CONTENTS.

VI. THE GERMAN OFFENSIVES, 1918.
THE OFFENSIVE IN PICARDY,
21ST MARCH TO 5TH APRIL 1918.

THE FIRST BATTLES OF THE SOMME, 1918	537
A NOTE ON THE GENERAL SITUATION IN MARCH 1918	537
THE BATTLE OF ST. QUENTIN, 21ST TO 23RD MARCH 1918	541
THE FIRST BATTLE OF BAPAUME, 24TH TO 25TH MARCH 1918	560
THE WITHDRAWAL TO THE OLD BRITISH FRONT LINE, 26TH MARCH 1918	583
THE LAST DAYS OF MARCH 1918 AND THE RESUMPTION OF TRENCH WARFARE	587
A NOTE ON THE GENERAL SITUATION BETWEEN 21ST MARCH AND 8TH AUGUST 1918	598

VII. THE ADVANCE TO VICTORY, 1918.
THE ADVANCE IN PICARDY.

THE SECOND BATTLES OF THE SOMME, 1918	607
THE SITUATION UP TO "ZERO" ON 21ST AUGUST	607
THE BATTLE OF ALBERT, 21ST TO 23RD AUGUST 1918	615
THE CAPTURE OF MORY COPSE, 24TH AUGUST 1918	622
THE CAPTURE OF BEHAGNIES AND SAPIGNIES BY THE 5TH INFANTRY BRIGADE, 25TH AUGUST 1918	624
FROM 26TH AUGUST TO 1ST SEPTEMBER 1918	627

THE BREAKING OF THE HINDENBURG LINE: THE SECOND BATTLES OF ARRAS, 1918.

THE BATTLE OF THE DROCOURT–QUÉANT LINE, 2ND TO 3RD SEPTEMBER	635
OPERATIONS FROM 4TH TO 8TH SEPTEMBER	640

THE BATTLES OF THE HINDENBURG LINE.

THE BATTLE OF HAVRINCOURT, 12TH SEPTEMBER 1918	647
THE BATTLE OF THE CANAL DU NORD, 27TH SEPTEMBER TO 1ST OCTOBER 1918	656
THE BATTLE OF CAMBRAI, 1918 (8TH TO 9TH OCTOBER): The Capture of Forenville by the Second Division	669
THE BATTLE OF THE SELLE, 17TH TO 25TH OCTOBER 1918	676
THE RETURN TO MONS, THE MARCH INTO GERMANY, AND THE BREAK-UP OF THE SECOND DIVISION	689
APPENDICES	697
INDEX	715

LIST OF MAPS.

1. The Courcelette Sector in January 1917 356
2. The Actions of Miraumont, 17th–18th February 1917 . 364
3. The Capture of Grevillers Trench, 10th March 1917 . . 376
4. The German Retreat to the Hindenburg Line . . . 398
5. The Battle of Arleux, 28th–29th April 1917 . . . 436
6. The Third Battle of the Scarpe: the Capture of Fresnoy, 3rd–4th May 1917. The Operations of the Composite Brigade, 2nd Division 438
7. The Battle of Cambrai, 1917: the German Counter-attacks, 30th November–3rd December . . . 484
8. The Rat's Tail: Rearguard Action by the 17th Royal Fusiliers on the 30th November 1917 486
9. The German Offensives, 1918: the Battle of St. Quentin, 21st–23rd March 1918: Operations of the 2nd Division 540
10. The First Battle of Bapaume, 24th–25th March 1918, and the Withdrawal of the 2nd Division to the Old British Front Line, 26th March 1918. 560
10a. A Fight to the Finish: Action of the 2nd Battalion, Machine Gun Corps, in front of Rocquigny, 24th March 1918 568
11. The Advance to Victory: the Battle of Albert, 21st–23rd August 1918. The Capture of Moyblain Trench and Ervillers 614
12. The Capture of Mory Copse, 24th August 1918 . . . 622
13. The Capture of Behagnies and Sapignies, 25th August 1918 624

LIST OF MAPS.

14. The Battle of the Drocourt–Quéant Line, 2nd–3rd September 1918: Action of the 2nd Division on the right of the Battle Line 634
15. Operations of the 2nd Division from 4th–8th September 1918 640
16. The Battle of Havrincourt, 12th September 1918: and Preliminary Operations by the 2nd Division on the night 11th September 646
17. The Battle of the Canal du Nord, 27th September–1st October 1918, and the Capture of Mont sur l'Œuvres by the 2nd Division. 658
18. The Battle of Cambrai, 1918: the Capture of Forenville by the 2nd Division. 668
19. The Battle of the Selle, 17th–25th October 1918 . . 676

IV.
THE ADVANCE TO THE HINDENBURG LINE.

OPERATIONS ON THE ANCRE.
   Trench Warfare, 13th January to 16th February 1917.
   The Actions of Miraumont, 17th and 18th February 1917.
   Capture of Irles, 10th March 1917.

GERMAN RETREAT TO THE HINDENBURG LINE,
   14th March to 5th April 1917.

THE COURCELETTE SECTOR.

(Facing p.

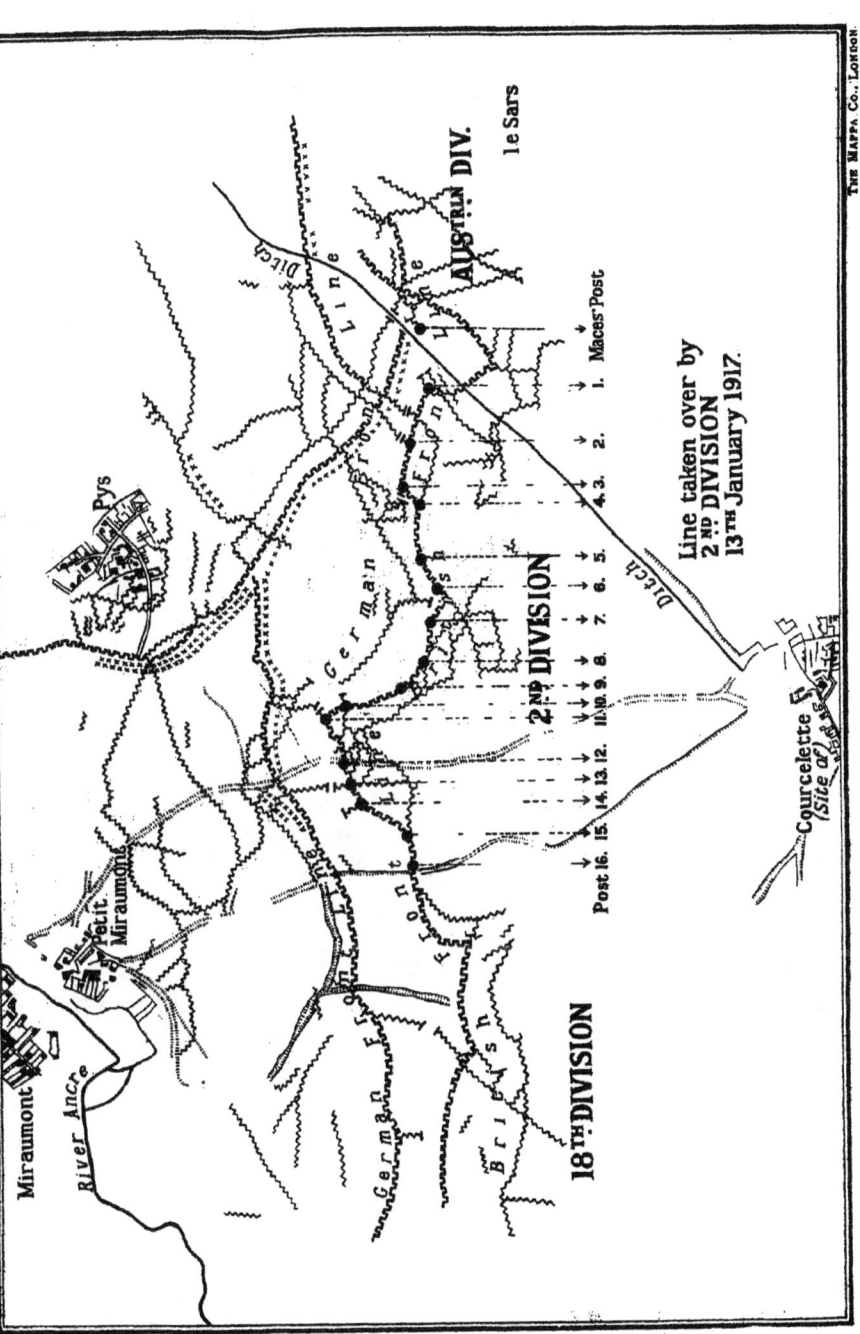

OPERATIONS ON THE ANCRE.

Trench Warfare, 13th January–16th February 1917.

NEW YEAR'S DAY, 1917, still found the 2nd Division training and resting in the Brailly area, north-east of Abbeville. The Division had been transferred from the Vth Corps, and on going into the line would be in the IInd Corps area. On 6th January the Divisional Artillery relieved the artillery of the 51st Division in the line, and at 7 p.m. on the same day 2nd Divisional Order No. 181 was issued: " On the 9th January the 2nd Division (less R.A.) will march to the Bernaville area . . . on the 11th January it will march to the Marieux area . . . on the 12th and 13th it will move up to take over the line now held by the 51st (Highland) Division." The 51st Division held the Courcelette sector—a line somewhat resembling in shape an arrow-head, about 2,000 yards due north of the remains of the village of Courcelette, and between Le Sars and Grandcourt.

1ST JAN. 1917.

And here, between the move forward and the arrival of the 2nd Division in the Courcelette sector, it is desirable to introduce an outline of the general situation and the scheme of operations in which the Division was to take part.

" At the conclusion of the operations of the 13th November and the following days," said Sir Douglas Haig, " the enemy still held the whole of the Ancre Valley from Le Transloy to Grandcourt, and his first line of defence lay along the lower northern slopes of the Thiepval Ridge.

" North of the Ancre, he still held the greater part of the spur above Beaumont Hamel. Beyond that point the original German front line, in which the enemy had established himself two years previously, ran past Serre, Gommecourt, and Monchy-au-Bois to the northern slopes of the main watershed, and then north-east down to the valley of the River Scarpe east of Arras.

" Besides the positions held by him on our immediate front, and in addition to the fortified villages of the Ancre Valley with their connecting trenches, the enemy had prepared along the forward crest of the ridge north of the Ancre Valley a strong second system of defence. This consisted of a double line of trenches, heavily wired, and ran north-west from Saillisel past Le Transloy to the Albert-Bapaume road, where it turned west past Grevillers and Loupart Wood, and then north-west again past Achiet-le-Petit to Bucquoy. This system, which was known as the Le Transloy-Loupart line, both by reason of its situation and as a result of the skill and industry expended on its preparation, constituted an exceedingly strong natural defensive position, second only to that from which the enemy had recently been driven on the Morval-Thiepval Ridge. Parallel to this line, but on the far side of the crest, he had constructed, towards the close of the past year, a third defensive system on the line Rocquigny-Bapaume-Ablainzevelle.

"The first object of our operations in the Ancre Valley was to advance our trenches to within assaulting distance of the Le Transloy-Loupart line."

These operations were begun on 18th November on the German line overlooking the villages of Pys and Grandcourt: "Valuable positions were gained on a front of about 5,000 yards, while a simultaneous attack north of the Ancre considerably improved the situation of our troops in the Beaucourt Valley." But the bad weather of the latter part of November and December had put a stop to offensive operations, and the improvement of trenches and of the roads and communication trenches occupied the attention of the troops. A rearrangement of the artillery, so as to take full advantage of the new positions for the concentration of fire, also took place.

Early in January the weather improved, and a number of small operations were possible, the most important of which was the capture (on 11th January by the 7th Division) of 1,500 yards of the enemy's trench along the crest of the spur east and north-east of Beaumont Hamel.

At this period the 2nd Division [1] was in the process of marching forward to take up its new position in the Courcelette sector. Divisional Headquarters were opened at Marieux at noon on the 11th, and in the evening final orders for the relief of the 51st Division were issued.

"The 2nd Division will relieve the 51st (Highland) Division in the line on 12th and 13th January. The 5th Infantry Brigade will

[1] The fighting strength of the 2nd Division on 6th January 1917 was given as: Officers, 422; other ranks, 13,733.

THE COURCELETTE SECTOR.   359

relieve the 154th Infantry Brigade in the front brigade area on the nights 12th-13th and 13th-14th. The General Officer Commanding 2nd Division will assume command of the right sector at 11 a.m. on 13th January. The 6th Infantry Brigade will be brigade in support area; the 99th Infantry Brigade will be brigade in reserve area."

The new front to be taken over by the 2nd Division was very different from the line held in the Beaumont Hamel-Hebuterne sector. In the latter the front line was held in trenches; in the Courcelette sector the front line consisted of " Posts." The sector was well described in a private diary thus: " The frontage is 2,500 yards, and the right of our line is about 1,000 yards west of Le Sars; the left, a mile south of the eastern edge of Miraumont, Pys being about 1,200 yards north of the centre of our line. The front line consists of 18 disconnected posts and platoons in close support—total, 10 platoons. Behind this there is nothing until one reaches the dug-outs in the West Miraumont road just north of Courcelette, where there are three platoons. There are three platoons in Courcelette, two companies west, and two south of it: total, two battalions. Ironside Avenue runs forward 800 yards from the West Miraumont road. That is the sole communication trench forward. There are brushwood tracks to near the front line, but they can only be used at night." [1]

The 24th Royal Fusiliers and the 2nd Highland Light Infantry of the 5th Infantry Brigade were detailed as the relieving battalions, the former on the right, the latter on the left. The 2nd Oxford and Bucks were ordered to remain in support at Wolfe Huts and the 17th Royal Fusiliers in reserve in Ovillers huts and dug-outs, near Ovillers La Boiselle Village. The 5th Machine-Gun Company was to take over the gun-positions held by the 154th Machine-Gun Company.

The relief began during the late afternoon of the 12th, when guides from the 51st Division met the relieving troops at 4.30 p.m. The strength of the garrison of each post varied from 9 to 20 men. The reliefs were completed without incident, the General Officer Commanding 2nd Division assuming command of the sector at 11 a.m. on the 13th January. Divisional Headquarters were now established at Usna Hill. The 2nd Division had on its right the 15th Division, and on its left the 18th Division. Nothing of importance happened on the Divisional front during the remainder of January—no tactical incidents of interest are reported in the

12TH JAN 1917.

[1] Diary of Major-General C. E. Pereira, C.B., C.M.G.

diaries. But much hard work was done on the defences and communications. When the Division took over the line none of the posts forming the front line could boast adequate head-cover, the tracks to the posts, made of brushwood, were out of repair, and as for Ironside Avenue, the main communication trench, it was impassable. But the brigades not in the line detailed large working parties, and these, in conjunction with the Sappers and Pioneers, rapidly improved conditions in the Divisional area. Cleaning, boarding, pumping, and deepening trenches occupied the troops day and night, whilst trench tramways were being built under the guidance of the Field Companies, Royal Engineers.

No raids were made by the Division during January, and only one was attempted by the enemy, and that did not materialize, for the attacking troops were caught by machine-gun fire ere they had cleared their own wire, and leaving 4 dead and 3 wounded men on the ground, they retired quickly to their own trenches.

The guns were less active, but hostile aircraft were very persistent, and considerable aerial activity prevailed.

The bitterly cold weather which froze the ground hard, interfered with building operations, and made life in the trenches generally unpleasant and uncomfortable.

On the 20th January the IInd Corps took over command of the front.

On the 21st January Brigadier-General A. C. Daly was invalided home to England, and Brigadier-General R. K. Walsh, D.S.O., assumed command of the 6th Infantry Brigade.

Towards the end of the month the Divisional area began to assume a very different appearance, though the communications were as yet far from perfect. So bad were the latter when the Division took over the line that (and it may seem strange to write it) no one possessed an accurate knowledge of the actual positions of the front-line posts. " It was not," said the General Officer Commanding on the 29th January, " until we got these photographs [air photographs of the Divisional area] that we had an accurate knowledge where our front posts really were." Reliefs often failed to find the posts they were sent out to relieve. And heavy snowstorms frequently added to the difficulties.

North of the 2nd Division the chief gain during January was the remainder of the Beaumont Hamel spur, the possession of which afforded splendid facilities for observation.

A certain number of casualties amongst officers and men were incurred. Captain H. W. Hill, M.C., of the 2nd Oxford and Bucks,

DIVISIONAL ARTILLERY REORGANIZED. 361

was killed by a shell whilst the battalion was relieving the 24th Royal Fusiliers on the evening of the 16th. Lieut. W. W. Edwards of the 17th Royal Fusiliers was wounded on the 18th, and died of his wounds on the 22nd.

Orders for the re-organization of the Divisional Artillery were received on 25th, and were carried out as follows:

Headquarters, R.A.: Brigadier-General S. H. Sanders, C.M.G., D.S.O., G.O.C., R.A.
    Major C. R. B. Carrington, D.S.O., Brigade Major.
    Captain R. H. R. Scott, M.C., D.T.M.O.
    Captain A. Kirby, Staff Captain.
    Lieut. A. H. Gillingham, Staff Lieut.
XXXVIth Brigade R.F.A.: Lieut.-Colonel A. A. Goschen, D.S.O.
    15th Battery, 6–18-pounders: Major V. Walrond.
    48th Battery, 6–18-pounders: Major H. F. Grant Suttie, M.C.
    71st Battery, 6–18-pounders: Major A. A. M. Durand.
    C/36 + Right Section D/34, 6–4.5-inch howitzers: Major F. L. V. Mills.
XLIst Brigade, R.F.A.: Lieut.-Colonel J. G. Dooner.
    9th Battery, 6–18-pounders: Major B. B. Quiller-Couch, M.C.
    16th Battery, 6–18-pounders: Major G. Messervie.
    17th Battery, 6–18-pounders: Major A. T. Sloan.
    47th Battery + Left Section D/34, 6–4.5 howitzers: Captain W. D. Dyson, M.D.
Divisional Ammunition Column. Lieut.-Colonel St. L. L. H. du Plat Taylor, D.S.O.

The XXXIVth Brigade R.F.A. (Lieut.-Colonel C. F. P. Parry, D.S.O.) became an Army Artillery Brigade under the new organization scheme. At this date it was formed of 50th Battery, 6–18-pounders; 70th Battery, 6–18-pounders; A/60th, 6–18 pounders, which became C/34; 56th Battery – $\frac{1}{2}$ of C/60th, 6–4.5 howitzers.

On the 1st February the 1st East Anglian Field Company R.E. was re-named the 483rd Field Company R.E.

The month opened fine and cold, with the ground still frozen hard, hampering digging operations. Carrying parties were, however, better able to bring up material. Preparations for the next offensive were in active progress.

On 1st February 2nd Divisional Order No. 187 ordered the 1st Royal Berks (99th Infantry Brigade) to carry out a raid on the enemy's trenches on the night 4th–5th February. The objec-

1ST FEB

tive was the "enemy's salient at the point of Guard and Desire Support Trench in M.13,b." Besides inflicting damage, the objects of the raid were to secure prisoners or obtain identifications, destroy or capture machine guns, and observe the state of the enemy's trenches, and his method of holding the line.

No artillery preparation was to take place before "zero," but after that hour a box-barrage was to be put down round the objective. Other points in the operation order are interesting: "In the event of snow still lying, white suits will be worn by the raiding party; all identifications are to be removed from the party before they go up into the line; Stokes mortars will be employed prior to the infantry assault. An understudy to the officer commanding the party is to be selected; he will take over command immediately in the event of the latter becoming a casualty. All members of the party are warned that in the event of being taken prisoner they are only bound to give their rank and name; no other information is to be given."

The raiding party was to consist of 2 officers and 60 other ranks, exclusive of stretcher-bearers.

From the night 28th–29th January to the night 1st–2nd February the 1st Royal Berks held the right sub-sector of the line, which included M.13,b, the objective. The battalion was relieved by the 22nd Royal Fusiliers on the night 1st–2nd, and on going into support at Wolfe Huts near Ovillers La Boiselle Village existing trenches almost identical with the objective were found and improved, and five practices were carried out by the raiding party by day and by night.

At 6 p.m. on the 2nd, the party, under Second-Lieuts. Burgess and Aveline, moved to the Miraumont dug-outs, where a meal and accommodation were found for them.

"Zero" hour had been fixed for 3 a.m. on the 5th.

A personal reconnaissance of the enemy's wire was made by Lieut.-Colonel Harris, D.S.O., the Commanding Officer 1st Royal Berks, who subsequently placed the raiding party in position.

"Three small wooden tripods covered with canvas (black on our side, white on the enemy's side) marking the flanks and centre of the party, had been placed beforehand in No Man's Land, about 30 yards outside our wire, and parallel to the enemy's trench. The men, dressed in white smocks with white helmet covers, crawled out in pairs, and were on the alignment (in two waves of about 30 men each, about 15 yards apart) 15 minutes before 'zero.' Three similar tripods had also been placed parallel to the three already

RAIDING THE ENEMY.

mentioned, and 30 to 40 yards nearer the enemy's line. These gave the direction of the advance, and proved effective."

5TH FEB.

At "zero" hour the Stokes guns of the 99th Trench Mortar Battery opened fire on the objective; this was maintained for one minute. One gun had been specially detailed to fire "rapid" on the enemy post at M.13,b.4.9.

The Divisional Artillery (18-pounders and howitzers) then placed a box-barrage round the objective, and the raiding party moved forward to within 50 yards of the objective and lay down.

One minute after "zero," as the Stokes guns ceased firing, the party jumped up and rushed forward. The leading wave (Second-Lieut. Aveline) jumped the eastern arm of the salient on a front of about 40 yards, with its left about M.13,b.9.5, formed to the left, and then went for the western arm of the salient—its objective. The rear wave (Second-Lieut. Burgess) crossed the enemy's wire, jumped the trench, turned to the left, and ran down outside the parados, until they met the enemy, most of whom, including two German officers, they found near the front of the salient. A few Germans who offered resistance were shot. The men then jumped into the enemy's trench, and in a few minutes all resistance was at an end.

It is a pity that further details of this successful little operation were not available. The raiding party had to pass through three rows of concertina barbed wire, $2\frac{1}{2}$ feet thick. Two officers and 49 other ranks were taken prisoners, 14 were killed or wounded, and a German machine gun smashed. The Berkshires were only from fifteen to twenty minutes in the enemy's line, during which they searched all dug-outs and shelters before returning to their own trenches. The artillery barrage was very effective in deceiving the enemy.

Casualties were: 1 officer (Second-Lieut. Burgess) severely wounded; 1 other rank killed and 11 other ranks wounded.

No German counter-attack was attempted.

Later in the day telegrams were received from the Corps Commander and from the General Officer Commanding 15th Division, congratulating the gallant Berkshires on their exploit, and the officer in charge of the raid, Second-Lieut. Burgess, was awarded the D.S.O. by the Commander-in-Chief.

Another raid on similar lines was ordered to be carried out on the night of 8th–9th February. The attacking party was drawn from the 17th Royal Fusiliers, 5th Infantry Brigade, the latter having relieved the 99th Brigade during the night

5th–6th. The date was, however, subsequently altered to the night of the 10th.

The objective was a portion of Desire Support Trench for a distance of 200 yards south of the sap at R.12,c.95.15, and the sap itself. "Zero" hour was at 8.5 p.m.

The raiding party consisted of Second-Lieut. Joelson and Second-Lieut. Antill and 34 other ranks, exclusive of a covering party and stretcher-bearers.

10TH FEB. During the night of the 9th the 17th Royal Fusiliers were relieved by the 2nd Highland Light Infantry, and on the morning of the 10th the raid was practised over taped ground near Wolfe Huts. At 3 p.m. the whole paraded and marched to Fraser's Post, where tea was ready for them. Near Battalion Headquarters rum was issued to the men, white smocks and helmet covers put on, and the party marched in small groups to the position of assembly behind Posts 9 and 10. By 7.15 p.m. all were in position.

At 7.55 p.m. the raiding party crawled out and got into position in front of the wire. Ten minutes later the artillery opened intense fire for three minutes, while two parties of rifle grenadiers fired into the enemy's sap. During this time the raiders continued to crawl forward. At 8.8 p.m. both artillery and rifle grenadiers ceased fire, and the raiders rushed forward and jumped into the enemy's trench. A number of the enemy were seen running away, and these were shot down. Four dug-outs were found, and as the occupants could not be induced to come out and surrender they were bombed and blown to pieces. Seven prisoners belonging to the 90th Mecklenburg Regiment were taken.

The raiding party suffered 13 casualties: Lieut. Joelson and 6 other ranks were wounded, 3 other ranks killed, and 3 missing.

12TH FEB. The Germans next attempted a raid (on the 12th), and the story of it is admirably told in a condensed form in the 2nd Division General Staff Diary: "Usna Hill. 7.50 p.m. A party of Germans, wearing white, endeavoured to raid our trenches between Nos. 9 and 10 Posts, R.18,a.9.5, and R.12,c.7.1 (the point from which the 17th Royal Fusiliers made their raid). The party crossed our front line where it was unoccupied, when they were fired on from No. 10 Post. They then turned and went towards No. 9 Post, and then retired across No Man's Land. Five dead Germans were found between Nos. 9 and 10 Posts. The enemy's machine guns prevented our patrols from finding any dead Germans in No Man's Land. There were no documents or badges on any of the men. One wounded man of the 90th Regiment was taken prisoner. One N.C.O. and

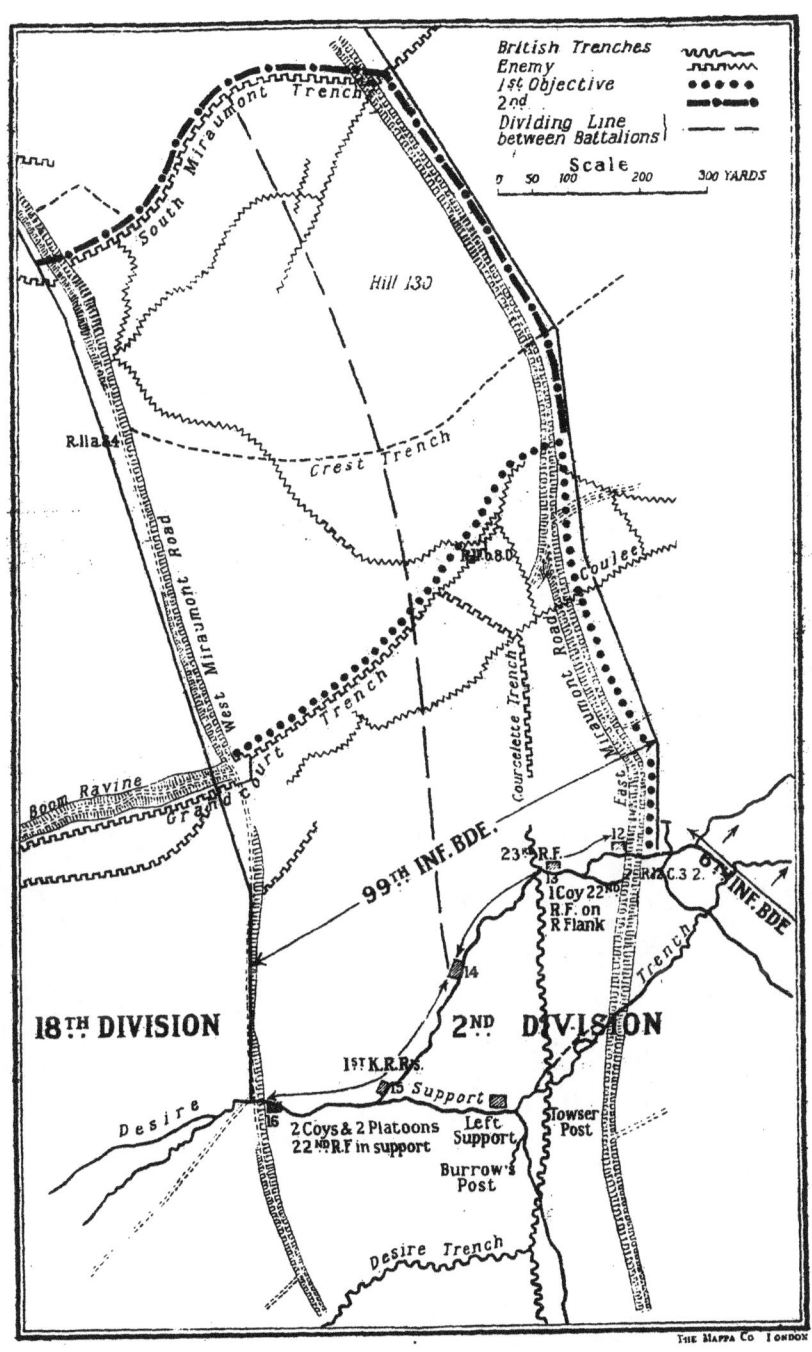

THE ACTIONS OF MIRAUMONT,
17th–18th February 1917.

(Facing p 364)

6 of our men were taken prisoners. They formed a Lewis gun detachment which was placed between Nos. 9 and 10 Posts."

The enemy raiding party consisted of about 70 men.

The Actions of Miraumont, 17th and 18th February 1917.

Early on the morning of the 12th February, at 7 a.m., 2nd Division Headquarters issued Operation Order No. 192, which stated that : " The IInd Corps will at an early date capture, with the 2nd and 18th Divisions, the approximate line : East Miraumont road from point R.12,c.3.2. to point R.5,a.8.0, thence along the road running to point R.10,b.2.9.–point R.4,c.8.0, and thence along the railway line to point R.9,b.2.3.

" At the same time the 2nd and 63rd Divisions will make subsidiary attacks, and capture the enemy's trenches on the approximate lines :

" 2nd Division—M.14,a.15.45, to R.12,c.90.15.

" 63rd Division—Sunken Road from point R.3,c.35.70 to its junction with Swan Trench (R.3,a.1.8.) and thence along Swan Trench to point R.2,b.05.65."

The operations on the Ancre begun on 18th November had already resulted in the gain of the Beaumont Hamel spur and Grandcourt. The task of driving the enemy from his positions in the Beaucourt Valley was resumed on the night of the 10th–11th February, and was successful. Determined counter-attacks by the enemy failed.

" The village of Serre now formed the point of a very pronounced salient, which further progress along the Ancre Valley would render increasingly difficult, if not impossible, for the enemy to hold. Accordingly an operation on a somewhat larger scale than anything hitherto attempted since the new year, was now undertaken. Its object was to carry our line forward along the spur which runs northwards from the main Morval–Thiepval Ridge about Courcelette, and so gain possession of the high ground at its northern extremity. The possession of this high ground, besides commanding the approaches to Pys and Miraumont from the south, would give observation over the upper valley of the Ancre, in which many hostile batteries were situated in positions enabling their fire to be directed for the defence of the Serre sector. At the same time arrangements were made for a smaller attack on the opposite banks of the river designed to seize a portion of the sunken road lying along the eastern crest of the second spur north of the Ancre, and so obtain control of the approaches to Miraumont from the west." [1]

Such were the intentions of the Commander-in-Chief.

The objectives of the 2nd Division were :

    1st : Grandcourt Trench from the eastern end of Boom Ravine to East Miraumont road.

    2nd : South Miraumont Trench between the East and West Miraumont roads.

    3rd : The road skirting the south-east edge of Petit Miraumont.

This was to be the main attack.

On the capture of each objective a defensive flank was to be formed facing north-east along the East Miraumont road.

The objective of the subsidiary attack was the Desire Support Trench, which formed the south-western face of an enemy salient.

Both attacks were to be simultaneous.

The 99th Infantry Brigade was ordered to carry out the main attack, and the 6th Infantry Brigade the subsidiary attack on Desire Support.

The two brigades disposed the following troops in the front line : 99th Infantry Brigade—23rd Royal Fusiliers on the right, with one company of 22nd Royal Fusiliers to form the defensive flank ; the 1st King's Royal Rifle Corps on the left, with two platoons 22nd Royal Fusiliers and two companies of the latter battalion in support, with orders to go through and capture the third objective ; the 1st Royal Berks were in support. The 6th Infantry Brigade—2nd South Staffords in the front line, to make the subsidiary attack.

The assaulting parties for each objective were ordered to go forward in four waves, each about 50 yards apart—*i.e.*, one assaulting wave followed by one " mopping up " wave, and then two more assaulting waves.

Some idea of the development of warfare may be gathered from the following extract from Brigade Orders laying down the fighting kit and other matters connected with the attack : " All officers will be dressed and equipped in the same manner as the men—badges of rank may be retained ; rifle, bayonet, scabbard, entrenching tool, box-respirator and helmets as issued ; haversacks and mess-tins on back ; 170 rounds of small arms ammunition per man—bombers, signallers, scouts, machine and Lewis gunners, and the personnel of the Stokes Mortar Batteries will carry 50 rounds only ; three grenades per

[1] Official Dispatches.

A SOLDIER'S EQUIPMENT IN 1917.

man; steel helmets; one aeroplane flare per man to be used at certain stated times after reaching the objective, or in reply to a call from a contact aeroplane; two sandbags per man; the unexpended portion of the day's rations, water bottle filled with tea and rum; one iron ration; and a bread and cheese ration; wire cutters and flares will be carried by the assaulting waves; Véry pistols and cartridges and S.O.S. cartridges for same will be carried by officers. Red, green, and white cartridges, in addition to being used for the authorized S.O.S. signals, will be employed to communicate information in accordance with a code which will be issued later; one Tommies' Cooker per man; fusees will be distributed amongst the leading waves; runners will carry out their duties stripped—*i.e.*, no arms, or equipment excepting the box-respirators and tube helmets; greatcoats for runners will be kept at Relay Posts or at Headquarters; greatcoats or jerkins, or both, will be worn underneath the equipment at the discretion of the battalion commanders—if greatcoats are worn, the coats will be folded back off the knees; shovels and a percentage of picks," completed the outfit of the British soldier about to make an attack in February 1917.

"Zero" hour had been fixed for 5.45 a.m. on the morning of the 17th. There was no preliminary artillery barrage, 50 per cent. of the guns opening at "zero" on the enemy's front line, and the remainder on 200 yards in front of the British line, with lifts of 100 yards every 3 minutes; 30 minutes' halt on each objective.

17TH FEB. MAP.

Great care had been exercised in getting the troops into their assembly trenches punctually and correctly. This was no easy matter, since the elements had again interfered—a rapid thaw having set in which caused seas of mud to collect along the communication trenches. Thus rapid progress was considerably hampered.

During the forming-up operations the enemy kept up a continuous barrage of varying intensity which seemed to reach a climax about 5 a.m. Showers of coloured lights went up from his support and reserve lines: he was evidently in a very jumpy condition. The effect of the barrage was not very serious, excepting so far as it concerned the 99th Trench Mortar Battery, which had all its stores destroyed and rendered useless for the purpose of the operations. The Commanding Officer of the battery was also wounded some time before "zero."

It was still dark at 5.45 a.m. when the assault was made on

the first objective, and the rapid thaw had made the ground very muddy.

" It was practically a night attack," said one of the Brigade Diaries. Darkness, added to the very heavy going occasioned by the sudden thaw, made progress very slow, and the distance between the troops and the barrage gradually became more pronounced.

A and C Companies of the King's Royal Rifles went forward in four waves, followed by B and D Companies, by sections in single file. The two first-named companies went forward well, but the two latter lost direction quickly, being pushed to the right by troops of the 18th Division, who were out of their alignment. The mopping-up parties of C Company pushed straight up the Boom Ravine, along the West Miraumont road, and cleared some dug-outs of the enemy both there and in the West Miraumont road. Many prisoners were taken and sent back to the cages.

With but little loss A and C Companies reached the first objective though very heavy machine-gun fire was opened on them from both flanks. The enemy's guns were fortunately trained too high and did little damage. The artillery barrage, however, caused many casualties, practically every senior officer and N.C.O. being put out of action at the commencement by shell-fire. In spite of almost unsurpassable difficulties, however, the first objective was won, and A and C Companies began to dig themselves in. B and D Companies should now have gone forward to the second objective: they did, in fact, set out, but D went far away to the right, fetching up eventually on the East Miraumont road, where it was heavily counter-attacked by the enemy and driven back. B Company, which had also lost direction too far to the right, was also forced to retire.

The two platoons which were mopping-up along the West Miraumont road had become mixed up with the 18th Division, and, as the latter retired, fell back with it.

The Rifles then consolidated the line of the first objective.

D Company of the 22nd Royal Fusiliers, which had been ordered to push forward on the right of the 99th Infantry Brigade and form a defensive flank, advanced along the east side of the East Miraumont road. On reaching the enemy's wire it was found uncut. A hostile machine gun opened from the north-east, and Major R. Walsh and a subaltern were wounded and both put out of action. The company had now lost all its officers, but No. 731 Lance-Sergeant F. W. Palmer assumed command, and with six other men very gallantly cut his way through the wire and, rushing the trench, drove the enemy back and established a block. No less than seven determined counter-attacks were made by the enemy during the next three hours, but they were repulsed by Palmer and his brave comrades.[1] Three other posts with Lewis guns were established along the East Miraumont road between the Old British line and the hostile wire.

On the left, however, A and C Companies of the 22nd Royal Fusiliers had advanced towards the Brown line (the third objective), but in crossing the Boom Ravine moved north-west and thus lost direction. Captain Powell (commanding A Company) fortunately discovered the mistake, and brought his company back, together with three platoons of C Company, to the West Miraumont road and continued his advance along the latter. The remaining platoons of C, under Captain L. Simons, M.C., had advanced to the enemy's wire west of the West Miraumont road. Here the entanglements were found to be uncut, and whilst gallantly attempting to force it he and his party were surrounded by large numbers of the enemy and forced to surrender. The enemy now attempted to outflank the 22nd Royal Fusiliers from the direction of the East Miraumont road, but the Fusiliers withdrew in good order. It was during this retirement that No. 18,337 Corporal Wilmott, the only survivor of his gun team, opened fire upon the enemy with such good effect that the latter was held up, and the withdrawal was carried out safely.

The 23rd Royal Fusiliers, on the right of the Rifles, appear to have been held up by the enemy's barrage and unable to move. The Diary of the battalion contains no account of the operation, and

[1] Lance-Sergeant F. W. Palmer (afterwards Second-Lieut.) was awarded the Victoria Cross for his gallantry on this occasion. "For most conspicuous bravery, control, and determination. During the progress of certain operations, all the officers of his company having been shot down, Sergeant Palmer assumed command, and having cut his way under point-blank machine-gun fire through the wire entanglements, he rushed the enemy's trench with six of his men, dislodged the hostile machine gun which had been hampering our advance, and established a block. He then collected men detached from other regiments, and held the barricade for nearly three hours against seven determined counter-attacks under an incessant barrage of bombs and rifle grenades from his flank and front. During his temporary absence in search of more bombs, an eighth counter-attack was delivered by the enemy, who succeeded in driving in his party, and threatened the defences of the whole flank. At this critical moment, although he had been blown off his feet by a bomb and was greatly exhausted, he rallied his men, drove back the enemy, and maintained his position. The very conspicuous bravery displayed by this non-commissioned officer cannot be overstated, and his splendid determination and devotion to duty undoubtedly averted what might have proved a serious disaster in this sector of the line."—*London Gazette*, 3rd April 1917.

the only available information is contained in a Divisional narrative of the operations on the 17th and 18th February.

About 10 a.m. the position of the 99th Infantry Brigade was as follows : the 1st King's Royal Rifles were holding the first objective with a composite force of their own men, some 22nd Royal Fusiliers, and a number of men of the 23rd Royal Fusiliers; their right was protected by D Company 22nd Royal Fusiliers, and their left by the 18th Division.

Meanwhile the subsidiary attack by the 6th Infantry Brigade (2nd South Staffords) had failed to make headway, for the gallant Staffords had hardly left their trenches when they were met by a perfect hail of machine-gun and rifle bullets : the enemy had about 5 a.m. placed a very heavy barrage on the battalion's trenches. In face of this opposition the left and centre of the battalion could not advance, though many gallant attempts were made to rush the enemy's position. The right flank, however, was reported to have succeeded in reaching its first objective, and maintained itself for some time in the enemy's trenches. Eventually, however, finding itself unsupported, the right flank fell back to the Old British line.

Subsequently a captured German officer stated that the enemy had received information at least five hours before " zero " of the intended attack, and had barraged the British lines, mounted machine guns in all his positions, and had filled his trenches with troops ready to meet the assaulting troops. That progress was made and the first objective captured is an eloquent tribute to the fighting qualities of the troops of the Division.

The effect of the failure on the right flank of the Division made itself felt on the left, where the Rifles of the 99th Infantry Brigade were making excellent progress, until it was discovered that their right flank was in the air, and machine-gun fire from the north-east began to take heavy toll of the advancing troops.

On the left and right of the 2nd Division the 18th and 63rd Divisions had also made good progress, the former at nightfall on the 17th being on the south-western outskirts of Petit Miraumont, the latter (north of the Ancre) having gained all its objectives on a front of about half a mile.

At 9 p.m. on the 17th IInd Corps Headquarters ordered the ground gained to be consolidated ; no further attacks were to be made without further instructions.

Heavy losses had been sustained by the 6th and 99th Infantry Brigades. Of the former the South Staffords lost 5 officers killed, 3 wounded, and 1 missing, and 109 other ranks killed, wounded, and missing. Of ten officers who "went over the top" only one remained uninjured. Of the 99th Infantry Brigade the Rifles lost 5 officers killed and 4 wounded, and 186 other ranks killed, wounded, and missing; the 22nd Royal Fusiliers lost 3 officers killed and 9 wounded, but the casualties amongst other ranks were not recorded; the 23rd Royal Fusiliers had 8 officers killed, 4 wounded, and 1 missing, and 227 other ranks killed, wounded, and missing; the 1st Royal Berks lost 1 officer killed and 2 wounded, and 12 other ranks killed and wounded; the 99th Machine-Gun Company had 1 officer killed and 3 wounded, and 32 other ranks killed and wounded. Altogether the losses of the 99th Infantry Brigade were 42 officers[1] and 737 other ranks. The Brigade captured 200 prisoners.

The official Diaries which record the action of the 17th record also the splendid work of the R.A.M.C., whose devoted work so often remained unnoticed in the narratives of the battles. The Battalion Aid Post of the 1st King's Royal Rifle Corps was in an open trench just by No. 15 Post. This was early struck by a shell, which killed the N.C.O. in charge and 12 other men; the post was then moved to a dug-out in Boom Ravine. Captain W. M. Coad, R.A.M.C., Medical Officer to the 22nd Royal Fusiliers, went out after dark and himself brought in Major R. Walsh,[2] who was lying mortally wounded in a shell-hole close to the German wire.

The Divisional Commander, in reporting the operations, said: "That a considerable success was achieved is, in my opinion, due to the magnificent heroism of all ranks. The officers fell almost to a man, and the troops continued under their N.C.O's until checked by overwhelming odds."

A deliberate attack at dawn on the 18th, proposed by the General Officer Commanding 2nd Division with five fresh companies of the 99th Infantry Brigade, was vetoed by IInd Corps Headquarters. The Corps Commander, however, ordered battalions to advance where they could by pushing forward posts and patrols.

Early on the morning of the 18th the 6th Infantry Brigade was ordered to take over the whole of the 2nd Divisional front on the night 18th–19th. The 2nd South Staffords were to be withdrawn from the line to Wolfe Huts. The three remaining battalions were then to occupy the following line: right sub-sector, the 1st King's; centre, 17th Middlesex; left, 13th Essex. The latter, with one company of the 17th Middlesex, was to relieve the 99th Infantry Brigade. The Machine-Gun Company of the latter Brigade was

18TH FEB.

---

[1] See Appendix for officers killed. [2] Died of wounds February 19, 1917.

relieved by the machine guns of the 6th Infantry Brigade. During the night these moves took place.

The line taken over by the 13th Essex on the right was in a terrible condition, for previous to the attack on the 17th this part of the line had been in the enemy's possession and had been very heavily bombarded by the British artillery; the earth had been ploughed up by the explosion of shells, and the trenches had been pulverized and blown to atoms. Damp and foggy weather did not improve matters.

19TH FEB. At intervals throughout the 19th the front line was heavily shelled by the enemy. The Essex were ordered to push forward posts and patrols in advance of their line, a policy by which it was hoped gradually to increase the Divisional gains. This the battalion did on the night 20th–21st, adding another 50 yards and establishing two forward posts on the right. It was obvious, however, that as long as the high ground—Hill 130—south-east of Petit Miraumont remained in the enemy's possession heavy casualties would be suffered, for the hill afforded excellent observation posts, enabling the enemy to reconnoitre the British line without danger to himself. A thick mist still clung to the ground, making aeroplane and artillery observation difficult, and there seemed no prospects of the atmosphere clearing. It was impossible, therefore, for the Divisional artillery to shell the enemy out of his trenches on the hill or give the infantry sufficient support to enable them to push forward to their original objective.

Accordingly the Divisional Commander submitted plans to IInd Corps Headquarters for the capture of the German trench running from the West Miraumont road at Point R.11,a.8.4 to R.11,b.8.0 (the western portion of Crest Trench), and for securing a position on Hill 130 which would prevent the enemy using it for observation purposes. The attack on Crest Trench was to be delivered in a north-easterly direction to defilade hostile machine-gun fire coming from east of the East Miraumont road. The plan necessitated the attacking troops of the 2nd Division forming up in the 18th Division's area. Owing to the conformation of the front line, and the difficulty in employing artillery fire on the enemy's position, barrages of Stokes mortars and machine guns were proposed.

On Corps Headquarters approving this plan, the General Officer Commanding 6th Infantry Brigade was ordered to get into touch with the General Officer Commanding right Brigade of the 18th Division, in order to arrange plans for forming up and overlapping. But on the 20th the weather suddenly broke, and a thin drizzle, which began in the early hours of that day, developed into a steady downpour. In a little while the conditions became truly appalling; it was impossible for the troops to move without great difficulty. In consequence the operations ordered for the 22nd were postponed. On the 21st conditions had grown even worse. The 17th Middlesex, on the right, who had relieved the 13th Essex on the night 20th–21st, had a terrible time in getting to the forward line of posts. Three companies were in the line, C, B, and D, and A in support. The relief was not completed until early in the morning " owing to the obscure position and condition of tracks."

In spite of the heavy going, however, D Company, on the 22nd, actually advanced its line of posts 80 yards and gained touch with the 18th Division on the left flank; C Company also pushed forward its position slightly. The men were in shell-holes, and the condition of shell-holes after many hours of heavy rain can be better imagined than described. Every now and then a shout went up, and a man would be seen sinking gradually lower and lower into the viscous mud. Then followed a long process of either pulling him out with the help of rifles or digging him from the quagmire. He emerged filthy and abominable.

Meanwhile the Brigadier in the line had received his instructions to prepare for the attack. " Every yard of ground that we can make is of the greatest advantage in the attack which we hope to carry out. The position is as follows: The Division has been ordered to establish itself on Hill 130; as soon as it has been done, our present very extended front will be reduced by the 18th Division taking over from us up to the East Miraumont road.... As regards artillery work during the next few days, it is essential to hinder any work the enemy may be doing on the objective trench (Crest Trench) eastwards." Finally these instructions said: " Ground must be gained to-night without fail, and as the 13th Essex know the ground it is proposed that they should do this before relief." As already stated, the Essex *did* gain ground, all that was possible in that Slough of Despond!

The 6th Infantry Brigade received instructions that it was to be relieved by the 5th Infantry Brigade on the night 23rd–24th, and before his Brigade left the line the Brigadier sent in a report of his position: " The right flank is in what must be described as a bog; the ground being so false that about 10 men or more had to be dug out and pulled out with beams and ropes . . . the enemy is within 30 yards of our front posts."

The relief was duly carried out by the 5th Infantry Brigade on the night 23rd–24th, the General Officer Commanding that Brigade, being thoroughly in touch with the situation and having already formulated his plans, went into the line with the intention of carrying out offensive patrolling and the attack on Hill 130. But that attack was destined not to take place.

The ground gained by the attack of the 17th and 18th February, and by the minor operations since these dates, had given Sir Douglas Haig the observation he desired and complete command over the German artillery positions in the upper Ancre Valley, and the enemy's defences in and around Pys and Miraumont. But bombarded constantly by the British guns, and threatened by attack in which troops would be at great disadvantage, the enemy had decided to abandon both Pys and Miraumont.

The 5th Infantry Brigade reported that at 2.15 on the morning of the 24th the relief was complete. The 2nd Oxford and Bucks Light Infantry had relieved the 1st King's on the right of the Divisional front line; the 17th Royal Fusiliers were on the left.

Meanwhile a report had been received from the 18th Division that Divisional patrols patrolling up as far as Miraumont had found the enemy had vacated his positions. "Thus," the official reports state, "the General Officer Commanding the 5th Infantry Brigade was faced the first morning after the relief with the problem of clearing up the situation and moving over very difficult country against an enemy well supplied with machine guns and with whom touch had been temporarily lost."

The 17th Royal Fusiliers (on the left of the Divisional front) began pushing forward posts and patrols immediately, and a little later both Crest Trench and Coulée Trench were occupied. Strong fighting patrols from the 2nd Highland Light Infantry were next ordered to establish themselves south of Pys in Below Trench, with protective posts thrown out to the southern outskirts of Pys, and Grundy Trench.

By 10 a.m. on the 24th the 5th Infantry Brigade was advancing with the 18th Division on the left and the 2nd Australian Division[1] on the right. This advance was carried out in a thick mist, which rendered observation for more than 100 yards ahead impossible, and called for great caution as well as determination from those who were following the enemy.

At 8.38 p.m. the 5th Infantry Brigade was ordered to send out two companies of the 2nd Highland Light Infantry as advanced

---

[1] The 2nd Australian Division had relieved the 15th Division.

THE ADVANCE CONTINUED. 375

guards and to take up a line of outposts with a view to pushing the Divisional line still farther forward.

Throughout the 25th February the advance was continued with but little loss and opposition from the enemy. The two companies of Highland Light Infantry moved off towards the line laid down as the objective for outpost line at 6.10 a.m., with the 55th Infantry Brigade (18th Division) on their left flank. Owing to the great difficulty in getting reports back to Battalion Headquarters, the situation in the front line became obscure. For some hours the two companies of Highland Light Infantry were practically lost. At 9.15 p.m., no communication having been received from them, the Brigade Major visited the 17th Royal Fusiliers to try and discover the whereabouts of the Highland Light Infantry; but he was unsuccessful. About midnight messages were received giving the dispositions of the two companies; they had won forward in a most commendable manner. " Advanced," said the battalion Diary, " in thick mist from Below Support at 6.40 on the morning of the 25th, and reached Grundy Trench at 8 a.m. The two companies reached their objectives at 9.30 a.m. After D Company advanced to the final objective one prisoner was taken and a number believed to be wounded. Between Below Support and Grundy road a rear-guard of the enemy sniped us from the right flank, and on mist lifting our positions were heavily shelled. Touch was gained on our left and right flanks and maintained; 18th Division on left and 2nd Australian Division on our right."

On other parts of the front also between Gueudecourt and Serre the enemy had been forced out of his front system of trenches. Luisenhof Farm, Warlencourt, Eaucourt, Pys, Miraumont, Beauregard, Dovecot, and Serre had all fallen into British hands.

Visibility was better on the morning of the 26th, and the guns were able to shell Grevillers Trench, Loupart Trench, and Loupart Wood. The enemy's artillery replied vigorously, shelling Pys and Grundy road intermittently. The right company of the Highland Light Infantry had pushed up Gallwitz Switch Trench and had established three posts. Officers' patrols were now sent forward to reconnoitre Grevillers Trench, but the enemy was found to be holding it in considerable strength.

At 1 p.m. Divisional Headquarters issued orders that Grevillers Trench was to be occupied, and the necessary arrangements were made for this to be done after dark. At from 4 to 6 o'clock patrols again reconnoitred Grevillers Trench, and found it strongly held by machine guns and heavily wired. The wire was in good condition and uncut, and in places consisted of two belts each about 12 feet wide. The enemy was also observed busily engaged in strengthening the wire. An officer's patrol entered Pys, but found it deserted save for one company of the Buffs of the 18th Division.

From the patrol reports it was evident that Grevillers Trench formed part of a strongly fortified line of trenches stretching from Bapaume to Irles, connected south of Loupart Wood with another well-wired line called Loupart Trench, running from Loupart Wood to Achiet-le-Petit. The whole presented a formidable obstacle; it was not only well wired but well sited upon the forward slope of a steep hill which, overlooking the British position, made movement across the valley during the day impossible. The position was one which, if the enemy intended making a stand, would be very difficult to capture.

On the morning of the 27th a conference was held at IInd Corps Headquarters, and after examining the patrol reports, and the results of the numerous reconnaissances, an organized attack on Grevillers and Loupart Trenches was decided upon. Grevillers Trench was to be attacked first, and for this purpose the guns were ordered forward to begin wire-cutting operations.

"The Army Commander was most anxious to press on and gain the high ground between Bapaume and Achiet-le-Petit. So strong were the positions held by the enemy that it was decided to capture them by several minor operations conducted by different Divisions with the same final objective in view. Each operation would have a direct effect upon and simplify the next attack."

These operations were separately described under four headings:

1. The capture of Irles from the south and west by the 18th Division, and the establishment of a line west of Irles parallel to and 300 yards from Grevillers Trench.

2. The capture of Gamp and Malt Trenches by the 2nd Australian Division, and the establishment of a line parallel to and 300 yards from Grevillers line (Trench?).

3. A combined attack by the 2nd and 18th Divisions on Grevillers line. The capture and consolidation and the establishment of a good line parallel to and 700 yards from the Loupart Trench.

4. The combined attack by the 2nd Australian Division, 2nd Division, and 18th Division on Loupart Trench; its capture and consolidation, and the establishment of a line of strong posts all along the high ground east, south, and west of Loupart Wood.

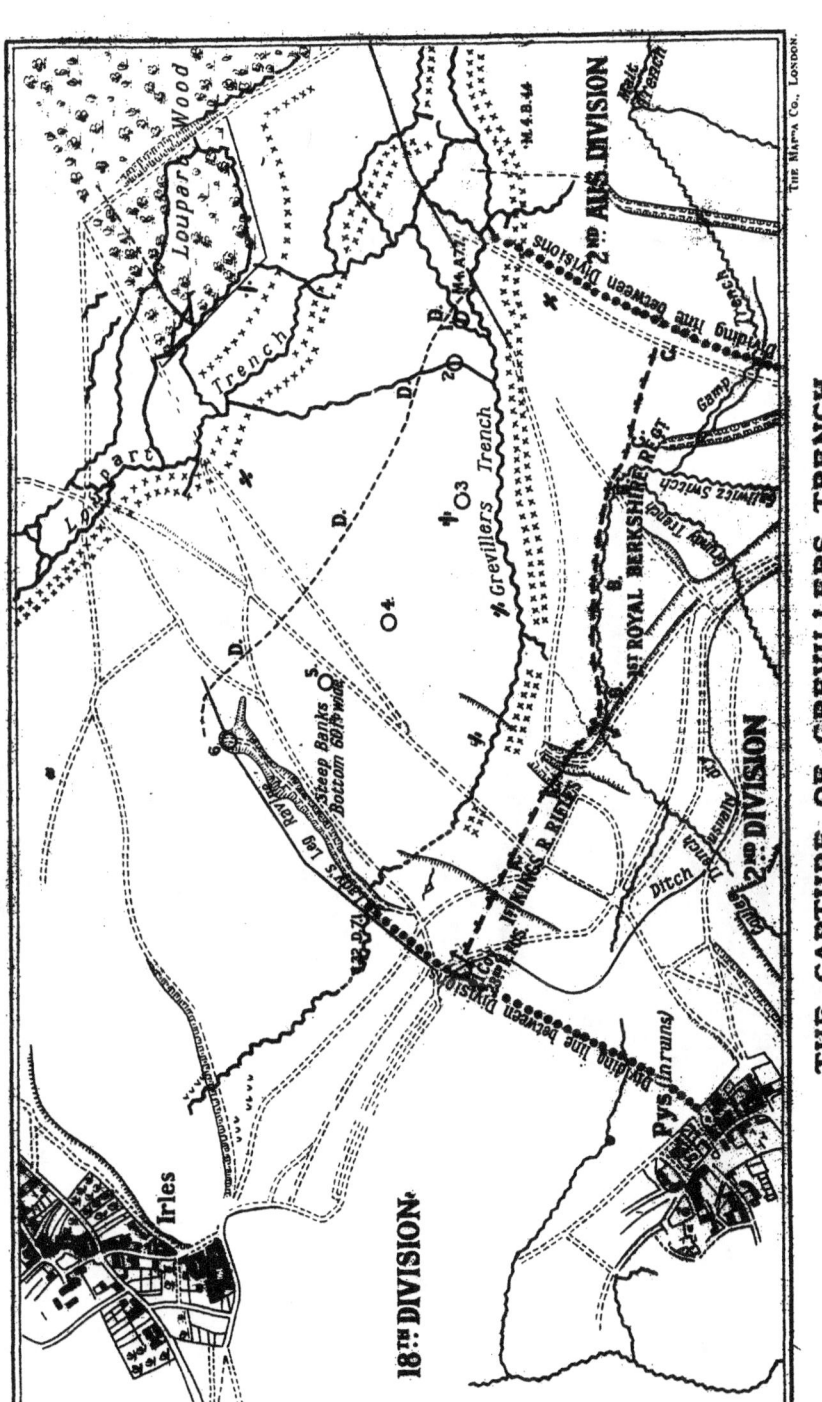

THE CAPTURE OF GREVILLERS TRENCH,
10th March 1917.

(Facing p. 376.)

GREVILLERS TRENCH.

The 27th and 28th February saw further progress on other parts of the line. At 10 o'clock on the night of the former date Gommecourt was occupied, and next day the capture of Puisieux-au-Mont was completed.

"The enemy had therefore," said the official dispatches, "been driven back to the Le Transloy–Loupart line, except that he still held the village of Irles, which formed a salient to his position and was linked up to it at Loupart Wood and Achiet-le-Petit by well-constructed and well-wired trenches."

The Capture of Irles,[1] 10th March 1917.

The operations against Grevillers Trench had been provisionally fixed for 5th March, but it was doubtful whether preparations and organization for the attack would be completed by that date. Much work had to be done, not only in the forward areas but behind the front line. Tracks had to be prepared over which the guns were to move forward for wire-cutting operations; the Divisional artillery at this period was at least 4,000 yards too far back for wire-cutting. The advance of the infantry had been rapid, but the guns could not be moved forward until the soft, spongy morass of mud and bog had been given a firm surface. Moreover, to find suitable gun positions on ground into which horses, men, guns, and limbers sank dangerously deep was no easy matter. Ammunition and other dumps had to be formed, and all the hundred-and-one things necessary completed ere an attack could be launched.

On the 2nd March, after severe fighting, the 2nd Australian Division captured Gamp and Malt Trenches. Twice the Division was counter-attacked, but on each occasion repulsed the enemy. Over 100 prisoners were captured. On the 6th March, as a preliminary to the capture of Irles, a portion of Resurrection Trench north of the village was captured by the 18th Division. This Division was then in position for the next operation, the combined attack on the village of Irles and Grevillers Trench by the 18th and 2nd Divisions.

Thus two of the four operations decided upon at the conference at IInd Corps Headquarters on 27th February had been carried out with successful results.

[1] This action is better known to the 2nd Division as the capture of Grevillers Trench.

And now for a while it is necessary to interrupt the narrative of the attack on Grevillers on 10th March in order to summarize briefly events which were taking place on the enemy's side of the line.

The Germans had decided upon a defensive rôle for at least the Spring of 1917. The Battles of the Somme, 1916, had weakened both the Allies and the enemy, whilst in war material and ammunition the latter especially was experiencing a temporary shortage. Both sides had suffered considerable exhaustion, though the Allies, profiting by the advantage gained in the previous year, had determined upon renewing the offensive in 1917. The enemy was, however, aware of their intentions, and fearing attacks both from the French on the Soissons–Rheims–Argonne front or between Roye and Noyon, and from the British either on the Somme or farther north, had definitely decided to shorten his line. On 1st March, however, he had concentrated his largest armies, the First numbering 20 divisions and the Fifth numbering $20\frac{1}{2}$ divisions, at two points—*i.e.*, in front of Albert and from Verdun to Ville-sur-Torbe respectively.

The German navy had on 1st February begun a submarine campaign in the hopes of preventing reinforcements arriving in France, and generally harassing communications with England. The enemy also wished to protect his coast line from Holland to Denmark, along the frontiers of which countries, fearing an invasion, he had massed troops. The protection of his coasts was effective, and he was able to release the troops massed along the frontiers of the above-named countries and employ them in France and Belgium. But even with these reinforcements he considered he had not enough men available for adequately defending his line from Verdun to the Belgian coast. He therefore decided to withdraw his troops from the huge salient between Soissons and Arras to a prepared position known as the Siegfried Line.

"The general situation," said Ludendorff, "made it necessary for us to postpone the struggle in the West as long as possible in order to allow the submarine campaign time to produce the desired results. Tactical reasons and a shortage of ammunition provided additional reasons for delay. At the same time it was necessary to shorten our front in order to secure a more favourable grouping of our forces and create large reserves. In France and Belgium we had 154 divisions facing 190 divisions, some of which were considerably stronger than ours. In view of our extensive front this was an exceedingly unfavourable balance of

A DOUBTFUL HONOUR.

forces.[1] Moreover, we had on certain sectors of our line to endeavour to avoid heavy enemy attacks as long as possible, by preventing our adversaries from concentrating strong forces in front of them. At the same time we secured positions in which weaker divisions, wearied by fighting, could be employed. These considerations, taken in close connection with the opening of the submarine campaign, led to the decision to straighten our front by withdrawing to the Siegfried Line, which was to be in a state of defence by the beginning of March, and methodically to carry out the work of demolition over an area of 15 kilometres in breadth in front of our new positions."

To the Army Group of the Crown Prince Rupprecht belongs the doubtful honour of carrying out the work of demolition and wanton destruction, much of which was *not* warranted by military necessity. The name given to this wholesale programme of destruction was "Alberich." The work was to extend over five weeks, and "if an attack on the part of the enemy made it necessary we could at any moment interrupt this programme and begin our retreat. Our first object was to avoid battle; our second, to effect the salvage of all our raw material of war and technical and other equipment that was not actually built into the position, and finally the destruction of all high roads, villages, towns, and wells, so as to prevent the enemy establishing himself in force in the near future in front of our new positions. . . . The decision to retreat was not reached without a painful struggle. It implied a confession of weakness bound to raise the *moral* of the enemy and lower our own. But as it was necessary for military reasons we had no choice; it had to be carried out." [2]

The 4th February saw the order given to carry out "Alberich"; the first day was 9th February. According to the Chief of the German General Staff: "The retreat was to begin on 16th March, but under enemy pressure might start at any earlier date." It did! For on 6th February Grandcourt was evacuated; on the 10th–11th February the enemy was driven out of the Beaucourt

---

[1] Ludendorff's figures of the comparative strength of the opposing forces must be received with caution. Many British divisions were as weak, if not weaker, than the German divisions opposing them. As an instance, the actual fighting strength of the 2nd Division on January 6, 1917, when the Division went fresh into the line after the Battle of the Ancre, was 13,561; on the 3rd February it was 13,055; and on the 3rd March, 11,684. These totals are the number of troops in the three infantry brigades, each consisting of 4 battalions with a brigade machine-gun company; the pioneer battalion is also included.

[2] Ludendorff.

Valley; Pys, Miraumont, and Serre were next evacuated, and successively Le Barque, Ligny-Thilloy and Thilloy, Gommecourt Village and Park, and finally Puisieux-au-Mont fell into the hands of the British. Thus the enemy had been driven back willy-nilly to the Le Transloy–Loupart line, though he still clung to the village of Irles. "Accordingly," said Sir Douglas Haig, " our next step was to take Irles, as a preliminary to a larger undertaking against the Le Transloy–Loupart line itself."

The "Alberich" plan had so far succeeded in that before Irles could be attacked much work had to be done on the roads and communications before any advance could be made. But Ludendorff's statement that "the 'Alberich' programme was carried out according to plan" is open to question. The enemy was forced to retreat before the 16th March, as already shown; the fancied secret had been discovered by Sir Douglas Haig's airmen and Intelligence Corps before that date. "For some time prior to this date a number of indications had been observed which made it probable that the area of the German withdrawal would be yet further extended. *It had been ascertained that the enemy was preparing a new defensive system known as the Hindenburg Line.* . . . It was also evident from the preparations he was making that he contemplated an eventual evacuation of the greater salient between Arras and the Aisne Valley, north-west of Rheims."

From frequent reconnaissance of the enemy's wire in front of Grevillers Trench it was evident that without considerable artillery preparation the thick entanglements were practically impassable.

1ST MARCH. On 1st March, therefore, the Heavy Divisional Artillery began wire-cutting operations. Only a few guns were in action, as the German retirement had been rapid and fresh gun positions had to be secured and registration completed before the Field Artillery could also take part in the operations. The terrible nature of the ground over which the guns had to be moved made progress very slow. But by 2nd March all batteries were registering, and the Loupart line was kept under fire practically all day long.

At 7 on the morning of the 3rd orders were issued for the attack on Irles and Grevillers Trench. The 2nd Division was to secure the latter position, including the Lady's Leg Ravine; the 18th Division, on the left of the 2nd Division, was to assault Irles; and the 2nd Australian Division, on the right, was also to co-operate in the attack with artillery, Stokes mortar, and machine-gun fire.

The 99th Infantry Brigade of the 2nd Division had been detailed for the assault on Grevillers Trench and the Lady's Leg Ravine.

The 1st Royal Berks (right) and the 1st King's Royal Rifles (left), with one company of the 23rd Royal Fusiliers, were the assaulting battalions of the Brigade. The latter relieved the 5th Infantry Brigade during the evening of the 3rd March, the relief being completed by 10 p.m., which, seeing the nature of the ground, was a very fine performance. The 5th Infantry Brigade then passed into Divisional Reserve; the 6th Infantry Brigade moving to Ovillers Huts as support brigade.

The wire-cutting proceeded slowly, and the proposed attack for the 5th March was delayed until the formidable belts of entanglements were sufficiently smashed to allow the passage of infantry. There were three rows of wire—the first about 8 feet deep and waist high; the second similar to the first; and the third higher and stronger than the first two, having an " apron " in front. But all day long the guns pounded the enemy's position with but little retaliation, for the Germans had also begun to withdraw their forward artillery in accordance with " Alberich."

The Intelligence reports during these early days of March 1917 are interesting, bearing as they did on the attack about to take place. From the statements of prisoners taken on the 2nd March it was learned that orders had been issued by Ludendorff to his troops to hold Grevillers Trench for fourteen days—*i.e.*, until the 16th March. These prisoners also stated that Beaumetz and Hermies, six and eight miles respectively east of Bapaume, were to be evacuated, and that both places were already being cleared of civilians.

To keep up the *moral* of his troops, which had been seriously affected by the retirement, the enemy issued frequent reports of the " success " of his movements. On 3rd March one report stated: " The fact that our movements have been universally successful during the last few days, and have cost us practically nothing, is due to the skill and bravery of our troops. Regimental historians will tell us in the future how delighted our officers and men were to return once again to open warfare."

Strange that troops who fought bravely, as undoubtedly the Germans did, should be " delighted " to retire from positions which had been soaked with the blood of their comrades in gallant efforts to maintain them. Queer mentality that could see " success " in an enforced retreat, the abandonment of much war material, and the loss of thousands of troops—killed, wounded, and missing. But humour was never a part of the German temperament.

For a week the general attitude of the enemy had been " inactive." He had made no attempt to mend his wire, which day by day was being blown to bits, or even repair Grevillers Trench itself, which, as "zero" day drew near, more and more resembled tumbled and shapeless masses of earth. Few enemy patrols were seen. Hostile sniping and machine-gun fire were alone kept up from Grevillers Trench, but these were checked and did not cause much trouble. There was, however, considerable aerial activity, the enemy's machines flying continually over the Divisional area, and were as constantly engaged by British airmen.

"Zero" hour was finally fixed for the morning of the 10th March, 5.15.

8TH–9TH MARCH.

On the night of the 8th–9th the 23rd Royal Fusiliers sent out three patrols, the battalion then holding the front line previous to being relieved by the 1st King's Royal Rifles before the assault took place. These patrols found the wire well cut in places, but in others practically intact. There were, however, sufficient gaps to make an assault possible, and there was still a whole day in which to carry out "final preparations."

The objectives of the 2nd Division were the line of Grevillers Trench between points (approximately) M.4,b.4.4 to G.32,d.7.1, and the line of strong points beyond.

The portion of the line allotted to the one company of 23rd Royal Fusiliers which had been placed under the orders of the Officer Commanding 1st King's Royal Rifles was the Lady's Leg Ravine; the company had orders to capture the ravine, consolidate the position there, and establish a post at the northern end.

9TH–10TH MARCH.

Thus on the night of the 9th–10th March, when the assaulting troops were all assembled ready for the attack, the line ran as follows: On the right, the 1st Royal Berks; on the left, the 1st King's Royal Rifle Corps, with one company of the 23rd Royal Fusiliers on the extreme left flank of the Rifles. The three remaining companies of the 23rd Royal Fusiliers were in reserve. The attack was to be supported by the 22nd Royal Fusiliers, organized into three companies—one company with eight Lewis guns in Grundy Trench, one company to carry for the Berkshires, and one company to carry for the Rifles. The 99th Machine-Gun Company was ordered to "Sweep Grevillers Trench; cover the ground between Grevillers Trench and Loupart Trench and prevent the enemy issuing from Loupart Trench; cover the flank of the attacking battalions, and especially to bring heavy fire to bear on the trenches on the right front of the attack; bring enfilade fire from the direction of Pys on to the Lady's Leg Ravine." The 99th

READY TO "GO OVER." 383

Trench Mortar Battery was to follow up the attack and assist the infantry in clearing the Lady's Leg Ravine, repelling bombing attacks, and in dealing with the enemy's machine guns and strong points reported in the vicinity of the junction of Coulée and Grevillers Trenches. The 5th Field Company R.E., one company of the 10th Duke of Cornwall's Light Infantry (Pioneers), and two sections of the 6th Infantry Brigade Machine-Gun Company, were also attached to the 99th Infantry Brigade.

The Sappers had begun work immediately the 99th Infantry Brigade relieved the 5th Infantry Brigade. Tracks were "trench boarded," dug-outs were built and others repaired, twelve "trench bridges" were placed over ditches "usually dry" (as the maps stated), and much hard labour was put in in preparing the way for the assault. In this work the Pioneers ably assisted the Sappers, who were commanded by Major Robinson.

The two assaulting battalions had relieved the 23rd Royal Fusiliers, who had held the position until it was taken over by the Berkshires and the Rifles. Between 1 and 4 a.m. on "zero" day hot soup and rum were issued to the troops. Each man carried, besides his arms and ammunition, bombs, iron ration, sandwiches, and water-bottle filled with rum and water, a flare and a Véry light and sandbags, and either a pick or a shovel slung over his back, for consolidating purposes; no light weight. *10TH MARCH. MAP.*

The artillery and machine-gun barrage had been timed to begin at 5.15 a.m., during which the infantry were to creep forward as close as possible to the barrage line. At "zero" plus 6 minutes the barrage was to lift to the next line 100 yards ahead, thence at the rate of 100 yards per 4 minutes, the barrage at "zero" plus 34 minutes becoming protective. At "zero" plus 1 hour and 22 minutes the barrage was to lift on to Loupart Trench, the infantry moving forward as close as possible to take up a line as near as they could get to Loupart Trench.

At 4 a.m. all ranks were in position ready for the attack. The previous day had been intensely cold, with a hard frost which had frozen the ground and would have made the "going" easy. But during the night atmospheric conditions had changed (as frequently they had an unhappy knack of doing whenever an attack was to take place), a rapid thaw set in, and a thick mist hung over the trenches. When "zero" hour arrived it was impossible to see more than 30 yards ahead, and the ground had again become a slimy disgusting morass of mud.

Punctually at 5.15 a.m. the artillery and machine guns opened fire, putting down a heavy barrage on and beyond Grevillers Trench. The assaulting waves at once moved forward to within 60 yards of the barrage. As the infantry neared the enemy's wire it was seen that the guns had done their work splendidly; the entanglements, which had been of considerable strength, were admirably cut and proved no obstacle to the advance. Six minutes after " zero " hour the barrage lifted to 100 yards beyond, and with a rush the Berkshires and the Rifles were into Grevillers Trench.

The extreme right of the enemy's line, south of Loupart Wood, was strongly held. Here heavy machine-gun fire caused the Berkshires some trouble and a number of casualties. But, assisted by rifle-grenades and a Stokes gun which came into action with excellent results, the battalion pushed on, silenced the machine guns and formed a block at M.4,a.7.7. Numbers of the enemy were killed and 49 prisoners were taken, including 1 officer; 3 machine guns and 2 large trench mortars were also captured.

The left of the attack, carried out by the 1st King's Royal Rifle Corps and D Company of the 23rd Royal Fusiliers, was also successful.

The Rifles, who numbered only 280 men (and were therefore assisted by the Fusiliers), kept close on the barrage and were into Grevillers Trench almost immediately the guns lifted. The enemy made two attempts to bomb the Rifles out, but the bomb-throwers were at once killed. A machine gun on the right opened fire, but after firing a few rounds the gunner was shot through the head by Sergeant Jacobs.

On the capture of Grevillers Trench, previously detailed parties, consisting of 1 N.C.O., 3 men, and a Lewis gun team, pushed on behind the barrage with orders to get as far forward as possible. Mainly owing to the gallant efforts of Capt. E. M. Allfrey, M.C., who though twice wounded as he left the assembly trench, refused to give in, these orders were well carried out and a line of outposts was rapidly pushed out, the N.C.O's of the battalion interpreting their instructions almost to the letter.

D Company of the 23rd Royal Fusiliers, to whom had been assigned the task of capturing the Lady's Leg Ravine, had, owing to the skilful dispositions of its Commanding Officer, little difficulty in attaining its objectives, and establishing a strong post at the end of the ravine. Two Lewis guns, one on either side, just south of the southern end of the ravine, opened a heavy fire at " zero," which swept up the ravine and kept down the enemy's fire. Parties of Rifle Grenadiers and snipers with a Lewis gun team, then advanced on either side and along the upper edges of the ravine, towards the northern exit, whilst a party followed along the bottom, some distance in the rear. The enemy's strong point was at the northern end of the ravine. The grenadiers did excellent work, and the Fusiliers not only captured the ravine and the strong point as well, but 30 prisoners also and 2 machine guns; 20 of the enemy were killed.

Thus the whole of Grevillers Trench and the line of posts beyond it in front of the 2nd Division were captured in the first stride. As soon as these objectives had been reached " protective detachments " each consisting of 1 N.C.O., 3 men, and a Lewis gun detachment, pushed forward under the barrage and gradually gained ground until they formed a line (D....D....D) approximately parallel to and 300 yards' distance from Loupart Trench where, in shell-holes, they consolidated their position.

The " protective detachments " were followed by parties each consisting of a platoon and two Lewis guns, under an officer, detailed for strong posts. These parties, proceeding to positions previously pointed out to them (1, 2, 3, 4, 5, and 6), dug themselves in. At nightfall on the 10th of March the Division was in possession of a line of strong posts stretching from M.4,a.6.6 to the northern end of the Lady's Leg Ravine, and a protective line dug in in shell-holes—*i.e.*, D....D....D.

Casualties during the day had been slight, 3 officers and 27 other ranks being killed and 4 officers and 166 other ranks wounded. Of the enemy many were killed and wounded, 215 were taken prisoners, together with 7 machine guns and 4 trench mortars. Lieut. R. W. B. Lovett (6th Battalion attached 1st Battalion King's Royal Rifle Corps), Second-Lieut. N. S. Done (6th Battalion attached 22nd Battalion Royal Fusiliers), and Second-Lieut. A. D. C. Brazier (3rd Battalion attached 1st Battalion Royal Berks), were the officers killed.

The success of this operation was entirely due to careful preparation and close co-operation of all arms of the Division. All the official narratives of the capture of Grevillers Trench are eloquent in their praise of the great assistance afforded the infantry by the efficacy of the artillery barrage. " My Brigade," said the Brigadier of the 99th Infantry Brigade, " has implicit confidence in the accuracy and skill of our 2nd Division gunners which has never been misplaced."

The 22nd Royal Fusiliers, who furnished the carrying parties, performed their toilsome and dangerous duties with splendid tenacity. Their duties entailed continual movements to and fro through a heavy barrage; but in spite of this, all dumps in the objectives were fully stocked an hour after "zero." "The work done by these parties," said the Brigadier of the 99th Brigade, continuing his report to 2nd Division Headquarters, "cannot be too highly commended. All ranks carried out their most dangerous and important duty to the satisfaction and admiration of those whom they so ably supplied." The battalion's casualties were 1 officer killed and 27 other ranks wounded.

The 5th Field Company R.E. and the Pioneers (10th Duke of Cornwall's Light Infantry) likewise earned the gratitude of the assaulting troops by their devoted efforts. Besides digging trenches between the Old British line and the objective on the right flank, the repair of the existing communication trenches from the Old British line to the objective in the centre, and in assisting the garrisons of strong posts in constructing the latter and in wiring them, the sappers were ordered to mark out a line in front of the strong points (held as an outpost line) to be dug for a forming-up trench for subsequent operations. This latter task was carried out personally by the Officer Commanding 5th Field Company R.E. (Major Robinson) assisted by Second-Lieut. Downes, R.E., and eight sappers under circumstances of extraordinary difficulty. The position was under heavy shell-fire, yet in extreme darkness intensified by fog the line was laid, only three sappers being wounded.

Throughout the operations communication between Advanced Battalion Headquarters, Brigade Headquarters, and Divisional Headquarters was splendidly maintained. Relay posts worked without a hitch, and the wires carefully laid by the Signal section held remarkably well, with the result that communication was practically uninterrupted.

On the left of the 2nd Division the 18th Division had also succeeded in capturing its objectives—the village of Irles and the enemy's defences in the vicinity. The fire attack carried out by the 2nd Australian Division on the right of the 2nd Division greatly assisted the right flank of the latter (the Berks) during the operations.[1]

At nightfall on the 10th March Nos. 1, 2, 3, and 4 Strong Points

---

[1] During the evening of the 10th March the following message was received at 2nd Division Headquarters : " Corps Commander congratulates General Officers Commanding and all ranks of the 2nd and 18th Divisions on the result of to-day's operations. The dispositions of Brigadier-Generals Kellett (99th Infantry Brigade) and Higginson (53rd Infantry Brigade, 18th Division), the fine shooting of our artillery, and the dash and discipline of the 99th and 53rd Infantry Brigades, have resulted in the capture of Irles and the whole of our objectives, and of about 280

were held by the 1st Royal Berks, No. 5 by the 1st King's Royal Rifles, and Lady's Leg Ravine (with No. 6 Point) by D Company 23rd Royal Fusiliers, under the orders of the Officer Commanding 1st King's Royal Rifle Corps. The remaining troops of both the Berkshires and Rifles were disposed in Grevillers Trench and the Old British line. At 5.30 p.m. orders were issued for the relief of the 99th Infantry Brigade on the night 11–12th March by the 6th Infantry Brigade.

Preparations were begun on the morning of the 11th to continue the attack. Bombardments and wire-cutting were carried out by the "Heavies" along the Loupart line, many batteries of the Field Artillery were in the process of moving forward to new positions, but the "going" was terribly heavy. "The difficulties of this position," said an officer belonging to the Divisional Artillery, "are appalling, yards of mud to go through, and all ammunition has to be brought up to the Bapaume road and pulled up here in ammunition packs on horses."

11TH MARCH.

During the day the enemy opened a heavy bombardment with 5.9's, but did not hinder preparations for the attack.

Shortly after 2 o'clock on the morning of the 12th the relief of the 99th Infantry Brigade by the 6th Infantry Brigade was completed, and the former marched back to billets in Albert. The 6th Infantry Brigade was disposed in the following positions in front of the Loupart line: 1st King's on the right in Posts 1, 2, and 3; 13th Essex on the left in Posts 4, 5, and 6 (Lady's Leg Ravine); the 17th Middlesex Regiment was in support round Courcelette, and the 2nd South Staffords in reserve at Wolfe Huts. The 5th Infantry Brigade moved forward and occupied the Support Brigade area—Ovillers Huts.

Throughout the 12th preparations for attacking the Loupart line were pushed forward, and the battalions in the front line were engaged on the communication trenches from Gallwitz and Grevillers Trenches, and from Grevillers to the jumping-off trench from which the assault was to be made.

Details of the infantry attack and the intentions of the Army Commander were issued from 2nd Divisional Headquarters at 11 a.m.: The Fifth Army was to capture the Loupart line and Bucquoy; the 1st Anzac and the IInd Corps were to capture the

prisoners, 15 machine guns, and 4 trench mortars. The fine soldierly spirit, backed by hard work and careful thought, which brought us success to-day will win us many victories." The Army Commander (Fifth) also wired his congratulations to both Divisions.

388 THE HISTORY OF THE SECOND DIVISION.

Loupart line between G.35,a and the spur in G.26 with the 2nd and 18th Divisions. The objective of the 2nd Division was the Loupart line between G.34,d.5.0 and G.35,b.7.6, and the establishment of a line of posts on the line G.29,c.2.0 to G.28,d.1.9; the 5th and 6th Infantry Brigades were to carry out the attack. The Vth Corps was to capture Bucquoy. All arrangements for the attack were to be completed by the evening of 14th March.

At midnight, 12th–13th, Second-Lieut. Searl of the 1st King's and a patrol of scouts went forward for the purpose of reconnoitring the wire in front of the Loupart Trench. The night had been very quiet—so quiet, in fact, that suspicions were aroused that the enemy was again retiring. The patrol crept cautiously forward and penetrated a portion of the enemy's trench; but on attempting a reconnaissance of the wire in front of the wood was forced to retire, owing to the heavy shell-fire of the British guns, which were engaged in bombarding Loupart Wood.

13TH MARCH.

About 1.30 a.m. on the 13th information was received that Australian patrols on the right flank of the Division had entered Warlencourt Trench, joining up with, but east of, Grevillers Trench; and later reports showed that the enemy had vacated, or was hurriedly vacating, the Loupart line. The 1st King's and the 13th Essex were then ordered to gain touch with the enemy. At 4 a.m. A, D, and C Companies of the King's advanced, occupying Loupart Trench and Loupart Wood. Posts (Nos. 7, 8, 9, 10, 11, and 12) were established round the whole of the wood. B Company was in reserve in Grevillers Trench. The 13th Essex on the left and the Anzacs on the right then joined up with the left and right flanks of the King's respectively.

At 7 a.m. patrols reported the ground from about a mile north of the wood clear of the enemy, and A, B, and D Companies of the King's, under Lieut. Kynaston, advanced on the line Loupart Wood–Biefvillers. C Company was now in reserve.

Shortly before 12 noon on the 13th Lieut.-Colonel Norris, D.S.O., commanding the 1st King's, arrived at advanced Battalion Headquarters, and with the battalion advanced and consolidated a line on the Grevillers–Irles sunken road. The 13th Essex advanced on the left of the King's. Lewis gun posts were pushed out 200 yards in advance of the line. Whilst approaching their objectives the King's and Essex came under shell-fire, and while the Lewis gun posts were establishing themselves they were subjected to heavy machine-gun fire from the direction of Biefvillers; but few casualties were suffered.

THE GUNS AND THE MUD. 389

The Anzacs had advanced as the 6th Infantry Brigade went forward; but on the left of the 2nd Division the 18th Division was at first held up by machine-gun fire.

The advance of the 2nd Division had been so rapid that a pause was now absolutely necessary in order to allow the artillery to move forward to fresh positions from which the gunners could support the infantry. But the ground was in such a terrible condition that fresh tracks had to be laid down before the guns could be pushed forward.

The 17th Middlesex were moved up during the evening to Grevillers Trench (1 company and Battalion Headquarters) and Gallwitz Switch (3 companies) in close support to the King's and Essex; the 2nd South Staffords were in reserve round Lady's Leg Ravine.

An officer's patrol of the 13th Essex Regiment went out towards the enemy's position at 9.15 p.m., and definitely established the fact that he was holding the Bihucourt line, where sentries had been posted at intervals of every 25 yards. His wire was found in good condition and of considerable strength, being four feet in height and about twenty feet wide. This patrol returned at 4.30 on the morning of the 14th.

Throughout the latter part of the 13th, during the night, and early hours of the 14th, working parties of infantry, sappers, and pioneers had been hard at work preparing tracks over which the artillery could move forward. On the latter date the guns advanced to their new positions south-west of Loupart Wood. Some forward batteries were established in the Lady's Leg Ravine; others were along the Aqueduct road. All, in spite of the tracks, experienced great difficulty in reaching these positions. " Started off with the guns at about 9.30," said a gunner officer in his Diary, " over the most appalling bit of road up to the Aqueduct road. A and B were coming up, but we only managed to get A up there eventually. I rode up to the positions, and started the men off working, digging dug-outs off a new trench, and then returned to find the guns in a large 9.2 hole just above the Aqueduct road. We took half an hour getting it out, and also pulling the cook's cart out of difficulties, and then soon after landed in another. Another half-hour's hard work. Then over a trench bridge, over some appalling mud through which the ten-horse teams were pulling the guns about axle-deep, and finally came to rest over the second trench bridge, with the limber hanging over the side, one horse down on the bridge, another both wheelers in the ditch, all tied up in their harness with their legs in the air. . . . After an hour's hard work we extricated the horses from the mud, then we tried again, and the same thing happened over the other side of the bridge. This time the horse in the trench started sliding down a 30-foot dug-out, and was only prevented by the near wheeler lying on top of him and kicking his ribs. . . . Poor old horses, we can no longer look at them as the friend of man, but purely as beasts of burden. By this time the gun was axle-deep and almost past moving ; but we had a third try with a different team. All of us were caked with mud from head to foot by this time, and when half-way over the near limber wheel ran up on to the riband of the bridge and wobbled there. . . . It finally settled down on the bridge, and we finished our journey up to Loupart Wood about 3 o'clock. . . . Thank the Lord, no more guns are to come up until the Pys road is put in working order."

The German Retreat to the Hindenburg Line, 14th to 19th March 1917.[1]

14TH MARCH.

The official date of the beginning of the German retreat to the Hindenburg Line was given by the Allies as 14th March. Ludendorff states it began on the 16th March. " The great retreat," he says, " began on 16th March according to plan, and was carried through without a break in a few great stages." But neither of these dates appear correct, for from the foregoing pages it will be gathered that the enemy began his retreat early in March, if not towards the end of February. And his intentions were known.

15TH MARCH.

Early morning of the 15th March still found the 6th Infantry Brigade holding the front of the 2nd Division ; but the 2nd South Staffords had relieved the King's and Essex, and now held the posts north and north-east of Loupart Wood, from which the next advance would take place towards the Bihucourt line. The 17th Middlesex had moved up in close support, the 13th Essex were in support, and the King's passed into Brigade reserve.

Consolidation of the positions gained, which had been begun on the previous day, was continued on the 15th under very trying conditions. On the 14th it had rained incessantly, and the enemy's artillery, which had developed in activity, barraged any places

[1] The period during which the 2nd Division was following up the retreating enemy. The official period, covering the whole retreat, extends from 14th March to 5th April 1917.

where movement was seen. Many reports were received of the destruction of villages in rear of the enemy's position, and other signs of a further retirement were not wanting.

Upon the Field Companies Royal Engineers and the Pioneers the continual move forward entailed very heavy work, for as the Division advanced new front lines had to be consolidated, new defence posts erected, whilst behind the latter broad wood tracks to and from the back areas, the rebuilding of roads over which the artillery could move forward, the construction and improvement of dug-outs, and many other items inseparable from the process of moving a Division forward in pursuit of a retiring enemy, were carried out by the 5th, 483rd (originally the 1st East Anglian Field Company), and 226th Field Companies Royal Engineers and the Pioneers (10th Duke of Cornwall's Light Infantry) with ungrudging and cheerful energy. Every call upon their endurance and patience was responded to willingly in their endeavours to assist their comrades. The veteran Field Company of the Division (the 5th Field Company), with glorious traditions of the early days of 1914 behind it, was specially complimented by the General Officer Commanding 2nd Division for the gallant part it had played on the 10th March in the attack on Grevillers Trench.

An interesting note in the Divisional Intelligence Diary throws light upon the methods adopted by the enemy to cause casualties in the ranks of his pursuers :

" Enemy ruses. The dug-outs vacated by the enemy in the Loupart line have been found to contain many traps. As our troops were on their guard against these no harm was caused by them. The following were found : artificial flowers, bits of evergreen, pieces of shell or a bayonet on the floor or walls. A wire was attached to these, running to an explosive charge near the entrance. If the object is picked up the charge is ignited and the entrance blown in. Pieces of wood lightly fastened to the wall, as though intended for use as a hand rail when going down the steps. Wires with an electric spark attached to an explosive charge were attached to these rails."

Soon after 8 o'clock in the morning a report was received at 6th Infantry Brigade Headquarters that the 18th Division on the left had occupied part of the Bihucourt line. The 2nd South Staffords immediately sent out two strong patrols, under Lieut. Fluke and Second-Lieut. Aitken. As the first patrol (under Lieut. Fluke) approached the enemy's trenches it was heavily fired on, and between 20 and 30 casualties were suffered. The patrols then retired, but took up a position half-way between the Staffords' position and the enemy's wire, which was rapidly consolidated, and a telephone post established. This proved invaluable as a report centre.

At nightfall on the 15th the position remained unchanged, though all day long rumours had reached the Division of extensive retirements.

16TH MARCH.

On the morning of the 16th a warning was issued that the 2nd Division would shortly attack the Bihucourt line, and preparations for the attack were at once begun. The morning was misty, and under cover of the mist " the enemy," as the Diary of the South Staffords records, " worked hard on the line and on the wire—one of his ruses prior to retirement."

In discussing details for the attack on the Bihucourt line the General Officer Commanding 2nd Division stated : " The position held by the Division was not a good one for an offensive. Between the Bihucourt line and Loupart Wood lay a level plateau some 2,000 yards in extent, destitute of cover and communication trenches. Any movement north of Loupart Wood on a clear day was visible from Bapaume on the right and Achiet-le-Petit and Logeast Wood on the left, and it was apparent that preparations to attack the Bihucourt line would have to be made by night or advantage taken of a misty morning.

" Roads were in a very bad condition, and, except for two routes—Pys–Loupart and Warlencourt–Loupart—non-existent as anything but muddy tracks. Work was concentrated on these two tracks, but it was impossible in the time to get them into a condition to take any traffic but field artillery and limbers. The Royal Artillery had the greatest difficulty in moving their guns up to positions south of Loupart Wood ; but on the evening of the 16th eighteen 18-pounders and three 4.5 howitzers had come into action, the remainder of the Divisional Artillery covering the front at extreme range."

Orders had been received as early as the 14th as to the procedure to be adopted should the enemy evacuate the Bihucourt line, the purport of which was that patrols were to be pushed forward to the line joining spur north-east of Biefvillers with spur north of Bihucourt, on which line they were to establish themselves in the first instance. Two troops of Yorkshire Dragoons which had been placed at the disposal of the General Officer Commanding 2nd Division would then be sent through the infantry patrol line and move towards Sapignies, under orders of the

THE RED FLARES.

General Officer Commanding 6th Infantry Brigade, who would become responsible for finding an advanced guard from a force of all arms which would be placed at his disposal. Touch was to be maintained with the flank divisions.

Since the 17th February the 2nd Division had fought two actions, and had followed up two retirements, the total advance being 6,000 yards.

During the 16th the 2nd South Staffords were relieved by the 17th Middlesex, and moved back to the Lady's Leg Ravine in support. The 1st King's were moved up to replace the 17th Middlesex in close support, and the 13th Essex were ordered to remain in Aqueduct Camp in reserve. The reliefs were completed without incident by 9 p.m.

Throughout the night 16th–17th March red lights were observed burning in the enemy's lines. They were not the ordinary flares which suddenly grew brilliant and then flickered out, but a steady red light, and they were seen all up and down the enemy's line. Although it was not known at the time, those flares were signals for the general retirement to the Hindenburg Line. True to its reputation for theatrical demonstrations, the German Higher Command—" O.H.L."—gave the signal on the 16th March, though it knew the retirement had actually begun some days earlier.

Before dawn broke on the morning of the 17th orders for the attack on the Bihucourt line and all the intricate details connected with an assault on the enemy's lines had either been modified or altogether cancelled. For on the right of the 2nd Division the 2nd Australian Division had pushed out patrols, who had entered Biefvillers. It was evident, therefore, that the enemy had begun his retirement from the Bihucourt line.

17TH MARCH

At 6 a.m. the 17th Middlesex, holding the front line of the 2nd Division, received orders from 6th Infantry Brigade Headquarters to push on and keep in touch with the enemy. The battalion then advanced and occupied the Bihucourt line just west of Biefvillers.

About two hours later hostile shells began to fall in Bihucourt and Biefvillers, and from 8.30 a.m. onwards frequent messages arrived at 2nd Division Headquarters, giving particulars of the enemy's retirement all along the line: the Vth Corps had entered Achiet-le-Petit and the Australians Bapaume, which was in flames; the villages of Bihucourt, Biefvillers, Achiet-le-Grand, Favreuil, Sapignies, Behagnies, Vaulx, Beugnâtre, and Bancourt were burning, and the enemy was blowing up the roads behind him as he retired—the final act in the " Alberich " drama.

By 9.45 a.m. the 17th Middlesex had reported that the battalion held a line which ran from the level crossing at G.24,d.5.9 to junction G.17,d.6.2, with patrols pushed forward towards the Biefvillers–Bihucourt road. The enemy's machine guns and rifles were silent.

At 11.30 a.m. two troops of the Yorkshire Dragoons reported at 6th Infantry Brigade Headquarters, and were instructed to patrol forward to Sapignies and get into touch with the enemy. Battalion Headquarters 17th Middlesex now moved forward to the sunken road in G.29,b., and the 1st King's advanced to G.28,c. An officer's patrol belonging to the Middlesex Regiment penetrated a mile in front of the battalion's line, but found no signs of the enemy.

On the left of the 2nd Division the 18th Division had experienced a temporary check in front of Achiet-le-Grand, but at 3.50 p.m. the Division had cleared the village and was in occupation of the northern outskirts. The 29th Lancers of the Lucknow Cavalry Brigade of the 4th Cavalry Division, placed at the disposal of the General Officer Commanding 2nd Division by IInd Corps, were then ordered forward to Mory and Ervillers to establish themselves in these villages and maintain contact with the enemy, and effect, if possible, a junction with the cavalry of the Vth Corps, then reported to be advancing on Courcelles. These orders to the Indian Cavalry were supplemented by instructions to the 6th Infantry Brigade to follow, as advanced guard to the Division, one battalion moving to Behagnies with a battery of artillery.

The battalion selected was the 1st King's, whose Commanding Officer, Lieut.-Colonel G. E. Morris, D.S.O., was appointed Officer Commanding Advanced Guard.

The latter orders were subsequently cancelled for the time being, an advance being ordered for the following day; the 29th Lancers were, however, sent back to Aqueduct road, and the Yorkshire Dragoons ordered to patrol north of Biefvillers.

When darkness fell on the 17th, the general outpost line of the Fifth Army stretched east and west from the high ground west of Favreuil spur north of Biefvillers and Bihucourt to the high ground north of Achiet-le-Grand. A line to be consolidated from Bapaume to Achiet-le-Grand had already been ordered.

During this day the 2nd Division had advanced 1,200 yards.

At midnight orders were issued by 6th Infantry Brigade Headquarters to the Yorkshire Dragoons to move forward at daybreak and ascertain whether Sapignies and lines east and west of it were

THE DIVISION SQUEEZED OUT.   395

held by the enemy. In the event of the village and the lines on both flanks being unoccupied, the 1st King's, reinforced by one company of the South Staffords, were to move as advanced guard [1] on these positions. The South Staffords (less one company) were then to occupy the line of posts held by the 1st King's, one company remaining in Lady's Leg Ravine.

The night passed very quietly, Sapignies, in front of the 6th Infantry Brigade, still burned fiercely; only a few white and green lights were sent up by the enemy. At dawn on the 18th the Yorkshire Dragoons pushed forward, and by 6.30 a.m. had reported that all was clear up to a short distance south of Sapignies. At 8.45 a.m. a message was received from the Middlesex that one of their patrols had worked forward through Sapignies, which was unoccupied, the patrol remaining on the far side of the village.

18TH MARCH.

The advanced guard was therefore ordered to move forward, and at 9.30 a.m. Colonel Norris reported that the 1st King's, one company of the South Staffords, a battery of Royal Field Artillery, one section of the East Anglian Field Company R.E., one section of the 6th Brigade Machine-Gun Company, and two troops of Yorkshire Dragoons had entered Sapignies.

The situation at 11 a.m. as reported by the General Officer Commanding 2nd Division was: The 2nd Australian Division had entered Beugnâtre without opposition; the vanguard of the advanced guard had entered Sapignies. The cavalry had reported the country for over a mile north and east of Sapignies clear of the enemy; Ervillers had been entered at 10.45 a.m. by the 18th Division without opposition.

By 11.50 a.m. the General Officer Commanding 6th Infantry Brigade was able to report that the country for two or three miles to his front was clear of the enemy, and that he was advancing rapidly on Mory; he had, however, lost touch with both Divisions on his flanks.

D Company of the 1st King's had by 2.45 p.m. established itself on the high ground south of Mory, sending out patrols through the village. Three lines of strong posts were then constructed, covering Behagnies and Sapignies; these were occupied by D, C, and B Companies, and two sections of the 6th Brigade Machine-Gun Company; A Company and Battalion Headquarters were in Behagnies.

[1] The advanced guard was formed of 1st King's Regiment, one company 2nd South Staffords, one section 483rd (East Anglian) Field Company R.E., one section 6th Machine-Gun Company.

In the evening—at 6.20 p.m.—C Company was advanced to positions covering the north-west, north, and north-east exits of Mory. Touch, in the meantime, had been gained with the 2nd Australian Division and 18th Division on the right and left flanks respectively.

When night fell on the 18th March the 2nd Division was disposed as follows :

> Cavalry screens, supported by the 1st King's, on the high ground north-east of Mory, with patrols pushed out to keep touch with the enemy.
> An advanced consolidated line, covering Behagnies and Sapignies.
> A main consolidated line, covering Biefvillers and Bihucourt.
> 5th Infantry Brigade : Aqueduct road and Courcelette.
> 99th Infantry Briagde : Courcelette, Ovillers, and Wolfe Huts.
> Artillery : Two Brigades moving up to positions north-west of Grevillers, one Brigade to south of Sapignies.

Thus by the evening of the 18th the 2nd Division had advanced 14,000 yards from the Old British line.

But so far as the Division was concerned the advance was almost at an end, for during the 18th the Corps Commander had intimated to the General Officer Commanding 2nd Division that, owing to the converging movements of the flanking Divisions, the 2nd was being squeezed out of the line, and would be relieved by the 18th Division.

19TH MARCH.

The relief took place on the night of the 19th, Brigadier-General Walsh (General Officer Commanding 6th Infantry Brigade) reporting at 8.30 p.m. that his advanced guard had been relieved by troops of the 18th Division, only one battalion (1st King's) remaining behind as escort for the guns. At this period the 2nd Division had reached a line within 1,000 yards of Écoust St. Mein.

The 6th Infantry Brigade on relief was placed in Corps Reserve until the morning of the 21st, and moved back to Aqueduct road (Brigade Headquarters), Bihucourt line, and Aqueduct and Courcelette Camps.

The Divisional casualties throughout March, including those sustained in the capture of Grevillers Trench and the German retreat to the Hindenburg Line, numbered 23 officers and 466 other ranks killed, wounded, and missing.[1]

On 20th March the " 2nd Division Intelligence Summary " gave an excellent précis of the general situation : " The German

[1] See Appendix.

retreat on the Western front proceeds. No such war of movement has taken place on the Western front since the days of the Marne. From Monchy, south-west of Arras, to north of Soissons, a distance of 70 miles, and allowing for convolutions of the line—about 120 miles—the German armies are retiring towards the Belgian frontier, with British and French forces, including cavalry, in close touch. Not only Bapaume and Péronne, as already reported, but Nesle, Chaulnes, and over eighty villages, have come into British hands in the last few days. The enemy has been laying the country waste, and has poisoned the wells with arsenic. About 40 miles of French line are affected by the enemy's withdrawal from a point near Andechy to neighbourhood of Soissons. The retreat on this front has been so rapid that at Roye 800 French civilians escaped from German thraldom. At Nesle also troops were welcomed by French inhabitants, who had remained through the German occupation. French official reports state Guiscard (north-east of Compiègne) has been taken, and patrols have advanced along the St. Quentin road. East of the Oise the second German positions were captured. The number of townships and villages released by the French is about one hundred."

Not all Ludendorff's apologies can gainsay the fact that the Allies had so imposed their will upon the Germans as to necessitate the retreat to the Hindenburg Line.

Qui s'excuse, s'accuse!

In warfare he who imposes his will upon his enemy is usually adjudged the victor.

Before leaving the area the 2nd Division, influenced by the personal example of its General Officer Commanding, worked hard at salving war material, for since the beginning of 1917 salvage work had received a great impetus, and upon all ranks the necessity had been urged for saving whatever was possible in the way of equipment, arms, ammunition, etc. So successful were the efforts of the 2nd Division that for the twenty days of March—during which time the Division had been in the line—the value of material salved was no less than £23,000, and for the period 18th January–20th March, £121,000. This drew a private letter from General Headquarters to the " Q " Branch of the 2nd Division making inquiries as to the method adopted by the Division in attaining such splendid results.

On the 23rd March the Division was transferred from the IInd to the XIIIth Corps (First Army), and on the 24th began to move to its allotted area—Pernes and vicinity. On quitting the IInd

Corps area the General Officer Commanding 2nd Division received a letter from the Corps Commander (General Jacob) expressing his regret at losing the Division.

* * * * * * *

The formation of the 2nd Division at this period is interesting: the three Infantry Brigades of the Division consisted of the following troops:

5th Infantry Brigade (Brigadier-General C. N. Bullen-Smith, D.S.O.): 2nd Oxford and Bucks Light Infantry; 2nd Highland Light Infantry; 17th Royal Fusiliers; 24th Royal Fusiliers; 5th Brigade Machine-Gun Company; 5th Trench Mortar Battery.

6th Infantry Brigade (Brigadier-General R. M. Walsh, D.S.O.): 1st King's; 2nd South Staffords; 17th Middlesex; 13th Essex; 6th Brigade Machine-Gun Company; 6th Trench Mortar Battery.

99th Infantry Brigade (Brigadier-General R. O. Kellett, C.M.G.): 1st King's Royal Rifle Corps; 1st Royal Berks; 22nd Royal Fusiliers; 23rd Royal Fusiliers; 99th Brigade Machine-Gun Company; 99th Trench Mortar Battery.

The Division had now three field companies of Royal Engineers—the 5th, 483rd (1st East Anglian), and 226th.

The Divisional Train had three companies—2nd, 3rd, and 4th—and a Supply Column.

The Divisional Artillery consisted of XXXVIth Brigade R.F.A. (15th, 48th, 71st, and C/36 + right section D/34 Batteries); XLIst Brigade R.F.A. (9th, 16th, and 17th, and 47th + left section D/34 Batteries); the Divisional Ammunition Column, V/2, W/2, X/2, Y/2, and Z/2 Trench Mortar Batteries. The XXXIVth Brigade R.F.A. had become an "Army Artillery Brigade."

A Pioneer battalion (10th Duke of Cornwall's Light Infantry) had for some months been attached to the Division.

The Field Ambulances with the Division were still the 5th, 6th, and 100th.

* * * * * * *

Several changes had taken place in the Staff. Colonel N. L. Gray, A.M.S., the A.D.M.S., left to join the 22nd Division on the 5th January, and on the 19th of the same month Colonel H. Herrick, C.M.G., D.S.O., reported and took over his duties as A.D.M.S. Captain J. G. Halstead, the D.A.P.M., was evacuated sick to England on 20th January and was replaced by Captain A. H. Upton. The D.A.D.V.S., also Major A. N. N. Swanston, handed over his duties to Captain L. L. Dixon and left the Division on 13th January. The D.A.A. and Q.M.G. of the Division, Brevet

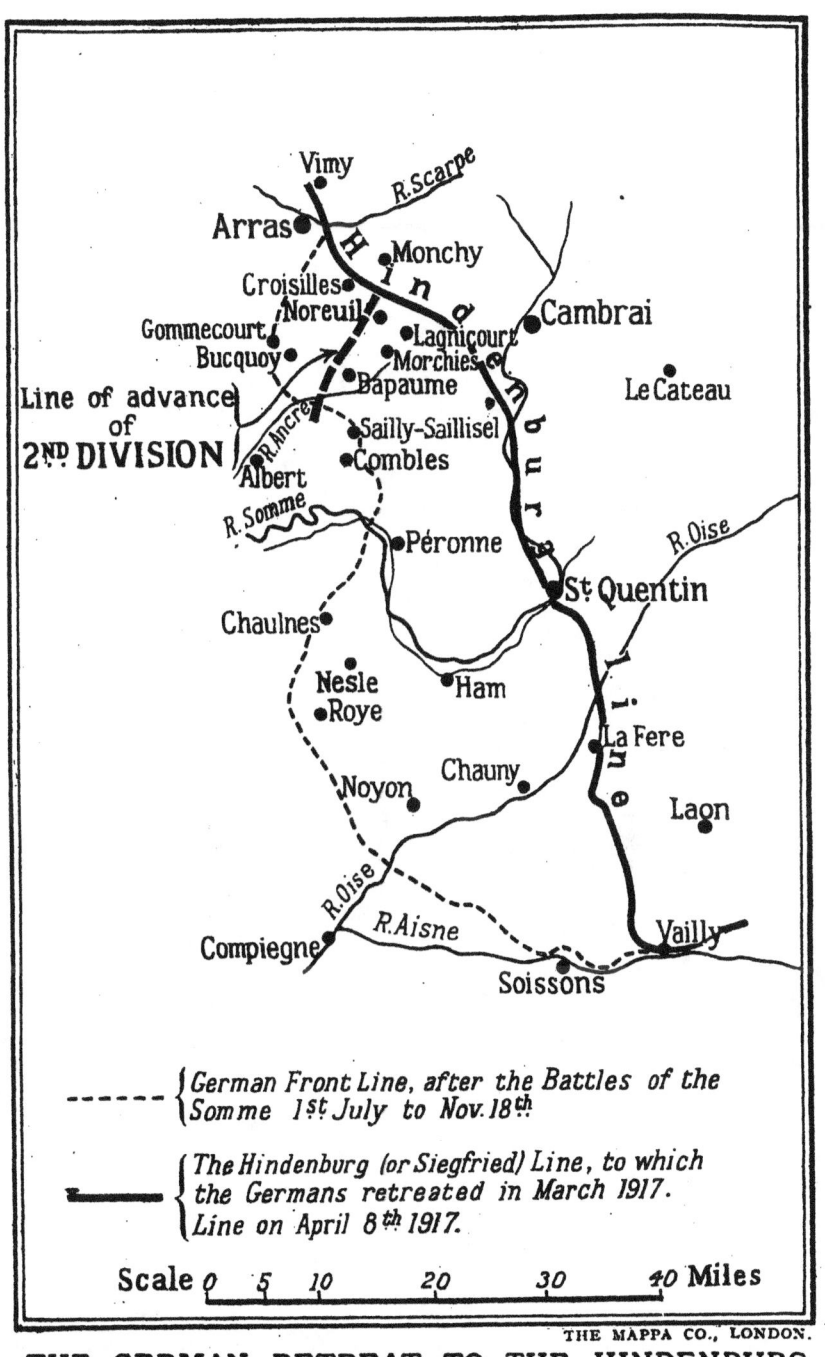

THE GERMAN RETREAT TO THE HINDENBURG LINE.

(*Facing p. 398.*)

STAFF CHANGES.

Major Viscount R. Feilding, D.S.O., left to join the 8th Division on 24th February and was succeeded by Major J. A. Pollock, who reported for duty on 11th March. On the 1st January Lieut. F. S. Arbuthnot, A.D.C. to the General Officer Commanding Division, was transferred to Headquarters Royal Artillery, 2nd Division, and was replaced by Lieut. C. D. W. Parish.

V.

THE ALLIED OFFENSIVES, 1917.

THE BATTLES OF ARRAS, 1917.

THE BATTLE OF VIMY RIDGE, 9th to 14th April 1917.
Trench Warfare, 15th to 27th April 1917.

THE BATTLE OF ARLEUX, 28th to 29th April 1917.

THE THIRD BATTLE OF THE SCARPE, 1917.
    Capture of Fresnoy, 3rd to 4th May 1917.
A Note on the Situation in the Spring of 1917.
The Second Division moves back to its old Sector, north and
    south of the La Bassée Canal.
Trench Warfare, 20th June to 4th October 1917.

THE BATTLE OF VIMY RIDGE,
9th to 14th April 1917.

AT 11 o'clock on the morning of the 30th March, 2nd Division Headquarters opened at Pernes; the 5th Infantry Brigade was also located in the same town. The 6th Infantry Brigade was at Monchy and Cayeux, and the 99th Infantry Brigade at Tangry. But the Divisional artillery was ordered to move up into the Canadian Corps area. Thus the gunners were again robbed of their much-needed rest.

30TH MARCH.

Having settled in its new area, the Division set to work to train and refit for the Allied Offensives of 1917, which were due to begin early in April. The weather was cloudy and cold, and the troops were not sorry to be away from the uncomfortable conditions prevailing in the front-line trenches. So within a few days of its arrival in the Pernes area the Division had settled down to alternate hard training and recreation, *both* necessary to make the men fit for the coming offensive.

At a conference of military representatives of all the Allied Powers held at French General Headquarters at Chantilly in November 1916, the general plan of campaign to be carried out by the Allied armies during 1917 was discussed and unanimously agreed upon; General Joffre was then Commander-in-Chief of the French armies.

A series of offensives on all fronts was to be launched, timed to assist each other by depriving the enemy of the power of weakening any one of his fronts in order to reinforce the other. The Battles of the Somme, 1916, had exhausted the enemy to such an extent that he was bound to wage defensive warfare in 1917, and the offensive had passed to the Allies.

Sir Douglas Haig was to attack the enemy's troops occupying the salient between the rivers Scarpe and Somme; the Fifth Army operating on the Ancre front, whilst the Third Army attacked from the north-west about Arras, including the Vimy Ridge, the possession of which was absolutely necessary, as it would deprive the enemy of valuable observation. If these operations were successful, the main attack was to be transferred to Flanders, where Sir Douglas Haig hoped to strike hard before the enemy realized that the attack in the south would not be pressed further.

The German retreat to the Hindenburg Line in the early weeks of 1917, however, necessitated certain modifications of these plans. Moreover, in December 1916 General Nivelle had succeeded General Joffre as Commander-in-Chief of the French armies, and a new plan of campaign was prepared and adopted by the French.

As a result of this new plan it was decided that the British offensive should begin early in April. " On as great a scale," said Sir Douglas Haig, " as the extension of my front [1] would permit, with due regard to defensive requirements on the rest of my line. The British attack, under the revised scheme, was, in the first instance, to be preparatory to a more decisive operation to be undertaken a little later by the French armies, in the subsequent stages of which the British forces were to co-operate to the fullest extent possible."

Preparations for putting these plans into execution had already been begun when the enemy, perceiving the danger in which he stood, laid waste the country between the great salient stretching from Soissons to Arras, and retired to the Hindenburg Line, thus shortening his front and securing better dispositions for his troops.

The Revolution in Russia had placed the Allies in the West in some difficulties, as it was obvious that the latter could not count upon their Eastern Ally in the coming spring, and the enemy would therefore be able to transfer troops from East to West and use them in stemming the tide should it go against him.

The point selected for Sir Douglas Haig's main attack was, however, north of the area included in the German retreat to the Hindenburg Line, and with slight modifications of his scheme of operations the British Commander-in-Chief decided that the retirement did not seriously affect his plans. Only the *rôle* of the Fifth Army was modified; instead of attacking the salient in the Ancre area, it had merely to follow up the enemy and establish itself afresh in front of the Hindenburg Line.

[1] When the new French plan was adopted, Sir Douglas Haig was asked to take over a large area from the French, stretching from a point opposite Lesbœufs and across the Somme west of Péronne as far south as Le Quesnoy-en-Santerre, on the Amiens–Roye road.

THE COMING OFFENSIVE. 407

Preparations for the British offensive in April were therefore proceeded with according to programme. Of these, the question of transport was of the foremost importance, necessitating the building of a considerable number of standard and narrow railways. Roads had to be improved, and an adequate water supply installed. For the building of roads wood planks of heavy beech, laid side by side, were of great utility. In this manner roads were built up rapidly and across almost any nature of ground. Over these roads vast quantities of stores and ammunition were moved up behind the front line from which the offensive was to take place. And the troops detailed for the attack had to be accommodated in huts and dug-outs in the battle area. The numerous difficulties inseparable from the launching of a great offensive were, however, overcome, and by the end of March all preparations for the attack had been made. There yet remained wire-cutting, bombardments of hostile trenches, strong points and gun positions, and in these important operations the guns were engaged night and day.

When the 2nd Division moved into the XIIIth Corps area in Pernes, and before the offensive began, the new German defence system—the Hindenburg Line—along the British front ran in a north-westerly direction from St. Quentin to the village of Tilloy-les-Mafflaines, immediately south-east of Arras. Northwards from Tilloy, the original German trench systems continued across the valley of the Scarpe river to the all-important dominating Vimy Ridge. The ridge, rising to a height of some 475 feet, commanded a wide view to the south-east, east, and north, and had been the scene of many a bloody contest between the opposing forces. From Vimy Ridge the British and German trenches left the high ground and, skirting the western suburbs of Lens, now battered and shell-blasted to ruins, stretched again northwards across a flat country of rivers, dykes, and canals, the dead line of which was broken only by the hills stretching from Wytschaete, north-westwards to Passchendaele and Staden, thence to the English Channel.

At a conference held on the 30th March the corps commander (Lieut.-General Sir W. N. Congreve) gave his Divisional commanders an outline of the operations which were to begin on 9th April. The main attack was to be carried out by the Third and First Armies.

The attack of the First Army on the Vimy Ridge chiefly concerned the XIIIth Corps; the Corps was then in First Army

Reserve. The future operations of the corps, however, depended upon the success of the Canadian Corps of the First Army and the XVIIth Corps of the Third Army; the Canadian and the XVIIth Corps having been detailed for the operations on and from the Vimy Ridge to the Scarpe.

The early days of April were spent by the 2nd Division in hard training; the Divisional schools were busy with bombing, Lewis-gun and other courses. In between times football matches, horse shows and other diversions by day, and performances by the Divisional troupe at night, kept the minds of the men from dwelling perpetually on the grim struggle which waged incessantly up and down the front line. The weather was still bad, and on 3rd April snow fell heavily, which meant a subsequent thaw and more mud.

Three weeks before the attack began the artillery opened with a systematic bombardment of the enemy's position. Whilst the "heavies" searched the back areas and communications, the light guns poured an almost continuous fire upon the enemy's wire and front-line trenches. Aerial activity on both sides was distinguished by its furious intensity, and combats in the air took place daily. British airmen, observing for the guns, were constantly attacked by large numbers of the enemy's machines, and losses on both sides were severe. But the British guns carried out their work effectively, unhindered by enemy aircraft. Aerial bombing raids against the enemy's dumps, railways, aerodromes, and billets caused him great loss.

Both the 2nd Divisional Artillery and the Trench Mortar Batteries took part in the preliminary bombardment. The gunners of the 2nd Division, instead of marching to Pernes with the Division, had gone into the line opposite the Vimy Ridge.

Concerning this bombardment an artillery officer's Diary said: "I have never seen anything like the way the ground is churned up—even the Somme front has nothing that it can show to beat it. Every dug-out nearly has been completely blown in, and numbers of Germans must have been buried in them. . . . What the difference in gun power is between this battle and the Somme I don't know, but the havoc each shell has done seems to be infinitely worse than anything further south. You cannot here walk between the shell-holes—you have to walk over and into them, and over vast parapets of clods of earth weighing over two hundredweights which the explosion causes. How any man could live in the hell it must have been I don't know."

On the 7th April the 99th Infantry Brigade moved to Orlen-

THE OFFENSIVE OPENS. 409

court, and the 6th Infantry Brigade to Ourton; the 5th Infantry Brigade still continued training. On the 8th the Division was located in the Hermin–Frévillers–Monchy Breton–La Thieuloye–Camblain Châtelain area, with instructions to be prepared to move at four hours' notice after "zero" hour on "Z" day. 2nd Division Headquarters were at Château de Boisennot. The Division was now twelve miles behind the front line.

Under cover of a most effective artillery barrage the attack by the First and Third Armies was launched on the 9th April at 5.30 a.m. Keeping close on the heels of the barrage, the infantry swept like a flood over the enemy's position, overwhelming his garrisons; and within forty minutes practically the whole of the German front-line system on the front attacked had been stormed and taken. Only on the extreme left on the slope of Hill 145, at the northern end of the Vimy Ridge, fierce fighting was still taking place. The first attack had surprised the enemy, and when, at 7.30 a.m., the advance towards the second objective took place, his resistance had stiffened. But eventually both British and Canadian troops overcame all resistance, and at nightfall on the 9th the line ran from north to south: a point just west of the summit of Hill 145 and La Folie Farm, along the eastern slopes of Vimy Ridge to the village of Pont du Jour, thence skirting the eastern exits of Fampoux back north of the railway, and round the eastern exits of Feuchy, just south of the Scarpe. From the latter the line zigzagged somewhat directly south, skirting the eastern edges of St. Martin-sur-Cojeul, and thence south-east to a point in the British line about half-way between Henin and Croisilles. Large numbers of guns and much war material fell into the hands of the victorious First and Third Armies; the prisoners were numbered in thousands, and at nightfall the British troops were in fine fettle.

9TH APRIL.

At midnight on the 9th–10th April the 2nd Division received orders to move during the 10th to the Marœuil area, preparatory to relieving the 51st Division in the front line on the night 11th–12th April. The march took place in the worst possible weather, and a driving snowstorm met the troops as they trudged along the slushy roads.

Meanwhile throughout the 10th the battle was proceeding. The Canadians stormed and captured the remaining portions of Hill 145, taking many prisoners, trench mortars, and machine guns. South of the Scarpe the western exits of Monchy-le-Preux were reached. More guns and more prisoners had fallen to the First and Third Armies.

410 THE HISTORY OF THE SECOND DIVISION.

On the 11th the attack was continued, and by 9 a.m. the whole of Monchy was in the hands of the British. An attack on the Hindenburg Line, in the neighbourhood of Bullecourt, made with great gallantry and at first gaining ground, was, however, beaten back, and the troops forced to retire to their original " jumping off " trenches.

Guides from the 51st Division had been ordered to meet the 5th and 99th Infantry Brigades of the 2nd Division at 3 p.m. on the 11th. The 6th Infantry Brigade was to relieve the 152nd and 154th Infantry Brigades of the 51st Division in the Reserve area round Roclincourt, the relief to be completed by 3 p.m. on the 11th.

Heavy snow again fell during the afternoon and the evening of the 11th, retarding the reliefs, which were not completed until the early hours of the 12th.

The 24th Royal Fusiliers of the 5th Infantry Brigade, and the 23rd Royal Fusiliers and the 1st King's Royal Rifle Corps of the 99th Infantry Brigade, were in the front line; the former on the left and the latter on the right. The 24th Royal Fusiliers joined up with the 8th Canadian Infantry (Canadian Corps), and the King's Royal Rifles with the 34th Division on their right; the 23rd Royal Fusiliers were between the Rifles and 24th battalion.

12TH APRIL. On the morning of the 12th Divisional Headquarters moved to Marœuil, and at 10 a.m. the General Officer Commanding 2nd Division assumed command of the line. At that hour the Division was disposed as follows:—

The front line of the Division extended from B.14,a.3.9 to (500 yards south-east of the Commandant's house) the railway in B.27,a. The 5th Infantry Brigade held the left sub-sector, between B.14,a.3.9 and Zenner Weg (exclusive) in depth with the 24th Royal Fusiliers in the forward trenches, the 2nd Oxford and Bucks in close support, the 2nd Highland Light Infantry in reserve, and the 17th Royal Fusiliers in the old German system. The 99th Infantry Brigade held the right sub-sector between Zenner Weg (inclusive) to the southern boundaries of the Divisional area, with two battalions in the front line, 23rd Royal Fusiliers (left) and the 1st King's Royal Rifle Corps (right); the 22nd Royal Fusiliers were in support, and the 1st Royal Berks in reserve. The 6th Infantry Brigade was in reserve about Roclincourt.

The 5th and 99th Infantry Brigades at once set to work to improve the trenches and take stock of their surroundings, whilst all battalions of the 6th Infantry Brigade were employed in laying

THE ENEMY RETIRES.

a duck-board track from Roclincourt to the forward areas, and in road-mending.

Hostile shells fell on the right of the 5th Infantry Brigade front during the day, but otherwise the enemy made no attack.

North of the Division, astride the Souchez river, attacks by the First Army met with complete success, and The Pimple and Bois-en-Hache were both captured with a number of prisoners and machine guns. South of the Scarpe, Heninel and Wancourt fell to the 21st and 56th Divisions, and the capture of some 2,000 yards of the Hindenburg Line was thus completed. These successful attacks created a marked salient in the enemy's line, placing the northern portion of his front from Liévin to Bailleul in jeopardy. And instead of continuing his preparations for a counter-attack from the direction of Givenchy-en-Gohelle and Hirondelle Woods, to recover the Vimy Ridge, he had perforce to consider a further retirement.

On the morning of the 13th April the Brigades holding the front line of the 2nd Division were making plans for an "aggressive defence" when a discovery was made that the enemy was withdrawing his troops from his forward positions. During the conference a telephone message was received from the 1st King's Royal Rifles saying that a patrol under Second-Lieut. G. H. Lee, D.S.O., with two N.C.O's and six men of A Company, had been out across No Man's Land. The patrol discovered that the enemy's defences on the railway embankment east of the Rifles' front line were unoccupied, and immediately entered into possession of them. With excellent initiative the patrol next pushed forward and occupied the railway station, where a strong point of ten men and one Lewis gun was established. *En route* a 77 mm. field gun was captured. Another post of twenty other ranks, with two Lewis guns, was then formed at B.21,c.4.5. Two platoons held a line from B.21,c.9.0 to B.21,6.4, with one platoon in support from B.27,a.4.8 to B.27,a.1.8.

13TH APRIL

The timely advance by the first patrol saved a heavy bombardment which had been timed for 2 p.m. in preparation for an attack by the 2nd Division on the following day. Corps Headquarters were immediately informed of the advance and the artillery ordered not to open fire.

Two companies of the left battalion of the 99th Infantry Brigade —23rd Royal Fusiliers—now pushed forward and joined up with the Rifles on the railway embankment from B.15,c.6.3 to the station.

On the left of the 23rd Royal Fusiliers the 24th Royal Fusiliers, about 3 o'clock in the afternoon, received a report of the advance of the 99th Infantry Brigade, and accordingly the whole battalion was ordered to move forward, covered by a screen of scouts (first) to the railway and (second) to a line drawn north and south through the eastern edges of both Willerval and Bailleul, crossing the Sugar Factory midway between the two villages. At 5 p.m. the leading waves of the battalion advanced, reaching both objectives. C Company, on the left, suffered somewhat heavy casualties but pressed forward. On approaching the Sugar Factory thirty or forty of the enemy fled from the buildings, which were then occupied by the Fusiliers. A German 6-inch naval gun was found in the orchard at the Factory. A line of posts was then dug on the second objective, and the battalion settled down for the night.

In their advance the 24th Royal Fusiliers lost Second-Lieut. H. Daft, killed, 3 other officers wounded, one of whom (Second-Lieut. C. F. Stafford) died of his wounds on the 14th, and 4 other ranks killed, 17 wounded, and 1 missing.

Meanwhile orders had been issued to the 23rd Royal Fusiliers and the 1st King's Royal Rifles to consolidate the line of the railway and push patrols forward into Bailleul, which was to be occupied and held. The Oppy line was then to be patrolled.

By 7 p.m. the 99th Infantry Brigade held Bailleul, two companies of the Rifles being extended on a line east of the village from B.28,b.1.1 to B.22,b.3.4, from which position posts were being pushed out to Hill 80—high ground between Bailleul and the Oppy line, in touch with the 23rd Royal Fusiliers on the left, who had established themselves in Ouse Trench, running from B.22,b. central north-west to Crucifix Corner, and who were also pushing forward to Hill 80. Both Bailleul and the front line were heavily shelled from the direction of Oppy Wood. The right flank of the 2nd Division was, however, somewhat in the air, as the 34th Division had been unable to advance with the Rifles; this necessitated the Rifles extending their line farther south in order to gain touch. The line, which was over 1,000 yards in length, was held by two companies and Lewis guns. During the night of the 13th–14th the 23rd Royal Fusiliers and the 1st King's Royal Rifles established posts on the ridge of Hill 80, and early on the morning of the 14th they held a line running from B.29,b.8.8 through B.22,d. and B.17,c. to a point about B.16,d.5.9. The crest of Hill 80 was consolidated. Patrols sent forward to examine the Oppy Line found the wire very thick and formidable, and were fired on by machine guns and rifles.

BRITISH GAINS AND GERMAN GROWLS. 413

In the meantime supports and reserves had been moved forward behind the advancing battalions.

In the afternoon, at 3 p.m., the 24th Royal Fusiliers (5th Infantry Brigade) pressed forward under orders to gain touch with the enemy and then dig in. The advance was continued to within 500 or 600 yards of the Arleux–Oppy line, where, under heavy artillery and machine-gun fire the battalion dug a front and support line of posts.

At nightfall on the 14th April the 2nd Division held a line running from about 1,000 yards east of Willerval, south-east for approximately 500 yards in front of the Oppy line, to the railway between Oppy Wood and Bailleul; thence the line turned back in a south-westerly direction across Hill 80, and slightly east again to point B.29,8.8.

North of the 2nd Division on the 13th, the enemy had retired from his forward positions, and Petit Vimy, Vimy, Givenchy-en-Gohelle, Angres, and Liévin were occupied by the Canadians. "Great quantities of ammunition of all calibres, as well as several guns, and stores and material of every kind, were abandoned by the enemy in his retreat." Hard fighting had taken place on the 13th and 14th south of the Scarpe, and the Hindenburg Line, south-east of Arras, for seven miles had fallen. Three fierce counter-attacks were launched against the gallant troops of the 21st, 29th, and 50th Divisions, but were repulsed with heavy losses to the enemy.

"The battle near Arras on April 9th," said Ludendorff, "formed a bad beginning to the capital fighting during the year. April 10th and the succeeding days were critical days. A breach, 12,000 to 15,000 yards wide, and as much as 6,000 yards or more in depth, is not a thing to be mended without more ado. It takes a good deal to repair the inordinate wastage of men and guns, as well as munitions, that result from such a breach." For seven miles the much-vaunted Hindenburg Line had fallen.

"At the end of six days' fighting," said Sir Douglas Haig, "our front had been rolled four miles farther east, and all dominating features forming the immediate object of my attack, which I considered it desirable to hold before transferring the bulk of my resources to the north, had passed into our possession. . . . In addition to the capture of more than 13,000 prisoners and over 200 guns, a wide gap had been driven through the German prepared defences." The operations had, moreover, drawn to this part of the Allied line the enemy's reserves from in front of the French attack which was due to develop on the Aisne. In brief, these were the results of the Battle of Vimy Ridge and the First Battle of the Scarpe in the Battles of Arras, 1917.

Trench Warfare, 15th to 27th April 1917.

15TH APRIL. On the morning of 15th April 2nd Division Headquarters moved from Marœuil to Roclincourt. During the previous night the 24th Royal Fusiliers (left sub-section) had been relieved by the 2nd Oxford and Bucks ; the 1st King's Royal Rifle Corps and the 23rd Royal Fusiliers (right sub-section) were relieved by the 22nd Royal Fusiliers and 1st Royal Berks respectively.

Active patrolling was begun immediately by all three battalions, but it was carried out under exceptionally trying circumstances. The hostile artillery was very active, whilst machine-gun fire and snipers harassed the troops as they moved about in their efforts to dig themselves in more securely and turn their new positions to the best account. The weather had also changed. The previous day had been one of glorious sunshine, with a fair wind under which the muddy ground rapidly became drier. But during the night of the 14th rain fell, and by the morning of the 15th a steady deluge had set in, changing the ground underfoot to thick, slimy morasses and inches of mud.

At 7.30 p.m. orders were received from 2nd Division Headquarters changing the southern boundaries of the Division, as the 190th Infantry Brigade (63rd Division) was to relieve the 99th Infantry Brigade on the right half of the line during the night. The new southern boundary of the 2nd Division ran from the southern end of Roclincourt to the railway crossing at B.27,a.9.4, along Iron Weg to the southern end of Bailleul, thence to the road and railway crossing at B.23,a.9.8 (inclusive to the 63rd Division), thence to the southern end of Neuvireuil. The northern boundary of the Division remained the same—*i.e.*, north of Roclincourt to the south-eastern corner of Willerval, thence to the road junction at B.11,b.7.5 to the corner of the wood south-east of Fresnoy.

The change took place during the night 15th–16th, when the 99th Infantry Brigade handed over its front to the 190th Infantry Brigade and the 5th Infantry Brigade, the latter extending its right as far as the new southern boundary of the Division. Two battalions of the 5th Infantry Brigade, the 2nd Oxford and Bucks and the 17th Royal Fusiliers, then held the whole Divisional front line, which, however, consisted of posts. The 99th Infantry Brigade moved back into support, the 6th Infantry Brigade remaining in reserve.

Throughout the relief the enemy's bombardment was particularly heavy. On the morning of the 16th the forward battalions received orders to reconnoitre the enemy's wire in front of the Arleux–Oppy line—a difficult matter in daylight. One patrol of the 17th Royal Fusiliers, consisting of Second-Lieut. S. E. Brodie and three other ranks, went out at 3 p.m. and proceeded north-east towards Arleux. The patrol pushed forward gallantly until it reached a point within 60 or 70 yards of the enemy's wire, having been sniped at during its advance. On arriving in this position six of the enemy appeared from the northern side of the Sugar Factory road and entered two houses close by. Shortly afterwards the enemy reappeared, and, lining the road, opened fire on the patrol. Lieut. Brodie then ordered his men to return the fire, and a regular duel ensued between the two parties. Three of the enemy had fallen, two had moved away out of range, and one had limped back to the houses, when the patrol was attacked by a second party of from thirty to forty Germans. Lieut. Brodie and one man fell wounded, another man was killed, and the fourth managed to get back safely though fired on heavily. Lieut. Brodie and the wounded man were captured by the enemy, the former dying of his wounds on the 17th. The patrol had, however, done its work well, and the man who escaped reported the enemy's wire as " thick and unbroken."

From the 17th to the 21st April inclusive the situation remained " normal." The 6th Infantry Brigade had relieved the 5th Infantry Brigade on the night 18th–19th. Wire-cutting continued, and the enemy's entanglements were kept under a heavy artillery fire. The 2nd Divisional Artillery, from being attached to the Canadian Corps, rejoined the Division on the 17th.

During this period the front line had been gradually advanced nearer the enemy's wire, and a few hundred yards now only separated the trenches of the forward brigade from the formidable Arleux–Oppy line.

On the night of the 21st the enemy made a daring raid on the trenches of the 6th Infantry Brigade. A new front trench within 300 yards of the Oppy line had been dug by the Brigade on the 20th, but a gap had been left in the centre between the two battalion sectors. The right sub-sector of the line was held by the 2nd South Staffords, and the left by the 13th Essex Regiment;

21ST APRIL

the 1st King's were in close support, and the 17th Middlesex in reserve.

The battalion raided was the 13th Essex. About 9 p.m., preceded by a heavy barrage, the enemy sent over two strong raiding parties against both flanks of the new forward trench. The Essex sent up an " S.O.S." to the artillery, who promptly opened fire. The enemy had, however, succeeded in getting round the left flank of the new trench, and had captured some men of the Essex Regiment, marching them back to his own front lines. Another company was immediately sent forward and reoccupied the trench, finding in it a wounded German officer of the 76th Bavarian Regiment. A number of enemy " other ranks " were also wounded. The Essex Regiment lost in this affair 5 other ranks killed, 3 wounded, and 22 missing. The enemy's barrage was particularly heavy.

During the night of the 21st–22nd the 6th Infantry Brigade extended its right flank to the railway at B.24,a., and took over that portion of the front line from the 63rd Division. On the following night the 5th Infantry Brigade took over the left half of the Divisional front from the 6th Infantry Brigade.

An assault on the Oppy line had been planned for the 23rd, but was postponed—the 2nd Division being ordered to co-operate by fire in an attack to be carried out by the 63rd Division on Gavrelle.

In the meantime the French had, on the 16th, launched their attacks between Soissons and Rheims, and many villages, some thousands of prisoners, and much war material had already fallen

23RD APRIL. into their hands. By the 23rd the time had arrived for Sir Douglas Haig to continue his plan of attack. Accordingly, at 4.45 a.m. on that date, the Fifth and Third Armies, as far north as (and including) the 63rd Division, attacked the enemy's position on a front of nine miles from Croisilles to Gavrelle. By the evening of the 23rd, Gavrelle, with 12 German officers and 350 other ranks, had been captured by the 63rd Division. An artillery officer of the 2nd Division, observing for his battery in an " observation post," said : " All of a sudden things began to get interesting. News came in that the first objective had been captured, and that Gavrelle was ours. The whole Boche countryside seemed to spring into life, and parties of men collected from everywhere— Boches marching out of Oppy, Neuvireuil, the rear trenches, and being shot at all the time. . . . Unfortunately most of our big guns were not up yet, and the majority of them could not reach. Wagon teams of ammunition streamed over the roads to their battery positions, motor-cars dashed up and down all the roads, and a continual stream of Huns wended their way, mostly at the gallop, from the support and front-line trenches—even " over the top "— towards Mauville Farm. Quite two battalions must have taken part in this retreat. . . . We plugged away at them for some time, until we got them well out of range, and then watched them all forming up for a counter-attack, three or four battalions of them all round Mauville Farm. Here they all sat down and waited, while each wave in turn was sent over. They marched right up to a flank, and then came on towards us, getting closer and closer into our range, while we plugged away at them hard." The principal feature of this attack was the extraordinary efforts made by the enemy to recapture Gavrelle. No less than six strong counter-attacks were launched against it, but all were repulsed with terrible loss to the attackers. Waves were annihilated as they advanced, and others were broken ere they reached the British trenches, only a few survivors returning to their own lines.

Again, on the 24th, the enemy tried to retake the village, without even the smallest success. By this time the British gains included Guémappe (as well as Gavrelle) and the whole of the high ground overlooking Fontaine-lez-Croisilles and Cherisy. Progress had been made east of Monchy-le-Preux, on the left bank of the Scarpe, and on Greenland Hill.

Over 3,000 prisoners were captured during the operations which took place on the 23rd and 24th. Valuable progress had been made by the French in Champagne and on the Aisne, but a continuance of the operations at Arras was necessary in order to attain the Allies' aims. Preparations were therefore pushed forward to begin the next attack.

On the 27th the French offensive came to a standstill—the enemy had reinforced his front, and further progress was impossible. But before this date it became necessary to attempt to divert his troops northwards, and with this intention orders for the final attacks at Arras were issued by Sir Douglas Haig.

The first of these attacks was to take place on the morning of 28th April over a front of eight miles, from Monchy-le-Preux northwards across the Scarpe, and against the villages of Oppy and Arleux. The Divisions to be employed for this attack were the Canadian, 2nd, 63rd, 37th, and 12th, from north to south in the order given. The Canadians and the 2nd Division were to capture Arleux and Oppy respectively.

THE BATTLE OF ARLEUX:

The Attack on the Oppy Line, including the Arleux Switch, by the 2nd Division.

26TH APRIL. During the afternoon of the 26th April 2nd Division Headquarters issued instructions (No. C.6) for the assault of the Oppy line, including Oppy Village and the Arleux Switch, the salient points of which were: the attack was to be made by the 5th and 6th Infantry Brigades, the 99th Infantry Brigade being in reserve; the Canadians on the left and the 63rd Division on the right of the 2nd Division would attack simultaneously. There were three objectives: the Blue (1st), Green (2nd), and Brown (3rd) Lines.

27TH APRIL. On the 27th "Z" day was announced as the 28th; "zero" hour was to be at 4.25 a.m. The brigades accordingly moved to their assembly positions, and on the evening of the 27th the 5th Infantry Brigade held the left of the Divisional front line and the 6th Infantry Brigade the right. Although the enemy's guns had not ceased shelling the Divisional area, the assembly positions were taken up without undue interference, and only a few casualties were suffered. At midnight on the 27th the 2nd Division was disposed for battle as follows:

The left sub-sector was held by the 2nd Oxford and Bucks and the 2nd Highland Light Infantry of the 5th Infantry Brigade. The 17th Royal Fusiliers were in close support, and had been ordered to furnish carrying parties and "moppers-up," and to assist generally the two attacking battalions. The 24th Royal Fusiliers were in Brigade reserve.

In the right sub-sector the front line was held by the 17th Middlesex Regiment (on the right flank of the 2nd Highland Light Infantry) and the 13th Essex of the 6th Infantry Brigade, with the 2nd South Staffords in close support (and to provide carrying parties), and the 1st King's in reserve.

Oppy Village and Wood were in the 6th Infantry Brigade area of attack, the 5th Infantry Brigade area lying between the villages of Arleux and Oppy.

To the attacking battalions were attached two sections of the 99th Brigade Machine-Gun Company and the 226th Field Company R.E. to the 5th Infantry Brigade, and one battalion of the 99th Infantry Brigade (the 1st King's Royal Rifle Corps), the East Anglian Field Company R.E., and two sections of the 99th Brigade Machine-Gun Company to the 6th Infantry Brigade.

EXPECTATIONS OF HEAVY FIGHTING.

The 23rd Royal Fusiliers were given the task of clearing the village of Oppy when captured.

Six Field Artillery Brigades under the command of the Commander Royal Artillery 2nd Division,[1] and Corps and Army Heavy Artillery were to support the attack.

Each attacking brigade was to establish strong points east and north and south of Oppy Village.

The artillery barrage was to be the guiding factor in the pace of the infantry attack. The troops were impressed with the urgent necessity of advancing close up to the barrage and attacking any portion of the enemy's trench opposite them immediately the guns lifted from it.

That stout opposition was expected may be gathered from the following paragraph in the " Instructions ": " All indications and information lead to the assumption that the enemy's troops have received orders to oppose strenuously our advance on the north bank of the river Scarpe, which, if successful, will not only bring us up to the Siegfried Line before it is completed, but also threaten his hold on the valuable mining area about Lens. Violent counter-attacks are, therefore, to be expected, and will probably develop very shortly after our capture of Oppy and Arleux."

In point of fact the enemy, owing to the Russian Revolution which had begun earlier in the year, had been able to transfer some of his divisions from the Eastern to the Western front, and to replace others, sending weak and worn-out divisions to Russia, and bringing back troops which were practically fresh to France and Flanders.

The attacking strength of the 2nd Division at this period was weak. The total length of front to be assaulted was 2,200 yards, and the troops available for the attack numbered only 3,518; this in spite of the fact that the strongest battalions of the two strongest brigades were to be employed. And the objective to be reached was 1,200 yards distant, no light task in the face of fierce opposition. The troops had been warned that " they may expect to find machine guns a few yards behind the trench line assaulted, as well as in front of it, and that they must go straight for these machine-gun emplacements immediately the barrage lifts off the trench."

Some idea of the preparation for the attack may be gathered from the Diary of the General Officer Commanding 2nd Division,

[1] The C.R.A. of the 2nd Division at this period was temporarily Lieut.-Colonel H. W. Newcome, R.F.A.

dated the 26th April: "During the afternoon I went up to the Farbus line to try and get a view, but visibility was extremely bad. There was considerable shelling on both sides, and the general appearance of the country under a leaden sky, mist, and smoke of bursting shells was that of a manufacturing district. Arleux was being shelled by our 15-inch howitzer, and looked a perfect inferno."

Air photographs of Arleux, Oppy, and Oppy Wood taken at this period show both villages practically in ruins, though beneath the tumbled masses of brick and masonry deep dug-outs sheltered the enemy's troops. The wood was a scorched and shell-blasted mass of tree stumps.

Nor were the British areas less shell-torn, for the enemy's bombardments had been continuous. On the day before the Oppy attack three battery commanders of the 2nd Divisional Artillery were killed in their dug-out.

28TH APRIL.
MAP.

By 3.30 a.m. on the morning of the 28th the assaulting battalions of both attacking brigades were all ready in their assembly trenches, the front-line trench having been adapted for this purpose; the forming-up line behind the front line had been taped out by officers of the Royal Engineers without a hitch.

The 1st King's Royal Rifles of the 99th Infantry Brigade, attached to the 6th Infantry Brigade, were found on arrival to number only one company with twelve Lewis guns. One company of the 1st Royal Berks—2 officers and 60 other ranks—was, therefore dispatched immediately, and arrived a few minutes before "zero" hour.

At 4.25 a.m. the artillery barrage opened on the enemy's trenches, and the troops moved forward to the assault. By the time the attacking troops reached the German wire the enemy's machine guns had opened a terrific fire on the advancing waves. Within one minute of the opening of the British artillery fire he had also put down an intense artillery and minenwerfer barrage about 150 to 200 yards behind the British front line.

Through this intense curtain of fire the troops pushed gallantly forward. The left flank of the whole attack progressed splendidly. The Canadians won through to Arleux, and despite bitter hand-to-hand fighting, the village passed quickly into their possession.

The 5th Infantry Brigade of the 2nd Division also made fine progress.

The 2nd Oxford and Bucks Light Infantry, the left flank of the Brigade, went forward in four waves, B and D Companies (Captain

Giles and Captain Barnes) on the right and left respectively, C and A Companies (Lieut. Dowson and Second-Lieut. Whitehead) forming the third and fourth waves in rear. The left flank of the battalion was covered by the 8th Battalion Canadian Infantry, and the right by the 2nd Highland Light Infantry, who disposed A and B Companies in the front line on the right and left respectively, with C Company on the right and D on the left rear—each company being in depth in two waves.

At 5.30 a.m. a message reached 5th Infantry Brigade Headquarters from B Company of the Oxfords: " My company has reached its first objective . . . thirty prisoners taken . . . we have a good many casualties . . . we are held up by machine-gun fire . . . enemy made fair resistance . . . I am in touch with 2nd Highland Light Infantry on my right, and am in front of Canadians going towards Arleux."

The left company of the Oxfords had likewise advanced, and with the Canadians had consolidated the Green Line, the second objective.

The Highland Light Infantry, however, found that the enemy's wire had been insufficiently cut, and were delayed in getting through. In consequence the barrage outstripped the advancing troops, and it was not caught up until it had reached the German support trenches (the Blue Line). By this time the battalion had lost touch on its right with the 17th Middlesex, the left flank of the 6th Infantry Brigade. The Highland Light Infantry then began an advance to the next objective, which was successfully reached, but could not be held owing to the right flank of the battalion being exposed to heavy enfilade fire from the direction of Oppy Wood and Village. The battalion finally consolidated the Blue Line.

In the meantime the Oxfords had won through to the northern apex of the final objective—*i.e.*, where the Brown and Green Lines joined; but finding that touch had not been gained with the 2nd Highland Light Infantry on the right, the battalion had to throw back its right flank until touch was obtained in the German support line. A line of strong posts was then established.

B Company of the 17th Royal Fusiliers (Captain Taylor), attached to the 2nd Highland Light Infantry, acting on the right of the latter, then formed a defensive flank to the 5th Infantry Brigade.

Meanwhile the right of the attack had been hung up.

The left flank of the 63rd Division (on the right of the 2nd

THE HISTORY OF THE SECOND DIVISION.

Division) had not found it possible to penetrate the enemy's wire. As a result the 6th Infantry Brigade, which had advanced with fine dash across the Blue to the Green Line, suddenly found itself attacked in flank and rear.

The Diaries of the two attacking battalions of the 6th Infantry Brigade—*i.e.*, the 17th Middlesex and the 13th Essex Regiments—are so complete that they are given in full: " The battalion," said the Diary of the Middlesex Regiment, " marched from Roclincourt on the morning of the 27th; formed up in its battle positions on the front allotted to the battalion, opposite Oppy Wood and the village of Oppy. The forming-up was carried out without a hitch and in perfect silence, in spite of heavy shelling of the front area. The attached company of 2nd South Staffords formed up also in their respective places either as ' moppers-up ' or as ' Strong Point Parties,' and the carrying parties also provided by the South Staffords formed up in rear. Touch was established with the 13th Essex on the right, and the 2nd Highland Light Infantry on the left.

" The battalion was formed up on a four-company front and in three waves, each wave having its own " moppers-up " immediately behind it. The five Vickers guns attached to the battalion took posts, two behind the right flank and three behind the left flank of the last wave. These guns were allotted duties of covering the flanks during the advance, until they should have reached the strong points which they were destined to garrison. The two Stokes mortars had instructions to move up behind the right flank. The order of companies from right to left was D, C, B, and A.

" At 4.25 a.m. our barrage came down, and at 4.33 a.m. the leading wave entered the enemy's front-line trench. The wire was found to be perfectly cut and the trench practically empty. The battalion pressed forward behind the creeping barrage, and the first objective (Blue Line) was reached with only a few casualties.

" Shortly after the advance commenced the Officer Commanding A Company on the left noticed that the battalion on our left had either lost touch or had been unable to make progress. He thereupon placed a Lewis gun section and some bombers in the enemy's front-line trench, with instructions to block the trench and prevent any movement of the enemy against the left flank. The right flank during the advance to the first objective appears to have kept well in touch with the 13th Essex.

" Fighting became much heavier on reaching the line of the first objective, very heavy machine-gun and rifle fire being opened

HEAVY COUNTER-ATTACKS.

from the houses in the village. Captain Parfitt of D Company had been specially charged with the consolidation of the first objective, and this was taken in hand by the first wave, while the remainder pressed on towards the second objective (Green Line). Very heavy fighting now ensued on the right; but on the left the German trench running north and south through C.7,c. (Crucifix Lane) was reached. The fighting had now become so serious that both the second and third waves were fully involved in the struggle for the second objective, whilst the first objective was still being consolidated. Up to this juncture reports from wounded men and reports by runners had been received at Battalion Headquarters confirming the capture of the first objective and of the struggle for the second objective; but owing to the hostile shelling all reports were somewhat late in reaching Battalion Headquarters, and the situation on the left did not seem clear, as, although A Company were known to have gained ground, a report came in from the Highland Light Infantry on our left to the effect that they were hung up by fire in the Sunken Road in the neighbourhood of the Crucifix.

" A senior officer was sent from Battalion Headquarters to clear up the situation on the left, and to locate a suitable forward position for Battalion Headquarters to move to. It was now nearly 8 o'clock (in the morning), and a few minutes later a report came in from the Officer Commanding A Company—the left company—to say that the enemy was working round both his flanks. The only available reserve inside the battalion—viz., the "moppers-up" of the first objective (who had reported the completion of their task)—had already been sent forward to strengthen the right, in the hope that the second objective might still be reached. Captain Edwards, the senior officer who had been sent out to clear up the situation, found that the enemy had pressed down in strength from the north, both down the German front-line trench and by the Crucifix Road, on the flanks of our two left companies, and had driven these back through the wood to the enemy front-line trench. Here these two companies were making a stand, but had by now sustained very heavy losses. The enemy also appears to have counter-attacked against the front and right flank as well, and had succeeded in re-entering the wood and getting in between the troops consolidating on the first objective and those who had been driven back to the Oppy Trench. The enemy had also worked up the Oppy Trench from the south, and were bombing up from that direction also. All communication with the remnants of the troops in the first objective was now cut off, and runners who attempted to get through to the troops still holding Oppy Trench were either killed or wounded.

"Lieut.-Colonel Martin, 13th Essex, Commanding, sent forward a company of the 1st Royal Berks to endeavour to relieve the situation, but these could not get beyond the Old British Line. The remnants of the two companies still holding on to the Oppy Trench finally exhausted all their bombs, and when reduced to about ten all told, made a dash for the Old British Line. One officer and three men succeeded in getting through.

"The troops on the first objective were not heard of again until a wounded officer succeeded in making his way back during the night (28th–29th). His evidence made it clear that these troops had fought till they were practically exterminated by the superior forces of the enemy; the few survivors probably surrendered. The few remaining men of the battalion, with some of the South Staffords' carrying party, remained for the most of the day in the Old British Line until relieved at night by the 23rd Royal Fusiliers."

Of the troops who "went over the top" in the morning, 1 officer and 41 wounded men eventually found their way back, whilst 3 wounded officers and 106 wounded other ranks were able to get back in the early stages of the fight. The pity is that details of that gallant fight on the first objective are not in existence.

The Diary of the 13th Essex Regiment is brief, but gives sufficient details conveying an idea of what happened on the extreme right flank of the 2nd Division :

"The battalion was formed up in their jumping-off positions without any hitch occurring about 2 a.m., in spite of heavy shelling. Companies were organized in three platoons, one platoon of each company representing the first, second, and third waves, each wave consisting of two lines: first line, bombers and riflemen; second line, Lewis gunners and rifle bombers. Moppers-up for each wave were formed up in rear of its second line. Carrying parties and garrisons for strong points were formed up in rear of the last wave. Close touch was gained with the 17th Middlesex and the Royal Marines (of the 63rd Division).

"At 4.25 a.m. our barrage came down, and at 4.33 a.m. the first wave crossed the enemy's front-line trench, with the exception of the extreme right of the battalion, which was held up by uncut wire, and lost heavily from machine-gun fire in endeavouring to get through it. At this period touch was lost with the Royal

THE SITUATION AT 9 A.M. 425

Marine Light Infantry on our right. It was maintained between the 13th Essex and 17th Middlesex, but was lost with the 2nd Highland Light Infantry, who were on the left of the 17th Middlesex.

"The advance continued under the barrage to the line of the practice trenches in C.13,d. (immediately south of Oppy Village), eastern end of Oppy Wood, and C.7,c. At this period a party of German bombers attacked our right flank. Heavy machine-gun fire and rifle fire took place from Oppy Village, and large numbers of the enemy were advancing down the Sunken Road at the Crucifix.

"At 5.50 a.m. I ordered one company of the King's Royal Rifle Corps (which company had been sent up by the 6th Infantry Brigade as support) to advance and form a defensive flank from B.18,d.3.5 to the southern end of the practice trenches. This company was unable to proceed farther than the British front line owing to hostile barrage and machine-gun fire.

"About this time the battalion on our left (17th Middlesex) was heavily attacked from the front and on the left flank, and large numbers of the enemy advanced through Oppy Wood, got in rear of the line, and reoccupied parts of the German front line. A senior officer was sent forward to clear up the situation about 7.30 a.m., but did not return, and no messages were received from him.

"The heavy fighting continued, and at 9 a.m. the troops were ordered to fall back and hold and consolidate the German front line. Small detached parties only succeeded in doing this, and were unable to cope with the enemy, who was then holding the trench. All the officers of the battalion had become casualties, and the majority of the non-commissioned officers, and what was left of the battalion was quite disorganized and exhausted. Small parties held out, but eventually, running from shell-hole to shell-hole, returned to the Old British Line."

So at 9 a.m. the situation was briefly this: the Canadians had captured Arleux; the 5th Infantry Brigade of the 2nd Division had won through to (and held) the second objective; but the 6th Infantry Brigade, having gone through Oppy Wood and entered Oppy Village, had been heavily counter-attacked, and driven back first to Oppy Trench and then to the Old British Line.

Had the flank of the 6th Infantry Brigade remained secure, the first objective might have been held against counter-attacks, and the second objective would in all likelihood have been gained in its entirety, though, in view of the strength of the enemy in the village, it is doubtful. The sudden onrush of the enemy from both flanks, combined with his vigorous counter-attack in front, enabled him to reoccupy the wood. In the confused fighting which followed it was impossible to ask for fresh artillery barrages, for friend and foe were intermingled, and much of the fighting was of a hand-to-hand nature.

The enemy was apparently quite unshaken by the barrage. The reason is interesting. A new system of holding his front-line trenches had just been introduced by the enemy, for his exhaustion from the middle of 1916 to the end of the year and in the beginning of 1917 had been severe. He had, therefore, to dispose his troops in such a manner as to minimize the number of casualties.[1] This he did by placing his men in depth, leaving machine guns to hold up any infantry attack launched against him, and keeping the bulk of his infantry back in their second and third lines for use in counter-attacks. But there was another factor in the partial failure of the first attack: the attacking battalions were very weak. With a long advance in front of them, the waves already weakened in the attack had not sufficient strength to get through to the final objective, and were unable to cope successfully with the enemy's strong counter-attack made with unshaken troops. The 2nd Division had a frontage of attack of about 2,200 yards, with only 3,500 rifles available. Finally, there is no doubt that had the 63rd Division been able to penetrate the enemy's front line and advance in alignment with the right flank of the 2nd Division, the 6th Infantry Brigade would not have been outflanked and driven out of Oppy Village and Wood.

From 8 a.m. the situation in the front line was obscure, and not until later in the day was the position of the 2nd Division definitely established. At 3.30 p.m., excepting on the left flank, the Division no longer held the positions gained in the morning.

---

[1] "Not the least important of these measures," said Marshal von Hindenburg, "were the changes we introduced into our previous system of defence. They were based on our experiences in the earlier battles. In future our defence positions were no longer to consist of single lines and strong points, but of a network of lines and groups of strong points. In the deep zones thus formed we did not intend to dispose our troops on a rigid and continuous front, but in a complex system of nuclei and distributed in breadth and depth. The defender had to keep his forces mobile to avoid the destructive effects of the enemy's fire during the period of artillery preparation, as well as voluntarily to abandon any parts of the line which could no longer be held, and then to recover by a counter-attack all the points which were essential to the maintenance of the whole position. These principles applied in detail as in general. We thus met the devastating effects of the enemy's artillery and trench mortar fire, and their surprise infantry attacks, with more and more deeply distributed defensive lines and the mobility of our forces. At the same time we developed the principle of saving men in the forward lines by increasing the number of our machine guns, and so economizing troops."

A FURTHER ATTACK ORDERED. 427

The 6th Infantry Brigade was back in the Old British Line. The 5th Infantry Brigade was consolidated on the line of the Sunken Road, with its right flank thrown back in alignment with that of the 6th Brigade.

Orders were then issued to the General Officer Commanding 99th Infantry Brigade to take over the right sub-sector from the 6th Infantry Brigade. At 5.40 p.m. the Brigadier of the 99th Infantry Brigade assumed command of the line. No portion of the German front line was handed over to the 99th Brigade, and touch with the 63rd Division on the right was uncertain. On the left the 5th Infantry Brigade, which had been counter-attacked, held a line north-north-east to the right flank of the Canadian Corps.

At 7.30 p.m. a further attack on Oppy by the 99th Infantry Brigade was ordered to take place on the morning of the 29th. The attack was timed to begin at 4 a.m. The objectives to be captured were the German front and support lines between the right of the divisional boundary and the left of the right brigade boundary about B.18,b.2.9.

The frontage on the objective assigned to the 99th Infantry Brigade was that from which the 6th Infantry Brigade had attacked on the morning of the 28th—roughly, 1,000 yards. And in view of the task it was called upon to perform, the strength and condition of the Brigade merits consideration.

The 1st King's Royal Rifles and one company of the 1st Royal Berks had been used in the first attack on Oppy (on the 28th), and were, therefore, not available for the second assault on the 29th. The 22nd Royal Fusiliers numbered 15 officers and 289 other ranks. To these were added 1 officer and 50 other ranks of the Rifles, making a total of 16 officers and 309 other ranks. The 1st Royal Berks (less one company) numbered 15 officers and 250 other ranks; the 23rd Royal Fusiliers, 16 officers and 225 other ranks. The 1st King's Royal Rifles were ordered to find two carrying parties, each consisting of 1 officer and 50 other ranks; one party was attached to the 22nd Royal Fusiliers, and the other to the 1st Royal Berks. The Brigade had 50 machine guns: 8 of the 99th Infantry Brigade, 10 of the 6th Infantry Brigade, and 32 guns of the 92nd and 94th Machine-Gun Companies; 4 guns were held in reserve near Bailleul railway station.

The 99th Infantry Brigade, therefore, had available for the attack 47 officers and 814 other ranks, supported by 46 machine guns. They had also recently passed three days in the front-line trenches, and had only reached the rear positions at 4.30 a.m. on the 28th; they were, therefore, still tired, having marched back again to the front line during the close of the 28th.

During the night 28th–29th all existing dumps of grenades, small-arms ammunition, and water were filled up and fresh forward dumps made, though the small number of men available made the work very difficult.

29TH APRIL.
MAP.

At 3.53 a.m. on the 29th all attacking troops were reported ready formed up for the assault—the 22nd Royal Fusiliers, with 1 officer and 50 other ranks of the 1st King's Royal Rifles, on the right, the 1st Royal Berks (less one company) on the left. Each battalion had, therefore, about 500 yards of the enemy's position assigned to it, which worked out at one fighting man for every $2\frac{1}{2}$ yards of the objective.

The 23rd Royal Fusiliers had one company in the Old British Support Line, and three companies on and just east of the Farbus–Bailleul railway embankment. The Rifles attached to the 22nd Royal Fusiliers had been entrusted with the making of a strong point at B.24,a.8.9, and the digging of a trench to the German front line for the protection of the right flank of the Brigade, should the attack of the 63rd Division fail.

Shortly before "zero" hour, two or three of the dumps formed by the Brigade were unfortunately blown up by enemy shell-fire; the loss of the grenades and small-arms ammunition so destroyed was later of serious consequence to the attacking battalions.

At 4 a.m. the artillery barrage began, and immediately the troops moved forward from their assembly positions. Six minutes later the enemy put down a severe barrage.

B Company (right) and D Company (left) of the 22nd Royal Fusiliers moved forward close on the barrage, but were at once hung up by the enemy's wire. B Company, after frantic attempts, managed to force a gap in the front line of entanglements and pressed through; but by the time the second belt was reached the barrage had lifted. The second belt of wire was impenetrable, and while trying to break a way through a whole platoon (with the exception of Second-Lieut. J. Steele and one man) was shot down; these two dropped into a shell-hole and remained there. Of the remainder of B Company, Major R. H. Gregg and all other officers with the exception of Second-Lieut. S. F. Jeffcoat, with most of the men, had become casualties. But Lieut. Jeffcoat and Acting Company Sergeant-major Hogan, finding a gap in the wire on the extreme right, collecting all the men they could find, jumped

"NO QUARTER WAS ASKED OR GIVEN." 429

through and into the German trench, capturing it with a number of prisoners. The gallant subaltern and his equally gallant acting company sergeant-major then bombed right and left up and down the German trench, endeavouring to get into touch with the 63rd Division and D Company of the battalion. Close and desperate fighting ensued. "No quarter was asked or given," said the battalion Diary, "and many Germans were killed. Lieut. Jeffcoat succeeded in bombing 400 yards outside the Divisional area, where he obtained touch with the Bedford Regiment (63rd Division)."

In the meantime Acting Company Sergeant-major Hogan had worked up about 100 yards to the left, where he established a block. Word was then brought to him that Lieut. Jeffcoat was being very hard pressed, and he set off down the trench and assisted his officer in repulsing a determined counter-attack. He then started back again up the trench towards the block he had established, only to find it had been broken down and the men driven in. The supply of bombs had given out, and the survivors of B Company, about 15 in number, had retired to the Old British Line. Nothing daunted, Hogan went after them, and organized them for an immediate counter-attack. He also sent a full message back to Battalion Headquarters giving the situation.

Lieut. Jeffcoat next found that his left rear was unprotected, and, placing a block in the trench, he sent back a message to Battalion Headquarters asking for assistance.

Meanwhile D Company advancing had also found the wire uncut. Of the right platoon only Second-Lieut. F. W. Palmer, V.C., survived, he having dropped into a shell-hole. Platoons 14 and 15 also suffered a similar fate, and Second-Lieut. Parks found himself up against impenetrable wire with only three Lewis gunners. He therefore retired to the Old British Line. No. 13 Platoon, however, had better luck. This platoon "side slipped" to the left, and finding a gap got into the German trench. The men then bombed up right and left, meeting with heavy opposition. On the right they formed a block, and on the left joined up with the Berkshires. This platoon was then placed under the latter battalion, and with it shared the fortunes of the day.

The left battalion of the 99th Infantry Brigade, the 1st Royal Berks, moved forward close on the barrage at 4 a.m. On the right the wire was imperfectly cut, but wide gaps were found on the left, and through these the troops rushed up the enemy's trench. Fifteen minutes from "zero" the Oppy line from B.18,d.4.7 to B.18,b.2.9 was in their possession. They then found that neither of their flanks was in touch with adjoining troops, excepting a few men (barely a platoon) of the 22nd Royal Fusiliers on their right. On the left a gap of about 200 yards existed between the battalion and the right flank of the 5th Infantry Brigade.

The Berkshires at once established blocks and flank defences, and snipers were pushed forward into Oppy Wood, where they also established themselves. Here three enemy machine guns were captured and used with considerable effect against the retiring Germans. A number of the enemy's troops were also captured, " some of whom," the official Diaries reported, " pretended to be dead until turned over in order to be searched. These prisoners were at once evacuated."

Thus far the Berkshires held all they had so gallantly won. The right flank of the battalion was heavily counter-attacked; the attack failed. Nothing daunted, however, the enemy with great courage came on again and again, his troops being decimated by the splendid marksmanship of the Berkshires. Between 5 and 9.30 a.m. he launched five separate counter-attacks against the battalion. Four were repulsed, but during the fifth the supply of grenades gave out, and, almost exhausted and much reduced in numbers, the Berkshires were forced to give ground. And then, as the men filtered back through the battered trenches, they came suddenly upon a store of German bombs. Arming themselves with these, they again faced the enemy, and attacking him furiously, won back all the ground they had lost.

Once more the enemy launched a heavy counter-attack against the right front and centre of the now very thin line of Berkshires. But ever as they came on the enemy's troops were shot down by rifle and Lewis gun fire, and this attack also was bloodily repulsed.

It was an Homeric struggle !

Fresh enemy attacks continued to develop, until at last, reduced to less than half their original strength, and scattered over a front of about 500 yards, the gallant Berkshires were compelled to withdraw to the line of the Sunken Road running south-west from the west corner of Oppy Wood.

The left company (C), holding its objective north of the Sunken Road, now numbering only 35 other ranks, moved north along the trench, taking with them their wounded and the three captured machine guns, until they joined hands with the 5th Infantry Brigade about B.12,d.0.4. Here the survivors of the company remained.

The remainder of the Berkshires, their left flank in the air, and all their bombs expended, retired to the Old British Line, and there maintained their ground. No wonder that the Brigadier of the 99th Infantry Brigade (Brigadier-General R. O. Kellett) said in his report to Divisional Headquarters: " During this severe fighting the action of the 1st Royal Berks was beyond all praise . . . towards the end practically all the Lewis gunners were killed or wounded." [1]

During the day's fighting the Berks had captured about 70 prisoners and 3 machine guns, and had killed large numbers of the enemy.

On the right flank of the 99th Infantry Brigade the 50 other ranks and 1 officer of the 1st King's Royal Rifles (D Company) carried out with great gallantry the duties of building a post and digging a trench across to the Green Line. They not only garrisoned defensive flank, but " parties of them got intermingled with the front-line fighters," said the Officer Commanding 22nd Royal Fusiliers, " and were of the greatest assistance."

The closing incident of this attack is the splendid fortitude of the young subaltern who in the dark hours of the morning, with Acting Company Sergeant-major Hogan, had fought so gallantly.

" At 9.30 a.m.," said Colonel Barnett Barker, commanding the 22nd Royal Fusiliers, " I received a message from Second-Lieut. Jeffcoat stating that (a) he was in touch with the Bedfords (63rd Division) ; (b) that I could dribble men up to him *via* the railway ; and (c) that if I sent him reinforcements and plenty of bombs, he could attack again, and probably capture the line."

Immediately on receipt of this message bombs and reinforcements were collected ; verbal instructions were given to Captain Bowyer of the 23rd Royal Fusiliers to take about 100 men of that battalion and proceed *via* the railway to the assistance of Lieut. Jeffcoat.

Captain Bowyer and his party set off up the railway, and reached the German front line with only insignificant casualties. Bombing operations were started at once. The gallant young officer who had held out for so long was able to give directions to Captain

[1] In this action No. 8763 Lance-Corporal James Welch, 1st Royal Berks Regiment, gained the Victoria Cross for most conspicuous gallantry. " On entering the enemy's trench he killed one man after a severe hand-to-hand struggle. Armed only with an empty revolver, Lance-Corporal Welch then chased four of the enemy across the open, and captured them single-handed. He handled his machine gun with the utmost fearlessness, and more than once went into the open fully exposed to heavy fire at short range, to search for and collect ammunition and spare parts in order to keep his guns in action, which he succeeded in doing for over five hours till wounded by a shell. He showed throughout the utmost valour and initiative."
—*London Gazette*, 26th June 1917.

Bowyer and his party, who, with the 23rd Royal Fusiliers leading, followed by the 7th Royal Fusiliers, Bedfords, and H.A.C. (all of the 63rd Division), bombed northwards up the trench to within 200 yards south of Oppy Wood. Here (at Point B.18,d.4.7) a post was firmly established. Beyond this point, however, the party did not go, for Captain Bowyer thought that the Berkshires were bombing southwards to meet him, and fearing a strong counter-attack, he had to conserve his supply of bombs. Every grenade upon which Colonel Barnett Barker (back at Battalion Headquarters) could lay his hands, was sent up to the front line. The shortage caused by the explosion of the dumps just before " zero " hour was very keenly felt, and had already resulted in the loss of ground and many valuable lives.

Meanwhile Captain Taylor, holding the Old British Line, had also been sent several boxes of bombs to enable him to get across No Man's Land to Captain Bowyer. Bombs, small-arms ammunition, and water now began to arrive at Battalion Headquarters from 99th Infantry Brigade.

At this period No Man's Land was being swept by machine-gun and rifle fire from Oppy Wood; but with great gallantry Captain Taylor's men rushed across the zone of death, and, reaching Captain Bowyer, maintained touch between that officer's attack and the Old British Line.

This brings the narrative down to 10 o'clock in the morning.

But while these incidents were taking place Second-Lieut. Jeffcoat had fallen mortally wounded. To him belonged the credit for having given information which led to the successful advance of Captain Bowyer and his party, and with the battalion Diary is a report by his Commanding Officer:[1] "I write to place on record the splendid gallantry of Second-Lieut. Jeffcoat (mortally wounded). It was entirely owing to the excellent report he sent me on the situation that I was able to push up the 23rd Royal Fusiliers, and so capture practically the whole of the objective given me."

In liaison with the Officer Commanding the Bedford Regiment (63rd Division), Colonel Barnett Barker (at advanced Battalion Headquarters) kept in close touch with the situation. Patrols were pushed out, but at 8.30 p.m. the enemy was found to be in possession of Oppy Wood.

In spite of the wire being practically uncut, and the difficulty

[1] Report by Lieut.-Colonel R. Barnett Barker, Commanding 22nd Royal Fusiliers, on the action of April 29, 1917.

experienced by the assaulting troops in finding (owing to the darkness) the few gaps, had the supply of bombs been sufficient the final objective would have been reached, and the troops would have been able to maintain themselves there. For it was essentially a bombing fight, rifles and bayonets being practically useless.

"The enemy," said the report, "were Guardsmen, and fought magnificently. The losses on both sides were, therefore, about equal. Their counter-attacks appeared to be splendidly timed and organized, and had unlimited bombs." And of the troops under him Colonel Barnett Barker wrote: "They were ready, eager and prepared to move at a moment's notice, quickly understood their orders, and carried them out to perfection."

North of the 99th Infantry Brigade, throughout the 29th, the 5th Infantry Brigade had not been subjected to infantry attacks; but the enemy persistently shelled the newly-gained trenches. The latter Brigade had been ordered to co-operate in the attack on Oppy, and two companies (A and B) of the 24th Royal Fusiliers were moved up to the left flank of the 22nd Royal Fusiliers, with the two remaining companies following in close support, to act as "moppers-up."

At "zero" the two companies followed close on the barrage, and reached their final objective—the Sunken Road running from Oppy Village to Arleux. It now became apparent that the left flank of the troops on the right had not been able to reach its objective, and in consequence the right of the 24th Royal Fusiliers was in the air. In the advance Captain Hooke, in command of the two companies, was wounded and Second-Lieuts. Barnes and Clifford were missing, but 1 officer and 64 other ranks had been captured from the enemy. Only 3 officers now remained with the two companies, and the senior—Second-Lieut. Kitmister—took over command. The companies were exposed to heavy machine-gun and rifle fire from Oppy Village and Wood, and gradually withdrew until touch was obtained on both flanks. The 24th Royal Fusiliers suffered heavy casualties in this attack, and at nightfall A and B Companies were drawn back into the support trenches, and C and D Companies took over the front line held by the two former companies, and also the trench line held by the 2nd Highland Light Infantry.

Thus ended the operations of both the 99th and 5th Infantry Brigades on the 29th April against Oppy Village and Oppy Wood.

Of the 22nd Royal Fusiliers there remained only Headquarters officers and 40 men who had gone into action in the early hours of the 29th. Nine officers and 144 other ranks were amongst the killed, wounded, and missing, whilst 19 other ranks were more or less severely gassed.

Interesting comments on the operations are contained in the private Diary of the General Officer Commanding 2nd Division: "The 99th Infantry Brigade relieved the 6th Brigade last night. In conjunction with the 63rd Division, they attacked and captured the front German line. Two pockets of Germans were dealt with, and then a series of most determined counter-attacks by bombing down trenches began, the enemy gaining a footing and then being driven out again. The attacks were made by a fresh battalion of the 1st Guards Reserve Division, and an officer in the front trenches described them as the most determined he had experienced; but the 99th Brigade had got their 'backs up,' and drove back all attacks and killed a lot of Germans.

"The 5th Brigade are all secure and settled down; they calculate their casualties at 600 and their present strength at 1,500. The 99th Brigade put their strength at 1,050. Our captures yesterday were 2 officers and 154 other ranks, including about 100 German Guards. During the bombing attacks to-day we bombarded Oppy Village with 8-inch, 9.2-inch, and 12-inch guns, and cut it off with a 4.5-inch barrage. This seemed to have the effect of cutting off reinforcements and bombs, and later a mixed party of 2nd Division and 63rd Division cleared 1,000 yards of German front trench, and we had no more trouble. The Germans were also seen evacuating Oppy Village in small parties, probably carrying parties or reinforcements, as the patrols we sent forward found there was no lightening their hold of the village."

Both on the 28th and 29th the Machine-Gun Companies of the 2nd Division were actively engaged,[1] and handled their guns with splendid effect. All four sections of the 5th Machine-Gun Company lent valuable assistance to the 5th Infantry Brigade during the attack which took place on 28th, A Section establishing guns at B.6,c.4.0 and B.6,d.2.1; D and B Sections guarded the right flank of the Brigade during the whole day, though subjected repeatedly to counter-attacks and heavy shelling. Some of the company's guns were knocked out of action, yet the gunners maintained their positions. C Section opened a heavy barrage on the enemy's

[1] The Machine Companies of the 2nd Division at this date were 5th Machine-Gun Company (Major W. M. Todd), 6th Machine-Gun Company (Major W. G. Hewett), 99th Machine-Gun Company (Captain A. P. Skevington).

OF THE DIVISIONAL TROOPS. 435

communication trenches in order to assist the attack at "zero" on the 29th.

On the 28th the 5th Machine-Gun Company lost 2 officers killed [1] and 1 officer wounded, 3 other ranks killed and 14 wounded; on the 29th 1 officer killed [2] and 1 other ranks killed and 9 wounded.

Of the 6th Brigade Machine-Gun Company, No. 1 Section was attached to the 13th Essex Regiment, and No. 2 Section to the 17th Middlesex. The two remaining sections were placed on the left and right of the reserve line, and carried out barrage fire, one team of each section advancing for the protection of the right and left flanks of the 6th Infantry Brigade as it went forward. The enemy's heavy barrage at "zero" on the 28th caught the 6th Machine-Gun Company, and caused the company the loss of 1 officer wounded and missing, 1 other ranks killed and 8 wounded and 8 missing. On the 29th the company co-operated with the 99th Machine-Gun Company in the machine-gun barrage. The 99th Machine-Gun Company was engaged in barrage work both on the 28th and 29th.

The Field Companies R.E. of the 2nd Division, to whom had been allotted the duties of constructing strong points on the line of the final objective, were unable to carry out their orders owing to the partial failure of the attack. The 226th Field Company was attached to the 5th Infantry Brigade, and the 483rd (East Anglian) Field Company to the 6th Infantry Brigade.

No. 3 Section of the 226th Field Company taped out the assembly lines for the 5th Infantry Brigade, and No. 4 Section of the 483rd Field Company the assembly lines for the 6th Infantry Brigade. The sappers were, however, kept back at the Headquarters of the attacking battalions until the situation in front should be sufficiently clear to permit of the strong points being built; but not until the 30th were they able to construct the posts. They were then assisted by the Divisional Pioneers (10th Duke of Cornwall's Light Infantry).

To the Pioneers fell none of the glories of the front-line fighting; but no attacking troops were ever served more faithfully than were the infantry of the 2nd Division by the 10th Duke of Cornwall's Light Infantry. For many hours on end, after strenuous labours on the communications within the Divisional areas, these men went cheerfully forward, and "carried" for the battalions in the front line. They had to pass across shell-swept areas, and at times came within the enemy's barrage, but they stuck to their

[1] See Appendix.   [2] See Appendix.

work with grim and splendid tenacity. A Company, for instance, which since the early morning of the 28th had been working on the railway, was sent up to Weston's and Tunnel Dumps at 1 p.m. From this point until 6.30 the following morning the company carried water, ammunition, and rations up towards Oppy Wood. All through the night the work continued. Another company—D—having already done seven hours' work on the Rolincourt-Thelus road, marched back to camp, had tea, and at 6.30 p.m. was also dispatched to Weston's Dump for carrying duties. Of C Company two platoons were attached to the Royal Engineers, another platoon carried wire for the Signal Company, and the fourth platoon marched forward to the Dumps for carrying duties. B Company did the same as D Company. On the following day (29th) the Pioneers were again employed in carrying, and continued working far into the night. One officer wounded, 6 other ranks killed and 16 wounded were the casualties suffered by the Pioneers.

Throughout the battle many of the guns of the Division were in action just north of Bailleul. The gunners had a very strenuous time, for the enemy's artillery was not only extremely active, but his range-finding was excellent. In consequence, both on the 28th and 29th, and even several days before the battle opened, the Divisional Artillery suffered heavy losses. On the afternoon of the 26th, as the officers of the XXXVIth Brigade R.F.A. were sitting in a dug-out at mess, a shell fell in the doorway and exploded with disastrous results: Major V. Walrond (Commanding 15th Battery), Major P. G. Bailey (Commanding 48th Battery), and Second-Lieuts. W. H. Manifold and H. J. Bell (both of the 15th Battery) were killed outright. During the preceding days, and including the 27th, the XXXIVth (Army) Brigade R.F.A. reported its losses as three 18-pounder and one 4.5-inch howitzer guns put completely out of action, and 20 casualties in personnel. The XLIst Brigade R.F.A. also suffered losses both in officers and other ranks.

On the 28th two officers of the 15th Battery (XXXVIth Brigade) especially distinguished themselves: Captain Claudet, who directed his guns with great coolness and courage; and Second-Lieut. Kershaw, who, though shot through both legs, continued for two hours after he was wounded to direct the fire of his guns.

The Battle of Arleux (the first of the final Arras attacks) ended on the night 29th-30th April. Very heavy losses had been inflicted on the enemy, but the British also suffered severely. The battle

THE BATTLE OF ARLEUX,
28th–29th April 1917.
(And to cover the period between 15th–27th April 1917.)
(*Facing p. 436.*)

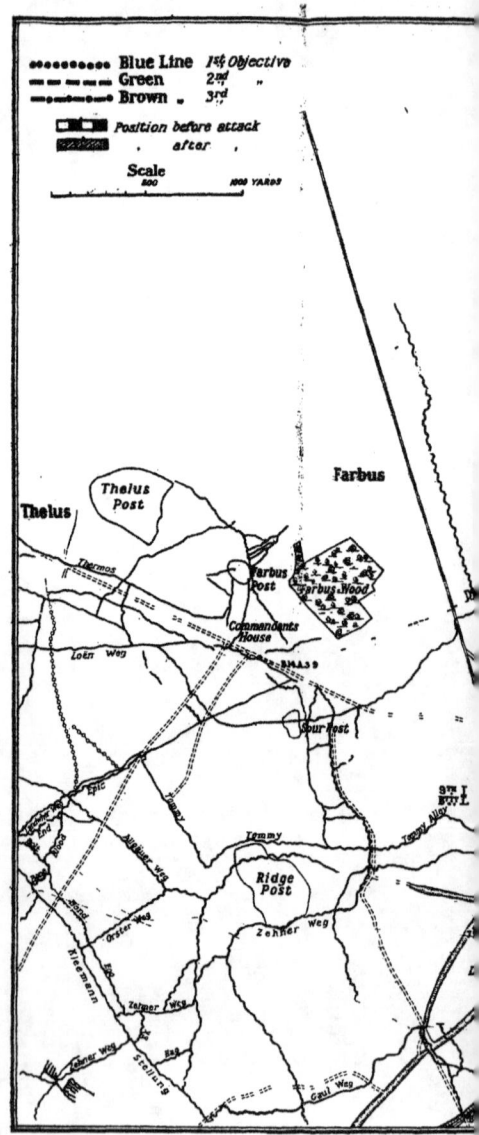

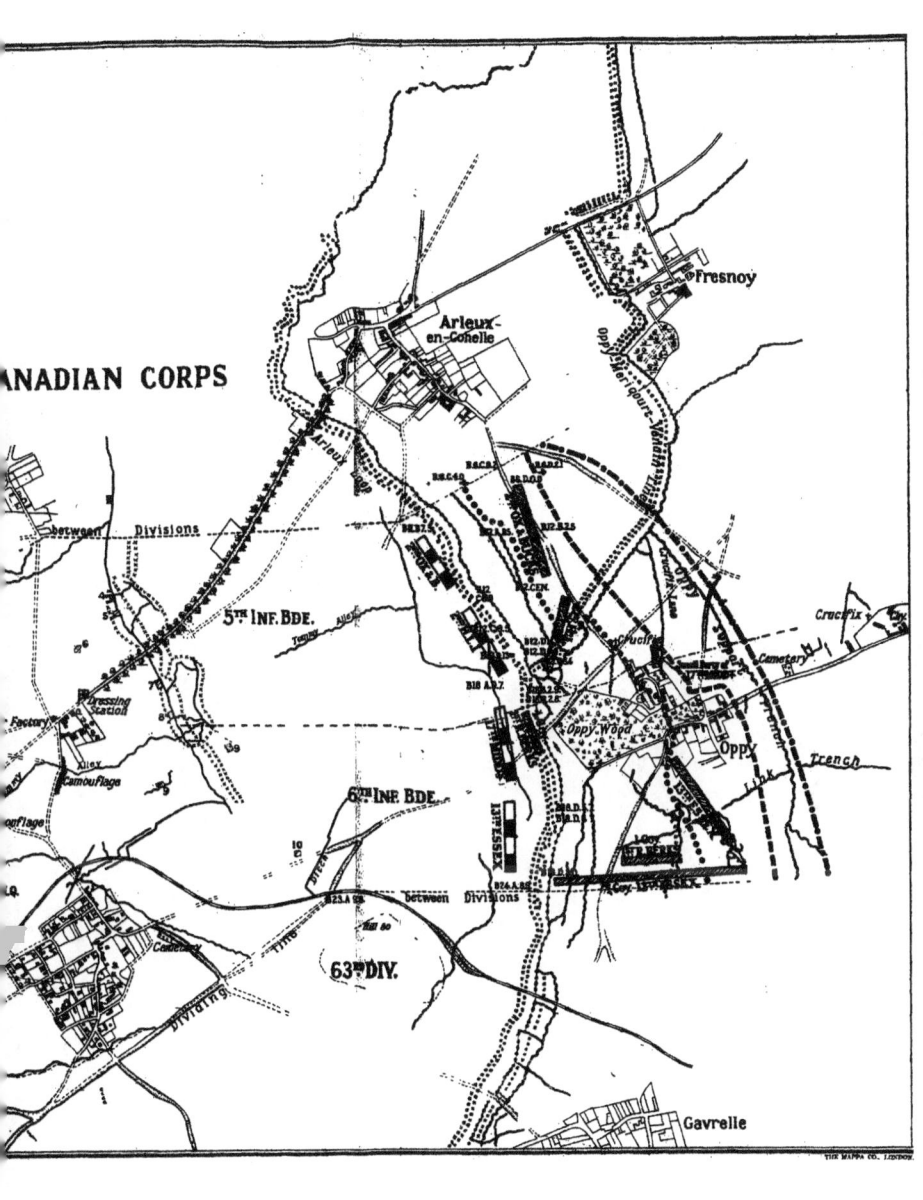

RESULTS OF THE OPERATIONS. 437

had been undertaken solely with the object of assisting the French, who were attacking on the Aisne and in Champagne. And these attacks were to continue until " such time as the results of the French offensive should have declared themselves."

The results of the operations on the 28th and 29th are thus summed up in the official dispatches : " In spite of the enemy's desperate resistance, the village of Arleux-en-Gohelle was captured by Canadian troops (1st Canadian Division) after bitter hand-to-hand fighting, and English troops (2nd Division, Major-General C. E. Pereira) made further progress in the neighbourhood of Oppy, on Greenland Hill (37th Division), and between Monchy-le-Preux and the Scarpe (12th Division). In addition to these advances, another 1,000 German prisoners were taken by us in the course of two days' fighting." Of this number over 250 officers and other ranks were captured by the 2nd Division.

The 2nd Division had, however, emerged from the battle very exhausted and much weakened in numbers. The actual fighting strength of the Division on the night of 27th April was only 518 officers and 10,986 other ranks, and although the exact number of casualties sustained on 28th and 29th was not given in the Divisional Diaries, the total number of casualties sustained by the Division from 15th to 30th April was :—officers : 39 killed,[1] 72 wounded, 28 missing ; other ranks : 349 killed, 1,504 wounded, and 1,089 missing—in all, 3,081. Almost all these casualties were sustained on 28th and 29th April. Many of the " missing " casualties were subsequently reported " killed."

THE THIRD BATTLE OF THE SCARPE:
The Capture of Fresnoy, 3rd to 4th May 1917.

The Third Battle of the Scarpe resulted in the capture of Fresnoy (3rd–4th May), the capture of Rœux (13th–14th May), and finally the capture of Oppy Wood (28th June). But with the first-named operations only was the 2nd Division concerned : " At 3.45 a.m. on the 3rd May," said Sir Douglas Haig, " another attack was undertaken by us of a similar nature to that of the 28th April, which in the character of the subsequent fighting it closely resembled."

The French had planned to launch their offensive along the

[1] See Appendix.

Chemin des Dames (on the Aisne) on the 5th May, and the British operations of the 3rd and 4th were undertaken solely to assist their Allies: " While the Third and First Armies attacked from Fontaine-lez-Croisilles to Fresnoy, the Fifth Army launched a second attack upon the Hindenburg Line in the neighbourhood of Bullecourt. This gave a total front of over sixteen miles."

30TH APRIL. On the 30th April a Corps Conference took place at the Headquarters of the 31st Division; the latter had relieved the 63rd Division on the right flank of the 2nd Division. The coming operations were discussed, and the 2nd Division was given 1,000 yards of front to attack. In view of the exhausted state of the Division, it must have been obvious that whether the attack between Oppy and Fresnoy was a success or a failure, the Division would emerge from the struggle fit only to be withdrawn immediately from the front line. " I explained," said the General Officer Commanding Division, " that the only way that the Division could do anything, now that we were so weak in numbers and so many of the men unfit for further operations, was by forming a Composite Brigade of the remnants of the three Brigades. . . . It was resolved that we should have to carry out our share of the attack."

For the first time during the war the 2nd Division was reduced to this extremity. The spirit of the Division was, indeed, all that it had been during the tremendous struggles it had passed through; but its numbers had been sadly diminished.[1]

Various orders were issued throughout the 1st May—*i.e.*, orders for the formation of the Composite Brigade, for the relief of the Brigade which was to take place after the attack, and numerous instructions (such as objectives and boundaries) concerned with the coming operations. But it was not until 12 midnight that " 2nd Division Operation Order No. 238 " was issued, which definitely laid down the lines of attack: " The 2nd Division, in conjunction with troops on either flank,[2] will attack the line Greenland Hill–Oppy Support Trench–Fresnoy. The attack by the 2nd Division will be carried out by a Composite Brigade under the orders of the General Officer Commanding 99th Infantry Brigade, and will be supported by three Field Artillery Brigades under the

---

[1] On the 1st May the available fighting strengths of the three Infantry Brigades were: 5th Infantry Brigade, 1,237; 6th Infantry Brigade, 1,322; 99th Infantry Brigade, 1,028.

[2] 1st Canadian Division on the left, 31st Division on the right.

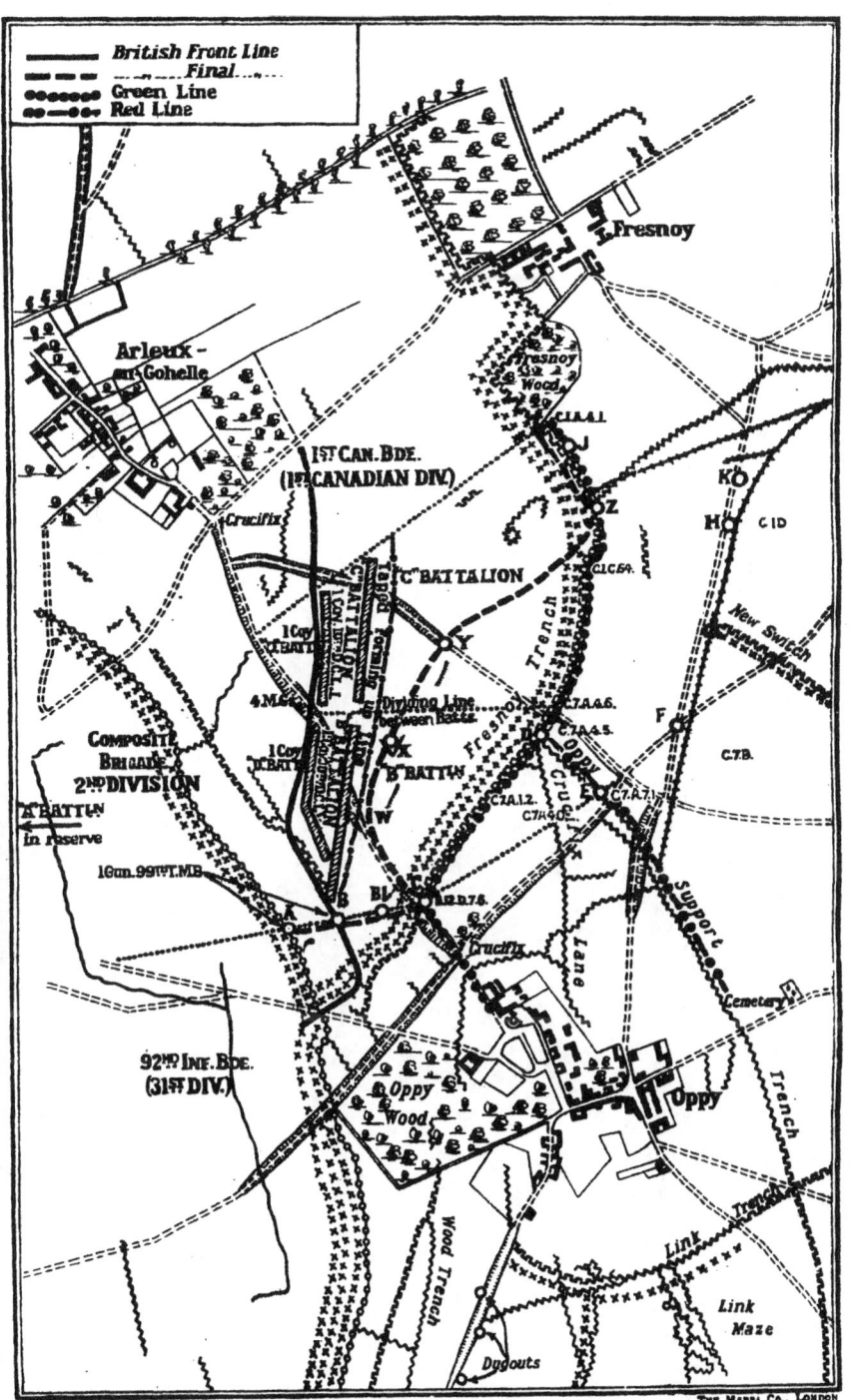

THE THIRD BATTLE OF THE SCARPE: THE CAPTURE OF FRESNOY, 3rd–4th MAY 1917. THE OPERATIONS OF THE COMPOSITE BRIGADE, 2nd DIVISION.

THE COMPOSITE BRIGADE. 439

orders of the Commander Royal Artillery 2nd Division, and by Corps and Army Heavy Artillery."

The Composite Brigade (formed at 12 noon on the 1st) was composed of the following :—

Composite Brigade Commander : Brigadier-General R. O. Kellett, 99th Infantry Brigade.
    99th Infantry Brigade Headquarters.
    99th Infantry Brigade Machine-Gun Company.
    5th Machine-Gun Company—2 Sections.
    6th Machine-Gun Company—2 Sections.
    99th Trench Mortar Battery.

A Battalion : Commanding Officer, Lieut.-Colonel S. V. P. Weston, D.S.O., M.C., 1st Royal Berks Regiment.
    (5th Infantry Brigade.)—
        1 Company, 17th Royal Fusiliers.
        1 Company, 24th Royal Fusiliers.
        1 Company, 2nd Oxford and Bucks Light Infantry.
        1 Company, 2nd Highland Light Infantry.

B Battalion : Commanding Officer, Lieut.-Colonel S. E. Norris, D.S.O., 1st King's Regiment.
    (6th Infantry Brigade.)—
        2 Companies, 1st King's Regiment.
        1 Company, 2nd South Staffords.
        1 Company, 13th Essex Regiment.

C Battalion : Commanding Officer, Lieut.-Colonel H. A. Vernon, D.S.O., 23rd Royal Fusiliers.
    (99th Infantry Brigade.)—
        2 Companies, 1st Royal Berks Regiment.
        2 Companies, 23rd Royal Fusiliers.

D Battalion : Commanding Officer, Major R. S. Stafford, D.S.O., M.C., 1st King's Royal Rifle Corps.
    (99th Infantry Brigade.)—
        1 Company, 22nd Royal Fusiliers.
        3 Companies, 1st King's Royal Rifle Corps.

The strength of each battalion was approximately 400.

More closely defined, the objectives of the Composite Brigade were : Fresnoy Trench between the points C.1,a.4.1 and B.12,d.7.6 ;

that portion of Oppy Support Trench lying between points C.7,a.4.5 and C.7,a.7.1 ; to establish a line of strong points (F, G, H, and K) on the road running through C.1,d. and C.7,b. Blocks were to be placed in Crucifix Lane and at a point where the latter cut through the southern boundary, and in Fresnoy Trench at about C.1,c.6.4.

The attack was to be made on a two-battalion front, B on the right, C on the left ; D battalion was in close support and A in brigade reserve, back at the railway embankment.

The 92nd Infantry Brigade of the 31st Division was attacking on the right, and the 1st Canadian Brigade on the left of the Composite Brigade of the 2nd Division.

"Zero" hour was to be 3.45 a.m. on the 3rd May.

1ST–2ND MAY.

On the night of the 1st–2nd May the Composite Brigade relieved the 5th Infantry Brigade, then holding the front-line trenches of the 2nd Division ; the 5th Brigade on relief was accommodated west of the Farbus–Pont du Jour line. On the following day (the 2nd) the Brigade, less the units with the Composite Brigade, moved back to hutments in Écoivres.

The day was spent by the Composite Brigade in completing arrangements and making all necessary preparations for the attack on the following morning. General Kellett had by no means an easy task. Indeed, the attack bristled with difficulties. The possibility of failure north and south of his line had to be considered, and dispositions made to protect his own flanks ; his brigade numbered at the outside 1,800 men, with which he had to capture Fresnoy Trench on a frontage of 1,400 yards, portions of the Oppy Support Trench and Crucifix Lane by bombing attacks, the formation of a defensive flank facing south on a front of 400 yards, and the making of eight strong points and four posts. In all, these operations covered a fighting front of about 1,800 yards.

The ground over which the attack was to be made was reconnoitred on the night 1st–2nd May. This dangerous task, carried out under heavy shell and machine-gun fire and through several barrages, was performed by Major A. E. Winter, second in command of the 23rd Royal Fusiliers. A line was taped out by the Royal Engineers on the following night.

At 9 p.m. on the 2nd May, as the troops were moving forward to their forming-up places, the Divisional Artillery put down a Chinese (feint) barrage on the enemy's trenches. This drew heavy retaliation on all the lines of approach to the forming-up area, and caused not only serious delay but many casualties, as well as interfering with the carrying forward of ammunition and supplies.

INITIAL SUCCESSES.

Moreover, it put the enemy on the alert. Both B and C Battalions were in consequence late in getting "lined out," for at 1.30 a.m. the enemy had put down a heavy barrage on the forming-up area, which continued until 2.30 a.m. At 3 a.m. the enemy again opened fire for half-an-hour. Finally, at 3.44 a.m. he put down another barrage, which gradually increased in violence until about three minutes after " zero " hour, when it became intense. The hostile artillery fire, which was accompanied by heavy machine-gun fire from Oppy and vicinity, was most intense on the southern area of the attack.

There was a bright moon, and the enemy no doubt observed the troops as they moved forward to the taped line and lay down ready for the barrage to open.

At " zero " hour—3.45 a.m.—the British artillery opened fire, and the attacking battalions of the Composite Brigade, with the flanking troops of the 31st and Canadian Divisions, went forward to the attack. Colonel Vernon (C Battalion) had disposed his troops in two waves of four platoons each—23rd Royal Fusiliers on the left, Royal Berkshires on the right. His orders were to capture Fresnoy Trench from C.7,a.4.6 to the southern corner of Fresnoy Wood, to form J and Z Strong Points, and Posts F, G, H, K.

3RD MAY.
MAP.

The whole of C Battalion gained its objectives immediately. The hostile wire was found to be well cut, and the enemy offered only a very slight resistance. Many of his troops were shot, some escaped across the open or down communication trenches, from 60 to 70 were made prisoners, and a machine gun was captured. Touch was obtained on both flanks.

B Battalion (Lieut.-Colonel Norris) was less successful. The battalion had been ordered to capture Fresnoy Trench from B.12,d.7.6 to C.7,a.4.6, that portion of Oppy Support from its junction with Fresnoy Trench to the southern divisional boundary at C.7,a.7.1; Crucifix Lane from its junction with Fresnoy Trench to the southern divisional boundary at about C.7,a.4.0, establishing a block at the latter point; and to form D and E Strong Points. With something less than 400 men, these were formidable tasks. Moreover, two companies of the battalion were unavoidably late in reaching the forming-up line, their guides having lost their way. At " zero," however, the King's, being the left and right attacking companies, advanced, and, although suffering severe casualties, succeeded in capturing that portion of Fresnoy Trench from C.7,a.1.2 to the right flank of C Battalion (the Berkshires) about C.7,a.4.6.

Captain N. J. Bannatyne of the King's, though severely wounded early in the fight, still remained in command of his company in the front line. Unfortunately this officer was later reported missing. The two companies of B which had been delayed arrived a few minutes after "zero" hour, and attempted to advance as ordered; but on reaching the Sunken Road in B.12,b. and d., they caught the full force of the enemy's artillery and machine-gun barrage, and were forced to take shelter in shell-holes, in the Sunken Road, and in whatever trenches in the vicinity they could reach. The right flank of the King's was, therefore, in the air.

A bombing attack southwards along Fresnoy Trench was made and from 50 to 60 prisoners and a machine gun were taken. Lewis guns were then pushed out to the front, and the trench—especially that portion of it near the junction of Oppy Support and Crucifix Lane—prepared for defence.

The enemy's counter-attack developed immediately. His bombers pressed forward down Oppy Support and Crucifix Lane. By 5 a.m. he had developed a very heavy attack with snipers and bombers, covered by machine guns, from Oppy Wood against the whole southern front of the line.

B Battalion, still fighting desperately, clung to its positions; but after thirty minutes' resistance against heavy odds, having exhausted its supply of bombs and lost many gallant men, was obliged to evacuate the trench and fall back. The battalion and its attached company from D Battalion then dug in astride the Sunken Road, and consolidated a defensive position facing south-east.

The development of strong counter-attacks against the right flank of the Composite Brigade was the result of the failure of the 31st Division to capture Oppy.

To D Battalion (Major Stafford) had been allotted the task of occupying A and B Strong Points with one platoon in each, on Y night (the night of 2nd–3rd May), and working on them continuously so as to have them in as strong a condition as possible by "zero" hour. Two platoons from the Pioneers (10th Duke of Cornwall's Light Infantry) had been detailed to assist the battalion in the work on these points, and right well did they carry out their duties. The gallant Pioneers (under Second-Lieut. A. G. Brian) performed very meritorious work not only in assisting to place the two points in a state of defence, but in carrying up through very heavy artillery and machine-gun fire a large quantity of small-arms ammunition, and formed a dump at the objective, suffering heavy casualties in so doing. Two more platoons of D Battalion were to move to B and C Strong Points at " zero " hour, and garrison them. Finally, two companies of the battalion were placed in support (one each) of C and B Battalions with the remaining company in support of the defensive flank on the right. These two companies had a stiff fight, but fought well. Both Captain G. F. Anderson, 1st King's Royal Rifle Corps, who with his company secured and safeguarded the right flank of the Composite Brigade, making strong points which resisted successfully all the enemy attacks hurled against them, and Lieut. G. Allen, M.C., who commanded the company of Rifles in support, assisted with their men in protecting most gallantly the vital points in the line. Captain Anderson later established a block 150 yards south of Strong Point B.

By " zero " hour the two platoons occupying A and B Strong Points had made splendid progress, and the two points were strongly held. The two platoons detailed to move forward at " zero " to establish strong points at B1 and C admirably carried out their tasks in the face of heavy hostile fire. The two mortars of the 99th Trench Mortar Battery in Points A and B by their effective fire greatly helped to stem the tide of the German counterattack.

Early on the morning of the 3rd B1 Strong Point was entirely destroyed by shell fire, and the survivors joined the garrison in C Point. Throughout the day the latter was steadily improved.

The remaining company of D Battalion was ordered to occupy the Old German Line and the British front line on news being brought to Major Stafford of the failure of the attack on Oppy.

As soon as reports reached Brigadier-General Kellett of the situation in the front line, and that the right and centre had been forced to fall back, he dispatched two companies of A Battalion (Lieut.-Colonel Weston), one to the Old German Line (Arleux Loop) in B.12.a, the other to the Old British Line west of the Arleux Loop; the two remaining companies had been absorbed for carrying duties and the evacuation of the wounded.

At 11.30 a.m. the line held by the Composite Brigade ran: Strong Points A, B, B.1 (obliterated by shell fire), C; thence north-west to trench W (across the Sunken Road), Points X Y; thence north-east to Point Z, whence the line ran north along Fresnoy Trench to Point C.1,a.4.1, where the left flank of the Brigade joined up with the right of the 1st Canadian Brigade, the latter having captured all its objectives.

The heavy counter-attacks had compelled withdrawal from the centre of the objective won by the Composite Brigade, and the 23rd Royal Fusiliers moved northwards along Fresnoy Trench to Point Z.

No further advance was made from this line during the day, and at nightfall the Brigade was relieved by the 13th Infantry Brigade (5th Division), the relief being completed without incident by 3.40 a.m. on the 4th May, the General Officer Commanding 5th Division assuming command of the line at 10 a.m.

4TH MAY.

The 2nd Division captured 138 prisoners and 2 machine guns. Casualties during the operations numbered 19 officers[1] and 498 other ranks killed, wounded, and missing. The trench strength of the Division was at this date: officers, 181; other ranks, 3,587.[2]

At 10 on the morning of the 4th May 2nd Divisional Headquarters closed at Roclincourt and opened at Bajus Château. The 5th Infantry Brigade marched to the Villers Chapel area, and the 99th Infantry Brigade to X Huts at Écoivres. On the 6th the Division was located in the Bajus Château–Dieval–Bray–Bajus area, in reserve.

The general results of the Third Battle of the Scarpe were thus detailed in the official dispatches: " Along practically the whole of this front (the first attack—sixteen miles from south of the Scarpe to Fresnoy) our troops broke into the enemy's position. Australian troops (2nd Australian Division) carried the Hindenburg Line east of Bullecourt; Eastern County battalions took Chérisy (18th Division). Other English troops entered Rœux (4th Division) and captured the German trenches south of Fresnoy

---

[1] See Appendix.
[2] The following details show the plight to which the 2nd Division was reduced:

		Officers.	Other Ranks.	
5th Infantry Brigade.—	17th Royal Fusiliers	23	252	
	24th Royal Fusiliers	16	334	
	2nd Oxford and Bucks	17	310	
	2nd Highland Light Infantry	13	341	
				1,237
6th Infantry Brigade.—	1st King's	17	298	
	2nd South Staffords	18	421	
	13th Essex	12	423	
	17th Middlesex	12	180	
				1,322
99th Infantry Brigade.—	22nd Royal Fusiliers	9	174	
	23rd Royal Fusiliers	17	230	
	1st Royal Berks	13	285	
	1st King's Royal Rifle Corps	14	339	
				1,028
		181	3,587	

RESULTS OF THE ALLIED OFFENSIVE. 445

(2nd Division). Canadian battalions (1st Canadian Division) found Fresnoy full of German troops assembled for a hostile attack which was to have been delivered at a later hour. After hard fighting, in which the enemy lost heavily, the Canadians carried the village, thereby completing an unbroken series of successes. Later in the day strong hostile counter-attacks once more developed, accompanied by an intense bombardment with heavy guns. Fierce fighting lasted throughout the afternoon and far into the night, and our troops were obliged to withdraw from Rœux and Chérisy. They maintained their hold, however, on Fresnoy and the Hindenburg Line east of Bullecourt, as well as upon certain trench elements west of Fontaine-lez-Croisilles and south of the Scarpe (12th Division)." [1]

The French attack on the Chemin des Dames (north of the Aisne) was delivered on the 5th, and was successful.

The Allies had now an opportunity of turning their attention to the Flanders front for an offensive east and north of Ypres.[2] The maintenance of activity on the Arras front was, however, necessary; raids and feint attacks were to form a principal part of these activities.

The German General Staff attempted to belittle the results of the Allied offensive of April and May 1917; but on the British front alone, during the operations which covered that period, some sixty square miles of territory had been wrested from the enemy, 19,500 prisoners (including over 400 officers) had been taken, and 257 guns (including 98 heavy guns), 464 machine guns, 227 trench mortars, and immense quantities of war material captured. The French had captured since 18th April 20,780 prisoners and 157 guns, besides considerable gains in territory.

A Note on the Situation in the Spring of 1917.

The spring campaign of 1917 on the Western front closed with the Third Battle of the Scarpe, the flanking operations round Bullecourt (11th April–16th June) being subsidiary to the main Arras offensive.

---

[1] Fresnoy was, however, lost again on the 8th May. Rœux was subsequently captured by the British on 13th–14th May, and Oppy Wood on the 28th June.

[2] It is unnecessary to enter into a discussion of the conference which took place in Paris on 4th and 5th May, or of the abandonment of General Nivelle's plan, and the retirement of that officer in favour of General Pétain, which took place a few days later.

Of far-reaching importance were events which had taken place during those early months of the year. Germany had begun her unrestricted submarine " warfare against mankind," [1] which eventually resulted in a declaration of war (6th April) between the United States of America and the German Empire, and brought into the war against the latter a number of smaller States ; the democrats in Russia had overthrown the Tsar's Government, and that country was in a state of revolution ; the German working-classes had begun to murmur against the lack of food, and strikes had taken place in Berlin and Leipzig.

Along the Western front the enemy had been able to reinforce his divisions with large numbers of troops transported from the Russian front, where active operations had, as a result of the Revolution, become practically stagnant.[2] The Allies, with no such opportunities of reinforcing their armies, were experiencing exhaustion following the offensives of 1916, and (especially where the British were concerned) the necessity of maintaining their positions in Asia and Africa. The question of man-power was acute, and although committed to a summer offensive in the Ypres area, the British Commander-in-Chief looked with no little concern on his diminishing forces. For in the United Kingdom the continual necessity for supplying reinforcements to the divisions in France and Flanders, East Africa, Mesopotamia, Palestine, and India had begun to drain the country to an alarming extent.

In its opening stages the German submarine campaign had no great effect upon the transit of troops or war material ; but vast quantities of food were sunk, and the want of it necessitated the retention of men for agricultural and other purposes connected with the production of foodstuffs, depriving the armies in France and other theatres of the war of much-needed reinforcements. Moreover, the quality of the troops had begun to fall off. Of the glorious Old British Army very few officers and men remained ; it had practically ceased to exist. And in spite of statements that trained troops could be produced in a few months, it was obvious to the commanders in the field that, though the men lacked nothing in *moral* or the will to fight, that staying power which alone comes from disciplined training spread over a long period

---

[1] President Wilson.

[2] How greatly the collapse of Russia favoured the Germans and affected the future conduct of the war on the Western front may be gathered from a statement by Ludendorff : " I could not help considering what our position must undoubtedly have been had the Russians attacked in April and May and met with even minor successes. We should then, as in the autumn of 1916, have had a desperate struggle."

THE RAW MATERIAL. 447

was at a low ebb. Exceptions to this rule there were, but they were few. Here and there amongst both officers and men born soldiers were discovered, men to whom the science of war came naturally. But it was not a fact that, as a whole, the new armies equalled the old regular army in discipline and fighting power. That both, to their eternal glory, gave of their best and to the utmost will for ever be remembered; but the historian must record that as the old regular army gradually passed away, and the numbers of the surviving officers and N.C.O's upon whom the duty of training the new armies devolved grew smaller and smaller, so it was impossible to maintain the standard of the troops who first faced the Germans at Mons in 1914.

Such, then, was the relative condition of the British army in France and Flanders in the spring of 1917; a condition common also among the French armies and the armies of the Central Powers —*i.e.*, the enemy. The serious nature of the situation may be gathered from a speech made on 4th April, just before the Arras offensive began, by Sir William Robertson, Chief of the Imperial General Staff, in which he stated that Germany was not beaten, her man-power was increased, and that the British army in France needed between April and July half a million men.

Behind the firing-line in France, where the divisions carried out their refitting, training, and resting, after strenuous periods in the trenches, reinforcements arrived, and something of the difficult task experienced by divisional commanders in fitting these troops for battle was expressed thus by a General Officer Commanding: " We recently got 700 reinforcements . . . most of them enlisted only seven to nine weeks ago. . . . Out of this short period one has to subtract the time taken for inoculation and leave, and it does not represent much time for turning the men into soldiers. At the training centre they get twenty-one days' sound training; but it is obvious that a division composed of 50 or 60 per cent. of such new and untrained material will not stand a very great chance in heavy uphill fighting, and chances of real, steady, and progressive training seldom occur. We have to fight, to provide whole brigades at a time for work, and at the same time instil the rudiments of soldiering into our drafts. . . . Meanwhile there is a shortage of officers, N.C.O's, and good instructors. It was a most depressing sight to see the attempts to train that were being made, *with very good will*, but with an absolute lack of the power of instruction."

Some divisions, however, which arrived in France having completed their training in England, were of greater fighting value, having received more instruction, and were better prepared for the strenuous life in the trenches. As late as the spring of 1917 divisions were arriving in France from England which had been formed in the early months of the War; these were excellent fighting material, and gave fine proof of their valour.

But whether trained, partly trained, or untrained, all fought gallantly, for gallantry comes not on the parade-ground, but is the very essence of the will to fight. Fearless courage is inborn (it cannot be inculcated), and this quality was not wanting in the British soldier. At periods, through no fault of his own, he may have lacked training, but his magnificent courage at all times is written on the battle monuments of France and Flanders which mark the site of many a bloody struggle in which he fought and died. Side by side, from the valley of the Somme to the apple orchards and cornfields of Picardy and Flanders, lie the trained and untrained soldier, to each his battle honours, to each a noble death.

The Second Division moves back to its old Sector, north and south of the La Bassée Canal.

7TH MAY.   On the 7th May all brigades of the 2nd Division began reorganization and training in the Dieval (5th Infantry Brigade), Bray (6th Infantry Brigade), and Bajus (99th Infantry Brigade) areas.

The recent operations had disclosed two important points. One was the urgent need of trained riflemen for sniping work as soon as an objective had been gained. It had been proved that the number of first-class shots was quite insufficient, and as a result some battalions in the front line had been worried by German snipers who had established themselves in various vantage points, from which they caused considerable casualties and impeded movement in the front areas. The want was met by the formation of a Divisional Riflemen's School at Magnicourt, in which the individual use of the rifle and the use of ground, sharp-shooting, and stalking were taught. The crucial point in these instructions was that after an attack every company in the front-line trenches would immediately push forward trained riflemen, who could (from concealed positions) cover the front in an intelligent manner, with full confidence in their own powers with the rifle

THE RIFLEMAN'S SCHOOL.   449

to pick off any enemy snipers bent upon similar work if they came within range.

The second point was the importance of the Stokes mortar. The effectiveness of these guns, when used intelligently, had been so strongly emphasized in the operations of April and May that special platoons were formed of men trained in the use of the mortar. They were to be kept out of the trenches, and their *rôle* in an offensive was to facilitate the advance of the infantry by bombarding enemy strong points.

Work on the roads and railways behind the front lines occupied the battalions at intervals in their training programme. On the 10th, for instance, the 99th Infantry Brigade marched to Écoivres, Bray, and Mont St. Eloy, coming under the orders of the C.E. XIIIth Corps for working duties. By the 18th some slight changes had taken place in the brigade areas: the 5th Infantry Brigade was in camp south of Roclincourt, the 6th Infantry Brigade at Dieval, and the 99th Infantry Brigade at Marœuil.

For a fortnight the Division had been working hard, training, refitting, and reorganizing, when orders were received to again take over the trenches of the 5th Division on the nights 23rd–24th and 24th–25th. Large numbers of men were still at the training centre, and companies with the Division at this period numbered only from 40 to 70 men each. Most of the companies were organized into two platoons. The Riflemen's School was in full swing, for in the Diary of the General Officer Commanding are the words: "I motored to the Riflemen's School. I got Gore to run it. He is making the men keen and cunning, and I am certain will develop in them all a spirit of self-reliance."[1]

Orders for the relief of the 5th Division were issued at 7.30 a.m. on the 22nd May, and during the night of the 23rd–24th the 99th Infantry Brigade relieved the 13th Infantry Brigade in the right sector of the 5th Divisional front.

23RD–24TH MAY.

During the time the 2nd Division had been training and reorganizing, the enemy had regained the village of Fresnoy (on 8th May) and the whole of Fresnoy Trench. The line held by the 5th Division on the night of the 23rd May ran from west of Oppy Wood (the Old British Line held by the 2nd Division during the first attack on Oppy on 9th April) northwards, then eastwards to Albert Trench, thence north again through B.12,b.2.5, east of Arleux-en-Gohelle along Britannia Trench to the joint post with

[1] Captain Gore was a Royal Fusilier officer who, as a Canadian "trapper," was a past master in the art of ground concealment, and a dead shot.

the Canadians; the point of division between the right and left sub-sector was the combined Brigade post in the Sunken Road north of B.12,b.2.5.

The 22nd Royal Fusiliers (99th Infantry Brigade) held the front line, which consisted of a line of posts and the trenches between the posts, and the Arleux Loop. The 23rd Royal Fusiliers were in immediate support, the 1st Royal Berks in support, and the 1st King's Royal Rifle Corps in reserve. All battalions were organized as two companies. The 190th Infantry Brigade (63rd Division) was on the right of the 99th Infantry Brigade. The relief was completed without incident by 2.30 a.m. on the 24th.

24TH–25TH MAY.

The relief of the 15th Infantry Brigade on the night 24th–25th in the left sub-sector did not, however, pass off as quietly. The 5th Infantry Brigade of the 2nd Division had been detailed to relieve the 15th Brigade. The 2nd Highland Light Infantry had been ordered to take over the right half and the 17th Royal Fusiliers the left half of the sub-sector. The 2nd Oxford and Bucks were in support, and the 24th Royal Fusiliers in reserve. As the two battalions moved forward to the front-line trenches the enemy put down a barrage. Two companies of the Highland Light Infantry (A and B) were at this period moving forward between the support and the front lines to relieve the 1st Norfolks, when the barrage came down. Following close on the barrage, a strong hostile raiding party of 80 Germans rushed towards the trenches of the left front company of Norfolks. They were driven off and counter-attacked, leaving several prisoners in the Norfolks' trenches, as well as a number of dead and wounded, the latter including an officer. The Norfolks had no casualties. The Highland Light Infantry, however, had 1 officer and 5 other ranks wounded. The relief was then completed. B and C Companies of the Highland Light Infantry were in close support.

The 17th Royal Fusiliers disposed D and C Companies in the front line, and A and B Companies in close support. The battalion, unfortunately, suffered the loss of 2 sergeants, 1 corporal killed, and 8 other ranks wounded during the relief.

The Canadians were on the left and the 99th Infantry Brigade on the right flank of the 17th Royal Fusiliers.

The 6th Infantry Brigade was in Divisional reserve.

The 2nd Divisional Artillery had not been out of the line; indeed, the gunners were relieved only at rare intervals.

At 10 a.m. on the 25th the General Officer Commanding assumed

ADVENTURES IN NO MAN'S LAND.

command of the line. The Divisional Commander had been informed that he was to hold the line for three weeks.

Patrol work began immediately. The 22nd Royal Fusiliers had hardly taken over from the 13th Infantry Brigade when an officer's patrol set out on its dangerous work. The adventures of this patrol are interesting :—

"An officer's patrol of the 22nd Royal Fusiliers (front battalion, 99th Infantry Brigade) went out on the night 24th–25th May. The patrol was fired on and heavily bombed from an enemy post. The patrol withdrew, but five men lost direction, and found themselves in rear of an advanced enemy machine gun and bombing post in a shell-hole. They then made a detour back along the enemy's wire, and on again advancing towards our lines encountered a second enemy post. Thinking they were going in the wrong direction, they turned about, and shortly found themselves in front of two belts of wire (which three of them crossed), when they were challenged in German ; the two men who had not crossed the wire retired, and succeeded in gaining our lines on the following night—25th–26th. The remaining three men were bombed from the trench, but kept out of reach in a shell-hole in front of the parapet, which was very high. During daylight on 25th May they remained in the shell-hole undisturbed. No. 54962 Private Place took charge of the party, and in spite of the critical position carried on with his observations. He confirmed the positions of his posts about 50 yards in front of a bright green tree ; both these posts were evacuated by day.

"Three of the enemy were on observation duty on the top of an embankment. This embankment is low at its southern end, growing steeper as it reaches the enemy's lines. A machine gun was heard firing apparently at aircraft . . . wire just north of this post was thick.

"On the night 25th–26th the party recrossed the enemy's wire unmolested ; but, keeping too much to the north, found themselves under the bank at M, where they stayed in a shell-hole during the night of the 26th. While here Private Place confirmed the position of their former shell-hole by a crashed aeroplane immediately east of it.

"On the night 26th–27th they made another attempt to reach their own lines ; but moving in a circle, found themselves on top of the embankment. Not knowing their whereabouts, they remained there throughout the following day.

"On the night 27th–28th they advanced straight to our wire,

crossed it, and regained our front line. As they had gone out on patrol, they carried no food or water, and had existed for three days without either."

To subsist for three days out in No Man's Land in 1917, subjected to their own artillery and machine-gun fire and trench mortar activity, was no mean feat. Unfortunately there are no records in the Diaries of these gallant men having been rewarded for their staunchness. The extraordinary thing was that these men were not discovered, though both the enemy and men of their battalion were out on patrol work during the nights Private Place and his companions were searching in vain for their own trenches. A fight between patrols of the 22nd Royal Fusiliers and the enemy had taken place in No Man's Land on the night 25th–26th, whilst another patrol from the 2nd Divisional front was working only a little north of the party on the night 26th–27th.

Work on the trenches and communications and patrol work at night continued to occupy the forward brigades of the 2nd Division during the remainder of May. There was considerable aerial activity along the whole front, the enemy's bombing planes causing some damage. One bomb dropped by a German aeroplane at Ecurie killed 31 horses and wounded 7 others belonging to the East Anglian Field Company Royal Engineers (483rd Company), but, as a Diary of one of the infantry brigades stated: "Our aerial supremacy on this sector is very marked, our machines making prolonged photographic and reconnaissance flights over the enemy's lines, and meeting with little opposition."

Hurricane bombardments were instituted by the Divisional Artillery on the 28th; they consisted of guns of all calibres firing for periods of three minutes. The effect on the enemy was apparently very worrying, as he soon began retaliating in a similar manner.

31ST MAY–1ST JUNE.

On the night of 31st May–1st June no less than five patrols went out into No Man's Land, and all of them drew the enemy's fire. The 2nd Highland Light Infantry (the right battalion of the left Brigade—the 5th) sent out two patrols. One of these, consisting of Second-Lieut. Blacker and five other ranks, located a hostile post manned by about twenty of the enemy. On retiring to its own lines the party encountered a hostile patrol of nine men, and a fight ensued. After killing three of the enemy, the remaining six got away, and Lieut. Blacker's party returned to its trenches without incurring casualties.

A severe thunderstorm on the last day of the month flooded

THE RETURN TO BÉTHUNE. 453

some of the posts and trenches to a depth of three feet, and for a while caused wholesale destruction of newly-made trenches, posts, and communications, as well as considerable discomfort to the troops in the front-line trenches.

No infantry attacks had been made either on or by the 2nd Division since it went into the line ; but activity had been maintained at other points of the Arras battlefield. Bullecourt, in which the 7th Division had gained a footing on the 7th May, was completely captured by the 58th and 62nd Divisions on the 17th. On the 20th the 33rd Division began a small attack between Bullecourt and the British line west of Fontaine-lez-Croisilles. These attacks were designed principally to keep the enemy occupied whilst Sir Douglas Haig was completing his preparations for the Messines attack, in which a feature, unique even in modern warfare, was to be furnished at the moment of assault by the simultaneous explosion of nineteen mines along the enemy's front.

On the night 3rd–4th June the 6th Infantry Brigade relieved the 5th Infantry Brigade in the left Divisional sector, the latter moving back into Divisional reserve. A battalion from the 5th Brigade was ordered to be placed in support of the 99th Infantry Brigade, which still continued to hold the right of the Divisional sector.

Hurricane bombardments, with active patrolling at night, and work on the trenches continued to occupy the Division throughout the early days of June. On the 14th the 99th Infantry Brigade was relieved by the 13th Infantry Brigade (5th Division), and moved to Acq ; the following night the 6th Infantry Brigade was relieved by the 95th Infantry Brigade of the 5th Division, and moved to Mont St. Eloy ; the 5th Infantry Brigade was relieved by the 15th Infantry Brigade, but remained in the forward area as working brigade.

The 16th June saw the 99th and 6th Infantry Brigades again in training ; but they had been warned that they would be required to relieve (in turn) the 5th Infantry Brigade as working brigade, beginning with the night 22nd–23rd June. Before, however, the time for that relief to be carried out came, the 2nd Division had received warning (on the 17th) that it was to relieve the 66th Division in the XIth Corps area (La Bassée sector) before 6 a.m. on the 23rd June, and on the next day the advanced parties of brigade groups moved to Béthune.

The 6th Infantry Brigade moved by 'bus to Béthune on the 19th ; the 99th Infantry Brigade followed on the 20th ; the 5th 19TH JUNE.

Infantry Brigade on the 21st. The Divisional Artillery, however, still remained in the line, and had been warned that it would move early in July.

* * * * * * *

On the 7th May Lieut.-Colonel C. P. Deedes, D.S.O., G.S.O.1, of the 2nd Division, left the Division to proceed to England to the War Office, and was succeeded by Lieut.-Colonel E. D. Giles. A new G.S.O.2, Major W. C. Wilson, D.S.O., M.C., had joined the Division on the 19th February in succession to Major C. A. S. Maitland, D.S.O., who had been transferred to the IInd Corps. On the 13th June the D.A.D.V.S., Captain L. L. Dixon, was evacuated sick to England, and was replaced by Captain F. R. Roche-Kelly.

Trench Warfare, 20th June to 4th October 1917.
A Period of Raids.

20TH–21ST JUNE.

During the night of 20th–21st June the 6th Infantry Brigade took over the left (Givenchy) sector from the 197th Infantry Brigade (66th Division).

The better part of two years (nineteen months to be exact) had passed since the 2nd Division was in the Givenchy–La Bassée Canal–Cambrin sector of the line. But as the 6th Infantry Brigade moved forward to relieve the 197th Brigade, many memories must have stirred the hearts of those officers and men who were with the 2nd Division during the operations of 1915. The very names of some of the trenches recalled those who had been or were still with the Division—Grenadiers Road, King's Road, Queen's Road, Glasgow Street, and Oxford Terrace were all named after units of the 2nd Division. But only two of the original battalions of the 6th Infantry Brigade—the 1st King's and the 2nd South Stafford—remained who trod familiar ground that night.

The 1st King's relieved the 2/7th Lancashire Fusiliers in the right sub-sector, and found themselves once more gazing out over No Man's Land towards the Duck's Bill. Many of them remembered that gallant attack of the 10th March 1915—a subsidiary operation to the main battle which was taking place farther north at Neuve Chapelle: one of the many operations in the war which necessitated the sacrifice of the lives of brave men—a " holding attack." All four companies of the King's were disposed in the line.

The 17th Middlesex relieved the 3/5th Lancashire Fusiliers in the left sub-sector. The 2nd South Staffords were in support, and

BACK IN THE OLD LINE OF 1915. 455

the 13th Essex in reserve. The 6th Machine-Gun Company and the 6th Trench Mortar Battery were also in the line. Both reliefs were carried out without incident. The 1st Portuguese Brigade was on the left of the 6th Infantry Brigade, and the 198th Infantry Brigade (66th Division) on the right.

On the 20th June the 99th Infantry Brigade proceeded north by motor bus to the new area : the King's Royal Rifles and the 23rd Royal Fusiliers to Beuvry, and the remaining battalions to Béthune. The Brigade went into the line on the night 21st–22nd, relieving the 199th Infantry Brigade in the Cambrin sector. The Rifles took over the right, and the 23rd Royal Fusiliers the left, sub-sector. The 22nd Royal Fusiliers were in support, and the 1st Royal Berks in brigade reserve in Noyelles.

This portion of the line was familiar to the Rifles and the Berkshires, who were last in this sector of the British front during the Battle of Loos in September 1915. The front line had changed very little so far as the actual position was concerned, but certain differences existed : " The battalion holds the right sub-section of the Brigade sector with a frontage of 1,300 yards. A continuous chain of mine-craters exists, however, along almost the whole length of the battalion front ; these craters are deep and impossible to cross except in one or two places. . . . The only part not thus protected is the left, where a small gap exists in one place. The front line is held by three companies, and consists entirely of posts. . . . Forward of the reserve trench communication is maintained by a complicated system of tunnels, lit by electric light, which have their exits in the posts themselves. Into these tunnels the major portion of the garrison is withdrawn by day, only gas sentries being left to guard the post against surprise. Once in the tunnel one is completely lost, and should anything happen to any of these posts, and Germans succeed in gaining an entrance, some most unpleasant and intricate underground fighting would ensue."[1]

The 5th Infantry Brigade arrived in Béthune about midday on the 21st, and during the night 22nd–23rd relieved the 198th Infantry Brigade in the canal sector of the new Divisional area. The dispositions of the Brigade on relief were : 2nd Oxford and Bucks in the right sub-sector south of the La Bassée Canal ; the 2nd Highland Light Infantry in the centre sub-sector ; and the 17th Royal Fusiliers in the left sub-sector.[2] The latter battalion

---

[1] Battalion Diary, 1st King's Royal Rifle Corps.
[2] The trenches taken over by the 17th Royal Fusiliers from the 2/10th Manchester Rifles were those in which the battalion received its baptism of fire in November 1915.

had on its left flank the 17th Middlesex (6th Infantry Brigade); and the Oxford and Bucks on their right (the Cambrin sector), the 23rd Royal Fusiliers of the 99th Infantry Brigade. The 24th Royal Fusiliers were in reserve in billets in Annequin.

Thus the three infantry brigades of the 2nd Division were in the line, flanked on the north by the Portuguese Division, and on the south by the 6th Division.

At 10 a.m. on the 23rd, 2nd Division Headquarters moved from Béthune to Locon, and the General Officer Commanding assumed command of the Right Divisional front, XIth Corps sector. " I met the Commander Royal Artillery of the 66th Division," said the General Officer Commanding, " and he reports that the last fortnight has been extremely quiet. In the previous twenty-four hours only 47 shells had fallen in the whole Divisional area, and we return about 1,000 daily ! What a different tale from December 1914 to May 1915 ! "

Each infantry brigade was ordered to prepare for a raid with the object of destroying mine-shafts, machine-gun emplacements, and causing casualties amongst the enemy's troops; prisoners were to be taken for identification purposes; active patrolling was to take place " so that every part of No Man's Land is systematically visited "; a Divisional system of observation and sniping was organized, and the vigorous use of medium and heavy and Stokes mortars ordered.

The 2nd Division had taken over the line quietly, but its arrival had evidently been noted by the enemy, for it was not long before he also began more active patrol work and a series of raids along the Divisional front.

25TH JUNE. The first of these hostile raids took place on the night of the 25th June, and was launched against the 1st King's in the Givenchy sector.

At 7.30 p.m. the enemy opened a very heavy minenwerfer bombardment of the whole front and support lines, accompanied by a certain amount of shrapnel on all communication trenches in the area. The bombardment was particularly heavy, and lasted for three hours, but slackened off about 10.15 p.m. A heavy shrapnel barrage was then put down behind the front-line trenches of the 1st King's, and a strong party of the enemy's " storm troops "[1] advanced to the attack at three points along the front of the battalion.

C Company of the King's was on the right opposite Red Dragon

[1] They belonged to the 1st Bavarian Reserve Division.

THE RED DRAGON CRATER. 457

Crater; A Company was in the right centre; D Company left centre; and B Company was holding Princes Island on the left, somewhat separated from the rest of the battalion. In front of C, A, and D Companies the German line ran close to the British front line and then away to a distance of about 300 yards in front of B Company: the two opposing lines were nearest about Red Dragon Crater.

The attacks against the Northern Craters in front of D Company, and the gap between Princes Island and Warwick South in front of B Company, were driven off by Lewis gun and rifle fire, and no enemy penetrated the line.

Owing, however, to the short distance which separated the British and German lines in front of C Company, and the rapidity with which he followed up his barrage, the enemy penetrated the trenches in front of the Red Dragon Crater. Captain F. F. Ryan, M.C., commanding C Company, was killed almost immediately whilst gallantly leading a few men with bombs against the enemy, who was working his way down a trench from one of the saps. In the extreme darkness, and a heavy rain, it was impossible for the officers to get a clear idea of what had happened, and in consequence the battalion reports of the situation are of necessity somewhat short. But two young officers, Second-Lieut. S. Lockhart and Second-Lieut. R. S. Tarran, organized a counter-attack with the supporting platoons who were in Gunner Siding. The enemy had by this period reached a line 150 yards behind the King's front-line trench, and when he was counter-attacked was near Marie Redoubt. The two officers and their men fell upon the advancing Germans and attacked them so vigorously that a number were cut off and captured. In the meantime the Commanding Officer of the King's had sent Captain E. R. Mace up to the front line in order to ascertain the situation. He returned with the information that Second-Lieuts. Lockhart and Tarran had driven the enemy back successfully, and the former officer had reorganized the position in the front line, Second-Lieut. Tarran organizing the support line from men he had collected in Piccadilly. Captain Mace also reported that all was correct along other parts of the front line, though the trenches had been very badly knocked about by the bombardment.

A company of the 10th Duke of Cornwall's Light Infantry (Pioneers) had reported to Battalion Headquarters about 9.45 p.m., and in view of the situation, as it was then, had been ordered to get ready for immediate action, as they might be needed. Some of the Pioneers were now set to work to rebuild the damaged posts, whilst the remainder carried bombs and small-arms ammunition up to the front line.

At "Stand to" in the early morning, the situation was once more normal. The King's lost in this affair 1 officer and 10 other ranks killed, and 7 missing. Twelve unwounded and 1 wounded prisoners were taken by the battalion, besides which a number of Germans were killed and some wounded who were not taken.

One corporal and three men of the King's maintained themselves in a sap throughout the whole operation, although practically surrounded by the enemy. With rifle and bombs they kept the enemy at bay until he had been driven back across No Man's Land to his own trenches.

Of the two gallant young officers by whose efforts the situation was saved, the Commanding Officer reported: " I wish to draw the attention of the General Officer Commanding to the extraordinarily gallant conduct of Second-Lieuts. Lockhart and Tarran, who are both extremely young and have only a few weeks' service."

Evidently smarting under his repulse and loss of prisoners, on the night of the 25th the enemy made another attempt to raid the 2nd Division in the early morning of the 27th. The point selected was a sap occupied by the 23rd Royal Fusiliers (99th Infantry Brigade) opposite Mad Point, in the Cambrin sector. At 3.15 a.m. the enemy put down a combined artillery, trench-mortar, and machine-gun barrage, the latter being particularly heavy on the sap. A party of from forty to fifty Germans then attempted to rush the post from the direction of the road running through Mad Point and the shell craters in front of it. They were observed, and were met by heavy Lewis gun and rifle fire, and after throwing a few bombs, which did no damage, were driven back to their own trenches. The Fusiliers sent up an " S.O.S." signal, and at 3.25 a.m. the Divisional Artillery put down a heavy barrage on the enemy's trenches: at 3.40 a.m. the situation was once more normal. No casualties were sustained by the Fusiliers, and the enemy's losses could not be ascertained.

On the morning of the 27th a German, who had belonged to the party which raided the 1st King's on the night of the 25th, gave himself up. He had been hiding since the night of the raid. His statements were interesting as showing the false information spread by the German commanding officers amongst their men. He said he was afraid to surrender because he had been told that the British would ill-treat him, make him work in their lines, and afterwards shoot him.

H.R.H. the Duke of Connaught (Colonel-in-Chief of the Regiment) inspected the 2nd Highland Light Infantry on the 27th. The battalion had been specially withdrawn from the line for the ceremony. Only about fifty men of the original battalion at Mons in August 1914 were on parade.

The 13th Essex Regiment was responsible for smart patrol work on the night 27th–28th. The battalion had relieved the 17th Middlesex in the left sub-sector (Givenchy sector) on the night 26th–27th. About midnight Lance-Corporal Jones, with three other ranks of the battalion, went out into No Man's Land and reached the enemy's wire at Canadian Orchard. Lance-Corporal Jones then halted his men and himself crept forward to reconnoitre. He discovered three of the enemy in a trench, whom he bombed and believed killed. He then entered the trench and, creeping along, found a sentry and two more men in a bay. On seeing Jones the two men ran away in different directions. Jones then threw a bomb at the sentry, and retired out of the trench, as the enemy had by this time turned a machine-gun on to him and had already begun to retaliate with bombs. In retiring he was wounded, but eventually, with his comrades, retired safely to his own lines, having been out five hours.

A careful survey of all diaries of the 2nd Division for July 1917 reveals one thing especially—the Division had only been relieved from one kind of warfare for another. In the Arras sector attack and counter-attack had been frequent; here in the Givenchy–La Bassée–Cambrin sector trench warfare of a very active nature began almost from the very first night the Division relieved the 66th Division. The Diary of the 99th Infantry Brigade for July gives something of the situation on July 1, 1917: " 99th Infantry Brigade holding the line known as the Cambrin sector from G.4,d.9.1 to A.27,b.5.4, a frontage of about 2,100 yards. Two battalions hold the front line, with one battalion in support and one in reserve. The front is held by a series of posts, those held by the right battalion being numbered and lettered L1 to L17, those by the left battalion M1 to M19. Most of the posts are reached through elaborate tunnels. In No Man's Land there are many large mine craters, the occupation of which is still a feature of this part of the line. Trench mortars and rifle grenades are much in evidence on both sides. The trenches in general use are in good condition, well duck-boarded and revetted in a useful manner. Some of the

1ST JULY.

communication trenches, having been disused for some time, are falling into a state of decay. It may be an advantage to retrieve these. Stokes guns and trench mortars very active during the day, firing on hostile working parties, machine guns, and trench mortars."

Along the whole Divisional front the same system of holding the line was in force—*i.e.*, each brigade having two battalions in the front line, one in support and one in reserve. All reserve battalions were employed in training when out of the line, for, owing to the influx of large numbers of young soldiers needing instruction in the use of bombs, Lewis guns, trench mortars, and in musketry, much hard work was necessary before the Division would be ready to take the offensive. So far as trench warfare was concerned these newcomers gained knowledge rapidly and often in a costly manner.

The centre (Canal) sector of the Divisional line (held by the 5th Infantry Brigade) seems to have been more heavily engaged with the enemy during July than either the northern (6th Infantry Brigade) or the southern (99th Infantry Brigade) sectors.

Throughout the 1st and 2nd July heavy intermittent shelling and trench-mortar activity took place along the whole Divisional front. Patrol work was general. At 12.30 a.m. on the 4th, under cover of a trench-mortar bombardment with gas shelling, accompanied by heavy machine-gun fire, Death or Glory Sap (held by C Company of the 17th Royal Fusiliers), just north of the Canal, was attacked by about thirty Germans. They approached in two parties. One party worked along the Canal bank and attempted to get through wire to the south of the sap; the other party tried to cross the wire to the north of the sap. Both parties were at once fired upon by Lewis guns and rifles, and after throwing a couple of bombs they retired, leaving two dead on the ground. One wounded prisoner was taken, who died as he was being carried down the trench. Groans were heard in No Man's Land, and on a patrol going out six wounded Germans were found, but they were too far out to bring in, and by this time it was getting light.

In the left sub-sector of the Givenchy sector the 6th Infantry Brigade had, since the beginning of the month, suffered heavy shelling from trench mortars. The 17th Middlesex had taken over this part of the line from the 13th Essex Regiment on the night of the 2nd July. The Battalion Diary for the 6th July contains the following entry: "Arrangements made with artillery to call certain 'Minnies' worrying our left front company by certain

"TINO," "FERDY," AND "KARL."

names. Those identified were called Tino and Ferdy respectively: Karl not definitely marked down. Raid expected on line where it joins the Portuguese; left flank accordingly strengthened. Trench mortars increased there, and eight more machine guns. Two companies 13th Essex brought to Old British Line. One platoon of 13th Essex in Pioneer Post; one platoon 2nd South Staffords in Cailloux Keep."

The expected raid on the Portuguese was made on the night of the 7th–8th. The enemy's minenwerfer had been active all day, but the Divisional 4.5 howitzers were turned on to them, the result being "Tino killed, Ferdy wounded—probably killed."

7TH–8TH JULY.

At about 12.55 a.m. the enemy suddenly opened a heavy barrage of light trench mortars, 4.2's, and 8.9's on the Portuguese and on the left flank of the 17th Middlesex—*i.e.*, Cover Trench, Canadian Orchard, Shetland Road, and Richmond Terrace. The enemy's barrage moved east to west to prevent the 6th Infantry Brigade reinforcing the Portuguese, who were being raided. A Lewis gun post in Canadian Orchard, under Corporal Searle, was so heavily bombarded that the gallant corporal pushed out under the barrage and re-established his post in No Man's Land. Leaving his men there, Searle then went out alone to reconnoitre. Suddenly he bumped into a party of eight Germans. At these he threw bombs until they retired. By this time the barrage had passed his post, and he also retired, withdrew his men from No Man's Land, and once more re-established himself in his old post in Canadian Orchard. The 17th Middlesex lost in this bombardment 4 other ranks killed and 10 wounded. "All was quiet by 3.20 a.m."

The next attempt was made on the 24th Royal Fusiliers (5th Infantry Brigade) in the Canal sector. At 3.10 a.m. on the 9th two hostile parties attempted to rush Posts 3 and 4 at Mine Point, astride the Vermelles–La Bassée road, held by the Fusiliers. The enemy advanced without artillery preparation, but unfortunately for him "Stand to" had just gone, so that his advance was immediately observed. The raiders, thirty or forty in number, were armed with automatic pistols and stick bombs, and wore forage caps. In the first rush all the garrison of No. 4 Post were either killed or wounded, but the enemy did not succeed in getting into the post, for machine-gun fire had been opened on him from the flanking posts. No. 3 Post held out, and a Lewis gun from No. 2 Post quickly forced the enemy to beat a rapid retreat. Two N.C.O's and two other ranks from No. 3 Post then left the post and chased the enemy back across No Man's Land, and only retired to their own position when all their bombs were expended. The Fusiliers suffered 3 killed and 6 wounded, but no men were captured by the enemy, whose casualties were not ascertained, though he must have lost heavily.

12TH JULY.   The 24th Royal Fusiliers were again raided on the 12th. At 3 a.m. the enemy put down a heavy barrage of trench mortars of all sizes on Posts 23 and 24, about half-way between the Cambrin–La Bassée and Vermelles–La Bassée roads. Tower Reserve Trench and Kingsway and the neighbouring communication trenches were also barraged. A large number of smoke bombs were fired into Tower Reserve Trench, and these gave off a dense cloud of smoke which floated over the trenches of the Fusiliers. A hostile aeroplane, flying low, "machine-gunned" the support trenches. Both posts were entered by the enemy's troops, but they were quickly expelled, and only one man of the 24th Royal Fusiliers was wounded.

The 24th Royal Fusiliers were relieved by the 2nd Oxford and Bucks about 4.30 p.m., and shortly afterwards the Oxfords were subjected to a long bombardment of gas shells. One shell unfortunately struck the parados of Kingsway, just opposite the entrance to a dug-out occupied by stretcher-bearers, and three old soldiers of the battalion, who had served from Mons 1914, were gassed and died later from the effects. On 16th July, at 3.30 a.m., the trenches of the 23rd Royal Fusiliers (99th Infantry Brigade, Cambrin sector), opposite Railway Point, were raided by a party of about fifteen of the enemy. The latter entered the Fusiliers' trench, but were immediately ejected by the battalion bombers, and were fired on as they left by the Lewis gunners. One man, a Corps cyclist attached to the Fusiliers, patrolling the trench, was wounded in the first rush and taken by the enemy into No Man's Land. Here they stripped him of his coat, and then made off. The wounded man's cries were heard, and Lance-Corporal Buery gallantly went out into No Man's Land and brought him in. Another N.C.O. of the battalion, who also went out into No Man's Land, found a dead German officer, but was unable to search the body owing to the enemy's machine-gun fire. Several of the enemy's troops were hit, and the Battalion Diary, evidently written just after the raid had taken place, stated : " Moans of wounded men can still be heard, although they are not visible owing to the long grass. Our casualties are 4 wounded."

17TH JULY.   On the 17th July, about 9 p.m., two German deserters (Alsa-

THE FIRST RAID. 463

tians) of the 65th I.R. (185th Division) crossed No Man's Land and surrendered to the 99th Infantry Brigade in the Cambrin sector. During the examination of these men various items of interest were revealed. The following sentence is taken from the report of the examining officer: "It is reported that the 185th Infantry Division will be relieved soon, as there are a great number of Lorrainers in the 161st and 65th I.R., and on that account the division cannot be trusted." On the 1st and 4th July other Alsatians from the same division, and in the same sector, had crossed No Man's Land and had given themselves up.

The identification of these men was "normal"—*i.e.*, no change had taken place in the enemy's dispositions since the 2nd Division took over the line. In the Givenchy and Canal sectors the capture of Germans, during the series of hostile raids between 1st and 16th July, had likewise shown no change in the line. In this lies the reason the Division, during the first half of July, made no reply (of similar nature) to the enemy's frequent raids, for the principal object of a raid was to obtain identifications: the Division could not afford to fritter away the lives of men. Every night the Divisional patrols had gone out and had carefully observed the conditions of No Man's Land and the enemy's wire, posts had been located, machine-gun emplacements observed, and shell-holes and mine-craters examined. In three weeks the whole of No Man's Land had been patrolled and reported upon.

So far as the enemy's trenches were concerned they had been damaged and crumbled by the artillery and trench mortars, and gaps had been made in his wire. But on receipt of information that the relief of the troops opposing the 2nd Division was imminent, it became necessary to obtain identifications as soon as the relief had taken place, and for this purpose 2nd Divisional Headquarters issued instructions for raids to be carried out on the enemy's trenches.

The first raid took place on the night of 20th July, the objects of the raid being, as stated in orders, "to kill the enemy and to take prisoners."

The Divisional Artillery had already begun wire-cutting. The gunners had been relieved by the 5th Divisional Artillery in the Oppy sector on 1st July. On the following day they had marched from Roclincourt to Béthune, staying one day in the town. On the 4th, Royal Artillery Headquarters moved from Béthune to Locon, and took over the defence of the La Bassée front from the 66th Divisional Artillery. Registration and check registration began immediately. The 47th Battery (XLIst Brigade R.F.A.) made good practice on the enemy's trench mortars, Tino and Ferdy, and promptly reduced them to silence. Hazy atmosphere, however, impeded good observation, and the result of wire-cutting bombardments were difficult to gauge.

The portion of the enemy's trenches to be raided on the night 20th–21st was Madagascar, the southern part of which was Mad Point, north of the Hohenzollern. Three officers and one hundred and fifteen men of the 23rd Royal Fusiliers formed the raiding party; these were split up into fourteen parties—*i.e.*, eight in the front rank, followed by four " mopping-up " parties; and two rear parties, one consisting of signallers and the other of stretcher-bearers.

At " zero " hour the artillery had been ordered to open a hurricane fire on the front line, and put down a box barrage round the objective. At " zero " plus 4 the barrage was to creep towards the enemy's support line. Three minutes later the barrage was to be protective, " continuing until ' zero ' plus 35, when it was to drop to slow, and finally cease at ' zero ' plus 50." Stokes mortars and the 99th Machine-Gun Company were also to co-operate.

" Zero " hour had been fixed for 10.30 p.m., 20th July.

The raid is memorable in that it was the first occasion on which the 2nd Division projected oil into the enemy's trenches.[1] No. 0, Special Company R.E., was responsible for manipulating the oil, and the records mention the work of the company in high terms, and of the confidence inspired in the raiding party, and the terror created in the minds of the enemy's troops.

20TH JULY. Four minutes before " zero " hour on the night of the 20th the raiding party left their trenches and formed up in No Man's Land. Gaps had been made in the wire in front of the Fusiliers' trenches, through which the troops crawled. The forming-up operations were undetected by the enemy, whose Véry light and machine-gun fire were normal. The artillery opened fire punctually at 10.20 p.m., and a hurricane of shells of all calibres fell on Madagascar

---

[1] " The projection of burning oil was a new form of ' hate,' an answer to the German flammenwerfer frightfulness, but in our case it was carried out by the Special Companies R.E., who had lately come into existence. The method was as follows: a large number of cylinders (often as many as 200 or 300) were discharged electrically and projected from mortars into the enemy's trenches. On impact with the ground they were ignited by a fuse and produced a most terrifying effect."—*The 5th Division in the Great War.*

The enemy first used liquid fire to support his attack on Hooge early on the morning of July 30, 1915.

THE CORPORAL'S PANTS.

and formed a box barrage round that system of trenches. The machine-guns and trench mortars poured a hail of bullets and bombs on the flank and support trenches.

Four minutes after "zero" the raiding parties jumped to their feet and rushed across No Man's Land. The enemy's wire had been well cut, and the Fusiliers passed quickly through the gaps and jumped into the trenches.

Very few men were found to be holding the front line, and these retreated as the raiding parties entered the trenches. Two of the enemy fired from a dug-out, but Mills and percussion bombs were thrown into the dug-out and there was no more opposition from that quarter. A mine-shaft entrance was also found and bombed. The blocking parties then went forward on either flank. The right party was bombed by the enemy, but retaliated, killing two Germans, and the block was established. Parties working forward "over the top" and up the communication trenches found two trench mortars in Madagascar Trench, which they blew up, using Mills bombs. An ammunition dump near one of the mortars was exploded. On the left, one party, working up a communication trench, encountered five Germans, and these were bayoneted. Here also another dug-out, in which a number of the enemy had taken shelter, was found. As the men refused to come out and surrender bombs were thrown into the dug-out, with a result which can be better imagined than explained. On reaching the enemy's support line two more dug-outs were found and bombed. Excepting for a party of Germans seen running up a communication trench on the left to their reserve line, no enemy troops were encountered. Having stayed the appointed time in the enemy's trenches, the raiding parties withdrew to their own lines.

The raid, carefully rehearsed over practice trenches beforehand, was carried out perfectly to programme, and it was sheer bad luck that more of the enemy's troops were not encountered and killed or captured. The Fusiliers had 2 other ranks killed, 15 wounded, and 5 wounded and missing. On the following day the raiding party was inspected and congratulated by the General Officer Commanding 2nd Division. "One corporal," said the General, "paraded in his pants, his trousers having remained on the Boche wire. I caused some amusement when I asked what he had done with them." Seven of the raiding party were subsequently awarded the Military Medal for gallantry.

Three nights later, on the 23rd, at 11 p.m., the enemy retaliated 23RD JULY. by a raid on Surrey Sap (east of Givenchy sector), held by the 17th

Royal Fusiliers. The post raided had been manned every night by an N.C.O. and two men. On the night in question, at 10.30 p.m., an N.C.O. and two men, as usual, moved into the post. Shortly afterwards, without any warning whatsoever, four Germans jumped into the post and, presenting their revolvers at the tiny garrison, ordered the N.C.O. and his two companions to surrender : five other Germans lined the parapet. The three men holding the post immediately fired on the enemy, and a severe struggle took place. One man succeeded in escaping back to the battalion front line and reported what was happening. Despite a vigorous resistance, the two men remaining in the post were eventually overcome and forced to go over towards the enemy's lines. The struggle was not, however, over, for one of the two men captured, No. 51343 Private H. Jordan, although wounded in six places, suddenly hit his German escort over the head with his fist and, turning round, succeeded in escaping back to his own lines. Meanwhile a party of bombers with a Lewis gun had re-established the position in Surrey Sap. One dead German was found in the saphead.

The next raid by the 2nd Division took place on the night of the 25th–26th. The objective was the enemy's trenches in the vicinity of Red Dragon Crater in the 6th Infantry Brigade area (Givenchy). "Zero" hour was at 10.30 p.m. But hardly had the Divisional barrage begun when the enemy put down a heavy barrage and also sent over large numbers of minenwerfer bombs, causing casualties and confusion amongst the party formed up for the raid. The raid was carried out by the 1st King's, and was unfortunately unsuccessful from the point of view of identifications and causing casualties amongst the enemy's troops. Two officers of the King's were wounded, 4 other ranks were killed and 12 wounded.

28TH JULY.
Finally the 2nd Highland Light Infantry (5th Infantry Brigade) carried out a raid immediately north and astride of the La Bassée road, on the night 27th–28th, "zero" hour being at 12.40 a.m. By means of an oil projection, barrage, and the exposure of a number of dummy figures ("Murray's Light Infantry," so named after the officer who was responsible for them [1]), together with the

[1] An interesting description of "Murray's Light Infantry" is given in the Diary of the 226th Field Company R.E. : " The figures, some half-length, some full-length, were made of half-inch wood painted and hinged to a wooden base, so that they laid down flat on the ground in No Man's Land. They were secured by a screw picket ; by pulling a string from the trench the figures were made to stand up at ' zero ' and then drop again. They drew a great deal of fire."

THE 242ND M.G. COMPANY JOINS THE DIVISION.

sending up of the German S.O.S. signal, the hostile barrage was largely diverted from the front from which the raid actually took place.

The raid was gallantly carried out, but no prisoners were taken. "It would have yielded a good bag of prisoners, but unfortunately the party which was to have headed off the Boche garrison, was delayed getting through the wire. They blew up some dug-outs, killed two Germans, and had only a few slightly wounded. Tapes to guide the withdrawal were very successful. The Boche attention was taken from our raid by a mine which was blown to the south, and a dummy raid to the north; and the Highland Light Infantry escaped a barrage which the Boche put on the other places."[1]

About midday on the 28th two more Alsatians of the 65th I.R. crossed No Man's Land and surrendered to the 99th Infantry Brigade in the Cambrin sector. Very soon afterwards the Lorrainers in the 185th Division were transferred to the Russian front, but XIth Corps Intelligence reported that the 2nd Division was still opposed by the 1st Bavarian Reserve Division north of the La Bassée Canal, and by the 185th Division south of the Canal.

About the middle of the month another unit had joined the 2nd Division—the 242nd Machine-Gun Company, as Divisional Machine-Gun Company, and on the 24th went into the line, A, B, and C sections being attached to the 99th, 5th, and 6th Infantry Brigades respectively.

During the 28th and 29th the 10th Duke of Cornwall's Light Infantry (Pioneers) left the 2nd Divisional area for the XVth Corps area—north—for temporary duty.

Bad weather set in towards the end of July, and on the 1st August heavy rain fell, causing considerable damage to the front-line trenches. Frequently the situation along the whole front was quiet, and the troops were able to set to work rebuilding and revetting the fallen parapets where the rain had tumbled them. The enemy was apparently engaged upon the same task, though all along the line patrols reported that many of the opposing trenches were generally in a bad state of repair.

The period of raids was over. Patrol work, however, continued to be actively carried out, and nightly incursions into the enemy's trenches took place up and down the line in all three sectors. This dangerous work was performed most gallantly by officers, N.C.O's, and other ranks, and much valuable information was obtained.

[1] Diary of Major-General C. E. Pereira, C.B., C.M.G.

1ST AUG.

    Barely two months had passed since the 2nd Division had come out of the Oppy sector utterly exhausted and terribly thin in numbers. But by the 1st August the Division had vastly gained in strength, and although many men were still required to restore it to its former establishment, constant training and weeks of vigorous trench warfare had worked wonders. Though all three infantry brigades were in the line, holding a greatly extended front, it was found possible to carry out the regular training of all units as they passed back into reserve; and hard work, wisely interspersed with sports and other amusements, had combined to revive the offensive spirit of the Division. Of the gallant troops of 1914 only a few survivors remained; of newly recruited men there were large numbers, and, in spite of statements to the contrary, it was found impossible to turn the average recruit into a highly disciplined soldier in a few months. Drawn mostly from quiet civil occupations, these men lacked nothing of the soldier's bravery—only his discipline and training; these they did their best to acquire, and acquitted themselves nobly whilst endeavouring to fit themselves for the great struggle upon which they had entered. In the trenches they learned fortitude; out in No Man's Land initiative and daring. From the Diaries of all units of the Division it is evident that unsparing efforts were made to bring out the best of, and inculcate the true soldierly spirit in, all ranks.

    During August, along the Divisional front at least, the ascendency of the Briton over the German in patrol work was very marked. Not only was night patrolling unceasingly carried out, but daylight patrols, greatly daring, crossed No Man's Land and entered the enemy's lines, bringing back valuable information, stealing even the enemy's rifles and damaging his trenches.

    Apart from the incessant shelling by field guns and howitzers, trench mortars, gas bombardments, and the exploding of mines, only one operation of a minor character took place.

10TH AUG.

    About 7.5 o'clock on the morning of the 10th, a section of the Tunnelling Company allotted to the 5th Infantry Brigade exploded a defence mine at the northern end of the Brigade sector, near Surrey Crater. No infantry attack followed, but on the evening of the 11th the enemy was found in possession of the crater. Orders were at once issued to the 17th Royal Fusiliers, who were then holding that section of the Brigade front, to capture, consolidate, and hold the near lip, on the night 11th–12th.

    An attacking party of seventy-five other ranks was formed under Major Hale, M.C., the party being divided into two waves, each under an officer. Six rifle grenadiers co-operated in rear to overcome any serious opposition. The attack, which began at 9.35 p.m., was preceded by an artillery barrage. As soon as the first wave advanced the enemy evacuated the crater, leaving two dead men behind. All objectives were reached, and three posts were established. Wiring parties wired the flanks of the posts, and carried out their tasks without interference from the enemy. At 2.45 a.m. the attacking troops were withdrawn, and the three posts were each manned by one officer, one N.C.O., and six other ranks, with Lewis guns. The Fusiliers had 3 other ranks killed and 6 wounded in this affair. The crater was later named Warlingham Crater, after the " birthplace " of the 17th Royal Fusiliers.

Mustard-gas shells were used by the enemy on the 10th—" a little of which," stated one Battalion Diary, " eventually drifted over part of the front line, making every one sneeze." But just as every sin brings its own punishment, so the use of mustard gas by the enemy brought swift retribution. Ten tons of lethal gas were successfully projected on the enemy's trenches, along the 99th Infantry Brigade front, on the night of the 15th, the enemy retaliating with trench mortars. Another projection on the same area took place on the night of the 23rd, the gas floating in a huge cloud over the enemy's position. It was followed by yet a third projection on the 31st. During the latter projection No. 10 Squadron of the Air Force dropped phosphorus bombs into the enemy's trenches.

On the 26th the 99th Infantry Brigade handed over the Cambrin sector to the 139th Infantry Brigade (46th Division), and marched back to Beuvry into Divisional reserve. The Brigade Diary contains an excellent comment on life out of the line : " It is worthy to record the high spirits and keenness of all ranks during this period of rest. This may be attributed largely to the care with which the programmes of training have been compiled and arranged by the Commanding Officers, ensuring that the work may be varied and interesting. Also to the attention paid to games and sports for the men. The regimental bands are again proving a very valuable asset."

Throughout September the situation along the 2nd Divisional front was normal. South of the Division (during the summer months) the Affairs South of the Souchez River (3rd–25th June), the Capture of Avion (26th–29th June), and the Battle of Hill 70 (15th–25th August) in the same area, had been fought. These offensives were undertaken in order to contain the enemy's troops and prevent him reinforcing other parts of his front (north of the 2nd Division). The Flanders Offensive had begun on 7th June, and by the 14th the Battle of Messines, 1917, and the Capture of Wytschaete had taken place. The enemy counter-attacked at Nieuport on the 10th and 11th July. On the 31st July the Battles of Ypres, 1917, opened, and by the end of August the Battle of Pilckem Ridge (31st July–2nd August), with the subsequent Capture of Westhoek on the 9th August, and the Battle of Langemarck, 1917 (16th–18th August), had been fought and won by the Allies. By the 20th September the enemy had been forced back to the line Hollebeke, Shrewsbury Forest, Clapham Junction (on the Ypres–Menin road), Westhoek, Frezenberg, St. Julien, Bixschoote, and he had suffered very heavy losses in men and material. "The fighting on the Western front," said Ludendorff, "became more severe and costly than any the German army had yet experienced . . . besides the loss of from two to four kilometres of ground along the whole front, it caused us very considerable losses in prisoners and stores, and a heavy expenditure of reserves."

Von Hindenburg also admitted the serious results of the Flanders Offensive : " It is obvious that these actions kept us in great and continual anxiety. In fact, I may say that with such a cloud hanging over our heads we were seldom able to rejoice wholeheartedly over our victories in Russia and Italy."

The French, by the end of August, had almost completely restored their position at Verdun to that before the great German attack on the fortress in February 1916.

On the 25th June the first fighting contingent of American troops landed in France and were undergoing training. No wonder that the German Higher Command began to look with anxiety on the approaching months, and long for winter in order that the mud of Flanders might put an end to the offensive which was draining the resources of the German army.

1st Sept. On the 1st September the 2nd Division held the Givenchy (6th Infantry Brigade) and Canal (5th Infantry Brigade) sectors ; the 99th Infantry Brigade was in Divisional reserve. Portuguese troops were now attached to the Division for training purposes, and were " sandwiched " in between troops of the 2nd Division. On the 20th September the 99th Infantry Brigade again took over the Cambrin sector from the 139th Infantry Brigade (46th Division). All three infantry brigades of the Division were once more in the line, the 99th on the right, the 5th in the centre, and the 6th on the left.

REUTEL—A MEMORY OF 1914.

Excepting for one small raid by the enemy on the 17th Middlesex on the night of the 24th, no incident of importance took place during the month. Much gas was projected into the enemy's trenches, and the artillery and trench mortars kept up an intermittent fire which caused considerable damage to the opposing trenches. Patrol work still continued active, but no infantry attacks on a large scale were made either by or on the 2nd Division.

Early on the 3rd October instructions were received at Divisional Headquarters stating that the Division would be relieved by the 25th Division, the relief to be completed by 6 o'clock on the morning of the 7th October. On relief the 2nd Division was to move to the Auchel area for training purposes. All officers and men attending schools and staffs of schools were ordered to return to their units. Only the Divisional Artillery was to remain in the line until a later date. The Division (it was believed) was destined for the Flanders Offensive.

3RD OCT.

The Battle of the Menin Road Ridge and the Battle of Polygon Wood had been fought on 20th–25th September and 26th September–3rd October respectively. "News to-day," said the General Officer Commanding 2nd Division, " of another most successful advance at Ypres. Our line is now firmly established on the eastern slopes of the high ground at Reutel and north and south of it. They have passed the line that the 2nd and 3rd Coldstream held for three weeks just before Reutel ! " The very mention of the name " Reutel " was sufficient to stir up memories of that pitch black night in October 1914 (three years previously) when the 4th (Guards) Brigade crept forward through the then dense and rain-sodden Polygon Wood towards the Reutel spur, and of the sanguinary fighting in which the 2nd Coldstream took part, until it was relieved in the line, terribly depleted, about the middle of November. Would the Division go back into the old line again ?

Before the relief of the 2nd Division by the 25th Division took place, the enemy was given a final " gassing." On the night of 4th October, at 11.30, 1,178 cylinders of gas were discharged on to the enemy's lines from the Divisional trenches east of Cambrin. Five hundred and forty-three drums were projected opposite the Givenchy sector, and 435 drums north of the Canal : in all, $112\frac{1}{2}$ tons of gas were discharged, while the 46th Division, on the right of the 2nd Division, also joined in the projection. The enemy's retaliation was slight. It was one of the biggest discharges of gas that had ever taken place, and the enemy must have cursed that unfortunate day in the Ypres salient in 1915 when he first introduced it against the Allies. On the same night no less than fourteen patrols crossed No Man's Land and reconnoitred the enemy's trenches, establishing the fact that no change had taken place in his dispositions.

8TH OCT.

By the morning of the 8th October all three infantry brigades were settled in the Auchel area, with 2nd Division Headquarters at Labeuvrière.

The 2nd Divisional Artillery was relieved by the 25th Divisional Artillery on the night 7th–8th and 8th–9th October. The " G. S. " Diary of the 2nd Division contains the following note for October 1917 : " From 7th to 31st October the Division was training in the Auchel training area. Particular attention was paid to musketry and to battalion and brigade formation in the attack. These formations were based on the experience of other divisions in the recent fighting on the Flanders front, more especially in the attack on isolated strong points.[1] Stress was also laid on the dispositions of machine guns, machine-gun barrages, and the various means of forward inter-communication. The training facilities were good, and the weather generally permitted of successful training programmes being carried out."

The Division had improved vastly, and particularly in one most important point : excepting those old soldiers who still remained with the Division, the new troops had been unable to fire their rifles rapidly with any certainty of scoring hits. But during this period of training practically all troops in the Division learned to fire at least 13 rounds per minute, and many of them the pre-war regulation rate of 15 rounds per minute : this with a certainty of gaining a high percentage of hits.

---

[1] An interesting comment on these isolated strong points (" Pill Boxes ") is contained in the Diary of the General Officer Commanding 2nd Division : " They (the new principles quoted above) appear to have absolutely defeated the pill-box, and now the (enemy) garrisons clear out on the first possible occasion."

THE CAMBRAI OPERATIONS,
20th November to 7th December 1917.

THE BATTLE OF CAMBRAI:
  The Tank Attack (20th to 21st November) and the Capture of Bourlon Wood (23rd to 28th November).

THE GERMAN COUNTER-ATTACK, 30th November to 3rd December:
  I. 30th November.
  II. 1st to 3rd December.
  The Withdrawal from the Bourlon Salient.
  Trench Warfare, 7th December 1917 to 20th March 1918.

THE BATTLE OF CAMBRAI, 1917:
The Tank Attack and the Capture of Bourlon Wood.

THE anticipations of the 2nd Division—that it would join the XVIIIth Corps and take an active part in the Flanders offensive—did not materialize. Training in the Auchel area continued until 5th November, when all three infantry brigades moved northwards under orders to join the IInd Corps of the Second Army. 5TH Nov.

The 5th, 226th, and 483rd Field Companies R.E. had been ordered to move on the 4th–6th November to the Fifth Army area. All three Companies proceeded to Poperinghe, thence to Brielen, where work on the roads was begun immediately. For the next few days the sappers were strenuously employed, suffering casualties from the enemy's barrages, which frequently came down upon the very roads on which the Engineers were working. On the 11th November, in the Diary of the 5th Field Company, the following entry occurs: "Anniversary of the 5th Field Company's charge against the Prussian Guard at Ypres, 1914." It was in the Battle of Nonne Bosschen (a day never to be forgotten) that the original 5th Field Company R.E., with cooks, orderlies, batmen, and whatever stragglers could be collected, charged the enemy and assisted in the repulse of the Kaiser's famous Guards.

The 2nd Divisional Artillery was already in the line, for on the 17th October the gunners moved from Amettes *en route* for Poperinghe. The latter place was reached on the 19th; on the 20th the guns again moved forward, and on the following day went into action, being attached to the 63rd Divisional Artillery (until 5th November), and later to the 1st Divisional Artillery.

The 5th, 6th, and 99th Infantry Brigades, marching according to orders, had on the 8th November reached the following areas: Houtkerque (6th Infantry Brigade), Zermezeele (5th Infantry Brigade), Herzeele (99th Infantry Brigade); 2nd Division Headquarters were at Wormhoudt. The 5th Infantry Brigade moved on the 13th to Winnizeele area. But none of the infantry of the 2nd Division were destined to take part in the operations round 8TH Nov.

Ypres. The 24th Royal Fusiliers were indeed attached to the IInd Corps Heavy Artillery as working parties for the purpose of moving forward guns and ammunition, but no other infantry battalions of the 2nd Division took part in the Flanders offensive.

18TH Nov. Finally, on the 18th, the 2nd Division received orders for the concentration of the Division in the IInd Corps area by noon, 21st November, ready to leave the Second Army. On the 21st the Division was once more complete (the gunners and sappers having been withdrawn from the line) and "stood ready" to move.[1] Throughout the 22nd the Division completed all arrangements, and on the 23rd moved by rail from the Wormhoudt area southwards, *en route* for the Third Army, where it was to join the Vth Corps at Haplincourt. But eventually the Division found itself in the IVth Corps area, of which it subsequently formed part.

26TH Nov. On the morning of the 26th the 2nd Division completed its detrainment—the 5th Infantry Brigade at Lebucquière, the 6th Infantry Brigade at Doignies, and the 99th Infantry Brigade at Beaumetz. At 4.30 p.m. orders were issued to the three infantry brigades to relieve the 36th Division in the line during the coming night. The notice was short, but fortunately the brigades had only a few miles to go in order to carry out the relief.

As the operations which followed the relief are of great and special interest to the 2nd Division, those parts of the original orders containing the details of the reliefs are given in full :—

"The 2nd Division will relieve the 36th Division in the line to-night, south-west of Bourlon Village, between the points E.17,b.2.3 on the right and E.20,a.2.0 on the left.

"The 99th Infantry Brigade will be on the right, and will relieve the 107th Infantry Brigade from E.17,b.2.3 to the Sains-les-Marquions road running north and south through E.21,b. and d. (inclusive). Headquarters 99th Infantry Brigade will be at K.4,d.5.4.

"The 6th Infantry Brigade will be on the left, and will relieve the 109th Infantry Brigade from the Sains-les-Marquions road (exclusive) to E.20,a.2.0. Headquarters 6th Infantry Brigade will be at K.7,c.9.4.

The 5th Infantry Brigade will relieve the 108th Infantry Brigade in Divisional reserve to-morrow, 27th November. Headquarters 5th Infantry Brigade will be at Hermies (J.29,b.).

[1] To the unbounded satisfaction of all ranks the Pioneers, 10th Duke of Cornwall's Light Infantry, who had been away from the 2nd Division for five and a half months, rejoined the Division on the 7th November.

WHY THE BATTLE OF CAMBRAI WAS FOUGHT. 477

"2nd Division Headquarters will open at Ytres at 10 a.m. Command will pass from General Officer Commanding 36th Division to General Officer Commanding 2nd Division at 10 a.m. on 27th November."

The 2nd Division would, on relief, be flanked on the right by the 62nd Division, whose Headquarters were at Havrincourt, and by the 56th (London) Division on the left, Headquarters at Fremicourt.

Machine-Gun Companies and Trench Mortar Batteries were to be relieved on the 27th, and during the night 27th–28th.

The 2nd Divisional Artillery had arrived at Haplincourt on the 25th, when some of the batteries went into action. On the 26th the guns were moved from Haplincourt to Ytres.

The famous Cambrai operations of 1917 had already opened when the 2nd Division arrived at Haplincourt. The two great offensives—at Arras and in Flanders—of the spring and summer of 1917 had served their purpose, and the enemy had been forced to concentrate his troops in the areas of the Allies' offensives, leaving other portions of his front relatively weak. The Battles of Polygon Wood, Broodseinde, Poelcappelle, the First Battle of Passchendaele, and finally the Second Battle of Passchendaele, concluded the Flanders Offensive which had opened on 7th June. The continuance of the Flanders offensive after 4th October was practically forced upon Sir Douglas Haig by a combination of circumstances over which the British Commander-in-Chief had little or no control. Since July the Russian armies had ceased to be a fighting force; the fighting capacity of the French armies had been seriously affected by grave internal troubles; the Italian reverse of October had greatly jeopardized the solidarity of the Allied front in the West; the American army was not yet in a position to lend the Allies assistance; the enemy was rapidly transferring large numbers of divisions from the East to the West—set free by the Russian *débâcle*. The British army was thus the only Allied army capable of conducting serious offensive operations at this period, and if that army ceased its offensive the enemy had every opportunity of regaining the initiative: he would be free to attack wherever he thought the Allied line weakest. The condition of the French armies made the latter risk impossible, and it therefore followed that Sir Douglas Haig had no choice but to continue the Flanders Offensive.

On the 10th November, when weather conditions had put an end to any further offensive operations in the north, the Allied forces north, east, and south of Ypres had advanced to the line Le Touquet (just west of Frelinghien), a point 1,000 yards west of Deulémont, thence almost direct north to Hollebeke, thence north-east to about 500 yards west of Gheluvelt, north again and east, including Reutel spur and village, and a line running approximately through the villages of Noordemhoek, Molenaarenshoek, Broodseinde, Passchendaele, Poelcappelle, north-west along the southern extremities of Houthulst Forest to west of the lake De Blankaart. Besides considerable gains of enemy territory, 24,000 prisoners, 74 guns, 941 machine guns, and 138 trench mortars had been captured.

The vigorous operations in Flanders had compelled the enemy to reduce his garrisons in other parts of his line to a degree bordering on weakness. This reduction and consequent weakness resulted in the Battle of Cambrai, 1917.

Although it was not involved in the first phase of the battle, in order that the *rôle* and significance of the operations carried out by the 2nd Division may be fully understood, the general plan of action is given with a brief outline of the events preceding the heavy German counter-attacks of 30th November, the date upon which the 2nd Division might be said to have entered fully into the contest.

"The object of these operations," said Sir Douglas Haig, "was to gain a local success by a sudden attack at a point where the enemy did not expect it. Our repeated attacks in Flanders, and those of our Allies elsewhere, had brought about large concentrations of the enemy's forces on the threatened fronts, with a consequent reduction in the garrisons of certain other sectors of his line.

"Of these weakened sectors, the Cambrai front had been selected as the most suitable for the surprise operation in contemplation. The ground there was, on the whole, favourable for the employment of Tanks, which were to play an important part in the enterprise, and facilities existed for the concealment of the necessary preparations for the attack.

"If, after breaking through the German defence system on this front, we could secure Bourlon to the north, and establish a good flank position to the east in the direction of Cambrai, we should be well placed to exploit the situation locally between Bourlon and the Sensée River and to the north-west. The capture of Cambrai itself was subsidiary to this operation, the object of our advance towards that town being primarily to cover our flanks and puzzle the enemy regarding our intentions.

"The enemy was laying out fresh lines of defence behind those which he had already completed on the Cambrai front, and it was to be expected that his troops would be re-distributed as soon as our pressure in Flanders relaxed. He had already brought large forces from Russia in exchange for divisions exhausted in the struggle in the Western theatre, and it was practically certain that heavy reinforcements would be brought from East to West during the winter. Moreover, his tired divisions, after the winter's rest, would recover their efficiency. . . . The general plan of attack was to dispense with previous artillery preparation and to depend instead on Tanks to smash through the enemy's wire, of which there was a great quantity protecting his trenches. . . . It was explained to all commanders that everything depended on secrecy up to the moment of starting, and after that a bold, determined, and rapid action. Unless opposition could be beaten down quickly no great results could be looked for."

Since the beginning of the April offensive the enemy's defences on this part of his front had been vastly improved and strengthened. They now consisted of three systems: the first, the Hindenburg Line proper, ran in a general north-westerly direction for a distance of six miles from the Canal de l'Escaut (the St. Quentin Canal) at Banteaux to Havrincourt. At Havrincourt it turned abruptly north along the line of the Canal du Nord for about four miles to Mœuvres. Thus between Banteaux and Mœuvres the German line formed a salient. A series of strong forward positions had been constructed in advance of the Hindenburg Main Line; these included La Vacquerie and the north-east corner of Havrincourt Wood. Behind the Hindenburg Main Line lay the second and third German systems, known as the Hindenburg Support and the Beaurevoir–Masnières–Marquion Lines respectively. The attack was to be made by the 36th, 62nd, 51st, 6th, 20th, and 12th Divisions of the Third Army (Sir Julian Byng).[1]

"Zero" hour had been fixed for 6.20 a.m. on the 20th November.

The necessary preparations were carried out in great secrecy, and at "zero" on the 20th, without any previous artillery bombardment, Tanks and infantry attacked on a front of six miles from west of Gonnelieu to the Canal du Nord opposite Hermies. "Demonstrations with gas, smoke, and artillery took place along practically the whole British front south of the Scarpe, and subsidiary attacks were launched east of Epehy, and between Bullecourt and Fontaine-les-Croisilles."

[1] In the order given from left to right.

Moving forward in advance of the infantry the Tanks, carrying fascines, tore huge lanes in the enemy's wire, crashed on to and over the German trenches, grinding his machine guns with their teams beneath them. Many Germans ran down into their dug-outs to escape being pulverized, but they were cleared out by the British "moppers-up," who followed close in the wake of the metal monsters, and, whilst the latter patrolled the line of hostile trenches, rounded up the enemy's surviving troops and passed them back to the prisoners' cages. "In this way both the main system of the Hindenburg Line and its outer defences were rapidly overrun, and Tanks and infantry proceeded in accordance with programme to the attack upon the Hindenburg Reserve (Support) Line."

Into all the details of the fighting which took place during the next few days it is impossible to go. Around Bourlon the battle waged with extraordinary fierceness. Again and again the village was won and lost by Sir Julian Byng's devoted troops. During the morning of the 24th the enemy twice attacked the north-east corner of Bourlon Wood, but was beaten off; in the afternoon he launched a third attack with like result, and in the evening, still determined to regain the position, he launched a fourth attack, but this also was bloodily repulsed. The British troops fought grandly, whilst their opponents were no mean foes, many of the Germans showing supreme contempt for death, which certainly awaited them as they advanced in vain efforts to regain their lost trenches.

26TH Nov. With barely two hours' notice the 2nd Division moved forward about 5 p.m. on the 26th to relieve the 36th Division, and the left flank of the 62nd Division, in the front line. Reconnaissance under the circumstances was impossible. Under the worst possible conditions the troops met their guides and advanced along the Bapaume–Cambrai road to take over the trenches. A heavy snowstorm and a pitch-black night both favoured and hindered the relief; the adverse weather conditions evidently prevented the enemy shelling the Bapaume–Cambrai road, which, under ordinary conditions, was a veritable death-trap. The snow, however, turned the trenches into slimy ditches six inches deep in liquid mud. But 27TH Nov. by the early hours of the 27th the 99th and 6th Infantry Brigades had taken over the new line and were disposed as follows :—

99th Infantry Brigade—Right Battalion: 23rd Royal Fusiliers; Left Battalion: 1st King's Royal Rifle Corps; Right Support Battalion: 1st Royal Berks; Left Support Battalion: 22nd Royal Fusiliers.

SITUATION ON 27TH NOVEMBER.

6th Infantry Brigade—Right Battalion: 2nd South Staffords; Left Battalion: 17th Middlesex; Right Support Battalion: 13th Essex; Left Support Battalion: 1st King's.

5th Infantry Brigade—in Divisional reserve in the Hermies area.

The 5th, 226th, and 483rd Field Companies R.E. were at work on the Bapaume–Cambrai road, the Pioneers being similarly engaged on the Doignies–Demicourt–Graincourt road.

The gunners of the Division had arrived at Haplincourt on the 26th, and had hardly settled themselves in billets when orders were received at 4 p.m. to take up positions in front of Havrincourt. Guides were to be met at 10 p.m. The batteries marched out of Haplincourt at 6 p.m., and with great difficulty, owing to the darkness and snowstorm, the guides were found and the gun positions pointed out, the batteries going into action about 2.30 a.m. on the 27th. At 10 a.m. on the 27th the General Officer Commanding 2nd Division assumed command of the line, Divisional Headquarters being at Ytres.

The general situation (as reported in the Divisional Diary) when the 2nd Division took over the line, is here given : " At this time the general situation on the battle front was that the advance was held up along the army front by strong enemy reinforcements. Bitter fighting had taken place for Bourlon Village and Bourlon Wood, both places having changed hands several times. Most of Bourlon Wood and the high ground north-west of it remained in our hands, but the village was still in the enemy's possession. More to the south the important heights by the village of Fontaine-notre-Dame were still holding up our advance. . . . Both sides appeared to be hurrying up new divisions to take part in the battle, and preparations were being made on our side with fresh troops to drive home our initial advantage.

" A big attack on our immediate right on Bourlon Village and Fontaine-notre-Dame, by the 62nd Division and the Guards Division, was to take place at 6.20 a.m. on the morning of the 27th with the object of capturing Bourlon Village and Fontaine-notre-Dame, and gaining all ground from which observation could be brought to bear on our batteries. . . . Should this operation be successful it was rumoured that we would consolidate our gains before carrying out any further operations on a big scale."

On taking over command at 10 a.m., the General Officer Commanding at once went up to the front line to visit the Brigades. The front line was found to be extraordinarily irregular. The greater part of it ran from north-east to south-west; it then took a turn almost north-west, finally running almost due west. From in front of the 6th and 99th Infantry Brigades a trench ran northwards, while the right flank of the latter ended in a series of posts. It was obvious that such a line would be difficult to hold.

The attacks of the 62nd and Guards Divisions, at first successful, were gradually being driven back to the jumping-off line when, at 10.30 a.m., Divisional Headquarters were rung up by IVth Corps Headquarters and asked to send reinforcements to the 62nd Division, then being heavily counter-attacked. The Division was ordered to place one battalion of the 99th Infantry Brigade at the disposal of the General Officer Commanding 62nd Division, but at that moment the Officer Commanding a cavalry dismounted battalion reported to the General Officer Commanding 2nd Division, and permission was obtained to attach this battalion in place of a battalion from the 99th Infantry Brigade.

By nightfall on the 27th the situation was, however, well in hand, but the 62nd Division had suffered severely during the day's fighting, and, in order to secure their position, were in need of reinforcements. At 9.15 p.m., therefore, the 2nd Division, acting under instructions from IVth Corps Headquarters, dispatched the 22nd Royal Fusiliers from the 99th Infantry Brigade to the Right Brigade 62nd Division. The 17th Royal Fusiliers (5th Infantry Brigade) were ordered to replace the 22nd Royal Fusiliers, and came under the orders of the General Officer Commanding 99th Infantry Brigade.

After the attacks of the 62nd and Guards Divisions, orders were issued to the troops to consolidate their positions before undertaking any fresh operations. The attack had one important result—it had improved the line in Bourlon Wood and on the high ground north-west of it, and the crest of the hill immediately west of the wood had been gained. But in order to safeguard the hill it was necessary for the 2nd Division to strengthen and advance the line it had taken over. The enemy salient produced by the extraordinary position in the centre of the 99th Infantry Brigade line had first of all to be bitten off. The Brigade was ordered to carry out this operation on the 28th, but the attack was later postponed until 6.25 a.m. on the following day.

29TH Nov. The attack was made by C Company and one platoon from each of A and B Companies of the 1st King's Royal Rifle Corps. Under a heavy bombardment by artillery and Stokes mortars the Rifles advanced gallantly and in the face of a heavy machine-gun fire,

GENERAL SITUATION ON 29TH NOVEMBER.

which mostly came from a gun posted in a sunken road on the right-centre of the objective. In spite of considerable losses, the Rifles gained 300 yards of the enemy's position, and although the attack did not succeed in cutting off all the salient, the greater part of it fell to the attackers. "Officers and men," said the Commanding Officer of the battalion, "who took part in the attack particularly distinguished themselves, as their losses will show." Lieut. Goodwin was killed, 2 other officers were wounded, 18 other ranks were killed, 53 wounded, and 3 missing—*i.e.*, 75 per cent. of the attacking force.

The remainder of the 29th November passed without incident. Thus far the Battle of Cambrai had progressed splendidly. Ten thousand five hundred prisoners had been captured and 142 guns, 350 machine guns, and 70 trench mortars. The British line from east of Gonnelieu to west of Mœuvres had advanced, and now formed a great bulge into the enemy's system of trenches. Over six miles of the redoubtable Hindenburg Main and Support Lines had fallen. On the evening of the 29th November the British line, from right to left, ran as follows: astride the Hindenburg Main Line, half-way between Gonnelieu and Banteaux, thence north-east, west of Bonavis ridge to the St. Quentin Canal, about 1,000 yards south-east of Masnières; from the St. Quentin Canal the line then ran north and north-west, taking in Masnières, until it reached the canal again at Noyelles-sur-l'Escaut; skirting the latter village, and running east and north-west again, the line ran east of Cantaing to the north-eastern corner of Bourlon Wood; practically the whole of the wood was included in the New British Line, which ran due west; north-west again, including Tadpole Copse, then dropped back south-west to the Old British Line, almost midway between Pronville (north) and Louverval (south).

But as the official dispatches said: "During the last few days of November increased registration of hostile artillery, the movements of troops and transport observed behind the German lines, together with other indications of a like nature, pointed to further efforts by the enemy to regain the positions we had wrested from him."

THE GERMAN COUNTER-ATTACKS, 30th November to 3rd December.

I. 30th November.

Since the 2nd Division took over the Mœuvres–Bourlon Wood front on the night 26th–27th November, inter-battalion changes had taken place, though the 6th and 99th Infantry Brigades still held the left and right sub-sectors respectively. The 17th Royal Fusiliers, of the 5th Infantry Brigade, however, still remained in the front line under the General Officer Commanding 99th Infantry Brigade. On the right of the Division the 62nd Division had been relieved by the 47th (London) Division, while on the left the 56th (London) Division had relieved the 51st (Highland) Division. The 22nd Royal Fusiliers, who had been dispatched to Bourlon Wood, returned to the 2nd Division on the night of the 29th and marched back to Hermies in reserve.

30TH NOV. MAP.

When dawn broke on the 30th November—the dawn of a day long to be remembered in the annals of the British army—the dispositions of units of the 2nd Division were as follows: 99th Infantry Brigade, in the right sub-sector, with three battalions in the front line; 1st Royal Berks, right; 17th Royal Fusiliers (of the 5th Infantry Brigade), centre; and 1st King's Royal Rifle Corps, left[1]; the 23rd Royal Fusiliers were in support about the Sugar Factory which stood along the Bapaume–Cambrai road. The fourth battalion of the 99th Infantry Brigade was still in reserve in trenches east of Hermies. The 6th Infantry Brigade, in the left sub-sector, disposed the 13th Essex Regiment on the right and the 1st King's on the left; the 2nd South Staffords were in support of the 13th Essex; and the 17th Middlesex in support of the 1st King's; one company (A) of the Middlesex was at the immediate disposal of the Officer Commanding 1st King's.

The Royal Engineers and Pioneers, who had been at work in the vicinity of Demicourt, returned to the Division on the 29th, and had been affiliated to the brigades in the line: the 5th Field Company to the 6th Infantry Brigade, and the 483rd Field Company to the 99th Infantry Brigade; the 226th Field Company was kept in reserve under the immediate orders of the C.R.E.

Two companies (A and B) of the 10th Duke of Cornwall's Light

---

[1] The Divisional maps show two companies in the front line (on the left of the 17th Royal Fusiliers) and two in support.

THE BATTLE OF ARLEUX,
28th-29th April 1917.
(And to cover the period between 15th-27th April 1917.)
(Facing p. 436.)

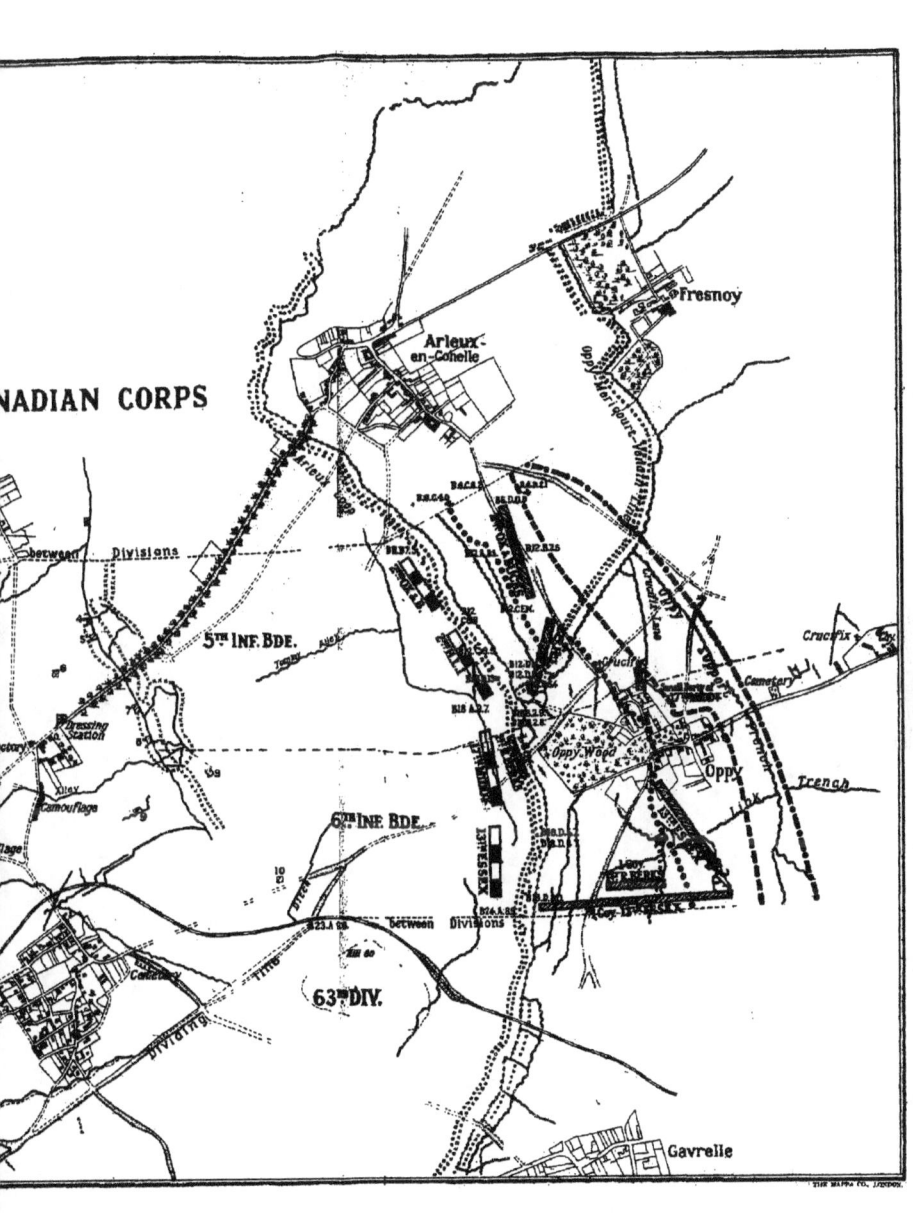

AN IMMORTAL STORY. 485

Infantry (Pioneers) were attached to the 6th Infantry Brigade, and two companies (C and D) to the 99th Infantry Brigade.

The guns of the XLIst Brigade R.F.A. were in action near the Canal du Nord, whilst the XXXVIth Brigade R.F.A. had gun positions in front of Havrincourt—*i.e.*, north of the village.

"From the first day in the line," said the Divisional Report of the German counter-attack on the 30th November, "all had worked hard to restore order to a line which had been taken over hurriedly during operations, and to replace chaos by organization. Had it not been for this it is doubtful whether, when the storm broke on the Divisional front on the 30th November, the line could have been maintained and the concentrated attacks of three German divisions broken up, with most severe losses to the enemy.

"The subsequent story is one so brimful of heroism that it deserves to take its place in English history for all time, and to be a proud day in the lives of all those splendid British soldiers who, by their single-hearted devotion to duty, saved what would have been undoubtedly a catastrophe had they given way.

"The troops can be said to have been already in action for three days, as constant movement and reliefs under shell-fire had had to be carried out."

At dawn on the 30th November the enemy opened heavy fire with his artillery on the battalions in the front line. Thence onwards, until between 8 and 9 a.m., he continued to shell the Divisional area. At about 8.45 a.m. the barrage fell particularly violent along the front of the 99th Infantry Brigade, the line of posts on the right of the Brigade, the line of the Bapaume–Cambrai road, and the Sugar Factory. All communication was cut between the two right battalions (the 1st Royal Berks and the 23rd Royal Fusiliers) and Brigade Headquarters, in the sunken road in the Hindenburg Support Line west of Graincourt. The 6th Infantry Brigade, on the left, was likewise subjected to very heavy shelling.

Shortly after 9 o'clock the enemy was reported advancing in force south and south-east from Quarry Wood. At 9.15 a.m. large bodies of hostile troops, estimated at a division, were reported entering the village of Mœuvres; the whole area north of the 2nd Division trenches, between Bourlon Wood and Mœuvres, appeared to be stiff with troops. On the ridge west of Bourlon Wood large numbers of the enemy were seen advancing against the junction of the 2nd and 47th (London) Divisions.

The S.O.S. signal went up, and the Divisional Artillery put down an intense barrage, tearing gaps in the grey masses as they pressed on towards the British trenches. But in spite of heavy losses the enemy's troops continued to advance.

The 17th Royal Fusiliers, holding that curious advanced sap which ran northwards, were ordered to thin out their line and concentrate for the defence of the main line of resistance. Two companies of the 23rd Royal Fusiliers were moved up into close support of the 1st Royal Berks.

The storm burst on the extreme right of the Division, at its junction with the left flank (6th London Regiment) of the 47th Division. Here the Londoners were gradually being pressed back; four posts of the 1st Royal Berks, immediately south of the sunken road, were wiped out, the survivors, under Second-Lieut. R. Palmer, getting into shell-holes farther back, where they held on. The situation on this flank was now critical. But the Lewis guns and machine guns, co-operating with three guns of the 140th Infantry Brigade, came into action with deadly effect, and, inflicting enormous losses on the enemy, successfully held up his advance. Again and again the Germans attempted to overwhelm the gallant defenders of the junction between the two divisions, but they were mowed down in hundreds, and eventually, after three hours' hard fighting, gave up the attempt.

MAP. Meanwhile at the saphead, held by the 17th Royal Fusiliers, a desperate and bloody conflict was being waged. The enemy's advance had broken upon the gallant Fusiliers just as they were in the act of withdrawing, the position being considered too exposed to hold in the face of very heavy attacks which had developed with unexpected speed and intensity. The rearguard—a platoon left to cover the withdrawal of the remainder of the company—under the command of Captain N. Stone and Lieut. S. Benzecry, assisted by machine guns, held up the whole of the German attacks in that part of the line, whilst the main position of the 17th Royal Fusiliers was being fully organized.

The splendid gallantry of this rearguard furnishes one of the most glorious stories of that day of fierce fighting. The two officers, Captain Stone and Lieut. Benzecry, had been ordered to withdraw to the main line, but elected to stay on with their men. With bullet, bayonet, and bomb they fought the enemy, inflicting terrible losses upon him. But one by one the gallant defenders fell, the survivors still fighting desperately. Lieut. Benzecry, who, when last seen, was wounded in the head, continued to fight until he fell dead. Captain Stone was then killed—shot through the head. There were no survivors: the rearguard died to a man,

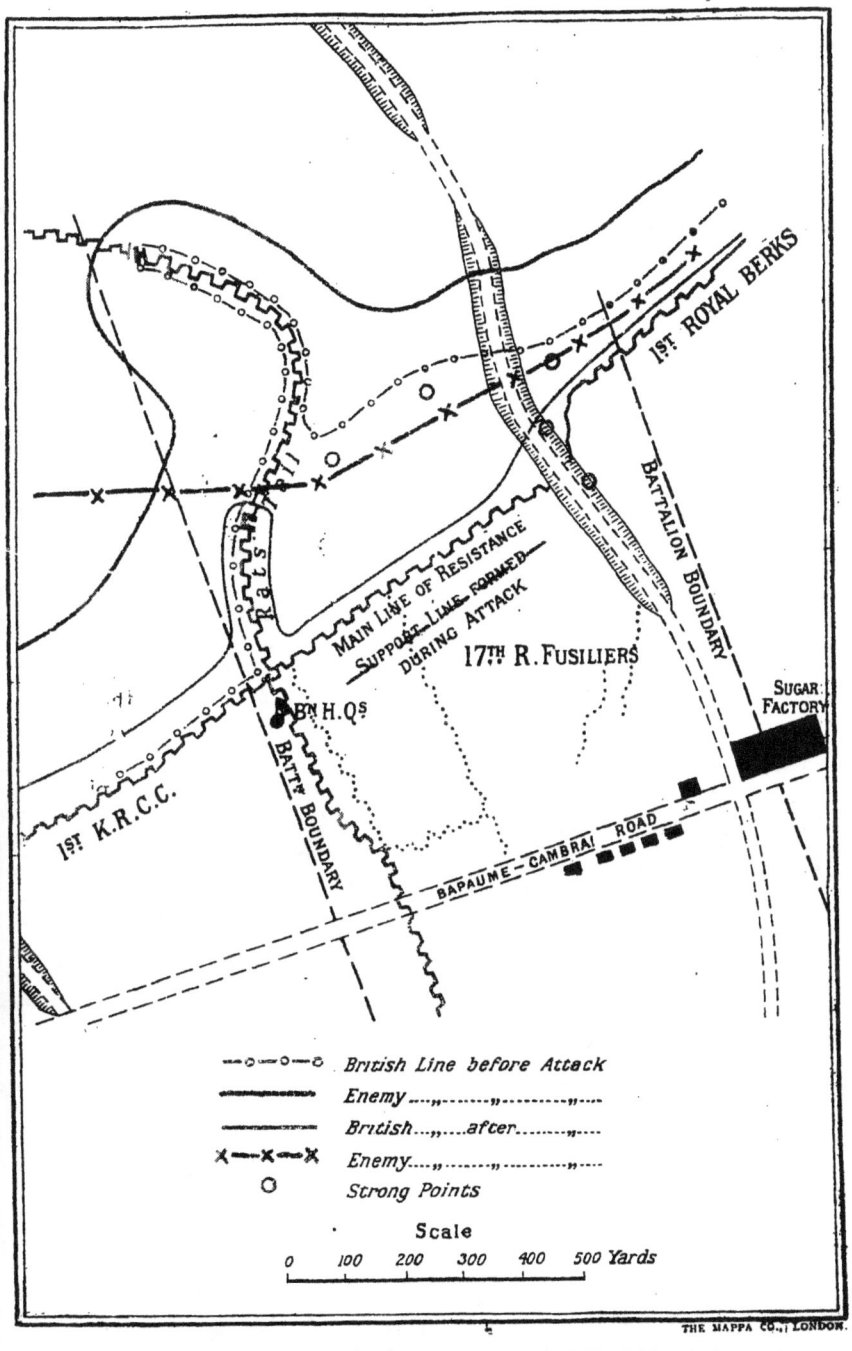

THE RAT'S TAIL: REARGUARD ACTION BY 17th ROYAL FUSILIERS on 30th November 1917.

(*Facing p. 486.*)

THE FIRST V.C. AT CAMBRAI, 1917.

facing the enemy. Captain Stone, by his invaluable information concerning the movements of the enemy prior to the attack, and his subsequent sacrifice with the rearguard, saved the situation at the cost of his life, and well merited the Victoria Cross (awarded him posthumously)—the first of the two Crosses won at Cambrai by the 2nd Division.[1]

Under cover of the splendid resistance put up by the rearguard, a block was formed in the trench some 500 yards from the saphead. Having wiped out the rearguard to a man, the enemy next attacked the block, but could not take it. Every attempt was met by a storm of bombs and a hail of bullets, and the enemy fell back exhausted, leaving the trench and the vicinity littered with his dead and dying. Lieut. Forbes Menzies, 17th Royal Fusiliers, with a party of bombers, followed up the enemy after a particularly violent but vain effort, and, driving him back about 200 yards, established yet another block which, though many times attacked in force, stood firm. The result of this action was to afford Battalion Headquarters a fine field of view, enabling the battalion to bring an enfilade fire on the line of the enemy's advance east and west of the trench. On the left of the 17th Royal Fusiliers the 1st King's Royal Rifles were hotly engaged. Wave after wave of the enemy advanced against the Rifles, but owing to the well-directed and intense volume of fire from rifles, Lewis guns, and machine guns, the enemy's troops were literally mown down. Now indeed were observed the splendid results of that period of musketry instruction through which the Division had recently passed. Topping a rise, as they advanced in massed formation against the Rifles, at about 200–300 yards' distance, the Germans throughout the day never got nearer. Seldom had the 2nd Division experienced such opportunities of testing its prowess with the rifle; the rifles were so heated from rapid fire that in

[1] "For most conspicuous bravery when in command of a company in an isolated position 1,000 yards in front of the main line and overlooking the enemy's position. He observed the enemy massing for an attack, and afforded invaluable information to Battalion Headquarters.

"He was ordered to withdraw his company, leaving a rearguard to cover the withdrawal. The attack developing with unexpected speed, Captain Stone sent three platoons back and remained with the rearguard himself. He stood on the parapet with the telephone, under a tremendous bombardment, observing the enemy, and continued to send back valuable information until the wire was cut by his orders.

"The rearguard was eventually surrounded and cut to pieces, and Captain Stone was seen fighting to the last, till he was shot through the head. The extraordinary coolness of this heroic officer, and the accuracy of his information, enabled dispositions to be made just in time to save the line and avert disaster."—*London Gazette*, 13th February 1918.

many instances inactivity was forced upon the men to the very evident annoyance of the latter. Some brave Germans endeavoured to creep forward to snipe the Rifles; they were promptly disposed of by the battalion snipers and Lewis gunners. The slaughter was prodigious !

At 11.25 a.m. the enemy again attacked all along the line of the right Brigade, his principal efforts being directed against the 17th Royal Fusiliers. The advanced post of the Fusiliers and the troops on the immediate right and left were momentarily driven in, but the situation was restored by a company of the 23rd Royal Fusiliers acting in support on the left of the 1st Royal Berks, and the enemy was again hurled back with great slaughter. At from 50 to 200 yards' range the Lewis and machine gunners and the riflemen had splendid targets, and swept the ground clear of the enemy.

At 1 p.m. the 17th Royal Fusiliers sent back a report that their line was intact, that they were in close touch with the units on either flank, and that " the men were really enjoying the novel experience of killing Germans in lumps at point-blank range." Only five Lewis guns, however, remained serviceable, and small-arms ammunition and bombs were needed urgently; the latter were dispatched forthwith.

From 12.30 to 1 p.m. there had been a slight lull, though the roar of the guns and the cracking of machine guns and rifles never quite ceased. In the last attack the enemy, in close formation, was under " very hot artillery, machine-gun, Lewis-gun, and rifle fire for about two and a half hours." They fought gallantly, those Germans !

But at 2.30 p.m. large masses of the enemy advanced south and south-east along the British front from the western edge of Bourlon Wood against the left flank of the 47th Division and the right flank of the 2nd Division, held by the Berkshires. Another deadly struggle ensued. South of the sunken road, at the juncture of the divisions, the attack was driven off with heavy loss. North of this road, however, the 140th Infantry Brigade, whose ranks were much thinned out through constant losses, were forced back by the enemy. It was here that three posts garrisoned by the Berkshires, on the extreme right of the line held by the 99th Infantry Brigade, were captured. The garrisons fell fighting to the last, and when later (on the 2nd December) an attempt was made to recover the bodies, there was such a heap of German dead in and around the posts that it was impossible to find the remains of those who had so gallantly given their lives. The remaining

GALLANT BERKSHIRES.

five posts north of the sunken road, held by the Berkshires (under Lieut. Valentine) stood firm and repulsed all attacks, until the 23rd Royal Fusiliers reinforced the line. The 140th Infantry Brigade also received reinforcements, and the enemy was driven back north of the ridge. " Too much praise cannot be given," said the Official Reports, " to this splendid company of the 1st Royal Berkshire Regiment, and its Commander, Lieut. Valentine, for their valour and steadfastness in this most critical time, extending over some six hours. They met attack after attack of the enemy, who was always in vastly superior numbers and who came right up to them time after time only to be mown down or to retire in disorder. The casualties in this company were 46 all ranks and a Lewis gun put out of action, but they never flinched. They claim to have killed over 500 of the enemy, and I well believe that this is no exaggeration."

At 3.10 p.m. (having preceded the attack by a barrage which opened at 2.45 p.m.) the sorely tried 17th Royal Fusiliers, as the unit on the immediate flank of the Berkshires, were again attacked, but once more threw back the enemy with frightful loss.

Finally, at 4.10 p.m., a last attempt was made to drive the very gallant Fusiliers from the block formed by Lieut. Forbes Menzies in the morning, in the trench running northwards (called the Rat's Tail). The enemy, massing in great force, advanced from the north, east, and west of the Rat's Tail. An 18-pounder battery of the 2nd Divisional Artillery got right on to the massed Germans, with disastrous results to the enemy. His troops were slaughtered in great numbers as the shells burst amongst the " bunched " men crowded together in the trenches east and north of the Rat's Tail. Like all other attempts, this attack broke down.

This seemed to finally quell the attackers, who made no further efforts, but commenced consolidating on the line which the 1st King's Royal Rifles had captured on the 29th—a very minor gain for the prodigious loss of life inflicted on the enemy.

This closed the right attack.

On the left—the Mœuvres sector—where the 6th Infantry Brigade held the line, events were happening similar to those already described as taking place along the front held by the 99th Infantry Brigade.

Here also, at 8.30 a.m., the enemy was reported massing, and at 9.20 a.m. he was observed advancing from the north and north-east, against the Canal du Nord. Half an hour later his troops were seen massed for the attack in Mœuvres Village.

The line of the 6th Infantry Brigade was ill adapted for defence. It was cut through the centre by the Canal du Nord—a kind of gigantic dry moat about 80 feet broad at the top and 40 feet at the bottom. The steep sides of this moat and the bottom of it were of brick. The canal ran from south to north, not only through the 6th Brigade line, but also through the enemy's position east of Mœuvres, and from his trenches he was able to enfilade the bridges, so that they could not be used. In consequence, communication between the British troops east and west of the canal was most difficult and hazardous. The bed of the Canal du Nord was dry, and if a man wanted to cross it he had to slide down a slippery 20-foot wall and climb up the other side by means of a rope—the while the enemy opened a galling fire on him with machine guns and rifles.

As on the front held by the 99th Infantry Brigade, there was in the centre of the 6th Infantry Brigade line a short trench running north-east along the western bank of the Canal du Nord. Lock No. 5 was also held and garrisoned.

East of the Canal the 13th Essex Regiment held Lock No. 5, Canal Trench, and a trench running from west to east, joining up with the 1st King's Royal Rifle Corps. D Company of the Essex held the short trench (about 500 yards in extent) on the western banks of the canal, joining up with the right flank of the 1st King's, the left-front battalion at the southern extremity of the trench. The King's held their front line on a two-company basis—C on the right, B on the left, with A and D in support.

The left flank of the 6th Infantry Brigade joined up with the Queen's Westminsters (56th Division).

The 17th Middlesex were in dug-outs just south of the Bapaume-Cambrai road, and the 2nd South Staffords were likewise in support.

About 9.50 a.m. an S.O.S. signal was sent up, and the Divisional Artillery opened on the enemy's troops massed in Mœuvres and on the left flank of the Division. The right flank of the 6th Infantry Brigade was engaged just before ten o'clock. The enemy in considerable force attacked the sunken road just west of the Canal du Nord, and although subjected to heavy machine-gun, Lewis-gun, and rifle fire, during which he suffered huge casualties, he succeeded in breaking the line.

At 10.25 a.m. B Company of the Essex, which held Lock 5 and the vicinity, had been attacked from the north-east, and after fighting desperately against great odds, had been forced back, the enemy occupying the lock and the sunken road. These two

THE SPLENDID KING'S.

combined attacks isolated D Company of the Essex, holding the short trench just west of the Canal du Nord. The story of the very gallant fight put up by these brave men will be continued later.

In the meantime B Company of the King's had been practically annihilated. The attack on the extreme left of the line had developed first of all against the Queen's Westminsters, holding the right flank of the 56th Division. As no attack had at that period been made on the left company of the King's, the Lewis gunners opened fire on the enemy as he advanced against the Londoners. Wave after wave of the enemy's troops were flung against the Queen's Westminsters, and eventually the line gave way. Thereupon Lieut. Taggart, commanding B Company of the King's, rushed down to the left flank of his company and arranged for its protection by building a block. " The enemy," said the Battalion Diary of the 1st King's Regiment, " now advanced in great numbers along the whole front of B Company, and by sheer weight of numbers succeeded in entering our line and practically wiped out the garrison. Out of 4 officers and 125 other ranks, only 2 officers and 24 men succeeded in getting back to our support trench down Donner Weg, being pushed back by a large bombing party." The enemy's triumph was, however, short-lived, for Sergeant Woods, organizing a bombing attack, went forward with his men and, after severe fighting, eventually succeeded in driving the enemy back up the communication trench to within 50 yards of the main line. Here a block was established, and despite repeated attempts by the enemy throughout the 30th and succeeding days to break through, the line here held fast.

A hostile attack on the King's was now made between Donner Weg and Edda Weg. The enemy—about a company—was impeded in his advance by old German wire, much of which still remained in this part of the line, and, as his troops were endeavouring to break a way through, they were caught by Lewis guns and machine guns and practically wiped out. The survivors jumped into shell-holes and began to snipe the King's. This was too much for the British troops! A number of men, without waiting for orders, climbed " over the top " and, with bomb and bayonet, disposed of the last remnants of that company of Germans.

About 10.20 a.m. the enemy made a heavy bombing attack down Edda Weg, and succeeded in getting to within 20 yards of the support line. Yet another bombing party of the King's, consisting of Sergeant Gannon and five men, drove the enemy back about 30 yards, but all excepting the N.C.O. were killed, and, still fighting, the gallant sergeant had to retire. A second bombing party was then organized under Company Sergeant-Major Jackson and Sergeant Gannon. Working their way up the trench, partly below and on top of the parapet, the second attack succeeded in driving the enemy back 150 yards, and the block was established. The officer commanding the enemy's bombers was killed, and for a while hostile activities in this trench ceased. Later, heavy bombing attacks over the open were made by the enemy, but all were repulsed.

Meanwhile the right-front company (C) of the King's was also engaged in desperate fighting against overwhelming numbers. The enemy's barrage, which came down on this part of the line, fell heavily upon three isolated posts held by the King's, between the two sunken roads and behind the sunken road held by the right-half of C Company. Fortunately only the left-hand post of the three was occupied, but of the gallant garrison not one escaped. The enemy now appeared at the north-western end of the sunken road, and was immediately engaged by the Lewis gunners and riflemen. Another large party of the enemy, having worked round the left flank of C Company, attacked from the rear. The right-half company was now in desperate straits. Only Second-Lieut. Scott and about a dozen other ranks remained alive, but this young officer successfully withdrew his men back into a communication trench running southwards from the rear of the sunken road, and tried to hold up the enemy working round his rear. The little band was again outflanked, and had to retire still farther down the communication trench. On reaching a bank which crossed Ernst Weg, the survivors of the right-half company lined the bank, and for some time succeeded in arresting the advance of the enemy, a Stokes gun, ably handled, rendering valuable assistance. Again and again the enemy tried to get across the embankment, but his attempts were annihilated by Lewis-gun and machine-gun fire.

Eventually he brought up a machine gun and, under cover of a heavy fire, he finally worked down the trench. Second-Lieut. Scott and his men, fighting all the way, then fell back and joined a party in Elsa Weg. The gallant resistance made by this officer and his men gained valuable time, during which supports were hurried up. The enemy now having broken the front line (he had, in point of fact, driven a wedge between the left and right battalions of the 6th Infantry Brigade), advanced southwards and occupied the ruined factory buildings, and also pushed men down the road for a distance of about 200 yards. He had reached the vicinity of Battalion Headquarters of the 1st King's. For nearly an hour heavy fighting had taken place in the immediate vicinity of Battalion Headquarters of the latter. Assisted by A Company of the 17th Middlesex, under Lieut. Munn, the enemy was bombed back along Ernst Weg, as far as the embankment, and here a block was established.

D Company of the 17th Middlesex, moved up to replace A Company, which had been placed at the disposal of the 1st King's, next closed with the enemy on the right, where he had also penetrated. Under the command of Captain McReady-Diarmid, the company immediately attacked the enemy, and with such success that 27 prisoners were taken, many of the enemy killed, and the remainder put to flight back up the trench down which they had at first forced their way.

East of the Canal du Nord, in Lock 5, and in Canal Trench, thence to the left flank of the 1st King's Royal Rifle Corps, B and A Companies of the 13th Essex Regiment had experienced hard fighting.

The enemy launched his first attack at 9.30 a.m. From the sunken road east of Lock 5 and his trenches running west to east through the road, he was seen debouching in great numbers. One report stated that he advanced in column of fours followed by field guns.

In Lock 5 B Company beat off this attack, but in doing so almost entirely exhausted the supply of bombs and rifle ammunition. At 10.20 a.m., however, the company still held its original position. A Company had formed blocks in the northern end of Canal Trench, also in Cable Trench. At 10.20 a.m. the enemy's barrage was intense, and included gas shells and "heavies." Under cover of this barrage another attack was launched, which resulted about 11 a.m. in B Company having to evacuate Lock 5 and retire through the sunken road by the bridge into Canal Trench; the strength of the company was then about forty rifles. The men had no rifle ammunition or bombs—all had been expended in a desperate effort to hold up the enemy's advance; but as the company evacuated the lock, it was immediately occupied by the Germans. Captain H. H. Duff, of A Company, rallied the survivors of B Company. Together with Captain F. R. Keeble, commanding B Company, some men of A Company and a platoon of the 2nd South Staffords (under Second-Lieut. C. T. Hinde), who had been sent up as reinforcements, Captain Duff now organized a counter-attack. The men were supplied with ammunition and bombs. They then attacked the enemy and drove him back to the sunken road. Again the supply of small-arms ammunition and bombs gave out, and the road could not be held; but Captain Keeble, B Company, formed a block in Canal Trench, a few yards south of the sunken road, and manned the parapet facing east and west. Small-arms ammunition and bombs were now beginning to arrive in plentiful quantities, and the enemy was prevented from advancing farther along the eastern banks of the canal. Another attempt later by Captain Keeble with a party of bombers to clear the sunken road failed.

By this time Canal Trench, from the bombing block southwards to where the trench joined the trench running west and east, was garrisoned by a platoon of A Company and three platoons of a company of the 2nd South Staffords. The trench running west to east was held by two platoons of A Company 13th Essex Regiment, and one platoon of the 2nd South Staffords under Captain Baxter.

"The conduct of Captain F. R. Keeble (B Company), Captain H. J. Duff (A Company) 13th Essex Regiment, and of Second-Lieut. C. T. Hinde, 2nd South Staffords," said the Official Report, "was beyond all praise. The determination shown by these gallant officers not to yield an inch to the enemy had a great stimulating effect on their men. The enemy made repeated attempts to sally from the sunken road and also to approach Canal Trench from the north-east, but was always beaten back by rifle and machine-gun fire."

During the afternoon the situation along the whole front of the 6th Infantry Brigade remained unchanged.

Throughout the 30th November the 5th Infantry Brigade (with the exception of the 17th Royal Fusiliers) had remained in Divisional reserve. During the day 5th Infantry Brigade Headquarters, under orders from the Division, had moved from Hermies to Lock 7.

At 10.10 a.m. the Brigade was ordered to get ready to move on a fighting scale at a moment's notice. The battalions were ready to move between 11.30 a.m. and 1.30 p.m.

Just before 1 p.m. the 24th Royal Fusiliers and the 2nd Oxford and Bucks were ordered to move forward and counter-attack in the direction of the Sugar Factory just south of the 99th Infantry Brigade line, where it was reported the enemy had broken through. "Most alarming reports were sent to us from outside sources. One stated that the enemy had captured the Sugar Factory and

THE 13TH ESSEX AND LOCK 5.   495

were advancing on the right Brigade's Headquarters. All communication between us (Divisional Headquarters) and the two forward Brigades was cut, and our line to the 99th Infantry Brigade was not re-established until 3 p.m." [1]

Fortunately the information proved incorrect, but the two battalions took up a line in support of the 99th Infantry Brigade. The 22nd Royal Fusiliers (99th Infantry Brigade) were also ordered to occupy the old German trenches in the Hindenburg Main Line, in the vicinity of Lock 6, and the 2nd Highland Light Infantry moved into Brigade reserve west of Lock 7. At 3.30 p.m. the 6th Infantry Brigade, having called for reinforcements, the Highland Light Infantry were sent forward to just south of the Bapaume–Cambrai road and came under the orders of the General Officer Commanding 6th Infantry Brigade. At 7 p.m. the position of the 5th Infantry Brigade was as follows: the 24th Royal Fusiliers were engaged in relieving the 17th Royal Fusiliers, who subsequently marched back into Divisional reserve; the 2nd Oxford and Bucks were in the Hindenburg Support Line south of the right Brigade front, under orders of the 99th Infantry Brigade; the 22nd Royal Fusiliers were in support south of the left Brigade front; the 2nd Highland Light Infantry were under the orders of the 6th Infantry Brigade.

At 8 p.m. the closing scene in this great day of fighting took place. Sergeant L. S. Legg and one man of D Company of the 13th Essex Regiment arrived at Battalion Headquarters and informed the Commanding Officer that they had escaped from the company, which had been isolated and surrounded by the enemy during the morning. The two men had been sent back with orders to try and break through and inform the Commanding Officer of the situation. They stated that when they crept out of the trench Captain H. T. Jessop, commanding D Company, was wounded but still alive; that when the action opened in the morning the company had not been attacked from the north or north-west; and that the platoon in the southern part of the trench, facing south-west and north-east, had inflicted very heavy losses on the enemy as he crossed the bridge, and as his troops were pursuing B Company from Lock 5. The enemy had brought three machine guns up to the road just east of the bridge, from which he had enfiladed the trench. One of these machine guns was knocked out, and the other two were retired. Again and again the enemy had tried to rush the trench, but had been beaten off, the company

[1] Diary of Major-General C. E. Pereira, C.B., C.M.G.

killing hundreds of Germans by enfilade rifle and machine-gun fire. The company had realized early in the day that they were cut off and surrounded, but, when the sergeant and his comrade left, the survivors were confident of being relieved, though ammunition had begun to fail. The company had a dug-out full of the enemy as prisoners, these having been captured in the southern end of the trench.

Before the two men left a council of war was held at 4 p.m.; for, realizing that, although they expected relief, there was still the possibility that relieving troops might arrive too late, a definite line of action was necessary. At this council of war the two surviving company officers, Lieut. J. D. Robinson and Second-Lieut. E. L. Corps, Company Sergeant-major A. H. Edwards, and Platoon Sergeants C. Phillips, E. C. Parsons, W. Fairbrass, R. Lodge, and L. S. Legg were present. "It was unanimously determined to fight to the last and have no surrender." Sergeant L. S. Legg and one man were then detailed as runners to get through to the battalion and inform the Commanding Officer of what had taken place.

Such was the story told by the two men of this very gallant company of Essex men.

"Throughout the night of 30th November," said the Report, "many efforts were made to effect the relief of these brave men, but all attempts failed against the overwhelming strength of the enemy. The last that is known of this gallant company is that it was heard fighting it out and maintaining to the last the bulwark against the tide of attacking Germans. It is impossible to estimate the valour of this magnificent fight to the death, which relieved the pressure on the main line of defence."

To fully appreciate the splendid action of those brave men, and the action of the Division as a whole on the 30th November, it is necessary to understand the enemy's plan of operations. He had selected two points at which to launch his counter-attacks, one north on the Mœuvres–Bourlon line, the other south between Masnières (on the Scheldt Canal) and Honnecourt. He thus hoped to cut off the salient driven into his line by the British attacks of and from the 20th November. What happened on the northern sector has already been related. On the southern sector the enemy at first succeeded in breaking through, but was later in the day counter-attacked, chiefly by the Guards Division.

"During the day news was received at the Division that the Germans had broken through our line farther south and had

ARTILLERY ACTION. 497

captured men and material, and had penetrated as far as Gouzeaucourt. Extravagant rumours reported them as being on the road to Metz. However exaggerated these rumours were, it was clear that the situation of all the troops in the Bourlon salient was critical, *and should the line break between Bourlon and Mœuvres the prospect of a big reverse would have to be faced.* The enemy, having massed his troops with unexpected speed, had struck with all his strength and regardless of cost, at the most vulnerable point in the big salient made by the successful attacks of the 20th November. . . . Fortunately there were resting divisions near Gouzeaucourt,[1] who counter-attacked with the greatest gallantry and drove him back nearly to our original front line." [2]

From the statements of prisoners captured by the Division, it was evident that three hostile divisions had been launched against the 2nd Division and its immediate flanks. These prisoners also stated that the Lewis-gun and machine-gun fire, and terribly accurate shelling by the Divisional Artillery, had caused enormous casualties.

From an artillery point of view the attack developed about 9 a.m., when large bodies of the enemy first began to appear about Quarry Wood and north of Mœuvres. Defence zones had been detailed in such a way that about two-thirds of the batteries covered the whole front, the remainder being superimposed upon them. This allowed the superimposed batteries to engage the moving masses of enemy troops as they appeared over the crest line, without leaving any gaps in the screen of fire on S.O.S. lines, and the losses inflicted on the enemy were heavy indeed. One or two sections were taken forward on to high ground and fired direct, doing great execution, until they were spotted by the enemy and so heavily shelled that they had to be withdrawn.

The two enemy batteries, a 77 mm. and a 10 cm. howitzer, which advanced with the hostile infantry and attempted to come into action within 1,000 yards of the Division's front line, were promptly knocked out by the 47th and D/173rd Howitzer Batteries, with "106" fuses; neither hostile gun fired again. Some of the Divisional batteries fired 500 rounds during the day, but ammunition was plentiful. The XLIst and XXXVIth Brigades R.F.A. made splendid practice, and the confidence felt by the infantry in

[1] The 5th Cavalry Division arrived from Monchy Lagache, the 4th Cavalry Division from Athies; the 2nd Cavalry Division was at Fins; the Guards Division was at Havrincourt; the 61st Division arrived from Le Transloy, and the 1st Cavalry Division from west of Péronne.

[2] 2nd Divisional Report.

the front-line trenches was a fine tribute to the work of the gunners. Many a time the line might have been broken had it not been for the devotion of the Divisional Artillery.

So far as the Lewis gunners and machine gunners were concerned, the 30th November was a day long to be remembered. Seldom indeed had the guns been trained on such fine targets. The 6th Brigade Machine-Gun Company (Captain C. H. Stampe), 99th Machine-Gun Company (Captain A. P. Skevington), and 242nd Divisional Machine-Gun Company (Captain H. P. Borlase) were in action practically all day.

Two guns of the 99th Company, which had done magnificent work in Lock 5 when it was first attacked, were surrounded and cut off later with D Company of the Essex Regiment. When the enemy made his first big effort against the 17th Royal Fusiliers, five guns of the company held their ground and were for a time wholly unsupported, but they maintained their position until the Fusiliers re-occupied the sap. All the enemy's attacks on the right of the Brigade, west of Bourlon Wood, were dealt with by the machine guns, which again and again caught the advancing masses in enfilade. Two guns had to be abandoned, but were completely destroyed by shell-fire, and three were damaged but were able to be used in emergency. One battery of eight guns of the 99th Machine-Gun Company fired over seventy boxes of ammunition— *i.e.*, 70,000 rounds.

The 6th Brigade Machine-Gun Company, on the left of the Divisional front, found splendid targets as the enemy debouched from the village of Mœuvres. The company fired over 100,000 rounds during the day, the guns being organized into two batteries of eight guns each. The casualties of the company were light.

The 242nd (Divisional) Machine-Gun Company was in action near the 6th Infantry Brigade Company. The 5th Brigade Company was just south of the Bapaume–Cambrai road.

Of the Pioneers (10th Duke of Cornwall's Light Infantry) the Divisional Report speaks with enthusiasm. These gallant fellows not only carried up ammunition and bombs to the sorely tried infantry, but at one period A and B Companies stood side by side with troops of the 6th Infantry Brigade and repelled the enemy during one of his most determined rushes. " I should like to mention," said the Commanding Officer 17th Royal Fusiliers, " the fine work done by a platoon of the 10th Duke of Cornwall's Light Infantry under Lieut. Smith, who made several journeys carrying up bombs at a time when they were most sorely needed.

THE FIELD AMBULANCES. 499

This platoon worked with the greatest cheerfulness and energy under heavy shell-fire." It was also at a desperate moment that another carrying party of the Pioneers arrived, when the 17th Royal Fusiliers were being very heavily attacked. "At this critical moment," said the Commanding Officer of that battalion, "a supply of bombs and ammunition arrived. Too much praise cannot be given to the work of this carrying party. They rushed up with the supplies, and the company cook of C Company (17th Royal Fusiliers) stood on the parapet hurling bandoliers to all the men around him." In addition the Pioneers, in conjunction with the Engineers, constructed strong points and wired the front in many places.

Eleven other ranks killed and 40 wounded were the Pioneers' casualties during the 30th November.

The 5th Field Company R.E., affiliated to the 6th Infantry Brigade, and the 483rd Field Company R.E., affiliated to the 99th Infantry Brigade, worked all day on strong points and in wiring the front, and were specially mentioned for their energy and skill.

The work of the Field Ambulances is seldom mentioned in the Divisional Diaries, but to their splendid devotion to duty special attention was drawn in the report of the operations of the 30th November :—

" The stretcher-bearers of all three Field Ambulances carried out their duties cheerfully and well, often under intense shell-fire, with the result that our aid posts were never choked with wounded. I would especially bring to notice the stretcher-bearers of the 100th Field Ambulance, who were on duty at our busiest time.

" The evacuation of the wounded was carried out without a hitch. Wounded passed through in a steady stream, taxing our bearers, who had a long, hard carry of many relays, to the utmost. As a precaution against a block in evacuation and, if required, to afford breathing space to our bearers, a large tunnel at Lock 6, capable of accommodating some thirty to forty stretchers, was placed in readiness. So steadily, however, were cases evacuated that there were never more than five or six cases there at one time. Evacuation was at first carried out by two bearer divisions in the line, and the third in reserve. By nightfall all three divisions had been used, and a party of fifty infantry were taken in on the rear relays, to allow one division to rest ; and thereafter a rotation of twenty-four-hourly reliefs of our bearers was carried out. The heaviest work fell upon the right section, evacuation from the aid post in the Sugar Factory being both hazardous and heavy. During the day the shelling of Demicourt, and the sunken road leading to it, became so severe as to render that route unsafe. A fresh track was reconnoitred and marked. . . . This track was used for the remainder of the time with great success."

All three Field Ambulances had casualties, and at least one gallant medical officer (Captain J. McD. Matheson, R.A.M.C., attached to the 17th Royal Fusiliers) was killed in carrying out his humane work.

The results of the German counter-attack of the 30th November along the front of the 2nd Division were: on the left front the 6th Infantry Brigade had fallen back to a depth of from 100 to 300 yards on a frontage of about 800 yards; on the right front the 99th Infantry Brigade retained all its positions of the morning, with the exception of about two-thirds of the Rat's Tail.[1]

The Division's casualties were estimated at about 2,000,[2] but the casualties amongst the enemy's troops were out of all proportion compared with those suffered by the 2nd Division; one battalion alone claimed to have caused the enemy 1,000 casualties.

In concluding, the Divisional narrative remarks: "It is difficult to write calmly of such events, and it can only be hoped that the Special Order of the Day by the Major-General Commanding the 2nd Division, in which this and similar deeds (the gallant stand of D Company of the 13th Essex Regiment[3]) are officially recognized, will one day be placed on record, so that Englishmen who come after may share in our pride and gratitude."

II. 1st to 3rd December 1917.

1ST DEC. When morning broke on the 1st December it was evident that the enemy had, for the time being at least, abandoned all attempts

---

[1] In *Die Schlachten und Gefecht des Grosen Krieges, 1914–1918*, compiled by the German General Staff, the total number of divisions used by the enemy in his counter-attacks from 30th November to 7th December is given as twenty-five. But some of these divisions were used between 20th and 30th November.

[2] See Appendix.

[3] It was afterwards ascertained that not all of this gallant company were killed. They fought to the last, until bombs and ammunition were utterly exhausted, and the survivors honourably surrendered to the enemy. The 13th Essex Regiment reported 4 officers wounded and missing, and 2 missing on the 30th November. Of the former, Second-Lieut. E. C. Hall was afterwards reported killed. The two officers who held the council of war—Lieut. J. R. Robinson and Second-Lieut. E. L. Corps—were the missing officers; they were captured by the enemy. There were also several men of the 1st King's Regiment with the isolated company of the Essex Regiment.

DISPOSITIONS.

to capture the right sub-sector of the Divisional area where the 99th Infantry Brigade held the front-line trenches. The 1st Royal Berks still held the right flank of the Brigade front, joining up with the left of the 47th (London) Division. The centre of the Brigade area—that portion held on the 30th November by the 17th Royal Fusiliers—had been taken over by the 24th Royal Fusiliers (5th Infantry Brigade), the 17th Battalion marching back into reserve to rest and refit after their truly bloody encounters with the enemy. The 1st King's Royal Rifles were on the left of the 24th Royal Fusiliers. Between 8 and 9 a.m., however, the Berkshires, who were somewhat intermixed with the 23rd Royal Fusiliers, reorganized their line, and as a result C Company of the Fusiliers took over the front and the two strong points north-east of the sunken road (joining up with the 47th Division), and B Company of the same battalion, with two platoons of D Company, filled the gap between C Company of the 23rd Royal Fusiliers and A Company of the Berkshires. C Company of the Berkshires was between A Company and the right of the 24th Royal Fusiliers. The fourth battalion of the 99th Infantry Brigade—the 22nd Royal Fusiliers—was in the 6th Infantry Brigade support area south of Mœuvres.

Throughout the day no attack developed along the front of the 99th Infantry Brigade. Hostile shelling of the front line was slight, but the enemy put down a heavy barrage along the Cambrai-Bapaume road, with concentrated fire on the Sugar Factory. During the day several enemy aeroplanes flew low down over the front-line trenches of the Brigade, and several times opened machine-gun fire on the troops; one of these planes was brought down by the right battalion, and crashed near Bourlon Village.

In the left (Mœuvres) sub-sector of the Divisional front (the 6th Infantry Brigade area) fighting had continued throughout the night of the 30th November-1st December. Here the enemy was still endeavouring to force his way southwards along both sides of the Canal du Nord and down the trenches of the Hindenburg Line west of the canal.

As with the 99th Infantry Brigade, the battalions in the left sub-sector were much intermixed. The 1st King's still held the left, and the 17th Middlesex the right of the line, with the South Staffords in close support south of the Cambrai-Bapaume road and west of the canal; the 13th Essex Regiment was back south of the Cambrai road, in support. The 22nd Royal Fusiliers (99th Infantry Brigade) were in close support behind the King's and

Middlesex. At 5.50 a.m. A Company and forty other ranks of D Company of the Highland Light Infantry (5th Infantry Brigade) relieved C Company of the Middlesex in the right half of the left sub-sector. C Company of the Middlesex and D Company of the Highland Light Infantry then went into close support. As the 2nd Highland Light Infantry had now been placed at the disposal of the 6th Infantry Brigade, the 22nd Royal Fusiliers were withdrawn into Divisional reserve. The 2nd Oxford and Bucks (5th Infantry Brigade) had likewise been placed at the disposal of the 99th Infantry Brigade, and moved to Kangaroo Alley in support of the 1st King's Royal Rifles.

During the night two attempts had been made to reach the isolated company (D) of the Essex Regiment, but without success. About 4.45 a.m. the enemy made a strong bombing attack down Edda Weg, but owing to the promptitude of Company Sergeant-Major Jackson and a party of C Company of the Middlesex Regiment, he was beaten back without occupying an inch of ground. At 8 a.m. the enemy again began a series of strong bombing attacks along the left sub-sector. One of these was made on B Company of the Middlesex (Captain Stansfeld). Full details of this attack were unavailable, but it appears that, despite the very gallant efforts of B Company and its commander, the enemy made progress. The company had expended its supply of bombs and was forced to give ground, the enemy advancing nearly 300 yards down the trench and attempting to cut off Battalion Headquarters of the 1st King's. A Company of the Middlesex, however, stopped the attempt by Lewis-gun fire. "All B Company officers," said the Battalion Diary, "were now missing, the men tired and shaken." It was at this period that what was probably the finest bombing exploit of the whole war took place.

Captain A. M. C. McReady Diarmid of D Company, 17th Middlesex Regiment, seeing the position, called for volunteers from his company. Arming himself with a plentiful supply of bombs, he rushed forward and attacked the enemy. With extraordinary gallantry, and with such splendid bomb-throwing as was seldom seen, he gradually drove the enemy back up the trench down which his troops had forced their way. "By throwing all the bombs himself," said the Official Report, "this officer killed and otherwise disposed of 94 of the enemy—67 dead and 27 wounded were actually counted after the recapture of the trench, a feat which can hardly, if ever, have been equalled in the past." Every foot of the 300 yards of lost trench was regained, and by

THE SECOND V.C. AT CAMBRAI, 1917.

his deliberate disregard of danger, his cheerfulness and coolness, Captain McReady Diarmid inspired all who saw him. It was a marvellous performance, but alas! the gallant officer, having won back for his battalion the lost ground, was himself killed by an enemy bomb almost at the moment of his final triumph. He had, however, by his very brave action, and by the same spirit of devotion displayed on the previous day, won for the 2nd Division the second Victoria Cross awarded to it during the Cambrai operations of 1917.[1]

The Lewis guns of the 1st King's and 2nd Highland Light Infantry also co-operated in this bombing feat by silencing the enemy's guns in the vicinity of Lock 5, which had caused many casualties. Captain Harrison, of the 6th Trench Mortar Battery, rushed a Stokes gun up to the junction of Elsa Weg with the main communication trench, and although having only ten rounds of Stokes ammunition, by his rapid and accurate fire completely demoralized the enemy, who began to retire. Very few, if any, of the enemy, whose strength was estimated at three companies, got back to the bridge near Lock 5, whence they had started. "One party of 15, who were caught in a bay which was overlooked from our position at Elsa Weg, was totally wiped out by the Lewis gun fired by Second-Lieut. J. A. Armstrong. A gun belonging to D Company, Highland Light Infantry, mowed down large numbers of Germans who had got out of the trench and tried to escape across the open."[2]

At 3.18 p.m. the enemy placed a very heavy barrage on the whole of the left sub-sector front line, and was reported massing in Mœuvres. An S.O.S. to the Divisional Artillery brought a prompt and extremely effective barrage on the enemy's lines, and although his troops advanced they finally abandoned the attempt, the stream of shells and bullets tearing gaps in the grey masses. No attack was made on the right sub-sector (99th Infantry Brigade).

At 3 p.m. orders had been issued to the 2nd Highland Light Infantry to take over the whole of the left sub-sector from west of the canal to the right sub-sector: to details of the 17th Middlesex . . . to withdraw, and with the remainder of the battalion reorganize in close support of the Highland Light Infantry; to the details of 2nd South Staffords . . . to withdraw from west of the canal to support the 13th Essex Regiment in the right sub-sector; and to the King's Regiment on relief by the 2nd Highland

[1] *London Gazette,* March 15, 1918.
[2] Battalion Diary, 1st King's Regiment.

Light Infantry, to withdraw south to the trenches occupied by the 17th Middlesex.

During the evening, however, the 22nd Royal Fusiliers, having been placed at the disposal of the 6th Infantry Brigade, a slight alteration took place in the dispositions of the battalions: the 22nd Royal Fusiliers were ordered to relieve the 13th Essex in the sub-sector east of, and including, the canal, with two companies in Canal Trench and the trench running diagonally south of Canal Trench, one company in Kangaroo Alley (relieving troops of the 2nd Highland Light Infantry), and one company just south of the Cambrai–Bapaume road; the 2nd South Staffords were to move into Brigade reserve in the vicinity, but just south of, Lock 7; the 1st King's on relief to move to Lock 7 in Divisional reserve, under the General Officer Commanding 5th Infantry Brigade; the 13th Essex Regiment, on relief, to move to Lock 6, in support of 22nd Royal Fusiliers. The 186th Infantry Brigade (62nd Division) was ordered to occupy and prepare for defence the Hindenburg Support Trench from Lock 6 (inclusive) and a portion of the Hindenburg outpost line to the sunken road forming part of the left Divisional boundary.

The 186th Infantry Brigade of the 62nd (West Riding) Division had been placed at the disposal of the General Officer Commanding 2nd Division during the day, but these troops, after very gallant fighting since the 20th November,[1] were worn out and badly in need of rest; they were therefore used to garrison certain back areas.

The moves and reliefs were carried out during the night 1st–2nd December, as ordered.

2ND DEC. At daylight on the 2nd December all four companies of the 2nd Highland Light Infantry were in the front line—*i.e.*, from right to left, C, B, D, and A; C Company had taken over a line which left B Company's flank in the air, but during the morning the former bombed up the trench which gave touch between the two companies.

On the right of the Highland Light Infantry the 22nd Royal Fusiliers were disposed as follows: one company in Canal Trench extended northwards as far as the block just south of the sunken road from the canal bridge; another company in the diagonal trench south of Canal Trench; another company in Kangaroo Trench, about Lock 6; and the fourth company in the Hindenburg Line west of the canal and just south of the Cambrai–Bapaume

---

[1] They had taken part in the Tank attack, when the 62nd Division made a record advance of 7,000 yards in one day.

ENEMY ATTACKS CONTINUE.

road. All these companies were very weak, and that in Canal Trench numbered only about seventy men.

Excepting a certain amount of intermittent shelling little happened on the 2nd Divisional front until late in the afternoon, when about 4 p.m. the shelling increased, and by 4.30 p.m. there was a definite and very heavy barrage along the whole Divisional front. At 4.35 p.m. an S.O.S. was sent up, the Divisional Artillery opened on the enemy, and soon the guns of both sides were engaged in a very heavy duel.

On the left sub-sector of the Division—on the Highland Light Infantry—the enemy directed a heavy machine-gun fire, and all four companies, including Battalion Headquarters, manned the fire-steps. Reinforcements from support companies were held in readiness. So heavy was the bombardment that within five minutes all telephonic communication between the front-line battalions, Brigade, and even Divisional Headquarters, were cut, and messages had to be sent by runners, and to the back areas by pigeons.

" About 4.50 p.m. parties of the enemy were seen to be massing in the sunken road on the right, running north and south through B Company's lines. The Stokes guns, with great promptitude—in fact before the S.O.S. rocket was put up—opened a heavy fire on the road and also in front of the right company. A Lewis-gun team of the right-front company rushed their guns right forward, and their fire, combined with the Stokes guns and resolute rifle fire, dispersed the parties in the sunken road. By this time bodies of enemy troops were advancing from their trenches all along the line. Our rifle and Lewis-gun fire, combined with a very strong and accurate artillery and machine-gun barrage, broke up the enemy masses, and their attack did not materialize. On the right company's front, our weakest point, the enemy was more determined, and succeeded in effecting an entry into our position. The Officer Commanding company rapidly organized his men for a counter-attack, and, with bombs and bayonet, the enemy was ejected from our trenches and pushed back beyond our position. This position was found unsuited for our use, and the company withdrew to our old position, and proceeded to consolidate. By 6.30 p.m. the position was quiet, and our line firmly held at all points." [1]

The 22nd Royal Fusiliers had also been attacked.

About 5.13 p.m. two parties of the enemy, each about thirty

[1] Battalion Diary, 2nd Highland Light Infantry.

strong, made a dash from their strong point (in the sunken road north of Canal Trench) down either side of Canal Trench. The hostile troops east of the trench were caught by Lewis-gun fire and driven back to their original starting-point. The party west of the trench gave more trouble. Here the enemy gradually worked south at a distance from the trench and bombed it vigorously. For some while the situation was critical, but eventually the Fusiliers' Lewis gunners gained the upper hand, and the surviving hostile troops bolted back to their strong point pursued by bomb and bullet.

The enemy's attacks now died down, and for a time all was quiet. Again throughout the day no hostile infantry attacks had been made on the 99th Infantry Brigade in the right sub-sector. Shortly before 8 p.m., however, the left Brigade of the 47th Division, on the right flank of the 2nd Division, attacked the enemy. The attack was made by the 7th and 8th London Regiments. In this attack the 23rd Royal Fusiliers (99th Infantry Brigade) joined. As the Londoners advanced the Fusiliers discerned the enemy bringing up a machine gun. They waited until the gun was in position, then rushed the team, whom they killed, and brought the gun back to their own lines. The 140th Infantry Brigade (47th Division) in this attack pushed on to just behind the crest of the hill which they had lost on the 30th November. Here the Brigade consolidated, after capturing in its advance several machine guns and thirty prisoners. The 23rd Royal Fusiliers then advanced their flank 75 yards in order to conform to the left of the 140th Brigade. The Berkshires, on the left of the Fusiliers, also advanced their line—A Company (in the centre) establishing new posts 150 to 200 yards in front of their original line.

3RD DEC. Late in the afternoon of the 3rd December the enemy, as on the previous day, made violent efforts to break through the left sub-sector of the Divisional front. The 2nd Highland Light Infantry was again involved, though on this occasion the brunt of the attack fell upon A Company.

" The hours of daylight were spent in improving our position, and a close watch was maintained on all enemy movements. About 4 p.m. the short winter afternoon was drawing to a close, and once again the enemy attacked with determination, this time on A Company—our left-front company.

" Their front line was the Hindenburg Main Line, 300 yards north, running parallel to the Hindenburg Support Line. The latter was (now) the enemy's front line. A communication trench joined the two trenches, and we held a bombing block 150 yards up this communication trench. At 4 p.m. the enemy made a sudden rush down the communication trench. At first he was repulsed, but numbers tell, and his attack was so determined and incessant that our block was lost and we were pushed back to within 50 yards of our front line. The fighting here was long and severe. In fact, the best idea of what took place may be judged by the number of boxes of rifle grenades and Mills bombs which were urgently called for and used—in all, about 150 boxes were got up from Battalion Headquarters. Right on till 9 p.m. the fighting was carried."[1] And although there is no report in the Divisional Diaries, it is evident that the gallant Scotsmen won back all they had lost, for a little later the Battalion Diary states: "By this time a battalion relief was in process.[2] The companies on the right were relieved by the 4th Battalion Seaforth Highlanders. The 9th Battalion Royal Scots had been ordered to side-slip a company and take over A Company's front. They did so, and the men of A Company, fighting for the sap, retired on our new line, having established a new bombing block near the main line. The relief was then completed, and the line had been handed over with a gain of 250 yards on the right and intact on the left."[3]

On relief the 2nd Highland Light Infantry marched back to Divisional reserve, and the General Officer Commanding 154th Infantry Brigade assumed command of the Mœuvres sub-sector up to, but exclusive of, the Canal du Nord. For three days the 2nd Highland Light Infantry had been engaged in killing Germans; the Scotsmen had fought magnificently, for the enemy's troops were no mean foes. "His new reinforcements," said the Battalion Diary on the 1st December, "are men of high fighting quality, and of considerable courage." The spirit of all ranks was that of the indomitable British soldier—wounded men begged to be allowed to stay rather than miss such a chance of killing Germans. Stories were told of men being propped up by their comrades and given rifles which they continued to use until too weak from loss of blood to hold them any longer. An official booklet[4] issued to the Army in France, describing the German counter-

[1] Battalion Diary, 2nd Highland Light Infantry.
[2] The 154th Infantry Brigade (51st Division) was relieving the 6th Infantry Brigade west of the Canal du Nord.
[3] Battalion Diary, 2nd Highland Light Infantry.
[4] *The Second Division at Cambrai.*

attack in the Battle of Cambrai, related that when approached by stretcher-bearers one of these wounded men "told them in simple soldierly language to go elsewhere," as he "wouldn't give up such a rare chance of killing Huns." And also "one wrathful Jock, who had been shot in both legs, had to be pulled away by main force, and was borne out of the trench cursing loudly because the bearers would not leave him at his work."

At midnight on the 3rd December the General Officer Commanding 5th Infantry Brigade assumed command of the left sub-sector of the Divisional front, which extended from and included the Canal du Nord to the left Brigade boundary, just west of the Graincourt–Mœuvres road. This sub-sector was held by the 22nd Royal Fusiliers (99th Infantry Brigade) and 13th Essex Regiment (6th Infantry Brigade), with the 17th Royal Fusiliers and 2nd Highland Light Infantry in support. The 99th Infantry Brigade still held the right sub-sector, and the 6th Infantry Brigade was Divisional reserve Brigade with the definite *rôle* of organizing and assisting tired battalions as they came out of the line.

The Withdrawal from the Bourlon Salient.

"The strength which the enemy had shown himself able to develop in his attack," said Sir Douglas Haig, "made it evident that only by prolonged and severe fighting could I hope to re-establish my right flank on the Bonavis ridge. Unless this was done, the situation of my troops in the salient south of Flesquières would be difficult and dangerous, even if our hold on Bourlon Hill were extended."

At a Corps conference, held at 2nd Division Headquarters, at which the General Officers Commanding 2nd, 47th, 51st, and 59th Divisions were present, the Vth Corps Commander—General Fanshawe—told his Divisional Commanders that a retirement had been decided upon, and gave them an outline of the new dispositions. "This retirement is due to the unsatisfactory position on the Gouzeaucourt side, which has made the Bourlon salient so pronounced."

The disastrous results of the Russian *débâcle* had again made themselves felt. The enemy had been able to bring divisions from the East and largely reinforce his front, whereas the Allies had no reserves with which to continue operations on a large scale, for the offensive of the early months and summer of 1917 had used them up.

RESULTS OF THE BATTLE.

On the other hand, the surprise offensive of the 20th November had yielded good results. Apart from considerable gains in men, material, and enemy territory,[1] German divisions had actually been diverted from Italy, where the Italians had suffered a reverse. Ludendorff's vaunted " victory " of the 30th November was a myth. All things considered, the Allies' gains on the Western front more than counterbalanced their losses.

On the 30th November the enemy had launched no less than six divisions against the right of the Third Army line, and had broken through at a comparatively weak spot held by two British divisions. He was stopped on the line of Gonnelieu and Vendhuille. On the Bourlon front seven German divisions had been hurled against three British divisions (56th, 2nd, and 47th), and on other parts of the battle front his strength was as four to three.

From captured German maps and documents[2] it was evident the enemy had planned three converging attacks—two to be delivered simultaneously about Gonnelieu and Masnières, followed by a third and more powerful attack on the Bourlon-Mœuvres front. The objectives of these attacks were Trescault and Beaucamp, behind the original Old British front line.

The results were as described, but with such statements as, " We have won a complete victory over a considerable part of the British Army," did the enemy delude himself and the German people, who were not far off collapse.

On the 4th December orders for the withdrawal from the Bourlon salient to a main line of resistance were issued. Details of the operation were issued in " 2nd Division Order No. G306 " : " The Bourlon salient, including the present front line held by the 2nd Division, is to be evacuated. This operation will be carried out to-day (4th December) and throughout the night 4th–5th December. The withdrawal on the front of the Vth Corps is to be made to the main line of resistance, or the ' A ' Line. This

4TH DEC.

---

[1] " We had captured and retained in our possession over 12,000 yards of the former German front line from La Vacquerie to a point opposite Boursies, together with between 10,000 and 11,000 yards of the Hindenburg Line, Hindenburg Reserve Line, and the villages of Ribecourt, Flesquières, and Havrincourt. A total of 145 German guns were taken or destroyed by us in the course of the operations, and 11,000 German prisoners were captured.

" On the other hand, the enemy had occupied an unimportant section of our front between Vendhuille and Gonnelieu."—*Official Dispatches*.

The extent of the enemy's casualties at Cambrai will probably never be known, but they must have been enormous. Another important, and not often appreciated, result of the Cambrai operations of 1917 was the proof of the efficacy of Tanks.

[2] The 2nd Division found a large quantity of German documents in Graincourt.

main line will be covered by an outpost line, or ' B ' Line. The main line will be sited to give mutual flanking defence, and will be well wired. A covering line, or ' C ' Line, will, as a temporary measure, be held in advance of the outpost line, so as to ensure all our rear dispositions being made quietly and undisturbed by the enemy. . . . The rearguards, which will consist of picked officers and men (about two sections and a Lewis gun per company in the line) will, by firing at intervals from different positions, keep the enemy unaware of our withdrawal."

The rearguards were to be withdrawn at 3.15 a.m. on the 5th December.

Immediately on receipt of these orders the Royal Engineers and the Pioneers, assisted by the 186th Infantry Brigade (62nd Division), were at once employed upon the preparation of a main line of resistance. The splendid devotion of the troops of the 186th Infantry Brigade drew the following report from the General Officer Commanding 2nd Division : " The highest praise must be given to officers and men of the 186th Infantry Brigade who, brought from a well-earned rest and marched hurriedly back from entraining stations tired, after days of heavy fighting, and handed over to a strange division, yet turned out willingly and worked with the greatest energy." By midday on the 4th the 226th Field Company R.E., and one company of the Pioneers, were hard at work digging and wiring an outpost line ; the 5th Field Company R.E., with the remaining three companies of the Pioneers, were at work on the main line of resistance ; and the 483rd Field Company R.E. prepared all forward dug-outs and observation posts for demolition.

During the afternoon all preparations were made for the withdrawal. Stores were salved, and the whole Divisional front cleared of anything which could be carried away. Some idea of the work this entailed may be gathered from the fact that in the 99th Infantry Brigade area 410,000 rounds of small-arms ammunition, 4,000 hand grenades, and about 500 Stokes bombs were collected. All these were removed.

Throughout the evening of the 4th, and the night of the 4th–5th, the Sappers and Pioneers were hard at work digging and wiring the new positions.

At 5 p.m. on the 4th, command of the main line of resistance, the outpost line, and the covering troops of the 2nd Division passed to the General Officer Commanding 5th Infantry Brigade.

The covering troops consisted of the 24th Royal Fusiliers on the right, and the 2nd Oxford and Bucks Light Infantry on the left; the 2nd Highland Light Infantry (left) and the 17th Royal Fusiliers (right) held the main line of resistance.

"Despite the bright moonlight," said the Brigade Diary, "the withdrawal was carried out without loss and unperceived by the enemy."

At 4.45 on the morning of the 5th December the 24th Royal Fusiliers and the Oxford and Bucks held "C" Line, and the 17th Royal Fusiliers and 2nd Highland Light Infantry the outpost line and the main line of resistance; the 6th Infantry Brigade was at Lebucquière, and the 99th Infantry Brigade in dug-outs and shelters in, and in the vicinity of, Hermies.

5TH DEC.

About 7 a.m. the enemy was reported to be shelling Kangaroo Trench, and about an hour later his troops were observed moving freely about the cross-roads just west of Lock 5, along the old Divisional front. He appeared to be collecting and organizing his troops for an advance, having apparently only just discovered the withdrawal. A small hostile patrol was observed by the 24th Royal Fusiliers entering the old support line of the 99th Infantry Brigade—*i.e.*, on the extreme right of the old Divisional line. Just before 12 noon information was received that the 140th Infantry Brigade (47th Division) on the right of the 2nd Division, was not north of Graincourt (as it was anticipated it would be), and a post of the 24th Royal Fusiliers, situated in the sunken road just south of the sugar factory, being "in the air," was withdrawn.

Half an hour later the enemy was observed advancing southwards in extended formation down the slopes of the high ground west of Bourlon Wood. The artillery was informed and opened heavy fire on the enemy's troops. From increasing movement all along the front it was evident that the enemy was making a general advance. The Lewis and machine guns of the Division came into action and joined with the artillery in checking a rapid advance. At 3 p.m. an S.O.S. went up from Kangaroo Alley, and a heavy barrage was put down on masses of hostile troops north of the Cambrai road and right across the Divisional front. Considerable losses were inflicted on the enemy, and after making repeated efforts to come on, all of which were frustrated, his attacks ceased. Only on the right flank did he succeed in getting within 300 yards of the Fusiliers, and here his troops were decimated by Lewis-gun and machine-gun fire. His attempts against the line held by the Oxfords and Bucks were similarly dealt with.

The attacks ceased at 4.30 p.m. At 5.30 p.m. and 7.35 p.m.

two patrols of the 24th Royal Fusiliers went out, and on return reported the enemy digging in, with his trenches full of troops.

Next morning, at 6.15 a.m., the enemy attacked a bombing post garrisoned by the 24th Royal Fusiliers, at the junction of the Hindenburg Support Line with Kangaroo Alley—*i.e.*, between the sunken road leading north-west from Graincourt and the Bapaume–Cambrai road. A sharp hand-to-hand fight ensued, during which No. 2620 Sergeant A. F. Wood, No. 55023 Sergeant E. Tarlton, and No. 479 Lance-Corporal G. Day showed admirable skill and courage. At the end of half an hour the enemy had been driven off with considerable loss.

During the morning a gap was reported in the covering line near Graincourt, through which parties of the enemy had worked their way into the village and to within a short distance of the Battalion Headquarters of the 24th Royal Fusiliers. To confirm this, No. 2966 Sergeant D. McCabe was sent out with two men. By the skill and daring bravery of his party Sergeant McCabe was able to locate the position of the enemy and return with valuable information. D Company of the 1st King's Royal Rifles was then placed at the disposal of the Officer Commanding 24th Royal Fusiliers, who used it to form a defensive flank west of Graincourt.

The left-front battalion—the Oxford and Bucks—was attacked during the 6th, and although there are no details of the action, the Battalion Diary stated it was "repulsed in a manner which reflects the greatest credit on Captain Fulbrook-Leggatt and his company (A)."

At 2.15 p.m. the withdrawal from the covering line was ordered to be carried out at 5.30 p.m. This was done, practically without loss. Lock 6 was blown up, and 65 dug-outs demolished in the evacuated area. In the sugar factory a "booby trap" was laid. The footbridge over the canal south of Lock 6 was likewise destroyed.

"The operation of withdrawing the covering troops was a delicate one," said the Divisional Report, "and the strain thrown on these two battalions was severe. Nevertheless the spirit of all ranks remained of the finest, and each situation was met with courage by the men, and with skill and spirit by their leaders. The integrity of the covering line owed much to the excellent and prompt treatment of Graincourt by the artillery. . . . Throughout this retirement not a man of the Brigade (5th) fell into the hands of the enemy."

The only variation in the withdrawal time-table was in the

blowing-up of Lock 6, which took place twenty minutes earlier, after a conversation between the R.E. officer in charge of the demolition party and the Officer Commanding Oxford and Bucks Light Infantry.

The 24th Royal Fusiliers and the Oxfords withdrew through B and A Lines (through the Highland Light Infantry and 17th Royal Fusiliers) to trenches and dug-outs south of the main line of resistance. The 2nd Highland Light Infantry and 17th Royal Fusiliers then held the Divisional front. " If by day things were quiet and movement at a minimum," said the Battalion Diary of the 2nd Highland Light Infantry, " by night it was a different story. The whole area of the Division was alive with workers— Sappers, Pioneers, and infantry—all working neck and crop to form a line which would baffle the numerous divisions the enemy was known to have put against this sector. A small point called Albert went out well in front of the advanced posts. By means of a telephone all movement on the front was registered. To-night, the 6th–7th December 1917, the advanced outposts withdrew through our lines, and so we remained as the main line of resistance, with advanced posts as outposts. Consolidation proceeded, and there was a busy night. Once more Albert did good work and telephoned through the general situation."

Throughout these withdrawal operations casualties were very small, for the enemy had received a severe lesson. He had been repulsed so often and with such terrible losses, that apparently he had no mind to take risks against troops who, even when wounded, refused to leave the battle line and who, when the word was given to retire, fell back reluctantly to positions in rear.

By the morning of the 7th December the withdrawal may be said to have been completed. " The new line taken up by us," said the Official Dispatches, referring to the situation along the whole front, " corresponded roughly to the old Hindenburg Reserve (Support) Line, and ran from a point about one and a half miles north by east of La Vacquerie, north of Ribecourt and Flesquières to the Canal du Nord, about one and a half miles north of Havrincourt.

7TH DEC.

In the Mœuvres–Bourlon fighting many gallant actions were recorded; many more will never be made known. But in a " Special Order of the Day," besides the gallant conduct of Captains Stone and McReady-Diarmid, which won for the 2nd Division the highest possible awards, other stories are mentioned.

One of these stories concerned a corporal and a driver of the

9th Battery (XLIst Brigade) R.F.A. On December the 1st, near Hermies, the team of which No. 12682 Driver J. Brodie was wheel-driver was hit by a shell. The lead and centre drivers were wounded and the team all down, some horses being hit and others entangled in the harness. No. 21390 Corporal E. Benfield and Driver Brodie extricated the two wounded drivers, and, while Brodie remained with the team, Benfield, with the assistance of some other men, took the two wounded drivers to the dressing station. He then returned and, with Brodie, extricated three unwounded horses. Benfield now remained with the wagon, whilst Brodie went off, returning presently with two pairs of horses from empty ammunition wagons then returning from the gun positions. The two men then took their wagon up to the battery, arriving at a time when ammunition was much needed. Corporal Benfield and Driver Brodie were over two hours rescuing their wagon, though persistent shell-fire swept the track the whole period.

On the same day another gallant action was recorded. In the enemy's lines, west of Bourlon Wood and about seventy yards from the trenches of the 23rd Royal Fusiliers, there was a derelict tank. This tank was being used by the enemy as a sniper's post. The battalion had already suffered many casualties when No. 1079 Lance-Sergeant J. Cochrane, M.M., and No. 2852 Private F. Hemington volunteered to put an end to the sniper's activities. Creeping out through their own wire, the two men, in spite of heavy enemy rifle fire, eventually succeeded in reaching the tank. They dropped two Mills bombs into it, and, when these had exploded, returned safely to their own lines, though on the way back they were again subjected to heavy rifle and machine-gun fire. No further sniping came from the tank. The gallant action of these two men undoubtedly saved many lives.

Just before the retirement of the covering force, on the 6th December, whilst the battalion was being heavily pressed by the enemy, No. 11963 Sergeant E. Constable (2nd Oxford and Bucks Light Infantry) was sent up to reinforce the garrison of Lock 6. The enemy, however, drove out Sergeant Constable's section, which was holding a post guarding the entrances to the lock, but the gallant N.C.O. led his men through a neighbouring trench and, going over ground, drove the enemy out and regained the lost post. When the post was again attacked Sergeant Constable, in conjunction with No. 8897 Lance-Corporal Easden, led a party round by the left flank and repulsed the attack. Subsequently, when

"COURAGE, INITIATIVE, AND COOLNESS." 515

orders had been issued to evacuate and blow up the lock, and after the fuses had been lighted, the intrepid sergeant voluntarily went down through the lock to the basement to make certain that all the garrison had withdrawn.[1] His action delayed the enemy's advance and facilitated the safe withdrawal of the whole line covering the outpost line.

Another N.C.O., No. 9794 Lance-Sergeant J. McInally, of the 2nd Highland Light Infantry, is twice mentioned for gallant conduct. The first occasion was on the 30th November. Sergeant McInally's platoon was carrying bombs up to the front line from a dump on the Cambrai–Bapaume road. The dump was in the open, and exposed to an exceedingly heavy fire from machine guns and artillery. When the platoon had finished its work Private McLuskie was missing. Sergeant McInally immediately returned and found McLuskie, who had been seriously wounded, and carried him to a place of safety. Again on 3rd December, when the enemy attacked his battalion south of Mœuvres, Sergeant McInally displayed fine courage, initiative, and coolness. The enemy had attacked in great strength and, forcing a block, succeeded in gaining an entrance to the front line. A counter-attack was at once organized, whereupon Sergeant McInally jumped on to the parapet and, bombing the enemy out of the trench, drove him back beyond the block—a distance of about 200 yards. The personal courage of this N.C.O. saved the right flank of the battalion from being turned.

Trench Warfare, 7th December 1917 to 20th March 1918.

During the night of the 8th–9th December the 5th Infantry Brigade (less 5th Machine-Gun Company) was relieved by the 6th Infantry Brigade (less 6th Machine-Gun Company) and marched back into camp in the Lebucquière area. "This completes a tour of fourteen days," records one Battalion Diary, "during which time the battalion has fought the fiercest battle in its history, and undertaken constant reliefs and continuous minor enterprises against the

[1] Sergeant Constable was not the last to leave, though he saw all of his own men clear of the lock. The demolition party consisted of Second-Lieut. W. E. Oliver and a small party of the 226th Field Company R.E. "A six-minute fuse was prepared, and also, in case the fuse did not work, an electric lead was laid to an explosion in spoil bank. At 5 a.m. the enemy made a second attack on the lock, and it was evacuated. No. 134953 Lance-Corporal Grinnell and No. 81529 Sapper T. Barratt remained in the lock until the last of the British troops had gone, and then fired the fuse. Six minutes after, when the enemy were well in the lock, the charge blew up."— *Diary of the 226th Field Company R.E.*

enemy's finest troops. On all occasions it has done magnificently and returns to a well-earned rest." And what was true of this battalion was true of all.

The 6th Infantry Brigade holding the main line of resistance, which had now become the 2nd Divisional front line, disposed the 17th Middlesex on the right and the 1st King's on the left; the 13th Essex Regiment was in support, and the 2nd South Staffords in reserve. The 99th Infantry Brigade was still at Hermies and Haplincourt.

Trench warfare now set in and it was not unwelcome, for the Division had passed through a very strenuous period, and all ranks were very tired and exhausted. Much hard work was, however, necessary before the front-line trenches would be able to stand the full severity of the winter. Wherever possible old German trenches were incorporated into the line, but for the most part new trenches had to be dug, wired, duck-boarded, and finished with shelters. And as the enemy was vigilant it followed that most of the work of building and revetting had to be carried out at night. Snow and frost had not yet made their unwelcome appearance, but the rain had already turned the trenches and the vicinity into quagmires. Even the battalions in support and reserve suffered greatly from the condition of the ground. Some battalions were still in tents, and their privations were truly terrible. Some idea of the measure of discomfort experienced at this period is contained in the Battalion Diary of the 1st King's Royal Rifles: " The Haplincourt camp proves to be a most uncomfortable spot. The mud is very deep, and the insides of the tents, which are without boards, are very wet. Headquarters mess consists of a bell tent, with a few boxes inside for use as chairs and tables. . . . Everybody very uncomfortable, but in good spirits considering the conditions are unpleasant. Living in newly captured trenches does not lend itself to comfort, and one has to make one's own arrangements, as little or no help is forthcoming." And then the battalion moved to Hermies: " Took over from the 1st Royal Berks and had a most enjoyable night. The men were comfortably and dryly housed in ' cubby holes ' and cellars. . . . The officers all had small but warm huts to mess in with good wood fires. This is the first time we have been really comfortable for ages. The degree of comfort is all a matter of comparison, for people at home would not have thought much of our present accommodation, but to us it is splendid. . . . To-day was spent by all ranks in getting rid of the mud brought from Haplincourt camp."

One of the most eloquent tributes to the endurance of the British soldier in France and Flanders during those terrible years is the almost total absence in the Battalion Diaries of any kind of complaint. His cheerfulness under all circumstances was at once the admiration of his French allies and the envy of his enemies. The point of view of the Divisional Commander at this time is not uninteresting : " Sunday, 9th December 1917.—I went up the line. I could not get to the front line owing to the considerable shelling. We can get quite a good communication trench right forward with comparatively little work by adapting old trenches. . . . Two of the Third Army Staff came to luncheon. Colonel —— who is on their Staff told us that on 30th November the Arras group of six divisions were employed on our Divisional front and immediate flanks ; that three of the six divisions were identified.[1] All six divisions had been relieved since the attack. . . . The army talk of there being an indication of a German effort to regain the lost Hindenburg Line. The task of making a new defence line in a hurry, and having to link up the Hindenburg Line with the old British line with a Divisional frontage of 3,500 yards and tired troops, is most exacting and requires the most careful organization. Owing to the wet weather our newly-dug trenches would have become impassable, and so by a special effort 2,000 duck-boards were carried up last night, and I hope they managed to lay them in the trenches.

" There are very weak spots in our new line, and for the moment it is a weak line throughout. Just west of the Canal, where we face the enemy, astride of some very big trenches, is a spot where there will always be trouble. Last night the 6th Infantry Brigade made special efforts to dig, wire, and establish more posts there. We have now been ordered to 'side-slip' to our right, and give up the least troubled section of our left to the 51st Division, and to take over 1,200 yards from the 47th Division on the left of the Canal. The Hindenburg Support Line runs into this bit—a source of weakness. . . . We have selected a very useful line for our machine-gun positions, but time is required to dig them in and get the telephone communication fixed up. . . . We have plenty to excite and interest us these days. Divisions from Russia keep on turning up, and the 25th[2] has just come into the line. Let us pray that our machine guns will be in position to give them a good baptism if they are due to come over the top."

[1] The 20th, 21st Reserve, and 49th Reserve Divisions.
[2] The 24th Reserve Division (?).

518   THE HISTORY OF THE SECOND DIVISION.

9TH DEC.   On the 9th December only the right sub-sector (held by the 17th Middlesex) of the 6th Infantry Brigade front was engaged with the enemy. Here, about 7.30 a.m., the enemy, with flammenwerfer, attacked the left bombing posts of the battalion, causing the garrison to fall back some 150 yards, and knocking out a Lewis gun. C Company was sent up to reinforce A Company, one company of the 2nd South Staffords taking the place of C Company. Continual bombing attacks took place during the day. The 1st King's (on the left) reported 'all clear.' The same post on A Company's front was again pushed in on the following day, "but," the Diary states, "the enemy was driven back apparently by Sergeant Glennie of C Company alone, who was wounded and probably captured in doing so." There are no further reports on the action of this gallant N.C.O.

On the night of the 11th, the 99th Infantry Brigade took over a portion (1,200 yards) of the line east of the Canal from the 142nd Infantry Brigade (47th Division), and the 6th Infantry Brigade handed over 800 yards of the Brigade front to the 51st Division. On completion of these moves the 99th Brigade front line was held by the 23rd Royal Fusiliers on the right, and the 1st Royal Berks on the left; the 22nd Royal Fusiliers and the 1st King's Royal Rifles moved to Hermies. On the 6th Infantry Brigade front the 2nd South Staffords had relieved the 17th Middlesex Regiment, the latter moving back into support; inter-company reliefs had also taken place between the 1st King's and 13th Essex Regiment. But on the 13th the Divisional front was again reorganized; the front was divided into two equal frontages, each forward Brigade having three battalions in the line and support, and one battalion in reserve at Hermies—the Reserve Brigade having three battalions at Lebucquière and one in the Spoil Heap south of Hermies. "Twelve days in the front line and six out," were the new orders.

An important scheme of work to be carried out by the forward Brigades was now mapped out and put into effect. The Brigades were ordered to carry out these various works according to their relative importance, and in the order given: "Complete front posts; give them duck-boarded communication trenches, and communication to the flanking posts; deepen and duck-board main line throughout; deepen and duck-board front communication trenches; deepen and duck-board support trenches; provide elephant shelters for the garrison; they will turn on all the available labour on each one in turn."

This programme of work, though of a very strenuous nature,

AN ENEMY RAID FAILS.

was absolutely necessary, for the enemy was in considerable strength opposite the Division. "Yesterday's Order of Battle," said the General Officer Commanding, " shows the area opposite us to be unduly thick with enemy divisions,[1] and I only hope they will give us time to get through our work set-pieces. As a further precaution I am making two strong points—Fort George and Fort Mary—one on either side of the Canal as soon as the forward work is complete. They will be made with real dug-out shelters for the garrison, and capable of being held against penetration by the adjoining trenches by means of series of straight trenches and protected loopholed blocks firing down them."

The 5th Infantry Brigade relieved the 6th Infantry Brigade in the left sub-sector on the night of 14th–15th December, the 2nd Oxford and Bucks taking over the right sub-section, and the 24th Royal Fusiliers the left, with the 2nd Highland Light Infantry in support and the 17th Royal Fusiliers in reserve. Patrol encounters, raids, intermittent heavy shelling, and discharges of gas took place during the remainder of December. Of several encounters with the enemy only four were of sufficient importance to relate.

14TH–15TH DEC.

The 22nd Fusiliers (99th Infantry Brigade) on the night 13th–14th, had relieved the 23rd Royal Fusiliers in the right sub-section. At 7.15 a.m. of the 15th a strong hostile raiding party of forty men attempted to raid a sap in the Fusiliers' line. The raid was preceded by a heavy rifle-grenade barrage which caused casualties. The enemy then attempted to rush the sap and gain a footing in the trench. This he entirely failed to do, being driven off by rifle and Lewis-gun fire. The Fusiliers' casualties were one officer wounded, one other ranks killed and ten wounded. Early in the afternoon between 2 and 3.30 an officer's patrol crept out and searched the area around the head of the sap. No enemy was found, but there was blood in the trench, eleven rifles, seventy bombs, and two steel helmets, all of which bore witness to the rout of the enemy.

Two days later a small party of the King's Royal Rifles was entrapped by the enemy. B Company of the Rifles held a somewhat isolated part of the line, in the front of which were posts held only at night. The battalion was due to be relieved by the 1st Royal Berks, and in the evening just before the relief took place an N.C.O. and four men went out to one of these posts to occupy

---

[1] The German divisions opposite the 2nd Division and flanking its front were, on the 12th December, the 49th Reserve Division, the 20th Division, and the 24th Reserve Division.

it. But no sooner had the party left the trench than the enemy opened fire from the post; his troops had forestalled the N.C.O. and his four men. Only one man escaped, the remaining three and the N.C.O. being captured by the enemy. During the night of the 20th–21st December the 99th Infantry Brigade was relieved by the 6th Infantry Brigade.

The 5th Infantry Brigade first established contact with the enemy in the left sub-section on the night of the 19th. Here the 24th Royal Fusiliers had sent out a fighting patrol of two officers and twelve other ranks. A hostile patrol, whose number was estimated at no less than fifty men, was met. A stiff fight with bombs, rifles, and revolvers ensued in which casualties were inflicted on the enemy. The Fusiliers then withdrew without loss.

The 17th Fusiliers at 10 a.m. on the 21st also repulsed a raid. The enemy, estimated at thirty rifles, attempted to raid a post covering the left flank of the battalion, but was beaten off and retired in disorder back to his own trenches. No casualties were sustained by the Fusiliers, who, however, captured one prisoner. "A new kind of automatic pistol was found afterwards," records the Battalion Diary, "probably belonging to the officer or N.C.O. in charge of the raiding party, with a magazine containing thirty-two rounds. Unfortunately the pistol was damaged by our fire. It is interesting to note that the enemy failed to pick off our post owing to the fact that they forgot to pull the strings of their bombs before throwing them. One man discovered and fired on the enemy before they threw, nevertheless these bombs fell in the trench at the feet of our men; D Company sustained the attack."

The Diaries of the 5th, 226th, and 403rd Field Companies R.E. show an extraordinary amount of work performed during December 1917. In the front line new trenches were dug, dug-outs built, hundreds of yards of wire entanglements erected, fire-bays cut, and trenches sandbagged; whilst behind the front line, in the support and reserve lines, communication trenches were dug, huts erected, shelters put up, officers' messes and cook-houses built, to say nothing of road repairs. In all this work the Pioneers ably assisted the Sappers. Little wonder that both were looked upon with affection by all ranks and units of the Division. In carrying out their orders they suffered many casualties, and many honours and awards fell to them.

On the night of the 19th the ground was frozen hard, and thence onwards to the end of the year seasonable, but terrible weather for campaigning set in.

THE DIVISION RELIEVED. 521

On the 1st January 1918 2nd Division Order No. 316 was issued: the Division was to be relieved on the night of 3rd–4th by the 17th Division. The enemy attacked during this relief and captured some advanced posts of the Division, but the main line intact was handed over to the 17th Division, and the 5th Infantry Brigade moved back to Beaulencourt, the 6th Infantry Brigade to Rocquigny, and the 99th Infantry Brigade to Barastre. The Divisional Artillery was at Haplincourt, and the Pioneers and Field Companies R.E. were left behind in the line.

1ST JAN. 1918.

The new area taken over by the Division for resting and training purposes was in a very bad condition, and much work was needed in order to make it anything like habitable. And the weather, which at the end of December and the beginning of January had been cold and frosty, began to break about the 6th of the month, interfering considerably with drill and movement about the camps. The area everywhere was littered with stores and equipment, and salvage operations on a large scale, well organized, were begun. The Salvage Reports for 1917 of the 2nd Division had showed an extraordinary amount of material salved, the total value of which was £252,644. Of this amount the Salvage Company of the 2nd Division alone salved stores valued at £167,000. During December 1917 the Division, though in the line, had salved material worth £12,000.

Enemy aeroplanes were very active during the second week in January, and the 6th Infantry Brigade, early on the morning of the 8th, had the misfortune to lose 2 other ranks killed and 43 wounded from bombs dropped by hostile aircraft. Eight horses were also killed and over 20 injured.

The weather consistently interfered with training, thaws followed by heavy rain reducing the ground in many places to an impassable condition. On the 11th all heavy motor transport was forbidden to use the roads.

For just under three weeks the Division lived under most uncomfortable circumstances, and then on the 22nd and 23rd took over the La Vacquerie sector from the 63rd (Naval) Division, the 5th Infantry Brigade relieving the 189th Infantry Brigade on the left, and the 99th Infantry Brigade the 188th Infantry Brigade in the right sub-sectors; the 6th Infantry Brigade was in the reserve area at Metz, Equancourt, and Etricourt.

At 10 a.m. on the 24th January command of the La Vacquerie sector passed to the General Officer Commanding 2nd Division. Divisional Headquarters were at Etricourt. On the same day

24TH JAN.

Brigadier-General R. Barnett-Barker, D.S.O., arrived at 99th Infantry Brigade Headquarters to take over command of the Brigade, *vice* Brigadier-General R. O. Kellett, C.B., C.M.G., who having gone on leave, owing to failing health, had been obliged to relinquish command of the Brigade which he had held since November 1915. The Division felt very keenly the loss of this gallant brigadier. The new brigadier was no stranger to the 2nd Division, having at one time commanded the 22nd Battalion Royal Fusiliers.

The new front line taken over by the Division was far from being a sinecure: " The sector extends north and south with the flanks resting on the spurs of the Fusilier ridge (right) and the Welsh ridge (left), the centre being in the valley which runs east and west between Villers Plouich and La Vacquerie. The front is approximately 2,300 yards; this includes Cornwall Trench 500 yards, which falls south to a flank. All the trenches are in a wet and very muddy state due to the melting of the snow-falls, and are impassable. The front is held by posts, the garrisons of which are relieved every twenty-four hours. Much work is needed to provide dry standings and shelters in the posts, and the fire positions need improving. The task of clearing the front and communication trenches from mud and water in order to make them passable will be extremely difficult under weather conditions in force."

The above description is of the 99th Infantry Brigade (taken from the Brigade Diary), where the distance between the British and German lines was some hundreds of yards. About the centre of the line, however—*i.e.*, the junction of the 5th and 99th Infantry Brigades—the British and German systems of trenches came suddenly closer together. Along the whole of the 5th Infantry Brigade front the trench-line was broken by saps, there being no less than eight up to a point northwards, where the left flank of the Brigade joined with the right of the 19th Division, the northern Divisional boundary. South of the 2nd Division the 9th Division VIIth Corps of the Fifth Army held the line. The 2nd Division was still at this period in the Third Army.

Fortunately the enemy remained fairly quiet, and with the exception of some intermittent shelling made no attack on the Division; his inactivity enabled the much-needed improvement of the trenches to be carried out satisfactorily. Patrols went out each night, but no enemy was encountered.

On the night of the 28th–29th January the 6th Infantry Brigade

THREE BATTALIONS DISBANDED.

relieved the 5th Infantry Brigade, the latter passing back into Divisional reserve.¹

28TH–29TH JAN.

Salvage work had made such progress by the end of the month that the returns for December were far outdistanced; war material valued at £31,000 had been collected in the Divisional area during January; the Division also had the satisfaction of knowing that it had salved more than all the other Divisions of the Vth Corps put together.²

Early in 1918 it became necessary for General Headquarters to consider the advisability of reducing the number of battalions in each division. Most divisions were lamentably weak in numbers. The man-power of Great Britain was at its lowest ebb towards the end of 1917, and battalions went into the line in France and Flanders barely 600 strong. Subsequently General Headquarters definitely decided to reduce the number of battalions in each infantry brigade to three, and on 2nd February the 2nd Division received orders to disband three battalions, the three selected being the 13th Essex Regiment, the 17th Middlesex Regiment, and the 22nd Battalion Royal Fusiliers. All three battalions had fought most gallantly; they had gained many battle honours, two of the three had won V.C.'s for the Division, and their going was very deeply regretted by all ranks of the Division. It was found possible to distribute the men of the 22nd Royal Fusiliers between the 23rd and 24th Battalions, and these troops thus remained with the Division. But the 13th Essex and the 17th Middlesex were dispatched to various other battalions of their own regiments. The 22nd Royal Fusiliers were broken up on the 5th February and the two other battalions left the 2nd Division on the 10th. As the Divisional Commander said: "The old soldiers who have survived many a fight are very hard hit by this disbanding."

5TH FEB.

As the Essex and the Middlesex had both belonged to the 6th Infantry Brigade the 17th Royal Fusiliers were transferred from the 5th Infantry Brigade to the 6th. On completion of these changes the three infantry brigades of the 2nd Division were as follows:

5th Infantry Brigade: 2nd Oxford and Bucks Light Infantry, 2nd Highland Light Infantry, 24th Royal Fusiliers.

6th Infantry Brigade: 2nd South Staffords, 1st King's Rifles, 17th Royal Fusiliers.

---

¹ Casualties for January: 1 officer (Second-Lieut. F. W. H. Barclay) killed, 3 officers wounded; 27 other ranks killed, 170 wounded, 16 missing.
² Corps Report.

99th Infantry Brigade : 1st King's Royal Rifle Corps, 1st Royal Berks Regiment, 23rd Royal Fusiliers.

During the latter part of January and the beginning of February weather conditions improved considerably, and the trenches gradually became more habitable.

The month of February opened quietly, the enemy being comparatively passive, though his artillery occasionally put down heavy bombardments of the front and back areas. In the early hours of the 4th, for instance, the 6th Infantry Brigade front was subjected to very heavy shell-fire, and the enemy's guns gave Metz an uncomfortable night. Orders were received on the 6th that the Divisional front was to be held on a three-brigade basis, the reliefs and moves to be carried out on the night of the 9th–10th. On completion the 99th Infantry Brigade was to hold the right, the 5th Infantry Brigade the centre, and the 6th Infantry Brigade the left sub-sectors. Each Brigade was to have one battalion in the front line, one in support, and one in reserve.

Considerable patrol work and a certain number of raids took place. Of the former over 120 reconnaissances and fighting patrols of the 2nd Division crossed No Man's Land, whilst several raids, both British and German, were carried out with varying results.

Towards the end of February a reorganization of the Vth Corps front took place. Hitherto four divisions had held the front line, but under the new orders only three divisions were to be in the front-line trenches, the fourth passing back into reserve. This reorganization necessitated the 2nd Division taking over part of the front held by the 63rd (Naval) Division. On the night of the 21st the 99th Infantry Brigade and the 6th Infantry Brigade closed inwards, taking over the front held by the 5th Infantry Brigade. The latter then moved north, and the 2nd Highland Light Infantry took over the right Brigade front of the 63rd Division, held by the 1st Royal Marine Light Infantry and Anson Battalion. Though of a very difficult nature—the whole Division being practically on the move at the same time—the relief was completed by 10 p.m.

Trench warfare was now of a strenuous nature, and on being relieved in the front line one battalion (1st Royal Berks) attached the following note to the Battalion Diary of the 22nd February: " This ended a memorable tour—six days in close support and seven days in the line, in all thirteen days without respite. The battalion can look back with pride on these thirteen days, for an immense amount of very useful wiring and digging was accomplished . . .

FORMATION OF THE MACHINE-GUN CORPS.

and at the same time, when in the front line, not a night passed without fighting and reconnoitring patrols going out on the whole front and, by sheer skill and boldness, obtaining valuable information and securing for us the absolute mastery of No Man's Land. This activity was inspired by a hint that an identification from the Divisional front was needed, and it was a genuine disappointment to all ranks that, in spite of our efforts, we were unable to secure a prisoner."

But an identification, which gallant efforts had failed to obtain, came to the Division without effort on the night of the 23rd–24th February, when a German deserter, belonging to the 80th R.I.R. of the 21st Reserve Division, crossed No Man's Land and gave himself up. He made one interesting statement: " Prisoner says a German offensive is certain, because everywhere the troops are practising the attack, but he has no idea where the blow is likely to fall."

On the night of the 24th the enemy poured no less than 3,000 gas shells into Havrincourt Wood, where the 24th Royal Fusiliers were in billets. This large expenditure resulted in the gassing of five men! Later, empty tents were purposely kept standing in Havrincourt Wood, which drew the enemy's fire most effectively: in blissful ignorance he regularly shelled the tents, blowing many of them to atoms.

24TH FEB.

Since the 1st of January a marked increase in hostile aerial activity had been noticed; enemy machines were everywhere encountered by British machines, and great air combats were frequent. But despite his efforts to bomb the British lines, his own lines suffered the most; for, whereas during January he dropped 2,206 bombs, the British dropped 11,851. In the Third Army area 780 bombs were dropped during January, whereas the Third Army airmen dropped 1,181 bombs on the enemy during the same period.

The 2nd Division was notified in February of the impending formation of the Machine-Gun Corps, and was ordered to form the 5th, 6th, 99th, and 242nd Machine-Gun Companies into a battalion, with the designation of the " 2nd Battalion Machine-Gun Corps." Until the 5th March there is no mention in the Divisional Diaries of this new organization, but on that date the details connected with the formation of the battalion are given as follows : " The four Machine-Gun Companies of the 2nd Division, consisting of 5th, 6th, 99th, and 242nd Machine-Gun Companies, were formed into 2nd Battalion Machine-Gun Corps, under the command of Lieut.-Colonel H. D. Buchanan-Dunlop, D.S.O., 1st Battalion Royal West Kent Regiment (attached Machine-Gun Corps)."

Lieut.-Colonel Buchanan-Dunlop was appointed to this duty and joined the 2nd Division on the 19th February, taking over the duty of Divisional Machine-Gun Commander from Major W. M. Todd, M.C., 9th Battalion Highland Light Infantry (attached Machine-Gun Corps) who had, up to this date, been performing the duties of Divisional Machine-Gun Officer. Major Todd was appointed second in command of 2nd Battalion Machine-Gun Corps; Lieut. A. Marshall, 5th Machine-Gun Company, Adjutant; Lieut. C. R. Forsyth, 6th Battalion Scottish Rifles (and Machine-Gun Company), 242nd Machine-Gun Company, Transport Officer; Second-Lieut. A. Winship (late 17th Battalion Middlesex Regiment), Signalling Officer; and Lieut. and Quartermaster R. D. Burgess (late 22nd Battalion Royal Fusiliers), Quartermaster.

Transport drivers and horses to complete establishment were taken from the 13th Battalion Essex Regiment, the 17th Battalion Middlesex Regiment, and the 22nd Battalion Royal Fusiliers. These battalions had been recently disbanded.

The original Machine-Gun Companies were now designated:

No. 5 Company—A Company, 2nd Battalion Machine-Gun Corps: Company Commander, Captain D. W. Bell, M.C.

No. 6 Company—B Company, 2nd Battalion Machine-Gun Corps: Company Commander, Lieutenant F. M. Richardson.

No. 99 Company—C Company, 2nd Battalion Machine-Gun Corps: Company Commander, Captain A. P. Skevington, M.C.

No. 242 Company—D Company, 2nd Battalion Machine-Gun Corps: Company Commander, Captain H. P. Borlase.

"It was necessary to form the battalion and take over the administration of the companies by degrees, owing to the fact that the Division was in the line . . . want of accommodation was also another difficulty which rendered the formation of the battalion slow. . . . The Division holds (1) the lower slope of the spur running north-west from Gonnelieu (commanding ridge); (2) the valley at the head of which stands La Vacquerie; and (3) the Welsh ridge. Parallel and in rear of the first runs the Couillet Valley. In rear of this is the Beaucamp–Highland ridge, about 2,500 yards from our front line on the right, and 1,800 yards in rear of the centre brigade. The Welsh ridge, commanding as it does the Couillet Valley, is of particular importance, and while the ridge is held by us close observation of the guns to the westward is denied to the enemy."

THE EVE OF GREAT EVENTS.

Each company was divided into four sections: three companies were in the line, and one in reserve.

In the strenuous times through which the 2nd Division was to pass in the coming months, the 2nd Battalion Machine-Gun Corps did splendid and gallant service.

On the 1st March the enemy opened a heavy bombardment of the extreme left of the Divisional line; the S.O.S. went up, and the Divisional Artillery replied promptly with a very effective barrage on the enemy's trenches. The hostile bombardment was accompanied by heavy trench-mortar and machine-gun fire. The bombardment ceased at 5 a.m., when the enemy raided an advanced post belonging to the 5th Infantry Brigade, held by the 24th Royal Fusiliers. One N.C.O. was subsequently reported missing.

1ST MARCH.

Careful reading of the Divisional Diaries for the beginning of March 1918 discloses the almost certain knowledge that great events were about to happen. The great German offensive had been expected on the first of the month, and the heavy bombardment in the early hours of that day was for a while looked upon as the preliminary bombardment to a big attack. "The rumours about a coming enemy attack," said one Battalion Diary, "circle thick and fast. Perhaps the reality of things is brought into bolder relief by the fact of the new works and dumps under construction in the reserve system of trenches. Then, too, the Intelligence information, culled from General Headquarters Summaries downwards, points to enemy action at an early date." After describing the bombardment in the early hours of the 1st March, the Diary states: "Has the offensive started? was the natural query which sprang to the lips of all. But the offensive had not started, and nothing eventuated except one of those raids by which the enemy seems at present to be testing the strength of our front."

It is rare in these Official Records to come upon a diarist whose notes are of psychological interest. But here is a note which throws into the limelight that queer feeling experienced by all who ever served in the front-line trenches—that "something" was about to happen. "Added to a certain apprehension difficult to diagnose," said the diarist, "there is a general restlessness all around." It was as a soft breeze stirring the leaves upon the trees before the storm burst.

The expected enemy offensive, as already stated, was not launched on the 1st nor until the 21st March, but in the meantime various raids and small operations took place along the Divisional front. The vital need was to keep General Headquarters informed of the dispositions of the enemy's divisions, and this could only be carried out effectively by raiding the enemy's trenches. But of the many gallant efforts made by the 2nd Division to obtain an identification, only one was successful.

16TH–17TH MARCH.

On the night of the 16th–17th March a fighting patrol of the 17th Royal Fusiliers, under Second-Lieut. Panting, crossed No Man's Land in order to obtain an identification. The patrol succeeded in entering Neptune and Anchor saps, but the only thing obtained was an enemy notice board. From the information gained by this patrol, a raid was planned for the night of the 18th. Throughout the afternoon of the 17th the 47th (Howitzer) Battery and the 6-inch "Newtons" cut wire at the point to be raided and on both flanks. The place selected for the raid was at the point of juncture between the 6th and 99th Infantry Brigades, opposite No. 1 Post. For some time past patrols had reported this locality held by the enemy at night.

The raiding party consisted of Second-Lieut. Fish, one sergeant, and ten other ranks of the 17th Royal Fusiliers. The forming-up tapes were laid early on the night of the 18th, this important and dangerous work being carried out by Second-Lieut. Panting, who from his patrol work had an accurate knowledge of the ground to be crossed and the sap to be raided. The tapes were put out about sixty yards from the enemy. "Zero" had been fixed for 11 p.m.

Forming up was begun at 10.30 p.m., but this operation was observed by the enemy, who opened fire with machine guns, rifle grenades, and bombs. But fortunately the fire was inaccurate, and caused no casualties.

At 11 p.m. the raiding party went forward in three groups, one to proceed north along Cover Trench, one south, and the remaining party along the communication trench running south-eastwards. A barrage of 18-pounders and howitzers, 3-inch Stokes mortars and 6-inch "Newtons" had been arranged, and immediately it opened the raiders dashed forward. The enemy, numbering about twenty men, fled. Second-Lieut. Fish was first into the enemy's trench and, seeing a German, held him prisoner at the point of his revolver, but some of the officer's party, not realizing that the man had surrendered, killed him. Lance-Corporal Bradley caught six of the enemy in a communication trench trying to get away. He promptly dropped one bomb in front of them and another in their midst, both bombs exploding. Of No. 1 party detailed to proceed along the trench northwards, some men rushed up the trench for about fifty yards, whilst others moved along the top, firing at the enemy as they ran. No. 3 party did the same on the south. At least ten Germans were killed, but it was found impossible to move the dead. Several pairs of epaulettes were, however, cut from the tunics of the dead men and brought back. The Fusiliers, in this raid, lost one man missing and one wounded.

"The artillery, Stokes mortars, and 'Newton'[1] barrages were most effective," said the Official Report, "and completely silenced the enemy's machine guns and trench mortars."

The identifications obtained were normal, showing that the men had belonged to the 88th R.I.R., 21st Reserve Division. "No live Germans were taken owing to the keenness of our men in the raid," said the Fusiliers' Diary. With pardonable pride the Diary also records the receipt of congratulations from 2nd Division Headquarters, 99th, 6th, and 5th Infantry Brigade Headquarters, "as so many other units had failed to gain identifications."

For the first few days of the month the enemy's artillery fire had been normal, but on the 5th his guns showed unwonted activity, which drew a "punishment shoot" from the Divisional Artillery. About midnight of the 6th–7th hostile gas was projected on to the Farm Ravine, the discharge being preceded by trench-mortar fire. Many casualties were suffered by the 1st Royal Berks. "The projection was by means of 'rum jar' trench mortars. High explosive was used, and the detonations were terrific, damaging the trenches badly and veiling the fact that gas was present. The gas used was of the 'phosgene' type. Second-Lieut. J. A. Grimes, M.C., died from the effects of the gas, after gallantly endeavouring to rescue his orderly, who had been buried in the trenches. Second-Lieuts. Beer and Foster and 29 other ranks were also casualties."[2]

On the 11th, 12th, and 13th, large quantities of gas shells fell in the Divisional area. Indeed, it soon became evident that if the enemy intended taking the offensive he was deliberately thinning out the forces opposed to him, by the use of gas shells of a particularly virulent type, known as "mustard gas."

For hours on end on all three days the enemy deluged Villers Plouich, Beaucamp, Farm Ravine, and other parts of the Divisional area, causing heavy casualties, all of which would take from four to six weeks to recover, if, indeed, the men were fortunate enough to escape a horrible death. On the 12th the 2nd

---

[1] The "Newton" was a 6-inch trench mortar lately issued to the armies in France and Flanders.
[2] Battalion Diary, 1st Royal Berks Regiment.

Division lost 400 officers and men, and on the 13th 13 officers and 686 other ranks "gassed." The mustard gas was very insidious, and it was only after several hours that the victims began to show signs of being affected, then in the eyes and throat; vomiting set in, and soon the man was in a terrible condition. "We met a party of the 60th and R.A.M.C. coming down gassed. Those who were temporarily blinded (who were in the large majority) were being led by those who could see. Some of the men were in considerable pain in their eyes and lungs, others being sick and throwing themselves on the ground when there was a halt and clasping their heads." [1]

All the Diaries are full of the frightful effects of this dastardly use of gas. "The most careful and thorough precautions had to be taken. For example, men who had been in the infected area . . . who, by wearing respirators, were not affected at the time, were found to be subsequently made ill by sleeping in their clothes to which the gas had clung; consequently clothing had to be removed outside billets, and sleeping in close proximity to other men became unsafe. A platoon of C Company, in Wood Trench, was transferred almost completely to hospital." [2] "The effects of the gas shelling on the night 11th–12th are now (13th) making themselves more apparent, and men not previously affected show symptoms, especially in the matter of sore eyes and sore throat. Clearly clothing has much to do in retaining this poison gas." [3]

The disastrous effects on the 99th Infantry Brigade are shown in the Brigade Diary: "Casualties—11th: killed, 1 other ranks; wounded, 3 officers, 111 other ranks. 12th: killed, 3 other ranks; wounded, 17 officers, 639 other ranks. 13th: killed, 1 other ranks; wounded, 2 officers, 49 other ranks.

"Although men wore their gas masks for six hours, as soon as they took them off they were gassed. The whole battalion was affected, though in the front-line companies only about four men in each had to be evacuated. But both the support companies, and the personnel of Battalion Headquarters were badly affected, and by noon (on the 13th) scarcely a man of them could see. The Commanding Officer who, in the morning, had gone round the line returned to find the whole road lined with blind and vomiting men, with eyes streaming and swollen. Most of Battalion Headquarters, and every officer and most of B and D Companies had

---

[1] Diary of General Officer Commanding Division.
[2] Battalion Diary, 2nd Oxford and Bucks.
[3] Battalion Diary, 2nd Highland Light Infantry.

THE ENEMY GASSED BY HIS OWN GAS.

to be led or carried out of the line—7 officers and 270 other ranks gassed."[1]

But on the 16th gas projectors were located north of Gonnelieu, and the Divisional "Heavies" opened at 6 p.m. with great success. Direct hits were obtained on the enemy's gas cylinders, which exploded, the gas drifting in low clouds over his own positions.

The trench strength of the 99th Infantry Brigade being only about 600 on the 16th, the 5th and 6th Infantry Brigades had to "side-slip" to reduce the frontage held by the first-named Brigade. But on the 17th the General Officer Commanding reported: "Gas shelling has decreased during the last two days. Yesterday there was practically none."

On the 18th March orders were issued for the relief of the 2nd Division on the nights 19th–20th and 20th–21st March. The 5th Infantry Brigade, on relief, was to move to Ytres; the 6th Infantry Brigade to Rocquigny; and the 99th Infantry Brigade to Manancourt and Equancourt.

20TH–21ST MARCH.

These reliefs were duly carried out, but before the command of the sector passed to the General Officer Commanding 47th Division, the long-expected German offensive had opened.

[1] Battalion Diary, 1st King's Royal Rifle Corps.

VI.
THE GERMAN OFFENSIVES, 1918.

THE OFFENSIVE IN PICARDY,
21st March to 5th April 1918.

THE FIRST BATTLES OF THE SOMME, 1918.
    A Note on the General Situation.
THE BATTLE OF ST. QUENTIN, 21st to 23rd March 1918.
THE FIRST BATTLE OF BAPAUME, 24th to 25th March 1918.
The Withdrawal to the Old British Front Line, 26th March 1918.
The Last Days of March and the Resumption of Trench Warfare.
A Note on the General Situation between 21st March and 8th August 1918.

THE FIRST BATTLES OF THE SOMME, 1918.

A Note on the General Situation in March 1918.

IN order to form some idea of the conditions prevailing in the Western theatre of the War, when the Germans opened their great offensive in March 1918, it is necessary to consider the relative strengths and the general situation of both the Allies and the enemy.

The offensives of 1917 had left the Allies weak, the strength of the British army in particular being at a low ebb towards the end of December of that year. The American armies, although growing, could not be expected to restore the balance in favour of the Allies, for they had not arrived in sufficient numbers, nor had they progressed sufficiently in training to take their place in the field. Early in 1918 it became necessary, therefore, to adopt a defensive policy in order to meet the strong and sustained hostile attacks which would certainly be launched by the Germans. Moreover, towards the end of January the British army had extended its front, and in March occupied 125 miles of the front line, extending from Barisis, south of La Fère, to a point just east of St. Julien, north-east of Ypres.

The adoption of a defensive policy necessitated a change in training methods, which for some time had been primarily devoted to offensive operations. Combined with the arrival of reinforcements of new troops the change of policy threw a great weight upon the army, for the adoption of a defensive attitude entailed the construction of new defences, work which had to be carried out simultaneously with the training of newly arrived troops.

Under such conditions the British army prepared for the enemy's offensive; and in spite of the vast amount of work and training necessary, and that time and labour were in no way adequate, when that offensive was launched the defences had been largely improved, and the troops were fairly well prepared to carry out what was required of them.

In contrast to the difficulties briefly referred to, the Germans, having transferred numerous divisions and large quantities of guns and munitions from the East, were able to carry out extensive training with units whose ranks were full of newly arrived and partly trained troops. The Russian *débâcle* has already been referred to, but it was not until late in 1917 and the early part of 1918 that the full extent of the blow dealt to the Allied Powers by that unfortunate country was felt. Divisions newly arrived from Russia had been used by the enemy in the Bourlon–Mœuvres operations of November and December; thence onwards he was continually being reinforced by divisions brought back from the East until his forces disposed along the Western front considerably outnumbered those of the Allies.

A vigorous enemy offensive was, therefore, certain. But where would the blow fall?

" Constant air reconnaissances over the enemy's lines showed that rail and road communications were being improved, and ammunition and supply dumps increased along the whole front from Flanders to the Oise. By the end of February 1918 these preparations had become very marked opposite the front held by the Third and Fifth Armies, and I considered it probable that the enemy would make his initial effort from the Sensée River [1] southwards. As the 21st March approached it became certain that an attack on this sector was imminent, and counter preparation was carried out nightly by the artillery at the threatened point. By the 21st March the number of German infantry divisions in the Western theatre had risen to 192,[2] an increase of 46 divisions since the 1st November 1917." [3]

The British line between the Sensée and the Oise, which ran north-east and south-west just north of Barisis, had been selected by the enemy on account of its weakness. " The weakest part was on both sides of St. Quentin . . . here the attack would strike the enemy's weakest point, the ground offered no difficulties, and it was passable at all seasons. . . . The centre attack seemed to lack any definite limit. This could be remedied by directing the main effort on the area between Arras and Péronne, towards the coast. If this blow succeeded the strategic result might indeed be enormous, and we should separate the bulk of the English army from the French, and crowd it up with its back to the sea. I favoured the centre attack, but I was influenced by the time factor and by tactical considerations, first among them being the weakness

---

[1] The Sensée River crossed the British line in the Third Army area, just west of Fontaine-lès-Croisilles.
[2] The actual number was 193 divisions and 3 brigades.
[3] Official Dispatches.

THE GERMAN PLAN IN MARCH 1918.

of the enemy. Whether this weakness would continue I could not know."[1]

Attacks at Verdun and in the Lys valley were discussed by the German General Staff and rejected: that at Verdun because of the difficult nature of the country, and that in the Lys valley because of the condition of the ground, which would not be favourable for attack until April.

Thus the British line from Arras to Barisis was selected, and on the 10th March final preparations were begun, and orders for the offensive issued from "O.H.L.,"[2] under the rubric of "Michael." The text of the German order was as follows:

"By His Majesty's orders—

"1. The Michael attack will take place on the 21st, 3. The first attack on the enemy's lines is fixed for 9.40 a.m.

"2. The first great tactical objective of the Crown Prince Rupprecht's Army Group is to cut off the English in the Cambrai Salient and reach the line Croisilles (south-west of Arras)–Bapaume–Péronne. If the attack of the right wing (Seventeenth Army) proceeds favourably this army is to press on behind Croisilles. The further task of this Army Group is to push forward in the general direction Arras–Albert, keep its left wing on the Somme at Péronne, and, intensifying its pressure on the right wing, compel the retirement of the English front facing the Sixth Army,[3] and release further German troops from trench warfare for the general advance. . . .

"3. The German Crown Prince's Army Group will first gain the line of the Somme south of Ormignon stream (this flows into the Somme south of Péronne) and the Crozat Canal (west of La Fère). By pushing on rapidly the Eighteenth Army (the right wing of the Crown Prince's Army Group) is to secure the crossings of the Somme and the Canal."[4]

The objective of the Seventeenth German Army was, therefore, the British positions opposite the line Croisilles–Mœuvres, and that of the Second and of the Eighteenth German Armies, the line from and between Villers Guislain and La Fère. The Cambrai Salient was to be attacked indirectly, but "the Seventeenth and Second were to take the weight off each other in turn, and with their inner wings cut off the enemy holding the Cambrai re-entrant,

---

[1] Ludendorff.
[2] German General Headquarters.
[3] North of the Seventeenth German Army.
[4] Von Hindenburg.

afterwards passing through between Croisilles and Péronne. This advance was to be protected on the south flank by the Eighteenth Army, in combination with the extreme left wing of the Second."

In comparing the forces opposed to his Third and Fifth Armies, Sir Douglas Haig said, " at least sixty-four German divisions took part in the operations of the first day of the battle." Actually the enemy employed seventy-six divisions. The Seventeenth Army consisted of seven corps formed of twenty-eight divisions; the Second Army of five corps formed of twenty-two divisions; and the Eighteenth Army four corps of twenty-six divisions.[1]

Against this formidable array Sir Douglas Haig could only muster thirty-four divisions, two armies each of four corps, formed of seventeen divisions each; more than half the total forces under his command in France and Flanders. Of the Third Army, consisting of the Vth, IVth, VIth, and XVIIth Corps, ten divisions were in the front line and seven in reserve; of the Fifth Army, consisting of the IIIrd, XVIIIth, XIXth, and VIIth Corps, eleven divisions were in line and three infantry and three cavalry divisions were in reserve. All reserves were within one day's march.

The British divisions in line from north to south were: Third Army—4th, 15th, 3rd, 34th, 59th, 6th, 51st, 17th, 63rd, and 47th; Fifth Army (joining up with the right flank of the Third Army at Gonnelieu)—9th, 21st, 16th, 66th, 24th, 61st, 30th, 36th, 14th, and 58th Divisions. The Third Army reserves were: 31st, Guards, 40th, 25th, 41st, 19th, and 2nd Divisions; the Fifth Army reserves were: 39th, 50th, and 20th Infantry Divisions and 1st, 2nd, and 3rd Cavalry Divisions.

The relief of the 2nd Division began on the night of the 19th–20th March, when a brigade of the 47th (London) Division relieved the 99th Infantry Brigade, which marched back to Equancourt (23rd Royal Fusiliers and 1st King's Royal Rifle Corps) and Manancourt (Brigade Headquarters, 99th, Trench Mortars, and 1st Royal Berks). During the 20th March the 5th, 226th, and 483rd Field Companies R.E. were relieved and concentrated in the Metz area.

[1] Seventeenth German Army on the 21st March consisted of 7 corps: 1st Bavarian Reserve, IIIrd Bavarian, VIth Reserve, IXth Reserve, XIVth Reserve, XVIIIth, XIth—28 divisions.
Second German Army on the 21st March consisted of 5 corps: XIIIth, XIVth, XXIIIrd Reserve, XXXIXth Reserve, LIst—22 divisions.
Eighteenth German Army on the 21st March consisted of 4 corps: IIIrd, IXth, XVIIth, IVth Reserve—26 divisions.
There were 13 divisions in the front line on the morning of the 21st; 28 divisions formed the first wave of the attack, 19 divisions formed the second wave, and 16 the third wave.

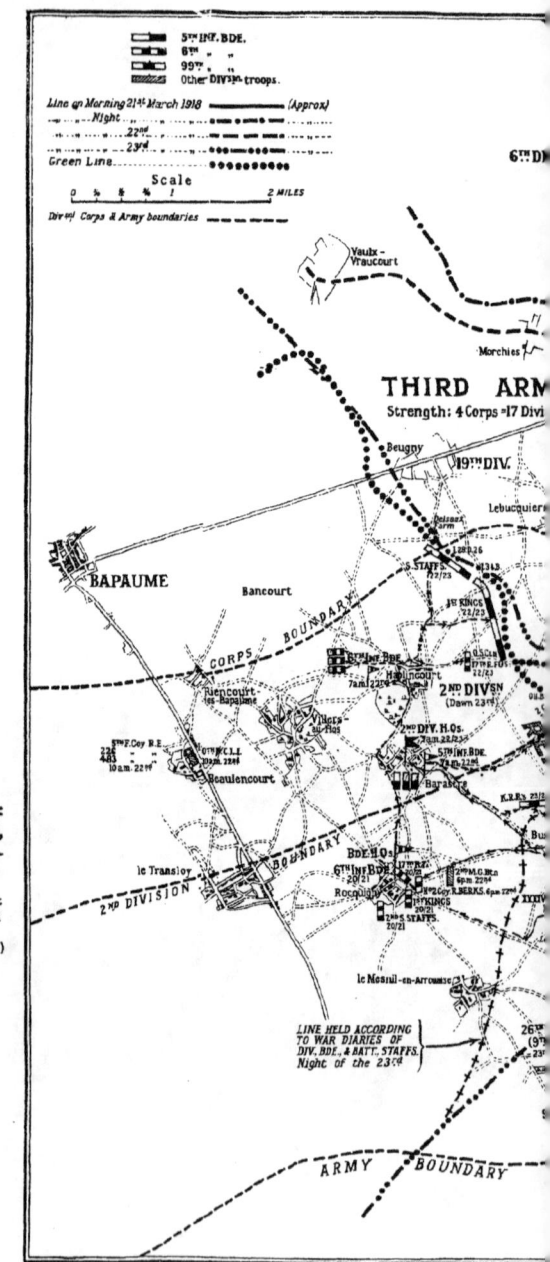

THE GERMAN OFFENSIVES, 1918:
THE BATTLE OF ST. QUENTIN,
21st–23rd March 1918. THE OPERATIONS OF THE 2nd DIVISION.

(N.B.—The difference between the line on the night 23rd March, as given in the Official Dispatches and the War Diaries, should be noted.)

(*Facing p. 540.*)

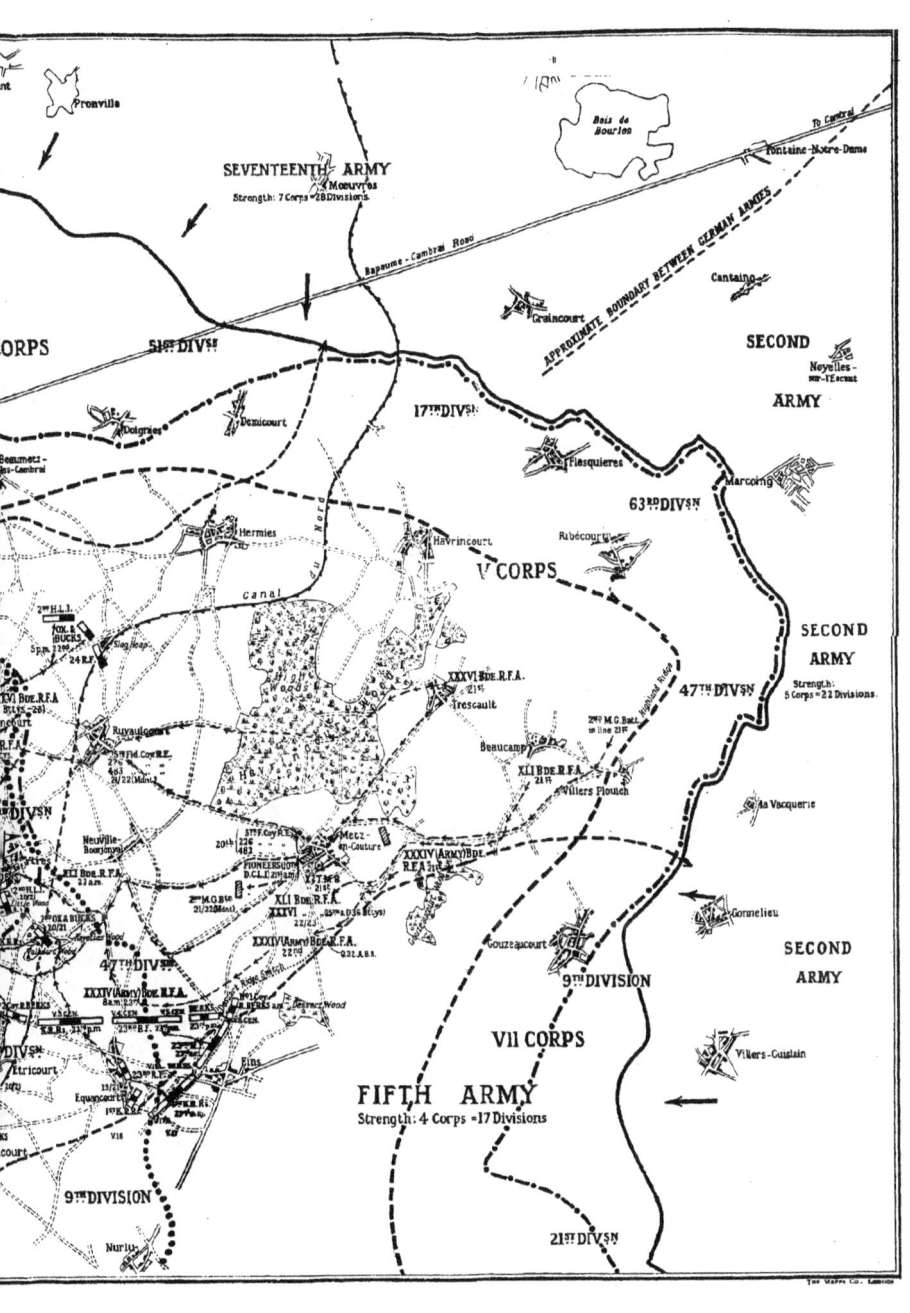

THE GERMAN OFFENSIVE OPENS.

The 5th and 6th Infantry Brigades were relieved on the night of 20th–21st March, the relief being completed at 2 a.m. on the 21st. The 5th Infantry Brigade moved back to Ytres, and the 6th Infantry Brigade to Rocquigny. The Pioneers (10th Duke of Cornwall's Light Infantry) on relief went into billets west of Metz.

The Divisional Artillery and the 2nd Battalion Machine-Gun Corps were still in the line.

THE BATTLE OF ST. QUENTIN,

21st to 23rd March 1918.

All accounts from the German side show the vital importance of the hostile offensive of March 1918. It was to be the enemy's great effort to break through the Allied line, and upon the results depended the very existence of the German Empire: failure would be the beginning of the end. Ludendorff had reported to the German Kaiser that "the army was assembled and well prepared to undertake the biggest task in its history." The balance of man-power was with the enemy; Von Hindenburg admitted this. "For the first time in the whole war," he said, "the Germans would have the advantage of numbers on one of their fronts."[1] The forces were more than two to one against the British, whilst the number of German divisions on the Western front was infinitely superior to the combined forces of the British and French armies, and thousands of guns of all calibres had been massed for the offensive.[2] The results of the German offensive, therefore, depended upon the fighting qualities of the opposing forces, though the enemy had an overwhelming preponderance in man-power and guns. It is well to remember that.

Before dawn on the morning of the 21st March, at 4.50 a.m., the enemy's guns opened fire on the IVth Corps front. The bombardment spread rapidly to the Vth and VIIth Corps areas and farther south. Soon along the whole front of the Third and Fifth British Armies shells of all calibres fell thick and fast on the British gun positions, whilst the rear areas far back were shelled with long-range guns. Large numbers of gas shells were used. General

21ST MARCH. MAP.

---

[1] Von Hindenburg seems to have forgotten Ypres 1914.
[2] According to Ludendorff from 20 to 30 batteries were allotted to each kilometre. On a 30-mile front (the front of attack) this amounted to from 1,000 to 1,500 batteries, "without trench mortars."

542 THE HISTORY OF THE SECOND DIVISION.

Headquarters had known of the enemy's intentions for weeks past, and, with the forces at its disposal, had made whatever dispositions were possible to meet the attack.

As dawn [1] broke, a dense mist obscured the whole battlefield-to-be, hiding S.O.S. signals sent up from the front-line trenches, and also preventing the machine gunners from obtaining that field of view which was absolutely necessary for the efficient working of their guns. The enemy blamed the fog for hiding the objectives given to his troops, but as the latter advanced in mass formation in enormous numbers, in practically continuous lines, his excuses are difficult to understand.[2] On the other hand, for troops on the defensive, the fog had disastrous results, for those in the front-line trenches could not see the enemy until he was within a short distance, nor could the machine gunners or artillery harass the enemy as he was massing for and advancing to the attack. Added, therefore, to the enemy's advantage in numbers must be that of protection by the fog.

At 5.30 a.m. Vth Corps Headquarters ordered the 2nd and 19th Divisions in Corps Reserve to "stand to and prepare to move to positions of assembly."

The relief of the 2nd Division had been completed by 2 a.m., but command of the sector was timed to pass from General Pereira (2nd Division) to General Gorringe (47th Division) at 6 a.m. On account of the impending attack, however, the 47th Division took over the front at 5.35 a.m., for there was no longer any doubt that an offensive on a large scale was about to be launched by the enemy. For two hours the enemy's artillery continued to shell the gun positions of the Third and Fifth Armies and as far back as St. Pol. And then, shortly before 9 a.m., the enemy's batteries were switched on to the trenches, minenwerfer joining in the bombardment. Under cover of an intense barrage the enemy's troops advanced to the attack.

[1] The actual time of the attack varied in different sectors, but by 9.45 a.m. the action had become general along the whole front. On the French front east and west of Rheims, and the British front between the Scarpe and Loos, violent bombardments were opened, whilst the trenches from La Bassée Canal to the Lys were heavily shelled with gas ; practically the whole line from Rheims to the sea at Dunkirk was ablaze with artillery fire.

[2] The enemy appears to have concentrated his artillery fire on certain tactical features—*i.e.*, the high ground—and then launched his infantry against them. Having captured them, the Germans enfiladed the British troops holding the lower ground, and then the whole line advanced to the next objective. The enemy failed because he expected his leading troops to go on *ad infinitum* instead of passing fresh troops through in order to capture succeeding objectives. Thus the leading troops became exhausted.

ACTION OF 2ND DIVISION ON 21ST MARCH.

With the exception of the Flesquières Salient,[1] from opposite the whole British line from La Fère to Croisilles, the enemy's troops surged across No Man's Land in vast numbers. There had been no such attack in the whole War. The battle-front was practically divided into two parts—northern and southern. In the former the Seventeenth German Army attacked from a point approximately south of Mœuvres to Croisilles; in the latter, from opposite Gouzeaucourt to La Fère. On the left-flank division (9th) of the VIIth Corps, Fifth Army, and the right-flank division (51st) of the IVth Corps, Third Army, the enemy's attacks fell heavily indeed, for a successful thrust at these two points would have entailed the immediate evacuation of the Flesquières Salient, held by the Vth Corps, Third Army.

The 2nd Division, however, spent the 21st March resting and reorganizing after two strenuous months in the front line. The last week (from the 13th to the 20th), during which the Division had suffered over 3,000 gas casualties, had played havoc with the men, who were, nevertheless, in good fettle despite their losses. The Division had to "stand fast" throughout the day, and assembly positions were detailed should it be necessary for the troops to move forward. The 10th Duke of Cornwall's Light Infantry were moved out in front of Metz (to the Metz Salient) during the morning, but in the afternoon were ordered to withdraw to billets in Lechelle.

On the night of the 21st March the 2nd Division remained in Vth Corps Reserve disposed as in the morning. The Divisional Artillery and the 2nd Battalion Machine-Gun Corps were in the line, still unrelieved, and the following extracts, describing the course of events, are from the official records of these two arms of the service: "A very heavy enemy bombardment started at 4.40 a.m., and all guns opened with counter-preparation, searching back from S.O.S. lines. During the early part of the bombardment the batteries in the Trescault valley all received attention, and also the 48th Battery in Bear Valley and Brigade Headquarters. A good deal of phosgene gas was used. The enemy attack was clearly mostly on the north and south, and on our front only a local attack of apparently small depth was made. The front line was, however, entered in one or two places, as it was, of course, lightly held, and after severe and partially successful counter-attacks, it was eventually decided to come back to the Highland Ridge line. This was done during the night (21st). The batteries were firing pretty

[1] Known to the enemy as the "Cambrai Re-entrant."

constantly all day for S.O.S. or counter-preparation, and a good many shoots were carried out at the request of the infantry. About midnight orders were received for two 18-pounder batteries to come out and rendezvous near Bertincourt under the 17th Divisional Artillery, and the 48th and 71st Batteries were detailed to fall out by 2 a.m. This was satisfactorily done without much interference. Wagon lines in Haplincourt were very heavily shelled all day with 4.2 and H.V. guns. Batteries were not much damaged, but 15th Battery moved into the open during the night." [1]

The XLIst Brigade R.F.A. was similarly engaged all day, and was successful in breaking up hostile parties of the enemy. "The 16th and 17th Batteries near Beaucamp were neutralised during the beginning of the attack with gas. . . . Both batteries fired for four and a half hours in their gas masks, the 16th suffering several casualties. . . . During the night 21st–22nd the forward batteries retired to the Metz positions covering the Highland Ridge line." [2]

The third account is taken from an official report by the XXXIVth (Army) Brigade R.F.A. This brigade had formed part of the 2nd Divisional Artillery which went out to France in August 1914, but in March 1917, on becoming an army brigade, had reluctantly severed its connection with the 2nd Division. For some while previous to the 21st March the brigade had been under the Vth Corps of the Third Army, and was in action in and around Gouzeaucourt Wood, Brigade Headquarters being adjacent to the Headquarters of 99th Infantry Brigade, and, on the relief of the latter, the 140th Infantry Brigade (47th Division). The brigade then "found itself once again fighting alongside its old comrades of the XXXVIth and XLIst Brigades R.F.A., and once again helping to support those same old well-seasoned infantry brigades, the 5th, 6th, and 99th. Many memories were recalled of former fights—notably Mons, the Marne, First Battle of Ypres, Festubert and Givenchy, Loos, Vimy, Serre and Beaumont Hamel, the Somme (1916), and that severe winter on the Ancre in 1916–17. Since then the brigade had been wandering about from corps to corps and from division to division, fighting throughout the Battle of Arras and Messines, and after that for a very arduous six months in the Ypres Salient throughout the Third Battle, when its casualties in officers alone amounted to 27." [3] The brigade consisted

[1] Diary of XXXVIth Brigade R.F.A.
[2] Diary of XLIst Brigade R.F.A.
[3] Narrative by XXXIVth (Army) Brigade R.F.A.

of the 50th, 56th, and 70th, and C/34th Batteries, and was commanded by Lieut.-Colonel C. E. P. Parry, D.S.O.

"Guns were well dug in and camouflaged; two deep mine shafts had been sunk by each position, connecting up underground. Each battery was armed with a Lewis gun for defence against low-flying planes or attacking infantry. A rifle squad was told off; a semicircle of barbed wire was planted 60 to 100 yards in front of the guns. A position for six guns was constructed for a reinforcing battery, or as an alternative position if needed; in this position 900 rounds of 18-pounder ammunition was dumped. Some 1,000 yards south of Metz each battery had constructed a dug-in position to which it could withdraw when ordered, and in which 2,400 rounds were dumped. Positions still farther in rear nearly 1,000 yards north of the village of Equancourt had been reconnoitred and fixed. All the above positions were subsequently occupied by the batteries, though unfortunately only for a few hours."[1]

The brigade had been engaged all day, though under difficulties, "all ranks suffering more or less from the effects of gas—loss of voice, sore throat, watery eyes, and all the symptoms, in fact, of a severe cold in the head. . . . Eventually, during the night, the forward sections of the 70th, 50th, and 56th Batteries were withdrawn (to their rear positions south of Metz). . . . These forward sections had been having a bad time, but had done good work and managed to fire off a large stock of ammunition. In withdrawing the forward section of the 56th (Howitzer) Battery, Lieut. Dunlop earned the D.S.O. This section all through the day had suffered severely, Lieut. Fetherstonhaugh and all the men, excepting two signallers and a sergeant, being put out of action by shell-fire and gas. Lieut. Dunlop went forward from the battery main position, and, although wounded, he restored the situation sufficiently to fire off the remaining rounds, evacuate the wounded, and safely withdraw the guns. By 5 a.m. the sections that had retired from the forward positions during the night were all in action in their new positions south of Metz."

From the diary of the 2nd Battalion Machine-Gun Corps it is evident the enemy put down a smoke barrage to mask his movements: "Owing to the enemy using dense smoke clouds which were suspected to be mixed with gas, all rations at Battalion Headquarters which were not in closed tins were destroyed. The smoke had been very dense for about half an hour, at Battalion

[1] Narrative by XXXIVth (Army) Brigade R.F.A.

546   THE HISTORY OF THE SECOND DIVISION.

Headquarters it being impossible to see more than about one yard."

During the night of the 21st–22nd March the 47th Division withdrew to the Highland Ridge, and the 2nd Battalion Machine-Gun Corps was relieved and marched back to camp west of Metz.

But it is apparent from Ludendorff's statements that the first day of the German offensive had not realized all the enemy's anticipations. In evident disappointment the Chief of the German General Staff reported: "The Seventeenth Army, which had the strongest enemy in front of it, *only reached his second line*. The barrage had gone too far ahead ; the infantry had lost touch with it. They remained in this position lying down, with no artillery support. In the Second Army attack the co-operation between the infantry and the artillery was better. The infantry penetrated into the enemy's second position. With the Eighteenth Army everything proceeded as intended. It was making good progress."[1]

At midnight on the 21st–22nd March the units of the 2nd Division were located as follows : Divisional Headquarters—Etricourt ; 5th Infantry Brigade—Ytres and Lechelle ; 6th Infantry Brigade—Rocquigny ; 99th Infantry Brigade—Manancourt and Equancourt ; 10th Duke of Cornwall's Light Infantry—Lechelle ; 2nd Battalion Machine-Gun Corps—in camp west of Metz ; 5th, 226th, and 483rd Field Companies R.E.—Metz ; XXXVIth Brigade R.F.A.—48th and 71st Batteries near Bertrancourt, 15th and D/36th Batteries at Trescault ; XLIst Brigade R.F.A.—Beaucamp ; XXXIVth (Army) Brigade R.F.A.—south of Metz.

22ND MARCH.

Half an hour after midnight—21st–22nd—2nd Division Headquarters received orders from Vth Corps to concentrate (less 99th Infantry Brigade and one machine-gun company) in the Barastre-Haplincourt area, the concentration to be completed by 7 a.m. on the 22nd. The Division was also ordered to be prepared to occupy the Green Line from the Haplincourt–Bertincourt road northwards, including, if necessary, that portion of the Green Line in the southern sector of the IVth Corps area. Divisional Headquarters were to be in Barastre, with one infantry brigade ; the other infantry brigade west of Haplincourt.

At 7 a.m. on the 22nd, 2nd Division Headquarters reported to Corps Headquarters the following dispositions : Divisional Head-

[1] The map shows the progress made by the enemy on both flanks of the Vth Corps on the 21st March and following days. The lines are as given in the Official Dispatches, with the exception of the night of 23rd March, when there is an important variation in the British line about Ytres and Bus. In the Official Dispatches the line given in this instance is incorrect.

THE GREEN LINE.

quarters and 5th Infantry Brigade—Barastre; 6th Infantry Brigade —west of Haplincourt; 99th Infantry Brigade—Manancourt and Equancourt; 5th, 226th, and 483rd Field Companies R.E., and 10th Duke of Cornwall's Light Infantry—Beaulencourt; 2nd Battalion Machine-Gun Corps in process of relief (in Metz) by Machine-Gun Battalion of the 47th Division and moving back to Rocquigny.

Hitherto, fighting along the Vth Corps front had not been heavy, and the 17th, 63rd, and 47th Divisions had little difficulty in holding the enemy. But immediately north and south of the Corps boundaries the enemy had succeeded in forcing back the flanking divisions of the IVth Corps (Third Army) and the VIIth Corps (Fifth Army), which necessitated the withdrawal of the Vth Corps to a line east of Hermies and Havrincourt, west of Ribécourt and the line Villers Plouich–Gouzeaucourt.

The 2nd Division had barely reported its concentration in the Barastre–Haplincourt area, when it became evident that the Vth Corps was preparing to move back to the Green Line. In this event the Division would be required to move forward and hold the Green Line from about P.2,B.3.1 to the northern Corps boundary about I.28,d.2.6, with the 5th Infantry Brigade on the right and the 6th Infantry Brigade on the left, the inter-brigade boundary cutting the line about O.11,b.9.6. The 63rd Division (Vth Corps) would be on the right and the 19th Division (IVth Corps) on the left of the 2nd Division.

The Green Line, or the rear zone, ran east of Equancourt, Ytres, and Bertincourt, thence due west to O.5 central, thence north-west to the northern Corps boundary, a mile and a half west of Velu.

During the evening officers of the 5th and 6th Infantry Brigades, and the officer commanding the Machine-Gun Battalion, reconnoitred the Green Line, the latter selecting gun positions in rear of each brigade. The Pioneer Battalion and two Field Companies were placed at the disposal of Third Army Headquarters for work in the Green Line.

Shortly before noon the 17th Division, holding the line in front of Hermies, was strongly attacked by the enemy, and at 1.30 p.m., on instructions from Vth Corps Headquarters, the 5th Infantry Brigade was sent to report to the 17th Division at Bertincourt. At 5 p.m. the three battalions of the brigade were disposed in the following line: 24th Royal Fusiliers on the right, astride the Canal du Nord; the 2nd Oxford and Bucks in the centre, facing north-east; and the 2nd Highland Light Infantry on the left, facing north, and about one mile east of Velu Wood.

About midday also information had been received that the enemy had broken through at Vaulx-Vraucourt, five miles north-west of Barastre, and the 6th Infantry Brigade, followed by two sections of the Machine-Gun Battalion, moved up to occupy the Green Line from I.34,b. to the Cambrai–Bapaume road. On arrival in the Green Line the 56th Infantry Brigade of the 19th Division was found to be holding the line south of the Cambrai–Bapaume road allotted to the 1st King's. The latter battalion, therefore, took up a position in artillery formation about 800 yards south-east of Fremicourt; the 2nd South Staffords occupied the line from Delsaux Farm southwards, and during the evening (at 8 p.m.) the King's moved up to their right; the 17th Royal Fusiliers remained in reserve east of Haplincourt.

Meanwhile the position of the 99th Infantry Brigade in Manancourt and Equancourt was not one to be envied. Cut off from its own Division and attached to the 47th Division, with an uncertain situation (rapidly becoming worse) on its right, constantly in receipt of orders and counter-orders, Brigade Headquarters in Manancourt had, at 1.50 p.m., received verbal orders from Vth Corps Headquarters to reconnoitre the Green Line from Nurlu to Equancourt; the Brigade was also from this time placed under the direct orders of Vth Corps. In the event of a move being necessary, the 1st King's Royal Rifles were to occupy a position on the right, the 23rd Royal Fusiliers on the left, and the 1st Royal Berks were to remain in brigade reserve.

At 4 p.m. the Green Line was reported to be about 3 feet deep, with three belts of wire in front and with support trenches also sited.

The situation was, however, still obscure on the flanks, and at 5.40 p.m. messages were sent to the 26th Infantry Brigade (9th Division) on the right, and to the 140th Infantry Brigade (47th Division) on the left, asking for details of the situation. A Staff captain of the 26th Infantry Brigade called at 99th Infantry Brigade Headquarters at 6.15 p.m., giving dispositions, and confirmed the report that his brigade would fall back to the Green Line that night. On receipt of this information Brigadier-General Barnett Barker decided to withdraw the 23rd Royal Fusiliers and the 1st King's Royal Rifles from Equancourt to Etricourt to facilitate the occupation of the Green Line. On reporting his intentions to Vth Corps Headquarters, however, he was told to keep the two battalions in Equancourt, as they might be required to occupy the Green Line Switch from V.17,a. to V.6 central, east of Equancourt.

A GAP IN THE LINE. 549

At 8 p.m. the 99th Infantry Brigade was attached to the 9th Division, Fifth Army.

The 23rd Royal Fusiliers and the King's Royal Rifles then set out to reconnoitre the Green Line Switch from east of Equancourt to Dessart Ridge, and to hold it with posts for liaison with the 9th Division (right) and the 47th Division (left). The Rifles, however, found the 9th Black Watch as far north as V.11 central, thus shortening the line allocated to the 99th Infantry Brigade.

At 10.20 p.m. a wounded officer of the South African Brigade informed the Officer Commanding King's Royal Rifles that his brigade on the right had been severely handled, and the Rifles at once set out for the Green Line Switch, this movement being made in conjunction with the Officer Commanding 23rd Royal Fusiliers, who moved up his battalion into V.11 and V.6, in order to form a defensive flank to protect Equancourt, into which bullets were already beginning to fall.

Streams of traffic through Manancourt, artillery and infantry, with considerable details from labour companies coming from the direction of Nurlu and Moislains, brought rumours of an enemy break-through on the right, and at 11.20 p.m. a dispatch rider was sent from 99th Infantry Brigade Headquarters, in Manancourt, to the 23rd Royal Fusiliers and King's Royal Rifles with a message to hold on to their line at all costs. The Berkshires in Manancourt were ordered to stand to arms and defend the village instead of reinforcing the 23rd Royal Fusiliers as they had previously been ordered to do. Two guns of the 2nd Battalion Machine-Gun Corps, attached to the brigade, were also sent to the Officer Commanding 23rd Royal Fusiliers.

At 11.30 p.m. it was ascertained that, though touch on the right had been established with the 9th Division and the line was held up to V.6 central, the left flank of the 23rd Royal Fusiliers had not yet gained touch with the right of the 47th Division. And it was not until 1.45 a.m. (23rd March), when a belated order (timed 6.50 p.m., 22nd March) reached 99th Infantry Brigade Headquarters, that the right of the 47th Division was found at Q.32,a.8.8, there being a gap of about 2,000 yards between the right of that division and the left of the 99th Infantry Brigade. On learning the situation, Vth Corps Headquarters ordered the 140th Infantry Brigade (47th Division) to fill the gap in the line before 5 a.m. on the 23rd.

Throughout the night the Fusiliers and the Rifles were busy consolidating their positions and in patrol work. The enemy was found to be holding Fins in strength, and was digging-in at about 300 yards from the front line held by the 99th Infantry Brigade, whilst from the machine-gun fire and constant shelling it was clear that, as soon as the day dawned, the enemy would attempt to advance his troops still farther west.

It will be observed that hitherto the 2nd Division had taken no active part in the fighting which since the 21st had been raging desperately on both flanks of the Vth Corps and only half-heartedly along the front of the Flesquières Salient. The constant movement had, however, tried the troops considerably, and having only just come out of the line after a two months' tour of a very trying nature, were in a somewhat exhausted condition when they became involved in the fighting. Their numbers were also greatly diminished. The approximate fighting strength of the 99th Infantry Brigade was: 23rd Royal Fusiliers—20 officers and 350 other ranks; 1st Royal Berks—20 officers and 404 other ranks formed into two companies; 1st King's Royal Rifle Corps—20 officers and 320 other ranks formed into three companies; the 99th Trench Mortar Battery had only 2 officers and 41 other ranks. The 6th Infantry Brigade numbered: 17th Royal Fusiliers—16 officers and 428 other ranks; 1st King's—20 officers and 410 other ranks; 2nd South Staffords—21 officers and 529 other ranks. The strength of the 5th Infantry Brigade was not obtainable, but the brigade was also much depleted.

During the night of the 22nd–23rd March the situation developed rapidly. At 10.15 p.m. the enemy, having broken through the IVth Corps front on both sides of Morchies, was reported advancing down the Cambrai–Bapaume road. This involved a general retirement to the Green Line, and in orders received from Vth Corps at 1.40 a.m. on the 23rd the 2nd Division was ordered to hold the Green Line from the Corps northern boundary to P.2,b.3.1; the 63rd Division would be on the right and the 19th Division (IVth Corps) on the left, and the 17th Division was to fall back through the 2nd Division in order to reform in the area west of Villers-au-Flos. The 5th Infantry Brigade, on receipt of these orders, returned to the 2nd Division.

23RD MARCH.
At dawn on the 23rd March the situation of the 2nd Division was as follows: " The order of units from right to left : 5th Infantry Brigade—52nd (Oxford and Bucks) Light Infantry, 24th Royal Fusiliers (less two companies), 2nd Highland Light Infantry; two companies of 24th Royal Fusiliers in reserve about the Bertincourt–Haplincourt road. 6th Infantry Brigade—1st King's, 2nd South Staffords, with the 17th Royal Fusiliers in reserve. 99th

THE ADVANCING ENEMY PAYS TOLL.

Infantry Brigade (at disposal of the 9th Division, VIIth Corps, Fifth Army)—23rd Royal Fusiliers and 1st King's Royal Rifle Corps from V.17,a. to V.6 central; 1st Royal Berks in reserve in Manancourt. Of the Divisional Artillery—all batteries of the XXXIVth (Army) Brigade R.F.A. were in action about a mile north of Equancourt; the XXXVIth Brigade R.F.A. was in front of Bertincourt and the XLIst Brigade R.F.A. was south-west of Neuville, with all batteries covering the retirement of the 142nd Infantry Brigade (47th Division).

The Pioneers (10th Duke of Cornwall's Light Infantry) were sent up during the morning to work at a line from 0.5 central northwards. They were assisted by the 5th and 226th Field Companies. The line was only spit-locked, and had a single belt of wire in front of it. Throughout the morning, under intermittent shell-fire, the preparation of platoon posts with Lewis-gun positions proceeded with great spirit, the infantry having to use their entrenching tools owing to a shortage of other implements. By the time the enemy reached Velu Wood, which was soon after midday, and could get his machine guns into position, all the men had sufficient cover. The guns of the 2nd Battalion Machine-Gun Corps were disposed in depth in three lines so as to bring cross-bands of fire in rear of the lines in front and also protect the flanks.

During the morning elements of the 17th and 19th Divisions had withdrawn from the high ground east of Lebucquière, which they had held during the night of the 22nd–23rd. These stragglers were stopped by company commanders of the 2nd Division in order to strengthen the thinly held line.

When the mist lifted at 10.30 a.m. hostile shell-fire was still heavy, but gradually died down, and during the afternoon the enemy's guns were fairly quiet. But as the enemy's infantry advanced over the ridge at Lebucquière with his machine guns and trench mortars he provided fine targets for the Divisional Lewis Gunners in the front line, and very heavy losses were inflicted on him. At one period the Germans got within 50 yards of the Oxford and Bucks, but there their line was broken and decimated, and they could get no farther. Unfortunately all communications were cut, and it was impossible to get into touch with the guns; thus splendid targets which frequently offered themselves could not be dealt with by the Divisional Artillery. The guns of the XXXVIth Brigade R.F.A., however, caught large numbers of the enemy advancing from the southern edge of Velu Wood, and, firing over open sights, inflicted considerable losses on him and held up his attack.

At 11.30 a.m. 2nd Divisional Headquarters opened at Beaulencourt.

Throughout the remainder of the 23rd no serious attack upon the 5th or 6th Infantry Brigades of the 2nd Division materialized, the situation being described in the Diaries as "quiet." But the 99th Infantry Brigade had been heavily engaged all day. It will be remembered that the brigade had been placed under the orders of the 9th Division. This division, which formed the left flank of the Fifth Army, had been hard pressed by the enemy, and had most gallantly frustrated every attempt to effect a break-through between the Third and Fifth Armies. But the left flank of the 21st Division (on the right of the 9th Division) had been forced back, and in order to conform the right of the 9th had also to be thrown back; this involved the centre and left, and early on the morning of the 23rd the General Officer Commanding 9th Division ordered a retirement to positions west of the Moislains–Manancourt road, "direction being taken from the right." This information (in the form of a copy of the order) reached the 99th Infantry Brigade at 7.50 a.m., and at 8.35 a.m. orders outlining the throwing out of a defensive flank were received by the 23rd Royal Fusiliers and 1st King's Royal Rifles, then holding the Green Line Switch from V.17,a. to V.6 central. Four (and later, two more) guns of the Machine Gun Battalion were sent up to take up positions in V.4 and V.2. A company, No. 1 (the battalion being organized into two companies, Nos. 1 and 2), of the 1st Royal Berks was sent off to the 23rd Royal Fusiliers to strengthen the left flank of that battalion.

Definite instructions for the formation of a defensive flank were issued at 9.50 a.m., the line running from the Beetroot Factory in V.2 central (which was to be the point of junction with the 26th Infantry Brigade, 9th Division) through V.3 to 4 and 5 to V.6 central. No. 2 Company of the Berkshires with Battalion Headquarters was ordered to hold from the Beetroot Factory to the railway; the 1st King's Royal Rifle Corps from the railway inclusive to V.4 central, and the 23rd Royal Fusiliers with No. 1 Company of the Berkshires from V.4 central to V.6 central; the length of line was about 4,000 yards. These dispositions were agreed upon both by the General Officers Commanding 99th and 26th Infantry Brigades and the General Officer Commanding 9th Division. The right flank brigade of the 47th Division later took over the line from V.4 to V.6 central, as the 99th Infantry Brigade was too weak to hold such a length of front, especially in view of the great strength opposed to it.

THE DEFENSIVE FLANK. 553

The formation of this defensive flank was a hazardous enterprise, for it involved the movement of troops in broad daylight over exposed ground to new dispositions across a valley and along the forward slope of the high ground above Equancourt, against which the enemy in wave after wave was rapidly advancing.

The closest reading of the official Diaries does not reveal exactly what happened from this time onward; there are no actual facts upon which to base comment. It is therefore impossible to give anything but a somewhat dislocated account of the day's fighting.

No. 2 Company of the 1st Royal Berks with Battalion Headquarters arrived at the Beetroot Factory (where they were to hold the right of the defensive flank) shortly before 12.30 p.m. Their arrival at the factory was followed immediately by that of the enemy in large numbers; the Rifles, who had been ordered to continue the line on the left towards V.6 central, had not yet arrived (that battalion having over 1,000 yards to move back), and as touch could not be obtained on either flank the Berkshires fell back, a bitter rearguard action ensuing. The withdrawal was carried out by stages via the Cemetery, Lechelle Wood, Le Mesnil-en-Arrouaise to Rocquigny. Each step was contested, the men fighting gallantly between the Cemetery and Lechelle all the afternoon. At dusk the village was reached, and here Lieut.-Colonel G. P. Hunt, C.M.G., D.S.O., commanding 1st Royal Berks Regiment, was killed " rallying and organizing his men," the records have it, " as he had done over and over again during the day to resist the incessant assaults of the enemy, who were at this time reinforced by cavalry." The survivors of No. 2 Company on reaching Rocquigny attached themselves to troops of the 47th Division. Here they spent the night.

The 1st King's Royal Rifles had received their orders about 11 a.m. The battalion was at this period organized in three companies—A, C, and D. Under heavy fire from field guns, machine guns, and low-flying aeroplanes the withdrawal was carried out, C Company moving back through A to the left of the new front, followed by A to the centre, and then D, who on retiring was to take up positions on the right.

The new position was occupied between 12.30 and 1.30 p.m. The next sentence in the Battalion Diary reads somewhat ironically : " 1 p.m. Our new position, which was on top of a hill, was subjected to intense machine-gun fire, and many casualties occurred while the men were digging in. This was particularly the case on the right, where no touch could be obtained with the 1st Royal Berks."

It should be remembered that when these two battalions received their orders to form the defensive flank, the Berkshires were in Manancourt and the Rifles just east of Equancourt.

From their position on the hill top the Rifles could see successive waves of the enemy advancing into the Etricourt valley in V.16 and V.17 with patrols and machine guns pushed out in front, and field guns and transport coming down in rear. Fire was opened on them with Lewis guns, but the Rifles were without Vickers guns, and although the enemy lost heavily his advance could not be checked. Touch had, however, been obtained with the right flank of the 23rd Royal Fusiliers. A little later Battalion Headquarters moved north to a spoil heap by the Canal du Nord. By this time a serious gap existed between the right of the Vth Corps (Third Army) and the left of the VIIth Corps (Fifth Army). Touch, as has already been shown, had not been gained between the 99th Infantry Brigade (1st Royal Berks of the 2nd Division) and the 26th Infantry Brigade (9th Division) at the Beetroot Factory. What happened to the Berkshires, at that period the extreme right of the Third Army, has already been shown; the extreme left of the Fifth Army—*i.e.*, the 26th Infantry Brigade— seems to have been withdrawn west of the Moislains–Manancourt road.[1]

The enemy rapidly exploited the gap between the two armies, and the right flank of the Rifles was attacked again and again, but held firm. The tenacity of these troops was splendid. The Rifles numbered only 320 men, and of these not more than 70 had been with the battalion more than a month.

At 2 o'clock the Commanding Officer of the 23rd Royal Fusiliers visited Lieut.-Colonel Stafford (King's Royal Rifle Corps), and told him that, in consequence of the enemy having forced back the right of the 47th Division, he was swinging back his left flank to conform. C Company of the Rifles (in touch with the right of the 23rd Royal Fusiliers), seeing the retirement of the left of the Fusiliers, and imagining that the whole of that battalion was retiring, fell back on to the eastern ridge of Vallulart Wood, thus leaving the right flank of the Fusiliers in the air. A and D Companies of the

---

[1] "At 7.30 a.m. on the 23rd orders from the 9th Division confirmed earlier rumours that the Green Line would not be held, but a retirement made to positions west of the Moislains–Manancourt road. At 11.30 a.m. the 99th Infantry Brigade Headquarters moved to Le Mesnil simultaneously with the 26th Infantry Brigade Headquarters, as machine-gun fire was already beginning to reach Manancourt and elements of the 26th Infantry Brigade were retiring in open order to the west of the Moislains–Manancourt road."—*Official Report*, 2nd Division Headquarters.

Rifles fell back with C, as the enemy was already working round the right flank of the battalion in large numbers. Behind Vallulart Wood the 142nd Infantry Brigade (47th Division) had taken up its position between the wood and Lechelle. Here Colonel Stafford placed himself under the command of the General Officer Commanding 142nd Brigade, and withdrew his men to the left flank of the latter, which, although in the air, was covered by troops seen to be retiring from Little Wood, Ytres.

From 5.30 p.m. until just before 7 p.m. the village of Lechelle and all ground in the vicinity was shelled heavily by H.V. guns and field guns. Many aeroplanes also circled low over the troops, coming down to within 100 yards of the ground and firing their machine guns wherever a target offered itself. No reply could be made to this machine-gunning, as the Rifles were short of small-arms ammunition. At 7 o'clock the situation was much quieter, but numbers of troops could still be seen withdrawing, and the enemy was still making frantic efforts to envelop the right flank of the Rifles. A retirement by companies was then ordered, and although the shelling was still heavy and the enemy's machine guns were very active, the battalion reached a point about 200 yards west of Bus. Here, about 7.45 p.m., the battalion reorganized. Just north of Bus were two companies and Battalion Headquarters of the 24th Royal Fusiliers. Leaving Major Brady in charge of the battalion, Colonel Stafford went over to Barastre and there interviewed the General Officer Commanding 5th Infantry Brigade. "It was obvious," said the Colonel in his report, "that that part of the 2nd Division facing north had no idea how serious the situation was south. This proved to be the case, as the Vth Corps flatly refused to believe that the enemy was in Lechelle." At 8.30 p.m. touch had been established on both flanks, and D and C Companies were ordered to picquet Bus. But half an hour later D Company's picquets on the left of the village were driven in by the enemy. A counter-attack was immediately ordered; but just as operations were about to begin a large dump of big shells north of Bus caught fire and blew up with a tremendous roar: the projected counter-attack was stopped. C Company's picquets were now driven in by the enemy, who had received large reinforcements. The position west of the village was then consolidated, and here, with two companies of the 24th Royal Fusiliers on the right, cold, hungry, and thirsty, and without rations, the Rifles proceeded to pass a most uncomfortable night.

Meanwhile the 23rd Royal Fusiliers and No. 1 Company of the

Berkshires on the withdrawal of the 1st King's Royal Rifle Corps had readjusted their line.

It has already been stated that on the retirement of the right of the 47th Division on the left of the 23rd Royal Fusiliers, the left flank company of the latter had necessarily to be thrown back: this was the movement which was mistaken by the Rifles for a general retirement. On seeing the Rifles retired, the Officer Commanding 23rd Royal Fusiliers had to move another company to protect the right flank of his battalion. An attack now developed against the Fusiliers and the Berkshires, but was beaten off. By 3 p.m., however, it was obvious that the line could not be maintained, for the enemy was working round the right flank, whilst on the left the 20th Londons, who were holding that part of the line, were retiring. Orders were then given to the Fusiliers and Berkshires to retire, fighting a rearguard action.

This withdrawal was effected through Hayettes Wood, on Ytres. North of Hayettes Wood the Fusiliers and Berkshires re-formed, and under brigade orders marched via Ytres, Bus, and Rocquigny to Le Transloy. About 60 casualties occurred during the rearguard action. In Le Transloy the 23rd Royal Fusiliers and the Berkshires went into bivouacs; the former now numbered 200 and the latter 60 men.

In spite of retirement in the face of overwhelming numbers the offensive spirit of the troops was excellent, as the following story demonstrates: When the Berkshires left Equancourt to take up their position north-west of that place, they found their entrenching tools insufficient with which to dig themselves in. Private Crabtree at once volunteered to take a party back to the village and draw tools from a dump. He set off and took his men to Equancourt. He found the dump in possession of the enemy; but without hesitation he and his men attacked the Germans, killed 6 of them and routed the remainder, about 10 men. His party then drew tools and returned with them.

In his summary of the operations of the 2nd Division on the 23rd March the General Officer Commanding Division said: " The fighting of 23rd March, therefore, mainly developed upon the 99th Infantry Brigade and XXXIVth (Army) Brigade R.F.A. The former was given a very difficult task—the hope of maintaining liaison between the Vth and VIIth Corps—and the battalions were out of touch with Brigade Headquarters from 11 a.m. until dusk. General Barnett Barker (General Officer Commanding 99th Infantry Brigade), with his Brigade Major, had ridden out in the early after-

THE GUNS RETIRE. 557

noon to attempt to reach his battalions, but this proved to be impossible, and it seemed unlikely that any unit of the brigade would manage to extricate itself from the rapid enveloping movements of the enemy. It is highly to the credit of the battalion and company commanders that, after holding on grimly till their flanks were completely turned, they continued to dispute every yard of ground with the enemy and to extricate their men from position after position. The brigade was disintegrated. At nightfall, when Brigade Headquarters with the transport was established near Windmill Mound on the main road south-east of Le Transloy, only the 23rd Royal Fusiliers, one company of the 1st Royal Berks, and the Trench Mortar Battery had been recovered; in all about 350 ranks. The 1st King's Royal Rifle Corps was in touch with the 5th Infantry Brigade, and was holding the ground just west of Bus, while the remainder of the 1st Royal Berks was at Rocquigny with troops of the 47th Division."

Although attached for tactical purposes to the 47th Division, the XXXIVth (Army) Brigade R.F.A. and its action of 23rd March are of peculiar and twofold interest to the 2nd Division. The fact that the brigade formed part of the 2nd Divisional Artillery at Mons in 1914 is in itself sufficient to warrant inclusion in the Divisional History; and on the 23rd its guns covered not only the 47th Division, but helped to beat off furious attacks on the hard-tried infantry of the 99th Infantry Brigade.

During the night of the 22nd–23rd the XXXIVth Brigade had retired to gun positions previously reconnoitred and selected, about one mile north of Equancourt. The 50th and 70th Batteries were the first to retire, followed by the 56th and D/34. Brigade Headquarters, however, did not move back immediately, and in consequence, in the early morning of 23rd, barely escaped capture, the enemy being on three sides of it when Headquarters moved back under cover of the 47th Divisional Artillery.

By about 6 a.m. all batteries were in action behind a crest north of Equancourt. Dessart Wood, reported strongly held by the enemy's machine guns and infantry, was shelled until 9.30 a.m. But during the morning it was evident that a further retirement would have to take place, as the gunners could see that the Fifth Army was retiring westwards. No authentic information was obtainable as to the position of the infantry, for at that period the defensive flank from V.2 to V.6 had not been formed. But from an infantry officer in charge of a body of men who were then falling back from north-west of Equancourt it was evident that already the situation in the front line was serious. " This line my men are holding," said this officer to the gunners, " will be the front line in a few minutes." The said line was the battery positions of the brigade. Machine-gun bullets had already begun to fall in rear of the guns. Thereupon some of the batteries limbered up and drew out of the line. The 70th, under Major Gaunt, moved off towards Ytres, where north of the station a section of howitzers came into action and opened fire on the approaches towards Fins and Metz. By this time the position north of Equancourt was critical; the 50th Battery was now under indirect machine-gun fire, and hurriedly limbered up. At noon a withdrawal was ordered to selected positions just east of Lechelle, from which the guns could cover the infantry. All the crossings over the Canal du Nord and the railway at Ytres were under a heavy artillery and machine-gun barrage, but the guns drew out to their new positions in an orderly and methodical manner.

By this time supplies of both ammunition and rations for the men and horses were causing anxiety. The ammunition dumps at Ytres were found empty, but the 70th, during the withdrawal to Lechelle, had a lucky find in six full but deserted wagons in a neighbouring field. This was a real godsend, for the battery was out of touch with the wagon lines, and the ammunition had almost run out.

The enemy's artillery fire continued very heavy, and the 70th barely came into action when a couple of shells from an H.V. gun fell in the centre of the battery. The first killed " No. 1," 3 gunners and 2 signallers, 1 complete gun team, and 3 horses belonging to another. While endeavours were being made to remove the wounded and hook in the remaining team, the second shell fell and burst, wounding 2 more men. Eventually 5 guns were removed to a position a little in rear, a team was made up, and volunteers soon found to bring in the remaining gun.

For two hours, from the Lechelle position, the guns poured " bursts " upon Equancourt and near neighbourhood; but the flanks of the 99th Infantry Brigade and of the 47th Division had begun to give way, and guns were again limbered up and retired to just south of Bus. Here the brigade once again found itself in touch with the XLIst Brigade R.F.A., 2nd Division. It was now 4 p.m., and as Etricourt was reported in the hands of the enemy, harassing fire on ground known to be in the enemy's possession, and on the village, was kept up by the 50th, 56th, and D/34 Batteries; " 70th Battery, owing to its crippled condition, retired

THE SITUATION AT NIGHT—23RD MARCH.

out of action, and the horses were put into empty limbers on the western edge of the village. It was all about this spot that the enemy's artillery suddenly, about 5 p.m., opened a venomous fire with uncanny precision ; the rounds burst on percussion with instantaneous fuze ; the casualties were heavy ; the fire lasted some ten minutes ; the 70th Battery finished the day with 60 horses deficient."[1]

Eventually, about 6 p.m., the brigade found itself marching via Rocquigny, along a road packed with transport, heavy guns, and impedimenta of every description, to take up a position some 2,000 yards south-east of Le Transloy. The brigade had had a strenuous day, and its losses had been very heavy. Major H. Whiteman, commanding C/34, was put out of action by a shell splinter, and two other officers, Lieuts. Lewis and Laycock, of the 60th, were wounded. The XXXVIth and XLIst Brigades R.F.A. had both been in action all day, and on many occasions had fired over open sights at large bodies of the enemy, who, at times, came within 700 yards of the guns.

When darkness fell on the 23rd March, the 6th and 5th Infantry Brigades (in the order given) held the Green Line from O.34 to P.2, and the remnants of the 99th Infantry Brigade were back at Le Transloy ; the 63rd Division was on the right of the 2nd from P.2 to about P.14,d., but here the line bent sharply back, Ytres and Bus being in the possession of the enemy.[2]

The British line along the front of the Third and Fifth Armies on the night of 23rd March ran approximately from just south of Rœux, thence north-west to just south of Fampoux, St. Martin, Henin, west of St. Leger, half a mile east of Mory, west of Beugny to half a mile east of Bertincourt ; from the latter village the line bent sharply back north-west of Ytres and Bus, then dropped again east of Rocquigny to the southern boundary of the Third Army at St. Pierre Vaast Forest. From the latter the Fifth Army front ran south, crossing the Somme at Cléry, and following the western banks of the river round Péronne to a lock south of the town. From Péronne the line followed the Somme southwards to Eppeville, thence to Golancourt and Eaucourt, and from the latter village south-east to Viry-Noureuil, crossing the St. Quentin Canal to the north-eastern edge of the Basse Forêt de Coucy.

---

[1] Diary of Captain A. T. Gooding, R.F.A., Adjutant XXXVth (Army) Brigade R.F.A.
[2] The Official Dispatches include these two villages in the British front, but they were without doubt held by the enemy on the night of the 23rd March.

The enemy's gains had been considerable, but the overwhelming number of troops launched against the Third and Fifth Armies on the morning of the 21st March had not obtained the results expected. A break-through between the two British armies had not been accomplished, neither had the Flesquières Salient been cut off as "O.H.L." (German Headquarters) planned it should be. But for the thick fog, which masked the enemy's massed troops and hid his advance from the British until his first wave was practically in front of Sir Douglas Haig's trenches, it is doubtful if even the ground gained would have been anything like that won by the evening of the 23rd March. Both the Seventeenth and Second German Armies were blamed by Ludendorff for not having achieved more; only the Eighteenth German Army, which, on the morning of the 21st, had attacked the Fifth British Army on the approximate line Pontruet (north of St. Quentin)–Beautor (south of La Fère), won the approval of the Chief of the German General Staff.

The Battle of St. Quentin (21st–23rd March) was over, but the First Battle of Bapaume was about to begin.[1]

THE FIRST BATTLE OF BAPAUME,

24th to 25th March 1918.

Throughout the night of the 23rd–24th March no respite was allowed the harassed troops of the Third and Fifth Armies. Sleep was impossible, the roads running westwards from the battlefront were crowded with transport of all units, motor ambulances and guns, stragglers who had lost their way and could not find their battalions, whilst worried and short-tempered Staff officers galloped across country with orders in vain efforts to deliver them. There was rearward movement everywhere.

Flames from burning dumps and buildings shot up into the dark skies, the almost continuous flashes from machine guns, rifles, and trench mortars, combined with the roar of big guns, so lightened their surroundings that the troops engaged with the enemy were able without difficulty to distinguish ready targets.

During the evening of the 23rd, 2nd Divisional Headquarters had moved back to an old Casualty Clearing Station west of Beaulencourt. Here the Division was in touch with 5th Infantry Brigade Headquarters at Barastre, and 6th Infantry Brigade Headquarters

---

[1] For casualties of 2nd Division, see Appendices.

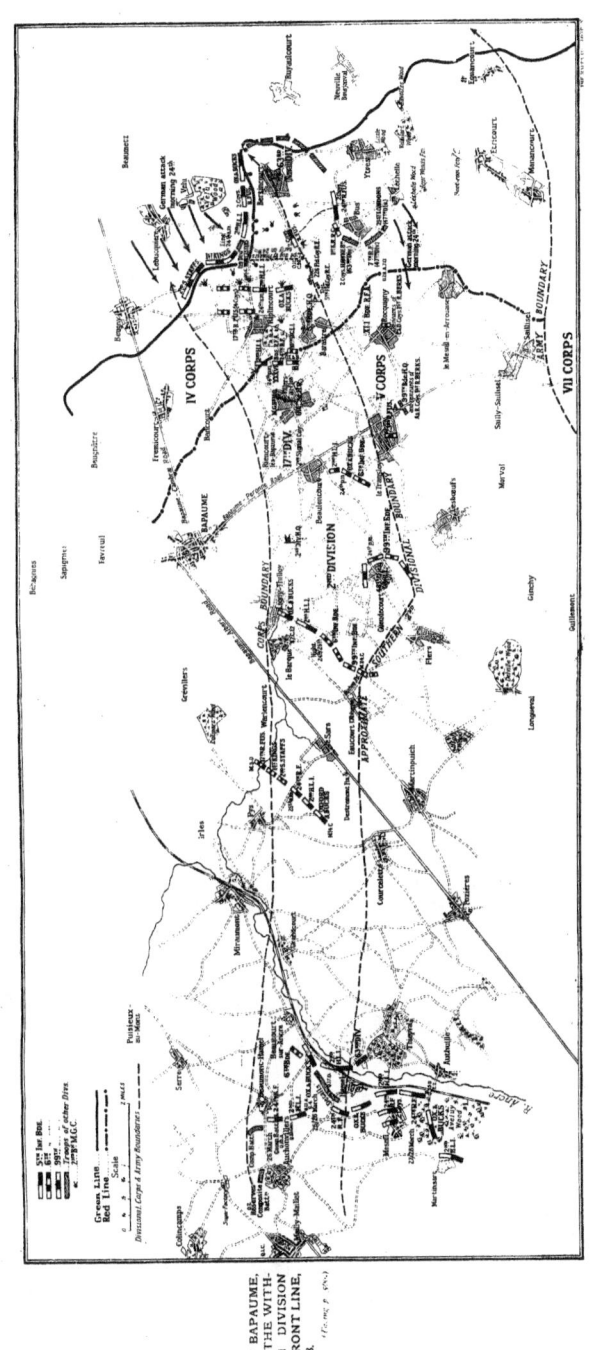

THE FIRST BATTLE OF BAPAUME, 21th-25th March 1918, AND THE WITHDRAWAL OF THE 2nd DIVISION TO THE OLD BRITISH FRONT LINE, 26th March 1918.

A NIGHT OF TROUBLE.

at Villers-au-Flos. All infantry battalions in the front line, assisted by the Pioneers and Field Companies R.E., improved their positions by digging and putting out wire wherever possible.

On the left flank of the Divisional front (6th Infantry Brigade), held by the 2nd South Staffords (left), and the 1st King's (right), the night was comparatively quiet. Patrols pushed out found the enemy in and about Lebucquière, and his troops were observed massing behind Velu Wood. The 17th Royal Fusiliers, formed up in two lines (two companies in each), were in reserve.

Between the right flank of the 6th Infantry Brigade and the left of the 5th Infantry Brigade a party of men belonging to a battalion of the Worcester Regiment (19th Division) filled a gap which had existed between the two brigades during the early period of the 23rd.

Of the 5th Infantry Brigade, which held the Green Line north and north-west of Bertincourt, the 2nd Highland Light Infantry was on the right; the next in line were two companies of the 24th Royal Fusiliers; and the right flank of the brigade was held by the 2nd Oxford and Bucks. The right of the latter battalion was in touch with the left of the 63rd (Naval) Division, whose troops formed a semicircle east and south-east of Bertincourt, to a point (very near Ytres Dump) about half-way between the latter village and Ytres. Half-way, also, between Bertincourt and Barastre (along the roadway) were the two remaining companies of the 24th Royal Fusiliers, near Battalion Headquarters, just north of Bus. Headquarters of the 5th Infantry Brigade were astride the Barastre–Bus road. Such was the position of the 5th Infantry Brigade when darkness fell on the 23rd March.

But about 8.30 p.m. Lieut.-Colonel Stafford (commanding the 1st King's Royal Rifles) arrived at Brigade Headquarters, and reported the retirement of his battalion and all that had happened during the day; Vallulart Wood and Lechelle were in the hands of the enemy, and the 47th Division had been driven out of its position. The gallant Colonel did not know that, even as he was relating the adventures of his battalion, the enemy was in Bus.

Soon after 9 p.m. Brigade Headquarters, astride the Barastre–Bus road, came under rifle-fire from the latter place. The two companies of 24th Royal Fusiliers, then north of Bus, were ordered to send out officers' patrols to reconnoitre Bus and the country beyond Lechelle. Colonel Stafford had returned from 5th Infantry Brigade Headquarters, and was at Battalion Headquarters 24th Royal Fusiliers explaining the situation by map to the two

THE HISTORY OF THE SECOND DIVISION.

officers detailed to carry out the reconnaissance, when brisk rifle-fire was suddenly opened from Bus and the slopes on the northern side of the village. Hastily collecting all spare men at Battalion Headquarters, some sappers, and men from the two Fusiliers companies who were going out on patrol, Colonel Pipon (commanding 24th Royal Fusiliers) rapidly formed a firing line a short distance up the slopes leading to the village. With a great deal of noise and singing, and shouting "Hoch! Hoch!" the enemy, in considerable numbers, rushed down the slopes. From the behaviour of his troops it was evident they had been looting the canteens in Ytres. As they advanced they fired several ammunition dumps, and these blazed up, lighting the valley around them. As the flames shot upwards, punctuated by loud explosions, the enemy was silhouetted against the glare, providing fine targets for Colonel Pipon's hastily collected party. For an hour or more the enemy endeavoured to gain ground, but finally, after his troops had been heavily punished and numbers of them killed and wounded, he was driven back on Bus, and throughout the night 23rd–24th did not attack again. Just as the situation was well in hand, the two support companies of Fusiliers arrived and dug in below the crest of the rise, in touch with the King's Royal Rifles (99th Infantry Brigade) on the right. A gap of 500 yards, however, existed between the left flank of the Fusiliers and the right of the 63rd Division.

Ytres was by this time burning freely, and the smoke and flames pouring from the village were visible for many miles around. About midnight the position on the left of the Divisional front was as follows: "The 63rd Division still held from the junction with the 2nd Oxford and Bucks Light Infantry to a point near Ytres Dump; then came a gap of 500 yards; then a rough line formed by Lieut.-Colonel Pipon (with two companies and Battalion Headquarters personnel of 24th Royal Fusiliers, and elements of four other units, 1/60th Rifles (99th Infantry Brigade, 2nd Division), Hawke Battalion (63rd Division), 7th Royal Fusiliers (the "Shiny 7th"), and a battalion (21st) of the London Regiment (47th Division)). This line ran across the north of Bus, and curled round the west and south-west of the village. Then came a gap, and then the Brigade Headquarters Company astride the Barastre–Bus road, with patrols pushed forward towards Bus and Rocquigny. The enemy was in Ytres and Bus, and south of the line Bus–Rocquigny."[1]

---

[1] Diary of the 5th Infantry Brigade. This statement is important, as the Official Dispatches show the British line on the night of the 23rd March *east of Ytres*, with that place and Bus and Lechelle still in the hands of the Vth Corps, Third Army.

THE BATTLE OPENS. 563

The remaining brigade of the 2nd Division (99th) at midnight on 23rd was disposed in the following positions : Brigade Headquarters and transport along the main road, 1,000 yards south-east of Le Transloy, protected by about 300 details of the 21st London Regiment (47th Division), guarding the Rocquigny–Sailly-Saillisel road ; the 23rd Royal Fusiliers (strength now about 200 all ranks) in Le Transloy ; A and B (No. 1 Company) Companies of 1st Royal Berks, all told about 60 strong, under Captain Pugh, were with Brigade Headquarters, whilst C and D (No. 2 Company) Companies, under Lieut. Crosbie, were at Rocquigny with troops of the 47th London Division, under Lieut.-Colonel Dawes ; elements of the 1st King's Royal Rifles were north-west of Bus. The XXXVIth Brigade R.F.A. was west of Haplincourt Wood, and the XLIst Brigade R.F.A. north-east of Rocquigny. Small detachments from the 226th and 5th Field Companies R.E. were astride the Bertincourt–Barastre and the Bus–Barastre roads respectively ; the 483rd Field Company R.E. was at Gueudecourt, and the 2nd Signal Company in Beaulencourt ; the Pioneers were disposed two companies in the front line and one company in reserve between Haplincourt Wood and Barastre, but in the early hours of the 24th were sent to assist the 5th Infantry Brigade and dig in on a line east of Barastre. The 17th Division, which had passed through the 5th Infantry Brigade, was now behind Villers-au-Flos.[1] The divisions flanking the 2nd Division were the 19th on the left, and the 63rd and 47th on the right. But despite gallant efforts to maintain it, touch between the right of the Third Army (47th Division) and the left of the Fifth Army (9th Division) had been lost. There is a limit to the endurance of all fighting troops.

Such were the dispositions of the 2nd Division and the flanking divisions of the Vth Corps when, early on the morning of the 24th March, the First Battle of Bapaume opened. " During the night of the 23rd–24th March the situation on the battle-front remained unchanged as far south as the neighbourhood of Ytres. Beyond that point divisions and brigades had lost touch in the course of their frequent withdrawals, and under the constant pressure of the enemy the rearward movement continued." [2]

The country over which the First Battle of Bapaume, 1918, was to be fought was well known to most of the troops of the 2nd Division, who during the past winter, when out of the front line,

24TH MARCH. MAP.

---

[1] The positions of other divisions are only approximate, though the details are taken from Diaries and other documents.
[2] Official Dispatches.

had spent their days in training and their nights in billets in the area west of Havrincourt Wood. It was hilly country, with a valley running south-west from Lebucquière towards Villers-au-Flos, with an offshoot along the Haplincourt–Barastre road; an undulating country of downs, sunken roads, old encampments, small villages, shell-shattered and tumbled, with here and there a copse of trees stunted and blasted by the holocaust of war, or a tangle of crumbling trenches—in all, admirable ground for open warfare, providing many opportunities to both officers and N.C.O's for the display of that initiative and ingenuity which had become so marked a quality of the British soldier.

When dawn of the 24th March broke a heavy ground mist again obscured the battlefield. Hidden by the mist, the enemy had massed his troops, machine guns, and trench mortars and artillery, ready to continue the advance.

Along the British front line the troops, knowing full well that long before the sun had risen the enemy would fling his masses against them, were on the alert. It was evident that the Bertincourt Salient would have to be evacuated, for the enemy was north, east, and south of it. Moreover, the position south of a line between Rocquigny and Bus was uncertain; what had happened to the left flank of the Fifth Army (9th Division) none knew; it was, however, fairly certain that Le Mesnil (47th Division area) was in possession of the enemy.

At 8 a.m. orders to evacuate the Bertincourt Salient were received from Vth Corps Headquarters, and were immediately issued to the brigades in line; "zero" for the evacuation was 9.15 a.m., but before that hour the enemy's shells had already begun to fall in the front line and back areas. Hostile guns opened fire from Velu Wood and from behind Lebucquière. Before the brigades in the front line had received their orders a very heavy barrage was put down by the enemy. The 63rd Division was the first to move, and began to retire about 9 a.m. The 5th Infantry Brigade had been ordered to follow the 63rd Division and form up on a line from O.5,c. to O.11,c.9.0; a brigade of the 17th Division was to move forward and occupy a line from O.11,c.9.0 to the Red Line about 0.29,a.7.0, whilst another brigade of the same division marched southwards from Villers-au-Flos towards Le Transloy. A small detachment of eight tanks moved off towards Bus in order to draw attention from the withdrawal of the 63rd Division and the 5th Infantry Brigade.

At 9.15 p.m. the brigade moved, the 24th Royal Fusiliers with-

A COUNTER-ATTACK.

drawing first to just west of Haplincourt Wood, in reserve; the Oxford and Bucks followed the Fusiliers, but instead of taking up their allotted position on the right of the line O.5,c. to O.11,c.9.0, moved too far back in the absence of any indication as to where the correct line lay, and a position was taken up by the battalion behind two belts of old German wire, 1,000 yards east of the Barastre–Haplincourt road. "Absence of all landmarks, pressure of time and shell-fire," said the 5th Brigade Diary, "all contributed to this mistake." The Highland Light Infantry was the last battalion to withdraw, and formed up on the left of the Oxford and Bucks, the left flank of the battalion resting between the left of the 5th and the right of the 6th Infantry Brigades. The small party of about 100 men of the Worcesters, who had filled the gap between the two brigades, had disappeared, none knew whither. Patrols were therefore pushed out by the Highland Light Infantry to try and gain touch with the right of the 6th Infantry Brigade (the 1st King's), and Second-Lieut. D. Sheridan took out a platoon to minimize the danger, and gave valuable assistance by maintaining covering fire whilst the 6th Brigade was brought more into line with the 5th.

At 9.35 a.m. the enemy's barrage lifted, and immediately his troops all along the line, in overwhelming masses, advanced from Lebucquière and Velu Wood against the 6th Infantry Brigade and the right flank of the IVth Corps. The ground-mist had by this time cleared, and four machine guns of the 2nd Battalion Machine-Gun Corps, under Lieut. Christopher, having splendid targets in the advancing masses of Germans, inflicted very severe casualties and, after terrible slaughter, drove the enemy in confusion back towards Velu Wood. On the left flank of the 2nd South Staffords, however, a battalion of the IVth Corps was forced back some 200 yards, but, with the assistance of a platoon of the Staffords, under Second-Lieut. Atkinson (who was unfortunately killed), they counter-attacked at 10.30 a.m., and forced the enemy back to the high ground just east of Lebucquière.

Although the first attack had been beaten off, the position of the 6th Infantry Brigade was desperate. Of the left flanking company of the 1st King's (C Company) only eight other ranks and no officers remained. Two platoons of the 17th Royal Fusiliers were therefore hurried up to reinforce this flank. At 10.45 a.m. the South Staffords, on the left of the brigade front, with a company of 17th Royal Fusiliers, formed a defensive flank. The line, however, had hardly been steadied when the enemy pushed forward another attack along the whole front, and penetrated the gap between the two brigades. Yet another attack on the left of the 6th Infantry Brigade again drove in the flanking troops of the IVth Corps, and thus a general retirement from the Green Line was imperative.

Both the 5th and 6th Infantry Brigades now began to fall back on the Red Line, which ran east of Rocquigny, west of Barastre, thence about half-way between Haplincourt and Villers-au-Flos. All units of the 2nd, 17th, 47th, and 63rd Divisions were now engaged in a fierce fight, standing or retiring as the situation demanded. No clear or adequate detailed records exist of those fierce rearguard actions and retirements, nor is it possible to give anything like an accurate description of the hundred and one gallant deeds performed that day. Neither can justice be done to the extreme gallantry of the machine gunners, " who," said the official report, " protected the withdrawal of the infantry ; and the unflagging energy and cool heroism of the officers and men who, for two and a half hours, without any rest, were endeavouring to stem the hostile flood and to dispute every yard of ground, and often rescue, at the hazard of their own lives, their wounded comrades in the open. Many stories were told, and it is invidious to select any particular episode."

One of the most astonishing things was the splendid way in which, throughout the day, Battalion Headquarters frequently covered the retirement of companies.[1] During the withdrawal from the Green Line, when the enemy was advancing upon Haplincourt, and the King's were struggling back towards the village, Second-Lieut. A. A. Armstrong, 1st King's, with about thirty men of Battalion Headquarters and two Lewis guns, took up a position on the high ground north of Haplincourt. Hostile machine guns swept this position, the ground about was pitted and pockmarked by shell-holes, and the enemy's artillery kept up an incessant volume of fire ; but, with two Vickers guns close at hand, commanded by Lieut. D. A. Lewis, this little party of officers and men successfully covered the retirement of the battalion, inflicting appalling losses on the enemy. Of the section which manned the two Vickers guns, only one officer survived, and this gallant subaltern spent the remainder of the day carrying his gun from place

---

[1] Most Brigade Headquarters were of considerable strength, comprising runners, signallers, and probably an L.T.M. section, to say nothing of the usual Staff, and, at this period, there were probably added stragglers from other units. Thus it came about that Brigade Headquarters was often stronger than a company in the field.

to place (the other had been knocked out), pausing, at every opportunity, to get his gun into action and kill still more of the enemy.

Never, throughout the four years of war which had gone before, had the gallant South Staffords proved themselves such stout soldiers as on March 24, 1918. "Further to the left," said the official narrative (which is given *in extenso* in order that it may be preserved), "the 2nd South Staffords were ordered to retire on their Battalion Headquarters, a mile north of Haplincourt. One company, following the Cheshires (a battalion belonging to the IVth Corps on the left of the 6th Infantry Brigade), was apparently cut off, as none of them have been seen since. Another company, in that splendid spirit in which grit and enthusiasm outran prudence, fought and fought on till retirement was impossible, and only one or two escaped to tell the tale of the last stand. The other two companies reached Battalion Headquarters in perfect order, though heavily pressed by the enemy. A further retirement, one company at a time, was directed towards Haplincourt, and, in extended order, the men faced the ordeal of crossing the valley down which concentrated machine-gun fire was poured from the direction of Lebucquière."

The commanding officer of the battalion, Lieut.-Colonel Alban, with a few Headquarters details, was the last to leave, the enemy being then in some huts less than 200 yards away. The gallant Colonel was wounded almost immediately the little party began to retire, and fell to the ground, but, with the assistance of Captain Williams, Medical Officer of the 2nd South Staffords, he was helped along until he was again hit, this time more severely. Captain Williams, Second-Lieut. Bona, and Private Gavin then managed to carry him, but before they reached a place of safety they had to cross an open space of 700 yards through a band of machine-gun fire.

The conduct of Second-Lieut. Sheridan of the 2nd Highland Light Infantry has already been referred to. With two platoons of his battalion he had been sent to close the gap between the 5th and 6th Infantry Brigades, east of Haplincourt. But the enemy had already penetrated the gap, and the only way of saving his battalion from being cut off was to lead his men against the vastly superior numbers opposed to him. Without hesitation this little band of gallant men set themselves to hold up the enemy's advance. One by one they fell; Lieut. Sheridan was himself wounded, but still directed a steady and heavy fire on the grey masses as they came on. Finally, when all but four of the two platoons had become casualties, and the retirement of the 6th Infantry Brigade had been accomplished, the survivors marched back.

Everywhere the machine gunners did splendid work. Their undaunted courage saved many a platoon and company from annihilation. Only twenty-two days had passed since the 2nd Battalion Machine-Gun Corps (Lieut.-Colonel Dunlop) had been formed, but its organization and fighting spirit was never higher than during those terrible days of the March retreat. A section (No. 4) which had been detached from the battalion, and supported the 99th Infantry Brigade at Equancourt on the 23rd when the brigade retired on Rocquigny, was just east and south-east of the latter village when the enemy attacked, fought its guns until they were either smashed or purposely destroyed, the gun crews killed, wounded, or prisoners, and the line they had defended so gallantly swept away by the onrush of the enemy.

The section was under the command of Lieut. Robinson, 2nd Battalion Machine-Gun Corps. When dawn of the 24th broke No. 4 Section was in occupation of an old German trench of the Somme days. The guns were placed so as to sweep the valley across which the enemy would have to advance. Before the first attack took place, hostile light trench mortars had worked their way forward south of Rocquigny and had registered on the old German trench, which sheltered also some machine guns of the 47th Division and some men of the Bedford Regiment belonging to the 9th Division. Two machine guns of the 2nd Battalion Machine-Gun Corps were on the left flank of this line under Lieut. Robinson. The gun at A, commanded by Lieut. Robotham, was mounted some yards in rear of the front line; that at B, placed in a sap off the main trench with a clear field of fire to the right flank, was under Sergeant Hubbard.

At 9 a.m. the first attack started. It offered, as a private account written by Lieut. Robotham when a prisoner of war in Germany stated, "a great chance for machine guns. Every move forward by the enemy could be seen by the alert machine gunners. A gun firing down the valley enfiladed the enemy's troops where a sunken road crossed the ridge, and not a German got through that way.

"The 19th Londons put up a fine show, and it was up to us not to let them down, for they hadn't a single Lewis gun at that time. Steady fire! Feeling of confidence, after his (the enemy's) first

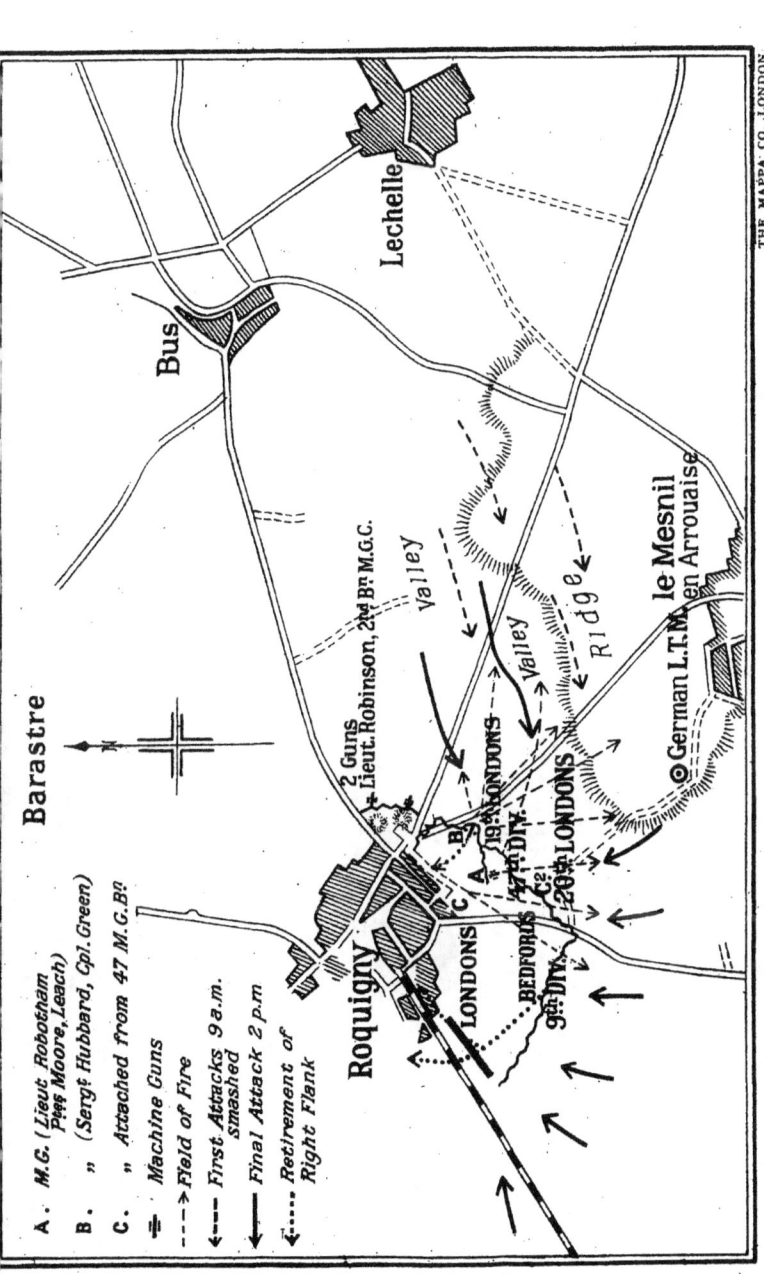

A FIGHT TO THE FINISH: ACTION OF 2nd BATT. M.G.C. IN FRONT OF ROCQUIGNY, 24th March 1918.

(Facing p. 568.)

A FIGHT TO THE FINISH.

attack was stopped. The enemy tried again and again to get through; the guns were tearing away as fast as the belts could be refilled. Ammunition was collected from the bandoliers of men in the trench who had become casualties. Petrol tins filled with water were brought from the railhead to cool the heated guns. We ran out of oil, but obtained some from a Lewis gunner of some supports which had just arrived.

" A gun suddenly stopped, the disk of the front cone had been smashed. There were (or had been) four guns of the 47th Battalion Machine-Gun Corps in a trench with the 20th Londons. We took one of the two still left in action, and mounted it on A's tripod. It was a dud. But a new disk was fixed on our own gun. The Officer Commanding 47th Battalion Machine-Gun Corps must have been killed, anyhow his guns were useless. A corporal of the 47th Battalion reported that the remaining gun was useless at C. It was placed at C2, to fire to the right flank and rear.

" It was now about 11.30 a.m. Sergeant Hubbard had been shot through the left shoulder and made his way back towards the village; he was a great loss, but I could see his gun still carrying on. The German light machine guns were very good; one tried to knock us out and got a burst right under the muzzle of our gun. One bullet through the socket (a clear hole without smashing it); but the gunner must have been sniped by our infantry, for he did not trouble us again. His (the enemy's) planes now began raking us with machine guns, but somehow didn't seem to hit any one.

" At 12.30 there was a distinct lull, lasting probably over half an hour. This was the worst stage of the whole show. When the attack commenced again, he was evidently behind us on the right. A platoon of the Londons lined the railway embankment, firing with their backs to us. A battery of 77 mms. (south-west of Ytres) opened on to us, but luckily the shells burst from 20 to 30 yards over, direct fire too, chiefly on to the road. Events now happened quickly. German trench mortars enfiladed the position; we got several bursts at them, then had to swing round to the front again. At 2 o'clock the people on our right were rushed by the Germans, and some tried to get away towards the village . . . the front still held ! Almost immediately afterwards, those who had retired came filing back again . . . hands up . . . C2 stopped. I ordered him to carry on. There was a parley at Point P. A German officer was making signs for us to surrender; no notice taken. Enemy artillery stopped. Seeing no desire to give up, the trench mortars carried on. Confusion now reigned—the trench was a shambles. I ordered the corporal of C2 to destroy his gun; asked Private Leach, who was at A gun, if he had a revolver, but he hadn't; told him to get away along the trench."

Hastily dismantling his gun and putting the trigger bar in his pocket, "for there still seemed a chance of getting it again," Lieut. Robotham went along to the trench to join up with the Londoners. But now the end came—"men were filing out of the trenches on the left, further resistance was hopeless."

Thus ended the very gallant action of No. 4 Section, 2nd Battalion Machine-Gun Corps. Lieut. Robinson was the only officer who succeeded in getting back from the trench; he brought with him a few men, but all guns were lost or destroyed. Second-Lieut. Craig, whose guns in front of Barastre fired over 100,000 rounds between 2 and 6 p.m.; Lieut. Christopher, facing Lebucquière and Velu Wood, and again in front of Haplincourt, where with two equally gallant men, Corporal Rooney and Sergeant Smith, he held up the advance of the enemy for half an hour under most extraordinary difficulties; and another N.C.O., Sergeant Callender, who himself accounted for no less than seven German machine guns—all these officers and men of the Machine-Gun Battalion played well their part on that terrible day.

From ridge to ridge, stumbling across country or along shell-swept roads, the tired infantry were settled in the Red Line by 2.30 p.m.; it was no more than a mark on a map, for of defences it had none. But having reached it, the exhausted troops paused for breath before pushing on to the Bapaume–Péronne road, for it soon became evident that the Red Line could serve only as a short halting-place, the enemy's pressure being very vigorous.

So at 3 p.m. the worn-out troops, fast dwindling in numbers, fell back again to the line of the Bapaume road between Le Transloy and Beaulencourt. Just east and north of the latter, a battalion of the 51st Division held the line of the road, and with these troops the 6th and 5th Infantry Brigades prolonged the battle-front towards the outskirts of Le Transloy.

To a spectator that retirement was a grim and extraordinary spectacle. Spread out like a chessboard on which the pieces moved at random, troops of several British divisions checked and counter-checked the enemy; here a gap and there a salient, at which, or against which, the enemy flung his troops in great numbers. British and Germans closed with one another in death struggles, the while the whole line, interlocked, drifted westwards. A sergeant runs forward to salve a Lewis gun; his action means death to a score or more of Germans. Combatants and non-combatants all are intermingled. It is no time for the niceties of warfare. A Herculean figure staggers along with a wounded man slung across his broad shoulders; it is Padre Gibson of the 17th Royal Fusiliers. Stretcher-bearers, seeing the gallant parson, bend to their work with redoubled energy. Three times Padre Murray of the 1st King's rushes back over 400 yards of evacuated ground, over which the bullets are falling like rain, to rescue wounded men who had, from sheer inability to carry them, been left behind to the tender mercies of hostile troops, many of whom were maddened by drink looted from abandoned canteens, or smarting under a score of costly rebuffs.

Scarcely had the troops settled down along the Bapaume–Péronne road when an order was received from Vth Corps Headquarters: " The enemy has taken Combles, and is advancing from Morval on Lesbœufs. The Corps is to withdraw . . . move at once with all military precaution."

Immediately 2nd Division Headquarters issued orders to the troops to retire to a new line from Thilloy–Ligny Thilloy road junction half a mile south of Eaucourt L'Abbaye–M.24,c.–High Wood : " 2nd Division holding from about Ligny Thilloy village to about road junction M.24,c. . . . 19th Division is on the left, 17th Division on the right."

The 5th and 6th Infantry Brigades were ordered to leave a rearguard on the Bapaume–Péronne road.

" So in perfect order, but with dragging feet, the 5th and 6th Infantry Brigades, the 10th Duke of Cornwall's Light Infantry, and about 400 men of the 51st Division, marched back through the brilliant evening sunshine over the shell-holes and long grass of the old battered battle-ground, due west. It was about 6 o'clock."[1]

But what of the 99th Infantry Brigade, and of the gunners and sappers of the Division, and those same gallant Pioneers now trudging wearily back towards the Ligny Thilloy–Eaucourt L'Abbaye line ? What had befallen them during this day of trial ?

After its splendid but vain efforts on the 23rd, under various commands, to maintain touch between the right of the Vth Corps (Third Army) and the left of the VIIth Corps (Fifth Army), the 99th Infantry Brigade had spent the night of the 23rd–24th March practically disintegrated.

As already stated, Brigade Headquarters with its transport,

---

[1] The 5th and 6th Infantry Brigades and the 10th Duke of Cornwall's Light Infantry (Pioneers) numbered in all only about 1,000 men.

the 23rd Royal Fusiliers (about 200 strong), and No. 1 Company, 1st Royal Berks (strength about 60), after considerable difficulty, had reached Le Transloy and a position on the main road 1,000 yards south-east of that village. Covering the front of the 99th Infantry Brigade, 200 details of the 21st London Regiment (47th Division) were on the Rocquigny and the Sailly and Saillisel roads. No. 2 Company of the Berkshires was at Rocquigny with troops of the 47th Division, whilst the 1st King's Royal Rifles were 200 yards north-west of Bus, between troops of the 5th Infantry Brigade and the 63rd Division.

At dawn on the 24th, 99th Infantry Brigade Headquarters, with the Fusiliers and Berkshires, set out for Gueudecourt, where, to the unbounded satisfaction of all ranks, the welcome news was received that the brigade had been returned to the 2nd Division. Orders were reissued to prepare to defend the village, and for this purpose a line round three sides of Gueudecourt—north, east, and south—was dug. During the day 150 men of the 17th Royal Fusiliers (under Major Pretty) and one company of the Pioneers arrived and were attached to the brigade. All day long streams of traffic and transport and artillery passed through the village coming from the direction of Beaulencourt and Lesbœufs.

By 2.30 p.m. the defences of the village were as complete as it was possible to make them, and command had been entrusted to Lieut.-Colonel E. A. Winter, 23rd Royal Fusiliers. The Fusiliers held the right flank of the line, south of the village in the direction of Lesbœuts; in the centre, facing east, were 40 men from the 99th Trench Mortar Battery and 100 of the Berkshires; on the left flank, Major Pretty, with 150 men, prepared to meet any attempt from the north and north-east. Fifty men of the Berkshires and some details of the Pioneers were in reserve.

At 3 p.m. orders were received for the Division to advance towards Morval, but they came too late. The enemy had already been reported not only in Morval but also in Lesbœufs, and an hour later the 63rd Division, retiring towards Martinpuich, was under fire of hostile artillery and machine guns from Lesbœufs. The line held by the 99th Infantry Brigade was now almost at right angles to that which the 47th Division was holding along the western exits of Le Transloy. It was in this situation, perilous to a degree, that the magnificent spirit of the British gunner once more showed itself.

The XLIst Brigade R.F.A. had been covering the front of the 47th Division, and when the Germans reached Lesbœufs, was

GENERAL BARNETT BARKER KILLED.

actually between that village and Gueudecourt, in front of the 99th Infantry Brigade. The enemy emerged from Lesbœufs, and at less than 1,000 yards range opened fire on the intrepid gunners, who, nothing daunted, fired round after round over open sights as the Germans advanced. Of the 17th Battery, two sections, under Lieut. Trapp, were withdrawn to Gueudecourt, covered by the third section, which, remaining in its position, poured shrapnel into the enemy and held up his advance. Finally, whilst this section was also being withdrawn, a section of the 9th Battery, some 700 yards east-by-south-east of Gueudecourt, remained in action, engaging the enemy over open sights at 1,400 yards, compelling the Germans to stop their advance, enabling the retiring infantry to withdraw unmolested. Even when all the guns had been drawn out of action, a limber belonging to the 17th Battery dashed back to within 1,000 yards of the enemy and, picking up a quantity of gear which had been left behind but which was absolutely necessary, returned safe and sound at a smart trot. Thus did the gallant gunners maintain the proudest traditions of the British artilleryman.

At 5.15 p.m. shells began to fall in Gueudecourt itself; in conjunction with the 63rd Division, Colonel Winter was to retire when both his flanks were exposed, but about 5.35 p.m. Brigadier-General R. Barnett Barker, D.S.O. (General Officer Commanding 99th Infantry Brigade), and his Staff captain, Captain E. Bell, were killed by a shell, and Colonel Winter, assuming temporary command of the brigade, withdrew Headquarters to a dug-out in Hexham road, east of Eaucourt L'Abbaye, the remainder of the brigade following.

Meanwhile the 1st King's Royal Rifles north of Bus had retired in conjunction with the Hawke Battalion (63rd Division) and the 24th Royal Fusiliers to a position south of Villers-au-Flos. Here the battalion organized. But during the retirement, which had been made in alignment and in full view of the enemy, D Company was entirely wiped out and the other companies suffered heavily. During the afternoon, when a further retirement had been ordered, Colonel Stafford marched his troops on Gueudecourt, but *en route*, hearing that 2nd Division Headquarters were at Destremont Farm, changed direction towards that place. Eventually, at 8.30 p.m., hardly able to stand from fatigue and utterly exhausted, the Rifles reached Divisional Headquarters, where they received orders to rejoin the 99th Infantry Brigade on the following morning.

Divisional Headquarters had moved back to Destremont Farm, near Le Sars, from Beaulencourt, at 1.45 p.m., and here, on the night of the 24th–25th, " we collected various parts of the Division and made them rest for the night and got their rations to them. There were Stafford and 100 of the 60th, Pipon and 85 of the 24th, Murray-Lyon and 100 of the 1st King's, and 60 of the 2nd Highland Light Infantry; they were ordered to rejoin their brigades at 8 a.m."[1]

Meanwhile the 5th and 6th Infantry Brigades had reached the Ligny–Thilloy line and were disposed, the former on the left, the latter in the centre, and the 99th Infantry Brigade on the right. The 19th Division was on the left of the 5th Infantry Brigade, and the 17th Division came into line during the night south of the 99th Infantry Brigade.

All through the night the 5th and 483rd Field Companies R.E. did magnificent work in organizing the defences of this line, and in assisting the tired infantry to fill gaps, where the latter existed, and to maintain touch on the flanks.

The Pioneers (10th Duke of Cornwall's Light Infantry), who all day had been gallantly fighting and digging alternately, marched out of Beaulencourt towards Martinpuich via Gueudecourt. About 7.45 p.m. the battalion reached Flers. Here, however, the pioneers found themselves under shell-fire, and snipers' bullets began to fall in the village. A move was therefore made to the valley north of the village. As the sky was illuminated by Véry lights going up from between Flers and Martinpuich, the position of the battalion, which had now been swollen to about 1,200 men by the influx of a company of a London Regiment, was obviously insecure. It was decided to push northwards towards Destremont Farm, where Divisional Headquarters were thought to be. By a great stroke of luck the Pioneers moved straight on to 99th Infantry Brigade Headquarters in the Hexham road, to which they had been properly attached. They were put into brigade reserve, and were able to snatch a few hours' sleep before dawn.

At 10 p.m. Divisional Headquarters moved back to Miraumont.

Thus, so far as the 2nd Division was concerned, ended the first day of the Battle of Bapaume.

Of the many deeds of gallantry performed during the day it has been possible to mention only a few; but everywhere the spirit of the troops was splendid, and although losing heavily as they withdrew, they inflicted enormous losses on the enemy, and the Seventeenth Germany Army, which on the morning of the 21st March had begun the great offensive with twenty-eight divisions,

[1] Diary of Major-General C. E. Pereira, C.M.G.

A DAY OF SUPREME TEST.

and the Second German Army with its twenty-two divisions, were already on the verge of exhaustion.

On the night of the 24th–25th the line of the Third Army north of the Somme ran from just west of Guillemont, Delville Wood, Bois des Foureaux, Eaucourt L'Abbaye, Ligny Thilloy, west of Bapaume, Sapignies, just west of Mory and St. Leger, through Henin-sur-Cojeul to Fampoux, then bent sharply back east to Rœux.

South of the Somme, the line of the river had enabled the Fifth Army to hold back the enemy temporarily, so that on the night of the 24th–25th March the battle-front from Hem to just west of Nesle took a sharp bend eastwards. But the existence of gaps between corps and divisions caused the greatest anxiety, as on every occasion they were rapidly exploited by the enemy, whose overwhelming numbers enabled him to push troops through wherever an opening presented itself.

Throughout the night 24th–25th March constant fighting took place on the northern positions of the battle-front about Sapignies and Behagnies, where the enemy made determined but unsuccessful efforts to break through. And on the morning of the 25th he still maintained great pressure on this front from Ervillers southwards.

Somewhat refreshed by a brief rest, but still very tired, the troops awakened to what (though they knew it not) was to be a day of supreme test, in which their fortitude, courage, and tenacity would be strained to the utmost.

25TH MARCH.

At midnight orders had been issued from 2nd Division Headquarters that "should a withdrawal be necessary from the present line held by the Division, the next line on which to retire would be Courcelette–Pys AAA, 63rd Division on the right, not 17th Division as previously stated."

Reconnaissances throughout the night had failed to gain touch on the flanks with the flanking divisions.

Before dawn, therefore, in order to take advantage of the friendly cover darkness provided, the 5th and 6th Infantry Brigades retired, and when eventually dawn broke the two brigades had halted and were snatching a hasty breakfast in the Dyke valley, north-east of Courcelette. But now a wide gap existed between the left of the 99th Infantry Brigade (1st Royal Berks) and the right of the 19th Division. The Pioneers (10th Duke of Cornwall's Light Infantry), who had been "standing to" since about 4 a.m., were therefore sent forward to fill the dangerous opening. When this "had been accomplished, the front line was then: 63rd Division on the right of the 99th Infantry Brigade ; 99th Infantry Brigade—10th Duke of Cornwall's Light Infantry and 1/4th Battalion Shropshire Regiment of the 19th Division. Two companies of the Pioneers (Y and Z) and three platoons of X Company reached their allotted positions in the line without incident, but the fourth platoon of the latter company met a large force of the enemy face to face in the Sunken Road about N.7,c.1.7, and a desperate bayonet fight ensued," and " there was a real good scrap. Both the officer commanding company and platoon officer were badly injured, and three-quarters of the platoon went down, but they wiped out the enemy to a man." [1]

In this gallant little exploit, one of those desperate encounters between small parties which were so frequent during the March retreat of 1918, the enemy's casualties were estimated at 50. This Sunken Road was seen to be a position of great danger, and a composite party of signallers, officers' servants, and runners, with two sergeant instructors, was organized, the gap was closed, and touch obtained with the 19th Division.

Whilst this miniature battle was proceeding, the 5th and 6th Infantry Brigades had been met by the General Officer Commanding Division, and were ordered to form a line from M.3,d. to M.14,c., 6th Infantry Brigade on the left and 5th Infantry Brigade on the right, through which the 99th Infantry Brigade and Pioneers could retire if driven from their positions. By 10.30 a.m. the enemy had been strongly reinforced and had launched heavy attacks against the whole line. It was very evident that the mere handful of troops comprising the 99th Infantry Brigade and the 10th Duke of Cornwall's Light Infantry would be unable to make a prolonged stand, and therefore, when about this period the 1st King's Royal Rifles arrived from Destremont Farm, where they had spent the night, Colonel Stafford disposed his men on the high ground west of Eaucourt L'Abbaye, from which position it would be possible to cover the clearly imminent retirement of the brigade and the Pioneers. For south of the 99th Brigade the flanking division had been pressed back farther. At once the Rifles came into action, and by a splendidly accurate covering fire harassed the enemy to such an extent that his troops were forced to advance very cautiously, which gave time for the retirement to take place. The left of the 10th Duke of Cornwall's Light Infantry was the first portion of the line to move. Fighting with dogged devotion, and contesting almost every foot of ground, the gallant Pioneers

[1] Report by Officer Commanding 10th Duke of Cornwall's Light Infantry.

fell back stubbornly, keeping touch with the troops on their left —*i.e.*, of the 19th Division. On reaching the Rifles the Pioneers helped to thicken the line, and together the survivors of the two battalions brought a very effective fire on the enemy, under cover of which the 1st Royal Berks and the 99th Trench Mortar Battery withdrew.

In spite of this admirable covering fire, however, the 23rd Royal Fusiliers, whose right had been uncovered by the retirement of the 17th and 63rd Divisions, were left in a precarious and isolated position. All the morning Hexham road, where Battalion Headquarters were situated, had been swept by machine-gun fire, and only small bodies of men were able to extricate themselves from their deadly situation; the remainder were either killed or wounded and taken by the enemy, whose advance had again by this time become very rapid.

West of Le Sars and the high ground the next stand was made. Small rearguards of Rifles, Berkshires, and Pioneers left behind in the village covered the withdrawal to the high ground. A handful of gallant Scotsmen belonging to the 51st (Highland) Division was also holding up the enemy from the Butte de Warlencourt. The rearguard put up a splendid fight, and the 99th Infantry Brigade (all that remained of it) withdrew towards Pys, through the 5th and 6th Infantry Brigades, who were holding the Pys–Courcelette road. Before the rearguard withdrew a German cavalry patrol was seen advancing south along the Le Barque–Eaucourt L'Abbaye road: the Pioneers turned a Lewis gun on to it, and not a man escaped.

No sooner had the rearguard evacuated Le Sars than the enemy entered the village, and in a little while his machine guns were harassing the 99th Infantry Brigade as it fell back.

The men were by now greatly exhausted; they could scarcely drag themselves along, and the want of sleep and food added to their sufferings. The shortage of ammunition had become almost acute, while the heavy losses sustained in officers made reorganization difficult, though the N.C.O's worked grandly, and the men were not anywhere near out of control.

By 1 p.m. the remnants of the 99th Infantry Brigade were disposed on a line west-south-west of Pys.

It now fell to the 5th and 6th Infantry Brigades disposed in line from M.14,c. to M.3,d. to hold up the enemy's advance. From right to left the battalions were placed as follows: 2nd Oxford and Bucks, 2nd Highland Light Infantry, 24th Royal Fusiliers,

2nd South Staffords, 1st King's, 17th Royal Fusiliers. On the left flank (left of the 17th Royal Fusiliers) the 51st Division, which had been holding the line about Logeast Wood, was being gradually pressed back; the right flank (right of the Oxford and Bucks) was entirely in the air, and at 2 p.m., in face of the enemy's advance, the two brigades began to fall back. For the enemy, as the 99th Infantry Brigade withdrew, had poured across the Bapaume–Albert road in large numbers, and with extraordinary rapidity had passed into and beyond Le Sars to the high ground, where his machine guns soon raked the British trenches. So, covering their own retirement, the 5th and 6th Infantry Brigades fell back through Miraumont on Auchonvillers. The units of the 99th Infantry Brigade, seeing their comrades retiring, likewise moved back on Auchonvillers.

One by one the battalions drew out of the line, over the ridge, down into the Ancre valley. Great difficulty was experienced by officers in co-ordinating the movements of their battalions, for the enemy's pressure was severe, and shrapnel in bursts swept the ridge across which the troops were retiring. Near Miraumont the exhausted men were collected, and in good order were marched back to Auchonvillers.

At 4.45 p.m. 2nd Division Headquarters issued orders to the brigades to form a defensive line east of Beaumont Hamel: " The Division will form a defensive line on the high ground east of Beaumont Hamel; 5th Brigade south of the Beaumont Hamel–Miraumont road; 6th and 99th Brigades north of the road AAA. Owing to the hurried manner in which these orders have to be given, it is impossible to lay down the exact position to be taken up by brigades; but the object is to cover the crossings of the river Ancre, and to delay the enemy's advance so as to give time for the fresh division to come up."

These orders had already been issued verbally. 2nd Division Headquarters were now back in Auchonvillers, having been speeded out of Miraumont just before 2 p.m. by two salvos of 4.2's which the enemy put down, all on the village, but without causing a single casualty.

But the story must be thrown back two hours, to the retirement which began at 2 p.m., for it was during this rearward movement that the 17th Royal Fusiliers on the left of the 6th Infantry Brigade fought a rearguard action with extraordinary stoutness and with great gallantry.

Lieut.-Colonel S. V. P. Weston, commanding the battalion, had

"AT ALL COSTS." 579

halted his rearguard on the Pys–Miraumont road in order to collect stragglers and to reorganize. Two companies, C and D, had passed through, and were already well out of reach. The remaining troops of the battalion numbered 2 officers and about 100 men, and 100 men of the 24th Royal Fusiliers had just passed.

A brigadier of the 51st Division rode up and asked for the senior officer, and on Colonel Weston going forward, was given these orders : " The Corps Commander's orders are that the Irles–Pys–Courcelette line is to be held at all costs. . . . The 51st Division is on your left." Colonel Weston pointed out that the whole of the 6th Infantry Brigade certainly, and, from all appearances, the whole of the 2nd Division, had gone back to Auchonvillers; that he had no men to hold such a stretch of line, and that his ammunition was almost exhausted. But he would do all that was possible. The brigadier then rode off.

The Fusiliers were not in touch with the 51st Division; but through field-glasses troops of the latter could be seen on a hill to the north. A cyclist orderly was dispatched to Brigade Headquarters asking for reinforcements and ammunition, and an officer was sent off hurriedly to fetch back the 100 of the 24th Royal Fusiliers who had passed but a little while before.

Colonel Weston then made his dispositions. They are given in his own words : " I then strung out my own two companies on the left flank in a series of posts in shell-holes at the top of the ridge. B, in a series of posts under Second-Lieut. Panting, I put on the left and ordered him to try and get in touch with the 51st Division. Next to him I put A Company, under Captain Aylmer. The company of the 24th Royal Fusiliers then came up, and I got them in position on the right. On my right flank I could see no troops of ours for miles."

In this position the gallant little band of men waited for the enemy to advance.

Shortly after 2.30 p.m. a heavy concentrated barrage came down on the ridge, which was also enfiladed by machine-gun fire. Under cover of this storm of shells and bullets, the enemy tried to rush the position. Though making desperate efforts to reach the thin line of defenders, the enemy was beaten off, and great losses inflicted on his troops. They were gallant fellows, those Germans, but they were faced by men whose courage had been so often tried and had not been found wanting. At one period it looked as if the line must break. Immediately the officers, rushing along the line of the ridge and exposing themselves fearlessly, rallied the men magnificently. Away on the left the 51st Division was seen to waver; but here also the Scotsmen were being rallied by their officers. The line held.

The XXXVIth Brigade R.F.A., in action on the Courcelette–Miraumont road, swept the enemy's positions with shrapnel and high explosive, and splendidly covered the infantry.

By 4 p.m. Captain Aylmer and Lieut. Panting had been wounded, but both officers refused to withdraw. The struggle was, however, drawing to a close. For no matter how bravely men fought, numbers told in the end, and the gallant Fusiliers had lost very heavily. Shortly after 4 o'clock Major Pretty, second in command, reached Battalion Headquarters, and reported that the enemy had worked round his right flank. Hastily collecting all Battalion Headquarters Staff, signallers, and runners, and any other troops he could muster, Colonel Weston rushed them up and formed a defensive flank, covering the Miraumont road. But now the left flank gave way, for the 51st Division had again been pressed back, uncovering the left of the gallant Fusiliers. The end came rapidly. No reinforcements were in sight, all ammunition had been exhausted, and it was physically impossible to do any more. Faced by that terrible but necessary standing order which imposed on every officer the responsibility of shooting any of his men who retired without orders, Colonel Weston stated in his report: "I could not shoot the remnants of the men, now reduced to about forty, who had fought so well." And no one could blame him.

At 4.30 p.m. a retirement down the road leading to the bridge under the railway at Miraumont was carried out, and Major Pretty with six men, with nothing but certain death staring them in the face, was left behind to cover the withdrawal. Major Pretty was killed, with five of his men, and only Sergeant Butterworth survived. "The officers," said Colonel Weston, "maintained the highest traditions of the 2nd Division. The men fought most gallantly; but, as was natural in their exhausted state, and in a completely isolated position, had to be rallied when they saw that there was a danger of their being surrounded. Touch was never secured with either flank. After the Brigadier-General rode away no word was received from the 51st Division. Touch was never secured with my own Brigadier. All the lightly wounded were man-handled and got away."

Thus ended another glorious episode in the history of the 2nd Division.

DISPOSITIONS AT NIGHT—25TH MARCH.

Meanwhile the three brigades were marching back in good order to the river crossings at Beaucourt and Hamel. Evening had begun to fall, and the enemy's pressure slackened, though his guns still shelled Miraumont and the Ancre valley heavily. The news that a fresh division was coming up to relieve them heartened the men considerably, even though they were dog-tired and worn out with fighting and fasting.

Just a little over a year previously the 2nd Division had advanced across much of the country evacuated that day. The ground between Miraumont, Courcelette, Le Sars, and Loupart Wood was familiar to those serving with the Division when it had followed up the enemy as he retired to the Hindenburg Line early in 1917. Indeed, just north of Courcelette, in a now disused trench across which the 6th Infantry Brigade had retired that very day, a gallant N.C.O. (who was later given a commission) of the 22nd Royal Fusiliers had won his Victoria Cross.

Back at Beaucourt, along the banks of the Ancre, the battalions as they arrived were, under Divisional orders, disposed so as to cover the river crossings and fill gaps. The 1st King's were on the right in touch with the 63rd Division on *their* right, at Hamel; the 2nd Highland Light Infantry were on the left of the King's. On the high ground, behind these two battalions, were the 24th Royal Fusiliers. The Oxford and Bucks were on the left of the Highland Light Infantry, with their left on the station road leading from Beaucourt, and crossing up the valley to Beaumont Hamel. Behind the Oxford and Bucks were the 17th Royal Fusiliers and the 2nd South Staffords. The northern side of the valley was held by the 23rd Royal Fusiliers, 1st Royal Berks, 10th Duke of Cornwall's Light Infantry, and about 120 men belonging to the 50th Brigade (17th Division), under Lieut.-Colonel Thomas, East Yorkshire Regiment, who had a strong flank guard facing north, as there were no troops in touch on that flank. The 1st King's Royal Rifles were in reserve, with a small party of stragglers from the 17th Division.

As on the previous evening, the enemy, as darkness fell, bivouacked on the ground he had won, and made no attempt to follow up his retiring opponents. His guns, however, continued to fire in a desultory fashion, with occasional furious bursts.

During this brief respite it was possible to bring up rations and serve out a hot meal to the famished troops, many of whom having fed, fell asleep where they sat ; the limits of human endurance had almost been reached. Ammunition dumps were formed by men who were less worn out. Divisional Headquarters, which had been at Auchonvillers all the afternoon, had moved back to Bertrancourt; but during the evening the General Officer Commanding Division went up to Beaucourt and visited all brigades in the line. " I saw all brigadiers and some commanding officers," said General Pereira; " nearly all of them are voiceless from the effects of gas and the intense fatigue they had undergone."

Thus, so far as it concerned the 2nd Division, the First Battle of Bapaume was over. On the night of March 25, 1918, the line of the Third Army, as reported in the Official Dispatches, ran from Curlu, on the left bank of the Somme, north-east of Maricourt, through Montauban, east and north-west of Contalmaison, Ovillers, and Thiepval, thence back to the east bank of the Ancre at St. Pierre Divion. From the latter village the line followed the river to west of Miraumont, north again through the Beauregard Dovecote to east of Puisieux, where it bent outwards south, south-east, and east of the two Achiets, north again midway between Behagnies and Gomiecourt, then north-north-east of Revillers, Hamelincourt, Boyelles, through Henin to Fampoux, thence to Rœux.

Heavy fighting had taken place during the 25th south of the Somme on the Fifth Army front, and although French troops were reinforcing Sir H. Gough's sorely tried men, and had been ordered to take over the Fifth Army front south of Péronne, some days had yet to pass before General Pétain could bring up troops in sufficient strength to arrest the enemy's progress. On the night of the 25th Sir H. Gough's line ran from Curlu southwards, through Herbecourt, just east of Ablaincourt, Chavines, Cremecy, thence due east to Billancourt, south of Nesle.

Ludendorff's summing up of the operations of his three armies is far from triumphant, despite the ground won: " On the 25th March," he said, " the Seventeenth and Second Armies had passed far beyond the line Bapaume–Combles, fighting hard all the way; the Eighteenth Army had taken Nesle, and met with but little resistance. The Seventeenth Army was already exhausted; it had lost too heavily on the 21st and 22nd, apparently because it had fought in too dense formation.[1] The Second Army was fresher, but was already complaining of the old shell-holes. It could get no farther than Albert."[2]

---

[1] An old fault, dating from the early days of Mons and the Battles of Ypres, 1914.
[2] It did not reach Albert until 26th.

The Withdrawal to the Old British Front Line, 26th March 1918.

About midnight on the 25th March Vth Corps Headquarters ordered a readjustment of the line which entailed a further withdrawal by the 2nd Division on the 26th. These orders defined the main line of resistance allotted to the 2nd Division as approximately the Old British Front Line from Q.17,d. to Q.10,a. The line actually occupied by the Division was much longer.

The hot meal issued to the battalions after they had settled down in the line on the previous evening, followed by a few hours' sleep, had worked wonders. The men, whose courage and cheerfulness had never deserted them even under the terrible strain of the anxious days through which they had passed, awoke in the early hours of the 26th March ready to meet the enemy again, no matter his overwhelming strength.

26TH MARCH.

Just before dawn the three brigades were again on the move, this time to take up a line which many of the troops knew well enough—the Old British Line held in the Somme battles of 1916, in front of Auchonvillers, a line from which there was to be no withdrawal. "It is distinctly to be understood," said Vth Corps orders, "that no retirement is to take place unless the tactical situation imperatively demands it."

By 8.30 a.m., unmolested by the enemy, whose exhaustion was apparent by the lateness of his morning activity, the 2nd Division was disposed as follows: the 6th Infantry Brigade on the right, holding the Hamel–Thiepval Bridge to Q.17,a.6.4; the 99th Infantry Brigade in the centre from Q.17,a.6.4 to Q.10,central; the 5th Infantry Brigade on the left from Q.10,central to east of and including Auchonvillers; a Composite Force of about 400 men, reinforcements under Major Smith (1st King's Royal Rifle Corps), was on the left of the 5th Infantry Brigade, facing north along the northern outskirts of Auchonvillers; the 2nd Battalion, Machine Gun Corps, was now moving to Mailly Maillet from Hénencourt. The order of battalions from right to left was: 17th Royal Fusiliers, 2nd South Staffords, 2nd Oxford and Bucks, 1st King's, 1st King's Royal Rifle Corps, 10th Duke of Cornwall's Light Infantry (Pioneers), 23rd Royal Fusiliers, 1st Royal Berks, 2nd Highland Light Infantry, 24th Royal Fusiliers, and the Composite Force.

The old trenches were found to be in fair condition, and the men settled down to await the enemy's next attack, which all ranks felt would not be long delayed. The men had refilled their bandoliers, and the machine gunners and Lewis gunners had plenty of ammunition. About 9.30 a.m. two battalions of Germans with transport were seen marching up the Miraumont road to Beaucourt, and the artillery at once got on to them; but ere long the Station Road Valley and the famous " Y " Valley were full of the enemy's troops, and in a little while they were occupying their old front line almost as if there had been no retreat to the Hindenburg Line a year before. The Lewis guns and the battalion snipers now got to work and took heavy toll of the enemy.

The left flank, however, was a great source of anxiety. Patrols pushing on as far as Hébuterne found no trace of British troops between the left flank of the 2nd Division and that place. " The gap to the north," reported the General Officer Commanding 5th Infantry Brigade to Divisional Headquarters later, " was found to extend to beyond Hébuterne, and the enemy was approaching that place and Serre by 9.30 a.m."

The situation was indeed serious, for a successful outflanking movement by the enemy would compel a further retirement of the Division. So the 5th Infantry Brigade had to prolong its line gradually northwards, but it was a hopeless task in the face of the enemy's numbers. By 12.20 p.m. the enemy was in possession of the Sugar Factory north-north-west of Auchonvillers, and by 2 p.m. he had established machine guns in Colincamps Cemetery. But once again the Divisional Artillery saved the situation. A section of the 15th Battery (XXXVIth Brigade R.F.A.), under Lieut.-Colonel A. A. Goschen, galloped out into the open and, engaging the machine guns over open sights, soon succeeded in knocking them out. The Pioneers were ordered to move their reserve company up to the north of Auchonvillers, while the 2nd Battalion, Machine Gun Corps, which had now arrived in Mailly Maillet, was ordered forward to a position on the railway line in Q.1,c with the object of covering the high ground in Q.2.

At 2.40 p.m. the enemy, supported by field artillery, was observed massing for an attack. But New Zealand troops had been arriving in driblets, and by the time the enemy was about to launch his attack along the line Sugar Factory–One Tree Hill, were about a brigade strong. They prolonged the left flank of the 5th Infantry Brigade, and with some tanks which had suddenly emerged from Colincamps, engaged the enemy and drove him back. But for the timely arrival of the New Zealanders there is no doubt the left flank of the 2nd Division must have been turned.

Along the front of the 99th and 6th Infantry Brigades the

enemy had been engaged all day. During the morning large bodies of German troops could be seen advancing along the Miraumont road, while no less than twenty-four hostile guns coming into action were counted. The two brigades were shelled intermittently and heavily during the day, but all attempts of the enemy to launch attacks were broken up. The Lewis gunners made fine practice, and with the infantry so obtained mastery over the enemy that not until dusk was he able to mount a machine gun.

The splendid fighting spirit of the troops that day is shown in the Battalion Diary of the 10th Duke of Cornwall's Light Infantry (Pioneers). The diary is dated March 26, 1918: "The position was splendid, and ample small-arms ammunition had now begun to arrive. The general outlook was very hopeful, and ' hang on ' was the idea and kill the Boche. True to time the enemy appeared over the opposite crest. Slowly he came, feeling his way; then he began to collect in the dead ground about Station Road. He then proceeded to advance, and the best of sport ensued. . . . Towards 5 p.m. the enemy dare not show so much as his finger, and movement died out in the enemy's lines altogether. He was undoubtedly beaten on this occasion and showed no enterprise at all. In ' Y ' Ravine some very fine sport occurred. A message was got through to the artillery that the enemy had collected in the ravine. The artillery did some fine shooting and soon the enemy started to run for it."

What will coming generations think of the word "sport" used in the above connection? Will they understand that the British soldier in the year 1918 was still the finest sportsman in the whole world?

The New Zealanders on the left of the 5th Infantry Brigade had advanced under the impression that the gap was much larger than it actually was, and in consequence advanced on the whole Divisional front, eventually taking over the sector. For, from 7.30 p.m. onwards on the 26th March, the three infantry brigades of the 2nd Division were withdrawn from the front line, and made their way back to Mailly Maillet Wood, where they bivouacked in bitterly cold weather.

"Such," said the Divisional summary of operations, which is here given on account of its excellence, "is the course of events as far as they concern the 2nd Division from 21st March to the 26th, a period fraught with peril to the Third Army as well as to the Fifth Army, and one which will live long in the memory of those who toiled painfully back over the twenty miles of country which had been wrested from the enemy since July 1916. Rearguard actions are recognized to be the severest test of the fortitude and ability of professional soldiers; and where the majority of officers and men have never known what it is to be a 'flank in the air,' the moral and physical strain is greatly enhanced. Tired and unfit at the outset, the Division fought its way back with stubborn and unflinching courage; stopped to strike, then turned and limped back a few more miles; again and again would have stood at bay and held its ground, but for the restless ebb of the tide to right and left, and the monotonous order to withdraw and to keep touch; till at last the men believed that they were playing a part in an ingenious plan to lure the enemy into a fatal trap. Nor can the measure of our men's achievements be taken unless due credit is given to our enemy. All ranks bear witness to his ordered mobility; his rapid enveloping movements; the patrols that signalled when they located our positions; the light machine guns that were instantly in action; the lamp-signalling from front to rear; the trench mortars with hand-carts of ammunition; the low-flying aeroplanes that dropped lights above our troops; the artillery that found us at once. All was carried out like clockwork. But these fresh troops, freshly trained, well equipped, could not have shaken the resistance if it had been adequately supported. Time after time the German advance was brought to a standstill by a handful of resolute men; and even at the end of it all, when at last there was to be no more retiring, 'every one agreed that it had been a top-hole day,' says one Commanding Officer. The one aim and object of all was to capture, kill, or maim the enemy. The spirit of death to the enemy was far greater, the *esprit de corps* far greater, the will to win was far more pronounced, the grim determination to conquer was far and away greater at the end than at the commencement of the operations." Brave words these, and well justified at any rate in the case of that particular battalion. Fine leadership and steadfast following brought the infantry back undismayed from Metz to Auchonvillers. In this brief summary little space has been given to the work of the Artillery, the Engineers, and the Machine-Gun Battalion, and the difficulties of the Signalling and of the Medical arrangements that were overcome. The evacuation of the wounded was immensely complicated by the shortage of motor ambulances, and the necessity for moving the dressing stations back in the general retirement; but the narratives of the fighting are everywhere punctuated by tales of the heroic and indefatigable work by medical officers and regimental stretcher-bearers. Prominent, too, amongst the golden deeds recorded are the acts of signallers, linesmen, and runners, whom the will to succeed carried through the days of acute danger and exhaustion. The machine gunners were hampered by circumstances; but whenever an opportunity occurred fine work was done, and many individual deeds of gallantry and perseverance, of deadly shooting and invaluable covering fire, have come to light. The sappers never failed the infantry when a chance was given to them to help; and on more than one occasion they were thrown into the fight to fill a gap. And the gunners in the vast turmoil of traffic and almost unsurpassable difficulties of locations and communications, maintained the reliance that the 2nd Division had always placed on its own artillery, and, especially by Le Sars and Auchonvillers, had some extremely fine and accurate shooting and scored heavily; open warfare did not catch them unprepared.

"But in the end we revert to the infantry, to the Lewis guns, manned often by one survivor and firing to the last, to the officers rallying their men and the men responding to the grim daring of the seasoned N.C.O's, and the spirit and grit of the young recruits; and with the same pride and the same assurance, as often before, we can say that the highest traditions of the 2nd Division were maintained."

And what of the Army Service Corps—the personnel of the Divisional Train—whose devotion to the troops in the front line during those terrible days of retirements is all the more eloquent because it is unrecorded! The difficulties of supply were enormous, and yet the " goods were delivered " at the refilling stations with fine regularity. Well, indeed, did the Corps serve its comrades during the March retreat of 1918.

* * * * * * *

On the 26th March the Governments of France and Great Britain decided to place the supreme control of the operations of the French and British forces in France and Belgium in the hands of General Foch, who accordingly assumed command.

The Last Days of March 1918 and the Resumption of Trench Warfare.

The 5th, 6th, and 99th Infantry Brigades, bivouacking behind Mailly Maillet, passed a wretched and uncomfortable night; the troops were without overcoats, and the bitterness of the weather made sleep impossible.

588 THE HISTORY OF THE SECOND DIVISION.

27TH MARCH.

During the night 26th–27th March the enemy captured Albert, and the position north of that town was by no means secure. He had also obtained a footing in Aveluy Wood, and from this position, on the morning of the 27th, he attacked the heights west of the Ancre, but met with no success. Throughout the morning several attempts made by him to debouch from Albert were immediately stopped, and he was driven back with heavy losses. About midday he attacked the New Zealanders on the line Serre–Beaumont Hamel, but was again repulsed. The 5th and 6th Infantry Brigades were, however, ordered to "stand to," though they were not called upon to join in the action.

At 8 p.m. on the night of the 27th, after a trying day, the 5th Infantry Brigade was on the move to Martinsart, under orders to relieve the 188th Infantry Brigade (63rd Division) in support of 12th Division; the 6th Infantry Brigade was on the road to Englebelmer, to relieve the 189th Infantry Brigade (63rd Division), and the 99th Infantry Brigade, with the Pioneers and two companies of the 2nd Battalion, Machine Gun Corps, at Forceville. The two remaining companies of the machine gunners were attached, one each, to the 5th and 6th Infantry Brigades.[1]

At 8.45 p.m. Divisional Headquarters opened at Varennes.

The reliefs by the 5th and 6th Infantry Brigades were completed at 5.45 a.m. on the 28th March without incident.

28TH MARCH.

The three battalions of the 5th Infantry Brigade were disposed: 24th Royal Fusiliers along the line of the railway north of Aveluy Wood, with their right flank partly in the wood and their left east of Mesnil, just opposite the Passerelle de Magenta; the Oxford and Bucks were in the wood, 500 yards from the northern exits, facing south, with their left in touch with the 24th Royal Fusiliers and their right in touch with the left of the 2nd Highland Light Infantry, who covered the eastern exits of the village of Martinsart. The brigade was now supporting the 12th Division, who had originally held the line from Hamel to Aveluy, but had been pressed back, losing both villages and also Authuille. The enemy's snipers had already penetrated Aveluy Wood.

At 10 a.m. the enemy attempted to advance in a north-westerly direction from the railway embankment on the east of Aveluy Wood. He succeeded in penetrating the wood for some distance, driving back troops of the 12th Division; but the 24th Royal Fusiliers

---

[1] On the 27th March Brigadier-General E. Ironside joined the Division as General Officer Commanding 99th Infantry Brigade, *vice* Brigadier-General A. Barnett Barker, killed during the retreat.

THE DEPLETED 2ND DIVISION. 589

counter-attacked and, driving the enemy before them, killed 40, and captured a light machine gun and two Germans.

About midday the General Officer Commanding 2nd Division was ordered to take over command of both Infantry Brigades (36th and 37th) of the 12th Division in the line; also to assume command of the front line from Hamel (exclusive) to about 1,200 yards due east of Bouzincourt. The 5th and 99th Infantry Brigades were then ordered to relieve the 37th Infantry Brigade in the line, the 6th Infantry Brigade to be in a position of readiness west of Martinsart.

These moves were completed by 2.20 a.m. on the 29th, and at 6 a.m. the 99th Infantry Brigade was on the right from Q.35,d.2.2, to and exclusive of Mesnil; the 5th Infantry Brigade on the left from Mesnil to Hamel, in touch at the latter place with the New Zealand Division.

29TH MARCH.

The exhaustion of all troops of the 2nd Division was still acute, but for a little while longer they were to hold on. Nothing of importance happened during the day of the 29th, and at night the 6th Infantry Brigade and the Pioneers moved up and relieved the 5th and 99th Brigades, the latter passing back into Divisional Reserve at Englebelmer and the 5th Infantry Brigade to Hedauville.

Reinforcements which had been arriving for the 2nd Division were formed into a " Composite Battalion," and on the night 30th–31st March relieved the 6th Infantry Brigade and Pioneers. At 2.30 a.m. on the 31st the Composite Battalion, under Lieut.-Colonel Murray-Lyon of the 1st King's, held the front line, the 99th Infantry Brigade and Pioneers were at Englebelmer, the 6th Infantry Brigade at Hedauville, and the 5th Infantry Brigade at Varennes.

Some idea of the depleted ranks of the 2nd Division may be gathered from the " Trench Strength " of the three infantry brigades on the 30th March. Of the 5th Infantry Brigade, the 2nd Highland Light Infantry numbered 14 officers and 516 other ranks; the 2nd Oxford and Bucks, 17 officers and 314 other ranks; the 24th Royal Fusiliers, 18 officers and 419 other ranks. Of the 6th Infantry Brigade, the 1st King's numbered 20 officers and 331 other ranks; the 2nd South Staffords, 9 officers and 387 other ranks; the 17th Royal Fusiliers, 10 officers and 481 other ranks. Of the 99th Infantry Brigade, the 1st Royal Berks had 18 officers and 543 other ranks; the 1st King's Royal Rifle Corps, 15 officers and 351 other ranks; the 23rd Royal Fusiliers, 15 officers and 498 other ranks. The three brigades together totalled 136 officers and 3,899 other ranks. Even including those who were not present with their units or at the disposal of their Commanding Officers the three brigades could only muster 249 officers and 5,819 other ranks. The casualties suffered by the Division during the recent operations were approximately 207 officers and 3,721 other ranks. The latter unfortunately included many senior N.C.O's.

Well, indeed, might the General Officer Commanding 2nd Division view with anxiety the state of his Division. " I saw the 99th Infantry Brigade march out," he said; " some of the men looked very drawn, and there are a lot of boys that had just joined them, and who look too immature to stand a long bout like the one we are just through. The only consolation is that many of the Boche prisoners are still younger."

2ND–4TH APRIL.

Orders for the relief of the 2nd Division were received on the 2nd April, and on the 3rd and 4th April the 5th and 6th Infantry Brigades and the Pioneers marched out of the line, handing over to the 63rd Division.

Divisional Headquarters closed at 10 a.m. on the 4th April, and during the day moved to Flers. Until the 11th the three infantry brigades were training and resting, and absorbing into their depleted ranks the reinforcements which from time to time came to hand. " Our chief difficulty now is experienced N.C.O's, company commanders, and specialists. We can do wonders if only we get two or three weeks' rest." But it was not to be. Fighting divisions with such fine records as that held by the 2nd Division were not allowed long out of the line, and on the 12th (Divisional Headquarters then being at Couturelle) a warning order was issued to the troops forecasting the relief of the Guards Division in the right sector of the VIth Corps area. Two days later, the 5th Infantry Brigade moved from the Saulty area and relieved the 1st Guards Brigade in the centre sub-sector of the right sector VIth Corps–Bertrancourt, south of Arras. On the 15th the 6th Infantry Brigade relieved the 2nd Guards Brigade, and the 99th Infantry Brigade the 3rd Guards Brigade in the left and right sub-sectors respectively.

All three brigades of the 2nd Division were now in the front line, with the 32nd Division on the right and the 2nd Canadian Division on the left.

It was a sector new to the 2nd Division. Across No Man's Land, in the enemy's lines, were the three villages of Moyenneville, Hamelincourt, and Boyelles, connected by a somewhat ragged, irregular system of trenches. Indeed in places the enemy's front line was held in a number of shell-holes. The British lines were very little better; there were few, if any, communication trenches,

A HEAVY RAID ON THE KING'S.

and behind the front line movement by day was impossible. A large amount of work was necessary before the line would be anything like secure or habitable. A number of sunken roads passed through both the enemy's and the British lines, and great vigilance was necessary. It was a sector admirably adapted to trench warfare and patrol fights out in No Man's Land.

Through the left sub-sector taken over by the 6th Infantry Brigade there ran a sunken road between the villages of Boyelles and Boisleux St. Marc. It was down this road that, early on the 16th April, the enemy made a heavy raid on the 1st King's, who had only a few hours previously taken over the left of the sub-sector. The 2nd South Staffords were on the right of the King's, and Canadian troops were on the left. *16TH APRIL.*

The night of the 15th–16th had been very quiet, but at 9 a.m. on the 16th the enemy opened a very heavy barrage on the King's front line. For half an hour "whizz-bangs," 4.2's, 5.9 shells, and light and heavy trench mortar bombs fell in large numbers. The bombardment lifted at 9.30 a.m. on to the support and reserve trenches, but by this time the King's had suffered heavy casualties, including the officer in charge of both front companies. The enemy now launched his infantry attack, advancing rapidly along the sunken road from Boisleux St. Marc to Boyelles and a communication trench leading to an unoccupied trench running parallel to the King's front line.

The Germans were in considerable strength, and were able to penetrate the front line in four places. From these positions the enemy began bombing operations, and soon established himself. The Divisional artillery had by this time opened fire and put down a very heavy barrage, which caused considerable losses amongst the enemy's reinforcements hurrying down the sunken road and communication trench.

By 10 a.m. the enemy held possession of a strip of front-line trench between 400 and 500 yards in length. At both ends of the strip of lost trench the King's had, however, built blocks, and from these two points presently counter-attacked the enemy. On the right B Company succeeded in driving him out of the trench, whilst on the left, with the timely assistance of the Canadians, 200 yards of the front line were recovered. Three fire-bays were all that now remained in the hands of the enemy.

Another attack up the sunken road towards the Picquet line was made by the enemy about 11 a.m., but it was completely broken up by Lewis gun and rifle fire. But by now the left bombing party of the King's (under Second-Lieut. H. Foster) was very weak, and formed a block in the trench; but before it could be completed, Second-Lieut. R. T. Symonds arrived with another party of eighteen other ranks and carried on the bombing fight. At 11.30 a.m. Second-Lieut. W. Wilson, with twenty-five other ranks of D Company, rejoined the line, relieving Lieut. Symonds and his party.

About 1.30 p.m. the enemy made a third determined attack on the line, and succeeded in driving the left bombing party of the King's back about 200 yards. In this attack Second-Lieut. Wilson was wounded.

Battalion Headquarters were now uncertain as to the exact position in the front line, and, owing to the nature of the ground to be covered, no messages could be got through. It was at this period that No. 94081 Private Jack Thomas Counter, 1st King's Regiment, volunteered to obtain the necessary information. The only way was from the support line along a sunken road, and then down a forward slope for about 250 yards, with no cover, in full view of the enemy and swept by his machine-gun and rifle fire. A small party had tried unsuccessfully to get through, but the leader was killed and another man wounded. Single men then attempted to get through, but on each occasion the runner was killed in full view of the position from which he had started.

"Private Counter, who was near his officer at the time and had seen four runners killed one after the other, then volunteered to carry the message. He went out under terrific fire and succeeded in getting through. He then returned, carrying with him the vital information with regard to the estimated number of the enemy in our line, the exact position of our flanks, and the remaining strength of our troops. This information enabled his Commanding Officer to organize and launch the final counter-attack which succeeded in regaining the whole of our positions."[1] Subsequently Private Counter carried back five messages across the open, under a heavy artillery fire, to Company Headquarters. This gallant man's extraordinary courage in facing what appeared to be almost certain death was most inspiring to his young and untrained companions, who had been with the battalion little more than a week or two.

At 2.30 p.m. Second-Lieut. R. T. Symonds, with a platoon of C Company and one of A Company, together with a platoon of 2nd South Staffords, reinforced the front line, and a counter-attack was made. The 19th Canadian Battalion sent half a company

---

[1] Private Counter was awarded the Victoria Cross "for most conspicuous gallantry and devotion to duty."—*London Gazette*, May 22, 1918.

ALL GROUND RECOVERED.

into the reserve trenches of the King's, who had by now only one platoon which had not taken part in the fighting.

Finally, at 3.15 p.m., Captains E. R. Mace and J. A. Armstrong arrived with twenty other ranks. A little while later the enemy began to dribble back to his front line, heavy toll being taken of the hostile troops as they retired. By 6.30 p.m. the whole line had been restored, and all the posts re-established. Two German machine guns and four wounded prisoners were taken. Eight dead Germans were left behind in the front-line trench. A large number of stick bombs, belts of small arms ammunition, picks, shovels, and much blood-stained equipment of all kinds were also left behind by the enemy, but he had been able to carry off the majority of his wounded.

The casualties suffered by the King's included Second-Lieut. G. P. Williams killed, Second-Lieuts. Purdon and Wilson wounded, 17 other ranks killed, 4 died of wounds, 61 wounded, and 20 missing.

The battalion was relieved later by the 17th Royal Fusiliers, and marched back to Blairville into brigade reserve. The Battalion Diary records that " Congratulations were received from General Officer Commanding 2nd Division, and General Officer Commanding 6th Infantry Brigade, on the excellent day's fighting of the battalion."

This raid was the first of many made by, or on, the enemy during the next few months. The period was one of great anxiety, and identifications were constantly required in order to keep touch with the movements of the enemy's troops. Raids for this purpose were also made by the enemy.

On the 22nd April a fighting patrol from the 2nd Highland Light Infantry crossed No Man's Land at 3.45 a.m. Three enemy posts were entered, but they had already been evacuated. From another post heavy rifle fire was opened on the patrol who, nothing daunted, rushed the post and carried off one prisoner, who supplied the necessary identification.

22ND APRIL.

Four days later the enemy again raided the King's in the left brigade sector, but on entering the trenches was immediately ejected. No identifications were obtained by either side.

The General Officer Commanding 6th Infantry Brigade (Brigadier-General R. K. Walsh) left for England on the 28th April for a six months' tour of duty, and Brigadier-General A. H. Hart Synnot took over command of the Brigade. But unfortunately the latter officer had both legs blown off on 11th May, and the

Brigade-Major, Captain E. L. Wright (of the same Brigade) was killed, both from shell-fire. On the following day Brigadier-General F. G. Willan, D.S.O., took over command of the Brigade.

12TH–13TH MAY.

The 2nd Division was relieved on the night of the 12th–13th May by the 32nd Division, and the three brigades were soon disposed in Barly (6th Infantry Brigade), Bavincourt (5th Infantry Brigade), and La Herlière (99th Infantry Brigade). The Division was now in VIth Corps reserve. At last an opportunity had been given the 2nd Division to train the large numbers of reinforcements but recently arrived. It was during this period of training that the American forces in considerable numbers began to arrive and train with their British comrades in arms. " It gave me a feeling of elation," said the General Officer Commanding 2nd Division, " to see the lines of Americans doing the attack, as they are the forerunners of millions that will now rapidly mature and redress the balance of men on the Western front and bring near the moment when the Germans will be overwhelmed." The German offensive on the Aisne had just begun (27th May), and although the enemy had penetrated fifteen miles into the French position, it was a desperate effort, and with the Americans arriving at the rate of a quarter of a million a month, did not cause the Allies untoward uneasiness. Early in June there were no less than eighteen American divisions on the Western front, totalling over half a million men.

6TH JUNE.

On the nights 6th–7th and 7th–8th June the 2nd Division again went into the line, taking over the Bazèque Wood area. For almost a month the Division had been out of the line, training and resting, but at the beginning of June received orders to relieve the Guards Division. On the 5th June Lieut.-Colonel Brett and one officer per company of the 1st Royal Berks went out to reconnoitre the forward area to be taken over by the battalion. But unfortunately the party was caught in an enemy bombardment. As a result Colonel Brett was wounded, and Second-Lieuts. H. M. Avery, S. C. Beresford, and A. L. Row were killed; Second-Lieut. J. H. Spencer was also wounded, and died later of his wounds.

The 6th Infantry Brigade took over the centre sub-sector of the line on the 7th–8th June, and the 5th and 99th Infantry Brigades the left and right sub-sectors respectively on the night 8th–9th. The 62nd Division was on the right and the 32nd Division on the left flanks of the 2nd Division.

The strength of the Division on the 8th June, including the Pioneers and 2nd Battalion, Machine-Gun Corps, was 296 officers and 8,561 other ranks. Officers and other ranks not present with their units, and therefore not at the disposal of their Commanding Officers, numbered 120 and 1,826.

On the 3rd June 2nd Division Headquarters had circulated a notice emanating from the Army Commander:[1] "The Army Commander has expressed a wish that frequent identifications should be obtained by the 2nd Division whilst in the line, the principal reason being to obtain constant information of the German divisions in the line. Fighting patrols will be most suitable for the purpose. Each brigade must aim at securing an identification every ten days."[2]

Thus began another period of raids and counter-raids.

Just a week after the Division had taken over the front line, on the night 13th–14th June, the enemy, after a heavy bombardment, tried to raid the 2nd South Staffords, but were repulsed with heavy losses. One German officer was left dead on the Staffords' parapet, and the enemy carried off a number of wounded. No identifications were obtained by the enemy, but in the bombardment the Staffords lost 5 other ranks killed and 9 wounded.

Two nights later, the 2nd Oxford and Bucks raided the enemy. The operation was carried out by two platoons of the Oxfords, artillery action taking the form of first a straight barrage on the enemy's outpost and main lines, followed by a box barrage at "zero," plus ten minutes, round the position to be raided. But the enemy observed the forming-up operations, and when the raiders, in two platoons, crossed No Man's Land, a heavy machine-gun fire met them, and the officer in charge of the raid, Second-Lieut. W. A. Creak, was wounded. In spite of gallant efforts (No. 7876 Sergeant Bennett and Lance-Corporal Wilson are especially mentioned in the report), and the killing of five of the enemy, no identification was obtained, and the parties returned almost all wounded.

On the 24th and 25th June the 23rd Royal Fusiliers and 1st King's sent out fighting patrols, but failed to get into touch with the enemy.

The 17th Royal Fusiliers carried out a raid on the night 28th–29th, but the enemy on this occasion took to his heels, and although (under cover of a perfect barrage put down by the Divisional Artillery) his positions were entered by all three parties, only empty trenches and dug-outs were found. But the report contains

---

[1] Sir Julian Byng, Commanding Third Army, to which the VIth Corps belonged.
[2] This order must not be taken as issued only to the 2nd Division, but to all divisions in the front line.

an interesting comment by the Officer Commanding raid: " A number of the raiders were recently joined lads, just of age, and it was proved beyond doubt that, perfectly led, they make splendid soldiers and will go anywhere." Not a single casualty was suffered by the Fusiliers.

These frequent raids and the almost nightly activities of fighting patrols began to tell on the enemy's *moral*, for early in July a Brigade Diary stated: " We continue to hold complete supremacy in No Man's Land, and enemy patrols are seldom seen." A surprise encounter, however, took place on the night of the 10th July, when five men of the Oxford and Bucks, who went out to cover a wiring party, were suddenly attacked by the enemy. A hand-to-hand fight ensued, during which two Germans were shot and one ran into the British trenches, where he was promptly captured.

About the middle of July (on the night of the 14th–15th) a very successful raid was carried out by the 1st King's. On the two previous nights Captain E. R. Mace, commanding D Company of the King's, with his section leaders and scouts, went out into No Man's Land and for several hours reconnoitred the positions to be raided, and the state of the enemy's wire. Enemy posts were definitely located and approaches to some decided upon.

On the night of the raid the normal organization of a company was adhered to. The raiders were formed into eight parties, each party being a complete rifle section, with two trained battalion scouts attached as guides across No Man's Land. Two Lewis-gun sections were disposed in rear and in echelon on each flank.

The raid was supported by eight batteries of 18-pounders, four batteries of 4.5 howitzers, the 6th Light Trench Mortar Battery, and " Y " Trench Mortar Battery. " Zero " hour was 11.30 p.m. on the 14th July.

14TH JULY.

At 10.30 p.m. the raiders, led by Captain Mace, left their trenches and began to crawl towards the enemy's lines, and when the barrage began to fall they had not been detected. " The combined Field Artillery and Stokes Mortar barrage was excellent," stated the report. Registration by the gunners had been extremely accurate, and from the very outset the precision of the gunfire inspired all ranks with the utmost confidence. The Artillery had so co-ordinated their fire that when the guns lifted at " zero " plus one to two hundred yards, it appeared to the raiders as if every gun and mortar had stopped and lifted together.

Without the slightest hesitation the troops rushed forward and jumped into the enemy's posts. Nine prisoners were secured, and

SUCCESSFUL RAID BY THE BERKS. 597

nine dead Germans were found in the posts. The raiders then returned, having suffered only 1 officer slightly wounded and 6 other ranks wounded, one seriously.

The King's had at last revenged themselves upon the enemy for his raid of the 16th April!

A week later, at 12.30 a.m. on the 23rd, the 1st Royal Berks 23RD JULY. raided the enemy's lines in the vicinity of Ablainzeville. The raiding party was of considerable strength, and consisted of 6 officers and 203 other ranks. Captain V. G. Stokes was in command. "The raid took place on the night 22nd–23rd July, and all the arrangements worked well. Five prisoners were captured, as well as one machine gun, and severe casualties were inflicted on the enemy, of whom it is estimated that 50 were killed by the bayonet and rifle. The artillery barrage, which was excellent, must have inflicted further severe casualties on the enemy who, it is known, had two reserve companies in his main line on which the heavy artillery and machine-gun barrages fell."

The casualties of the raiding party were Second-Lieut. F. C. Boshell and 3 other ranks killed, and 1 officer and 30 other ranks wounded.

One interesting feature of this raid was a searchlight (worked by Major G. F. Wood, A.I.S. Third Army), which, from Monchy, threw a beam of light on the clouds, giving a clear mark to the raiding party on which to withdraw; the light was exposed from 12.57 a.m. to 1.57 a.m. and drew no hostile fire.

Both of the above well-planned and executed raids drew congratulations from the Army, Corps, and Divisional Commanders.

An enemy raid on the 2nd Highland Light Infantry, at 2 a.m. on the 28th July, which was abortive, and another raid by the King's, on the 29th–30th, splendidly carried out by all ranks of A Company under the command of Captain E. Beesley, and accurately supported by the 6th Trench Mortar Battery (Captain Harrison) and the Centre Group Artillery (Lieut.-Colonel P. Barton), closed a month of difficult but highly successful trench warfare.[1]

So far as the 2nd Division was concerned, the culminating effort in trench warfare against the enemy line took place in the early hours of the 14th August, when by far the largest raid made by 14TH AUG. the Division was carried out by B and C Companies of the 1st King's (Captain R. E. Head and Captain W. J. A. Pratt), and two composite platoons of A Company of the 1st King's Royal Rifle Corps

[1] Casualties, Second-Lieut. Ellis and 2 other ranks killed, and 9 slightly wounded.

(99th Infantry Brigade) under Lieut. G. Fardell and Lieut. D. W. Robertson.

Complete success attended this operation, which, like the others preceding it, was finely organized and well carried out, with splendid co-operation on the part of the Stokes mortars and the Divisional Artillery. The King's captured seven prisoners and two light machine guns, and many of the enemy were killed. The King's Royal Rifles captured six prisoners and one light machine gun. The casualties were extraordinarily light : the King's had 2 officers and 3 other ranks wounded ; and the Rifles 1 other rank killed, and 3 wounded.

But north and south of the 2nd Division the British line was already pressing forward again, for on the 8th August about fifteen miles of the enemy's positions between Albert and Villers Bretonneux, and something over twenty miles of his front line, from just north of Béthune to Bailleul, had been captured—the Advance to Victory had begun.

A Note on the General Situation between 21st March and 8th August 1918.

To the military student the period between 21st March and 8th August 1918 is full of a consuming interest. Those momentous months, during which the Allies were heavily tried and practically fought with their backs against the wall, were also of vast consequence to the enemy. The two great German offensives of 21st March and 9th April—*i.e.*, the First Battles of the Somme, 1918, and the Battle of the Lys—had failed to bring about the results they were intended to produce. Those terrific blows, launched by troops in greatly superior numbers, had failed to shake the confidence of the Allies. Even the huge losses in men and material suffered by the British and French armies did not bring forth those immediate overtures for a peaceful (but one-sided) settlement which German arrogance still imagined could be imposed upon Great Britain and France.

No more interesting view of what was happening on the Western front during those anxious six months can be obtained than by reading (side by side) the official dispatches and Ludendorff's account of the German offensive in the West, 1918, and "The Last Phase—Summer and Autumn, 1918" contained in his book of War memories. In that book the successful efforts of the Allies are shown in bold contrast with the fruitless (though at times hopeful) endeavours of German Headquarters in the Field to snatch victory with soldiers whose ranks had already become permeated with Bolshevism and discontent, and whose Government was already on the downward path; Nemesis was drawing nigh unto the peoples of the Central Powers.

It is necessary to refer to these two interesting accounts, because they show how the Allied armies were not only able to win through, but how also, corps and divisions were able after years of truly terrible fighting to advance to victory.

The great German offensive in Picardy of March had hardly finished on 5th April, when the offensive in Flanders was launched (on 9th April), finishing on 29th April with the Battle of Scherpenberg. The enemy had been successful; he had bitten deeply into the Allied line in two places over many miles of front; he had captured many prisoners (whom he took good care to exhibit in Germany to try and hearten the German people); vast quantities of stores and munitions of which he was greatly in need had fallen into his hands. But of the March offensive Ludendorff said: "Strategically we had not achieved what the results of the 23rd, 24th, and 25th March had encouraged us to hope for." The failure to take Amiens was the enemy's most bitter disappointment. Of the offensive generally the Chief of the German General Staff stated: "The result was not satisfactory." And then occurs this pregnant phrase: "Our troops fought well, but the fact that certain divisions had obviously failed to show any inclination to attack in the plains of the Lys gave food for thought."

As long as Ludendorff's numbers were superior to those of the Allies along the whole of the Western front it was possible, by taking disaffected troops out of the line and replacing them by divisions which were to be trusted, to continue the struggle and even plan and launch further offensives.[1] But the enemy with anxious eyes had noted the arrival of American troops in ever-increasing numbers, and he knew it could not be long before the Allies would be in a position to launch an offensive which would be difficult if not impossible to survive. The initiative was still with the Germans, the difficulty was to hold it. "The initiative which we had seized on the Western front," said Ludendorff in another passage, "must be kept and the first great blow must be followed by a second as

---

[1] It will be remembered that when the great German offensive on 21st March was launched, the approximate strength of the Allies on the whole of the Western front, compared with that of the enemy, was as 155 to 190 some odd divisions. The enemy admitted his superiority in numbers.

soon as possible." His reserves had indeed made good his losses in March and April, but these could not be replaced, and unless he dealt the Allies a vital blow in his next attack, the weight of the American army would be thrown in against him. The outcome of this position was the German offensive in Champagne which began on 27th May and ended on the 6th June.

The state of the British and French armies at the end of April was serious. Although in splendid spirits, Sir Douglas Haig's forces had been greatly weakened by the heavy German attacks. Reinforcements in England had received orders to cross the Channel; considerable bodies of troops from other theatres of the war had been recalled. But these troops could not arrive at once, and when they did arrive they would need training and acclimatizing. In the meantime it had become impossible to maintain at full strength the number of British divisions in France and Flanders. Early in May eight divisions had been reduced to cadres, and two others could not be made up to establishment. Five British divisions forming the IXth Corps had been lent to the French. So that in May there remained on the British front only forty-five divisions, " most of which were below establishment."

So far as the French army was concerned, a number of divisions had been placed as reserves behind the British right flank, and to strengthen the Flanders front. And though rapidly increasing in numbers, the American army was not yet ready to take the field in sufficient numbers to materially affect the situation. The position, then, in May 1918 was such that another early attack by the Germans was absolutely necessary (from their point of view), if they hoped to retain the initiative; whereas the policy of the Allies was to tide over the difficult period which must elapse before the arrival of reinforcements, and the American armies could take the field.

On the British front the period of active defence lasted throughout May, June, and July, and passed with only two outstanding actions of minor importance; the first being the Action of La Becque on 28th June, by the 5th and 31st Divisions, resulting in the capture of German defences on a front of 6,000 yards with 450 prisoners; and the capture of Meteren on 19th July by the 9th Division.

The expected German attack had been launched on the 27th May, between Rheims and Noyon, and had pressed the French back to Château Thierry and the Forêt de Villers Cotterets (so well known to the 2nd Division in 1914). In this attack certain British

THE EVE OF GREAT EVENTS.

divisions which had been lent to General Foch were involved. And so well did they uphold the honour of the British army that General Maistre, the French Commander, said, "They have enabled us to establish a barrier against which the hostile waves have beaten and shattered themselves. This none of the French who witnessed it will ever forget."

Throughout those three months, a great change had taken place in the condition of the British armies. The newly arrived men had received a good insight into active warfare, the number of effective divisions had risen from forty-five to fifty-two, and in artillery Sir Douglas Haig had become stronger than he had ever been before.

Barring the minor operations already mentioned, every division in the line practically followed out the same plan of active defence, already described as taking place along the front of the 2nd Division. And in these operations American troops were first introduced to trench warfare on the Western front, battalions and brigades being attached to British and French divisions in the front-line trenches. Many American troops received their initiation into active warfare in the trenches of the 2nd Division; and their arrival had a splendid effect on the tired and worn British and French divisions.

By the end of July the Allied armies stood ready to advance. "The spirit of the men was as high as ever," said Sir Douglas Haig, "and the success of these various local operations had had a good effect." The American armies were also ready to advance.

The time had now come when the bitter iron of despair was to enter into the soul of Germany; when her Allies either deserted her or were soon to prove unequal to the task of rendering her any assistance.

Towards the end of July the French counter-attacked in Champagne,[1] and although British divisions were again involved, the Battles of the Marne, 1918, must be termed French operations, and it was not until 8th August that the Battle of Amiens began, the first operations along the British front in The Advance to Victory.

[1] On 18th July. This counter-attack was in reply to the German attack of 15th July which had gained ground across the Marne. This was Ludendorff's "Friedensturm" ("Peace" Battle) as he called it.

VII.
THE ADVANCE TO VICTORY.

THE ADVANCE IN PICARDY.
THE SECOND BATTLES OF THE SOMME, 1918.
    The Situation up to "Zero" on 21st August 1918.
THE BATTLE OF ALBERT, 21st to 23rd August 1918.
    The Capture of Mory Copse, 24th August.
    The Capture of Behagnies and Sapignies by the 5th Infantry Brigade, 25th August.
Operations from 26th August to 1st September.

THE SECOND BATTLES OF THE SOMME, 1918.

The Situation up to "Zero" on 21st August 1918.

FROM the foregoing account of the activities of the 2nd Division during May, June, and July—activities which were common along the whole front in France and Flanders—it will be gathered that from an enforced state of active defence, the Allies passed gradually to a period of offensive action, a period unparalleled throughout the whole course of the war.

In spite of Ludendorff's statement concerning the grave importance of the German offensive of 15th July—" We dare not risk failure "—the hope of weakening the Allies had not come about, and when three days later the French launched their counter-attack in Champagne,[1] with splendid success, there was no longer any doubt that the crisis which the chief of the German Imperial Staff feared, had come.

Pregnant with great things were the closing days of July 1918. " The definite collapse of the ambitious offensive launched by the enemy on the 15th July," said Sir Douglas Haig, " and the striking success of the Allied counter-offensive south of the Aisne, effected a complete change in the whole military situation. The German army had made its effort and had failed. The period of its maximum strength had been passed, and the bulk of the reserves accumulated during the winter had been used up. On the other hand, the position of the Allies in regard to reserves had greatly improved. The fresh troops made available during the late spring and early summer had been incorporated and trained. The British army was growing rapidly and had already given convincing proof of the high quality of its soldiers. At a conference held on the 23rd July, when the success of the attack of 18th July was well assured, the methods by which the advantage already gained could be extended were discussed in detail. The Allied Commander-in-

[1] British troops were also engaged in this counter-attack—*i.e.*, the XXIInd Corps (Lieut.-General Sir A. Godley), formed of the 51st and 62nd (West Riding) Divisions, operating with the Fifth French Army, and the 15th and 34th Divisions operating with the Tenth French Army.

Chief[1] asked that the British, French, and American armies should each prepare plans for local offensives to be taken in hand as soon as possible, with certain definite objectives of a limited nature. These objectives on the British front were the disengagement of Amiens and the freeing of the Paris–Amiens railway by an attack on the Albert–Montdidier front. The rôle of the French and American armies was to free other strategic railways by operations farther south and east.

"In addition to the disengagement of Amiens, the situation on the British front, such as the disengagement of Hazebrouck by the recapture of Kemmel Hill, combined with an operation in the direction of La Bassée. If successful, such an operation would have the effect of improving our positions at Ypres and Calais. The Lys salient would be reduced and the safety of the Bruay coal mines become less threatened.

"These different operations had already been the subject of correspondence between Marshal Foch and myself, as well as of the earnest consideration of the British General Staff. Ultimately I had come to the conclusion that of the tasks assigned to the British forces, the operation east of Amiens should take precedence, as being the most important and the most likely to give large results. It would depend upon the nature of the success which might be obtained in these different Allied operations whether they could be more fully exploited before winter set in. It was subsequently arranged that attacks would be pressed in a converging direction towards Mézières by the French and American armies, while at the same time the British armies, attacking towards the line St. Quentin–Cambrai, would strike directly at the vital lateral communications running through Maubeuge to Hersin and Mézières by which alone the German forces on the Champagne front could be supplied and maintained.

"As a necessary result of the advance of the British armies towards the all-important railway centres about Maubeuge, the group of German armies in Flanders would find their communications threatened from the south, and any operations which it might be possible for the Allies to undertake in that theatre at a later date would be powerfully assisted thereby. It was obviously of vital importance to the enemy to maintain intact his front opposite St. Quentin and Cambrai, and for this purpose he depended on the great fortified zone known as the Hindenburg Line."

Thus the general situation at the end of July 1918. By the

---

[1] Marshal Foch.

early days of August the Battles of the Marne, 1918, which included the Battle of the Soissonnais and of the Ourcq (23rd July–2nd August), and the Battle of Tardenois (20th–31st July), had been fought and won, and a sound blow had been dealt at the German Army. Indeed, the results of this battle forced the enemy to abandon any further idea of an offensive against the Allies, and he was now forced to assume a defensive attitude.

The situation was now favourable for the Battle of Amiens, which opened on 8th August and lasted until the 11th, with the subsequent Action round Damery, 15th–17th August. On the 18th August the Advance in Flanders was begun, the Action of Outtersteene Ridge being fought on that date.

In all these operations great captures of prisoners and war material were made, and the enemy had been heavily defeated. "August 8th was the black day of the German army in the history of this war," said Ludendorff. In the Battle of Amiens twenty German divisions had been defeated by thirteen infantry and three British cavalry divisions, assisted by one regiment of Americans. Four hundred tanks were used and nearly 22,000 prisoners and over 400 guns were captured.

At "zero" hour on the morning of the 8th a thick fog hung over the battlefield and hid the advance of the Allied troops; it was just such another morning as the 21st March. The tables were indeed turned.

The effects of this victory, following so closely after the Allied victory on the Marne, upon the *moral* both of the German and British troops, were very great. Buoyed up by the hope of immediate and decisive victory to be followed by an early and favourable peace, constantly assured that the Allied reserves were exhausted, the German soldiery suddenly found themselves attacked on two fronts, and thrown back with heavy losses from large and important portions of their earlier gains. The reaction was inevitable and of a deep and lasting character.

What a vain idea the "Friedensturm" must have seemed to Ludendorff on the evening of the 8th August!

Moreover, the terrible bombardments to which the Allies subjected the enemy's positions had shaken his troops and seriously disorganized his defences. German letters captured during this period are full of the awful effects of the continuous rain of shells of all calibres poured upon the enemy's lines. Many of these letters betray the constant fear of death, and a pitiful longing for peace; they were the letters of beaten and cowed men. And although it is only right to acknowledge that there were still many first-class fighting divisions in the enemy's front line, these captured documents are permeated with ideas and statements such as had seldom been read before. The Battle of Amiens and the Action of Outtersteene Ridge ended, the Second Battles of the Somme, 1918, began, the first of which was the Battle of Albert, 21st–23rd August.

On the 16th August, when the 2nd Division received orders from VIth Corps Headquarters for the capture of the Ablainzevelle–Moyenneville Ridge, all three infantry brigades of the Division were in the line from a point just north of Ablainzevelle to opposite Moyenneville: the 99th Infantry Brigade on the right, the 6th in the centre, and the 5th on the left. The VIth Corps (Lieut.-General Sir J. A. L. Haldane) was formed of the Guards, 2nd, 3rd, and 63rd Divisions; the Third Army of three corps, VIth, IVth, and Vth, in line from north to south as given.

The German main line of resistance (Moyblain Trench) lay some 1,000 yards from the 2nd Division's front line, the enemy's outposts being pushed forward to partially entrenched positions about 300 yards from the British lines.

On the afternoon of the 14th, both the 99th and 6th Infantry Brigades had pushed out strong patrols towards Moyblain Trench. The enemy's outpost line was occupied without resistance. Moyblain Trench was, however, found to be strongly held, and after killing some of the enemy and capturing a machine gun, the patrols withdrew, the old enemy outpost line was consolidated and posts pushed out in front. Subsequently the enemy established outposts a few hundred yards in front of Moyblain Trench, but to a depth of 800 yards in front of the 99th and 6th Infantry Brigades, No Man's Land remained under the control of the 2nd Division: a fact which facilitated the forming-up operations prior to the attack of the 21st August.

The preliminary instructions received from VIth Corps Headquarters on the 16th contained orders for the capture of the Ablainzevelle–Moyenneville Ridge by the 2nd and Guards Divisions, in conjunction with an attack by the IVth Corps (on the right of the 2nd Division) against Bucquoy and Ablainzevelle. The attack was to be a surprise operation. The 2nd Tank Brigade was to assist, and the Guards Division was ordered to take over and attack from the northern portion of the 2nd Division's front down to the northern outskirts of Ayette.

The 99th Infantry Brigade, preceded by tanks, was to attack from the 2nd Division front over a frontage of 2,200 yards; two

THE SPIRIT OF THE TROOPS.

battalions, each on a two-company front, were to assault the enemy's trenches; two companies of each battalion to take Moyblain Trench, the remaining two companies going through to capture and consolidate the Ablainzevelle–Moyenneville Ridge. The third battalion of the brigade to remain in brigade reserve. No creeping barrages were to be used.

On the night of the 17th–18th August the 99th Infantry Brigade was relieved by the 6th Infantry Brigade and withdrawn from the line to the St. Amand–Gaudiempre–La Cauchie area, in order to practise the attack with tanks, and to rest.

Further orders issued on the 18th stated that the proposed operations had been enlarged. The 3rd Division, in conjunction with the Guards Division on the left and the 63rd Division[1] on the right, was to pass through the 2nd Division on the Ablainzevelle–Moyenneville Ridge, for a further advance, and to capture the line of the Arras–Achiet-le-Grand railway, and if possible establish a line east of it. Cavalry with light tanks (Whippets) were to exploit any success in the direction of Bapaume. The 6th Infantry Brigade was to support the advance of the 3rd Division, whilst for this operation the 5th Infantry Brigade was placed under the orders of the Guards Division.

Six brigades of Field Artillery were to support the attack—*i.e.*, XXXVIth and XLIst Brigades R.F.A. (2nd Division); and the LXXVIth, XXXIVth (which originally belonged to the 2nd Divisional Artillery), XIVth, and XVIIIth Army Brigades R.F.A. The Heavy Artillery consisted of Sherer's Group—LXth Brigade R.G.A. (9.2 gun), LXXXIVth Brigade R.G.A. (mixed).

Between the 16th and the 19th August forward positions were selected for the six Field Artillery Brigades, and dumps containing 600 rounds per 18-pounder and 500 rounds per 4.5 howitzer were formed and camouflaged. Before 1 a.m. on the 21st all batteries had moved into their new positions, harassing fire being maintained meanwhile by guns near old positions and by anti-tank guns moved up to replace former harassing guns. At "zero" hour all guns were to open fire without previous registration.

The spirit of the troops was splendid. Every man was keen and full of expectancy, for every soldier in France and Flanders knew that the enemy had already been dealt a very serious blow, and that his troops were making a desperate attempt to ward off utter defeat.

Sir Douglas Haig had issued a Special Order, calling attention

[1] Subsequently the 37th Division was on the right.

to the changed situation since the victory of the Marne and the Aisne, and asking all ranks to put forward their greatest efforts in pressing the enemy back still farther. He did not appeal in vain.

The dispositions of all units immediately prior to the Advance to Victory are of historic interest, and those of the 2nd Division, on the night 20th–21st August 1918, are, therefore, given in full detail.

On the afternoon of the 20th, 2nd Division Headquarters moved from La Bazèque to the 99th Infantry Brigade's old quarters, south-west of Monchy, opening at 4 p.m.

Of the three infantry brigades, the 99th was detailed for the attack. The 1st Royal Berks left St. Amand at 8.15 p.m. in lorries, moving *via* Pommier to Monchy. Here the battalion debussed and marched forward to the " jumping-off " line, relieving the 2nd South Staffords in front of the Ayette–Bucquoy Road. The Berkshires were on the right of the line, two companies, B and C, having been detailed to capture the first objective and A and D Companies to pass through and capture and consolidate the second objective. The battalion was formed up by 1.30 a.m. on the 21st. The 23rd Royal Fusiliers were on the left, and on relieving the 17th Royal Fusiliers, assembled in the " jumping-off " trench in front of Ayette. The 1st King's Royal Rifle Corps was the reserve battalion of the 99th Infantry Brigade, and at 5.30 a.m. moved forward to take up its position.

On relief by the 99th Infantry Brigade, the 6th Infantry Brigade had withdrawn the 17th Royal Fusiliers to Stork Support trenches, and the trenches in the vicinity; the 2nd South Staffords to Sparrow Support and Rocket Trench; the 1st King's were in Rotten Ravine area.

Until the early hours of the 21st the 5th Infantry Brigade held the left sub-sector of the 2nd Divisional front, the 2nd Highland Light Infantry being on the right and the Oxford and Bucks on the left; the 24th Royal Fusiliers were in brigade reserve. But the brigade was under the orders of the General Officer Commanding Guards Division, who issued instructions to the Highland Light Infantry and Oxfords to withdraw at 3.30 a.m. on the 21st in order that the 2nd Guards Brigade, which was to make the attack, might form up on the " jumping-off " line. At " zero " on the 21st the Oxfords had been withdrawn to Hameau Switch, with three companies of the Highland Light Infantry; the remaining company of Highland Light Infantry was then located at Billy's Bank, with Battalion Headquarters. The 24th Royal Fusiliers were in brigade

GOOD WORK BY THE D.A.C.

reserve in Barclay's Bank, King's Cross, Cox's Bank, and Rabbit Wood. The brigade was still under the orders of the General Officer Commanding Guards Division.

Behind the "jumping-off" line the artillery had moved forward and had taken up their battle positions from which they were to open fire without previous registration. The whole area was thickly dotted with guns, and the enemy was in for a particularly heavy bombardment from batteries of all calibres. Once again the XXXIVth (Army) Brigade R.F.A. was to go into action with its old comrades of Mons days—the XXXVIth and XLIst Brigades R.F.A. The latter brigade was disposed along the ridge south-west of Douchy; the XXXVIth Brigade was north of the XLIst and of the XXXIVth (Army) Brigade, C/34 was on the ridge with the XLIst Brigade, the 50th Battery was east of Little Farm, the 70th Battery near Lewin Lane, and the 56th Battery north of Crawley Copse.

The X/2 and Y/2 Trench Mortar Batteries had gun positions on the southern boundaries of the Divisional front—*i.e.*, about the junction of Baden Avenue with the Ayette-Bucquoy Road.

These new gun positions necessitated great labour by the Divisional Ammunition Column, but all ranks worked with splendid vigour in forming new ammunition dumps.

The three Field Companies R.E.—*i.e.*, the 5th, 226th, and 483rd —throughout the early days of August had been working with the 6th, 5th, and 99th Infantry Brigades respectively. Strenuous days were those for the Sappers, but still more strenuous days were drawing near, when it would have been impossible for the army to move forward had it not been for the splendid devotion of all ranks of the Royal Engineers. Too often their part in the great advance to victory is forgotten; but their deeds, like those of their comrades the infantrymen and the gunners, are immortal, the more so as they are but rarely chronicled.

The 5th Field Company, on the night 20th–21st August, was hard at work in the Purple System, and the following is an extract from the Company's Diary: "Two cook-houses completed. Dug-outs partitioned, furnished, and completed for occupation. Track bridges over Purple System. Six 15 feet wide bridges over Purple System trenches now exist and the three tracks ready for traffic of a heavy nature. Sick Post, Douchy: second entrance completed and gangway connection to existing chamber finished off. Water posts: 40 feet of canvas troughing erected at Monchy Dump; 60 feet of canvas troughing erected at E.4,a.O.O; 400 gallon tank and L. and F. pump installed at Bienvillers. Prisoners' Cage at Humber Camp completed. Company standing by to take position in the attack on 21st. Fifth Field Company detailed " zero " plus twelve minutes, to commence repairs to the Ayette-Courcelles–Ervillers Road and make it fit for wheeled traffic."

The 20th August was spent by the 226th Field Company in erecting huts for the 6th Field Ambulance at Warlencourt, working on dug-outs making lamps for 5th Brigade, and covers for the Lewis guns. Ultimately this company also was detailed to prepare and clear the way for the advance should the attack on the morrow prove successful. Similarly the 483rd Company was engaged in preparing for the great movement forward.

The Pioneers (10th Duke of Cornwall's Light Infantry) were detailed to prepare two tracks from the British to the German lines, the work to be begun in the British sector immediately the attack went forward. Only one company was detailed for this work, the two remaining companies being held in reserve. One company spent the night at Bienvillers and the two remaining companies at Monchy Hill South.

Two strong sections of D Company, 2nd Battalion, Machine-Gun Corps, had been detailed to advance with the 99th Infantry Brigade, and in the event of the capture of the enemy's position, mount two guns at each of the following points : right section, F.18,c.5.2, and A.19, central; left section, A.8,a.8.2, A.9,a.8.2. As soon as the infantry had gained their objectives, C Company was to mount two 4-gun batteries at F.23,b.9.7 and F.17,b.5.5. B Company was to hold three sections in readiness to support the 6th Infantry Brigade should the latter receive orders to support the troops of the 3rd Division. A Company had orders to establish a 4-gun battery at about A.3,d.5.6 as soon as possible after the capture of Moyenneville and the ridge west of Courcelles; one section was also detailed to accompany the 5th Infantry Brigade should the latter be called upon to support the Guards Division.

The 5th, 6th, and 99th Trench Mortar Batteries were with their respective infantry brigades.

Behind the Purple Front Line the 2nd Divisional Train had for days been busily employed carrying stores and rations up to the Refilling Points, which were located for the 99th Infantry Brigade at Humber Camp, 5th and 6th Infantry Brigades at Pommier.

" Zero " hour had been fixed for 4.55 a.m. on the 21st, and before that hour, the tanks had gradually drawn nearer to their " jumping-off " line.

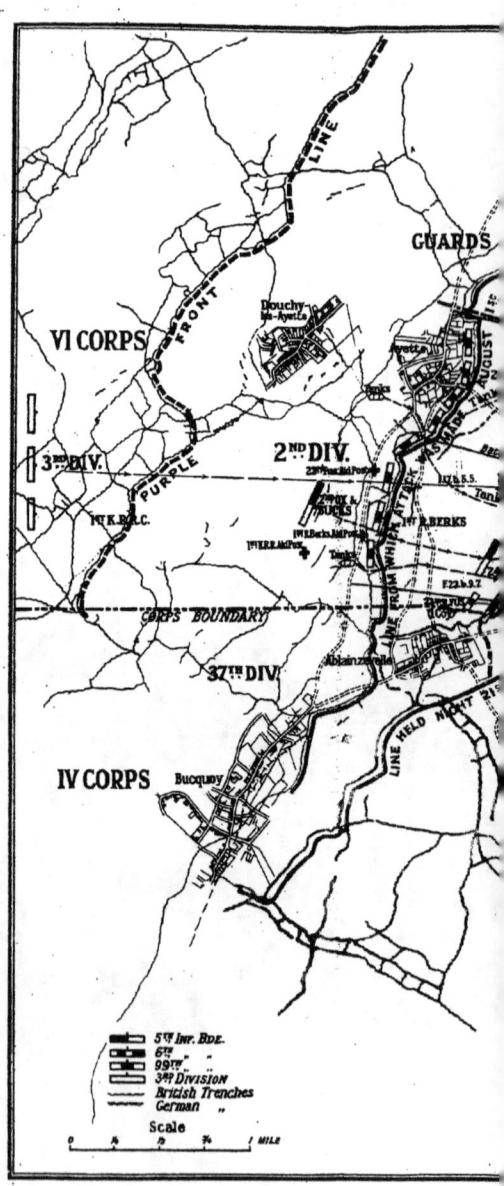

THE ADVANCE TO VICTORY: THE BATTLE OF ALBERT, 21st–23rd August 1918. CAPTURE OF MOYBLAIN TRENCH AND ERVILLERS BY THE 2nd DIVISION.

(*Facing p. 614.*)

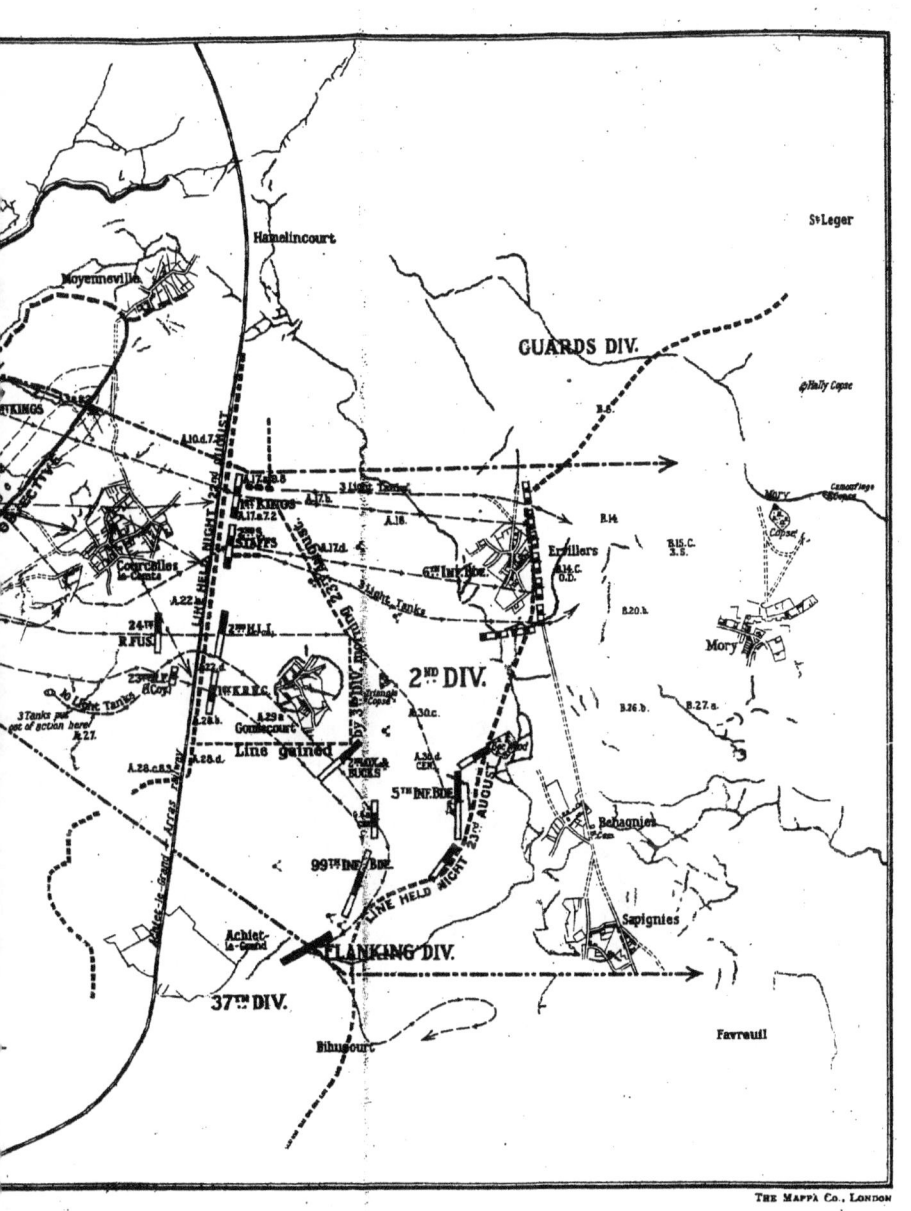

THE 23RD ROYAL FUSILIERS BADLY "GASSED."

The Seventeenth German Army held the line from Albert to east of Arras, north and south of the Scarpe; the Ist Bavarian Reserve Corps was north of the river, the IInd Bavarian Corps just south of it; next came the IIIrd Bavarian Corps and the XIVth Reserve Corps. The Guards, 2nd and 37th British Divisions, were opposed to the IIIrd Bavarian Corps.

The Battle of Albert, 21st August to 23rd August 1918.[1]

Punctually at 4.55 a.m., "zero" hour on the 21st August, the artillery barrage opened with a roar and came down roughly about 300 yards west of Moyblain Trench. Immediately nine tanks of the 12th Tank Battalion, moving along taped lines, passed through the assaulting troops of the 99th Infantry Brigade (23rd Royal Fusiliers and 1st Royal Berks), and advanced towards their objectives. They were regularly spaced out along the brigade front, the infantry advancing with their ungainly steel comrades, as the latter moved methodically in the direction of the enemy's trenches.

21ST AUG. MAP.

A thick mist hung over the whole battlefield, and although it caused the troops some slight loss of direction, this was soon rectified.

The enemy opened a weak barrage, causing little loss to the attacking troops, but the 23rd Royal Fusiliers, while in their assembly positions, had suffered serious losses from gas. The battalion had not only been badly shelled during the forming-up operations, but on moving across No Man's Land, the long grass through which the men had to pass was drenched with mustard gas, and as this soon came out, casualties rapidly occurred: 14 officers and 369 other ranks being put out of action by midday. But in spite of these serious losses "the attack," so the Divisional narrative states, "went like clockwork."[2] By 6 a.m. the 99th Infantry Brigade, without encountering any serious opposition, had won through to the second objective, capturing over 200 prisoners. Eight Vickers guns of the 2nd Battalion Machine-Gun Corps went forward with the 99th Infantry Brigade as "guns of opportunity." Both north and south of the 2nd Division, the Guards Division and the 37th

[1] The Official Dispatches name this operation the Battle of Bapaume, the period given being from 21st August to 1st September. The above title is that adopted in the official nomenclature of battles.

[2] The Battalion Diaries of the 1st Royal Berks and 23rd Royal Fusiliers contain no detailed account of this action.

Division respectively had also advanced in line, capturing their objectives.

Having captured its objective the 2nd Division set to work to consolidate its position, whilst the 3rd Division passing through pushed on to Courcelles, which place was taken without serious opposition. The latter division, in conjunction with flanking divisions, then advanced on the Arras–Achiet-le-Grand railway, where, however, the enemy made a stubborn resistance. At noon the situation at the junction of the Guards and 3rd Divisions being somewhat obscure, the 2nd Oxford and Bucks of the 5th Infantry Brigade were moved up to the Moyenneville–Ayette road, but by 6.30 p.m. the situation had been cleared up and the Oxfords were withdrawn.

Throughout the day the 6th Infantry Brigade had remained concentrated in readiness south of Douchy and Ayette, and had not been called upon to take part in the operations.

At 8.30 p.m. orders were issued for the 23rd Royal Fusiliers to be withdrawn immediately, and for the remainder of the 99th Infantry Brigade to draw out of the line as soon as the battalion had been relieved by the reserve brigade (76th) of the 3rd Division. During the early hours of the 22nd August, the 99th Infantry Brigade concentrated in the area just east of Ayette, and throughout that day all units of the 2nd Division rested and reorganized.

The " limited attack " which had been launched on the morning of 21st August, in order to gain the general line of the Arras–Albert railway, north of the Ancre, had been entirely successful. It had disclosed the fact that the enemy's main line of resistance was along the railway. From Miraumont to Moyenneville, the IVth and VIth Corps of the Third Army had carried the enemy's defences, while the Vth Corps had assisted by clearing the northern bank of the Ancre about Beaucourt.

The way was now clear for the next phase of the operation—an attack on a front of thirty-three miles from the junction of the British and French north of Lihons to Mercatel, " in which neighbourhood the Hindenburg Line from Quéant and Bullecourt, joined the old Arras–Vimy defence line of 1916."

Throughout the 21st August the principal hostile resistance had come from the enemy's machine gunners, who in several instances with considerable gallantry continued to serve their guns until both guns and men were crushed into the earth by tanks.

22ND AUG. The 22nd August was spent principally in bringing up bombs and getting guns into position. At nightfall the 2nd Division was

ORDERS FOR ATTACK ON 23RD AUGUST.

disposed in the following areas: 5th Infantry Brigade concentrated west of Adinfer; 6th Infantry Brigade, south of Ayette and Douchy; 99th Infantry Brigade in the Purple System in Quesnoy Farm area. Divisional Headquarters were south of Monchy.

The 3rd Division had gained the line of the Achiet-le-Grand railway from about A.10,d.7.3 southwards to A.28,c.8.3. But south of the latter point the enemy still held the railway and Achiet-le-Grand, the area north of the river being very thick with hostile machine guns. The Guards Division held the line of the railway north of the 3rd Division, but the line of the 63rd Division (which had attacked through the 37th Division) ran west of Achiet-le-Grand.

During the early morning the IIIrd Corps of the Fourth Army had forced the passage of the Ancre and had captured Albert by a well-executed enveloping movement from the south-east. The British line between the Somme and the Ancre was now advanced well to the east of the Bray–Albert road, and the way was thus cleared for the big attack which had been planned for the morning of the 23rd.

At 5.38 p.m. a telegram arrived at 2nd Divisional Headquarters from VIth Corps Headquarters, stating that the 3rd Division had been ordered to capture Gomiecourt during the night 22nd–23rd, and the 2nd Division was instructed to " close up " and be prepared to go through the 3rd Division and attack Ervillers, Behagnies, and Sapignies in conjunction with an attack by the IVth Corps on Achiet-le-Grand and Bihucourt. The 2nd Division was to be supported by light tanks.

At a conference held immediately on receipt of this telegram, the following plan of action was decided upon: The 5th Infantry Brigade, with ten whippet tanks and two sections of the 2nd Battalion Machine-Gun Corps, was to attack Behagnies and Sapignies and consolidate 200 yards clear of the eastern exits of the two villages; the 6th Infantry Brigade, with one battalion (1st Royal Berks) of the 99th Infantry Brigade, six whippet tanks, and two sections of the 2nd Battalion Machine-Gun Corps to attack Ervillers and consolidate 200 yards on the eastern exits of that village.

The 99th Infantry Brigade (less one battalion), with one section of the 2nd Battalion Machine-Gun Corps, to occupy the ridge running from Sapignies to Bihucourt, protecting the right flank of the 5th Infantry Brigade and maintaining touch with the 37th Division, which would be attacking Bihucourt.

The Pioneers were in reserve west of Douchy. The remaining

guns of the 2nd Battalion Machine-Gun Corps were to support the attack.

All attacking troops were to assemble by 8 a.m. on the 23rd on the Courcelles-Ablainzevelle Ridge and were to cross the railway at "zero" hour; the 5th and 6th Infantry Brigades to cross north of Gomiecourt. A barrage to suit the movements of the tanks, and a bombardment by the "Heavies" of the villages and selected points from which the enemy could observe the advance to and across the railway, were among the artillery arrangements.

"Zero" hour was 11 a.m. on the 23rd August.

23RD AUG. The 3rd Division attacked Gomiecourt at 4 a.m. on the 23rd with complete success.

By 8 a.m. the three infantry brigades of the 2nd Division were assembled about Moyblain Trench and the Courcelles-Ablainzevelle Ridge, the 99th Infantry Brigade on the right, just north of the Ablainzevelle-Courcelles road; the 5th Infantry Brigade in the centre with its left on Courcelles Alley; and the 6th Infantry Brigade north of the Ayette-Courcelles road.

As "zero" hour approached the troops were gradually moved to the line of the railway, crossing the latter at 11 a.m. All three brigades advanced on their objectives with the Guards Division on the left keeping touch with the 6th Infantry Brigade, and the 37th Division on the right attacking Achiet-le-Grand and Bihucourt, maintaining touch with the 99th Infantry Brigade.

For the sake of clarity the operations of the three brigades are described separately.

The 6th Infantry Brigade had disposed the 1st King's on the left supported by the 17th Royal Fusiliers, and the 2nd South Staffords on the right supported by the 1st Royal Berks (99th Infantry Brigade). All battalions advanced in artillery formation under a fairly heavy but fortunately ineffective shell-fire. The village of Courcelles was avoided as it was under fire of the enemy's artillery. Just before 11 a.m. the 1st King's and 2nd South Staffords were formed up east of the railway, each battalion on a two-company front. Three light tanks were attached to the Staffords, with orders to move round the south of Ervillers, and three were with the King's with orders to move round the north of the village.

Just after "zero" the enemy put down a heavy barrage on the line of the railway, but did not impede the advance of the 6th Infantry Brigade, whose leading waves rapidly broke down opposition, and by 12 noon had reached their objectives, capturing Ervillers and consolidating a line east and south of the village. Numerous

ACTION OF THE TANKS.

machine guns and trench-mortar nests were encountered along the Courcelles–Ervillers road, but these were soon captured, the light tanks doing splendid work in assisting the infantry in capturing the gun teams and putting the guns out of action.

"At 11.30 a.m., or thereabouts, it was seen that the leading platoons had crossed the spur running north-east through A.17,d and A.18,a.b.c, so one supporting company of 17th Royal Fusiliers was thrown forward to straddle the valley in A.17,b, and the north-west slope of the spur. The second supporting company of the 17th Royal Fusiliers was maintained on a north and south line from A.17,a.7.2 to A.17,a.9.8, thus safeguarding the left flank of the attack, which flank was judged to be the one offering the enemy the better opportunities of an immediate counter-attack, since a considerable gap existed between our advance and that of the Guards Division (on the left)."[1]

A little later white Véry lights went up from the village, and soon the King's and Staffords were consolidating their captured objectives, but severe machine-gun fire from the western slopes of Mory Copse and Hally Copse prevented the establishment of posts clear of the eastern exits of Ervillers as had been ordered.

In this advance the 6th Infantry Brigade lost 25 officers and 575 other ranks killed, wounded, and missing. A considerable number of prisoners were captured, besides many machine guns, some trench mortars, and several field guns.

The 5th Infantry Brigade crossed the railway at about A.22,b at "zero" hour, then, wheeling round the north of Gomiecourt, advanced in a south-easterly direction on Behagnies. The 2nd Highland Light Infantry, on a two-company front, led the advance, followed by the 24th Royal Fusiliers, and finally the Oxford and Bucks, in reserve. Behagnies was the objective of the Highland Light Infantry, Sapignies that of the 24th Royal Fusiliers, while the Oxfords (in reserve) moved to G.6,a to await orders.

Ten whippet tanks had been detailed to the 5th Infantry Brigade, with orders to move just south of Gomiecourt as an advanced guard to the infantry; three were to pass north of Behagnies, three between Behagnies and Sapignies, and four south of the latter village. But the intense barrage which the enemy put down three minutes before "zero" hour, a heavy machine-gun fire which was sweeping the line of the railway, and the operations of a hostile anti-tank gun caused trouble amongst the tanks. Three whippets were put out of action in A.27 by direct hits, and the remaining

[1] Battalion Diary, 1st King's Regiment.

seven wheeled to the left and passed south of Gomiecourt with the intention of joining up with the 5th Infantry Brigade in A.30,c. But heavy fire from Achiet-le-Grand and Bihucourt caused them to change direction again, and they appear to have turned south and south-west, rendering valuable assistance to the troops of the 37th Division, and it was not until 1.30 p.m. that any tanks were directed on Behagnies.

Meanwhile the gallant Highland Light Infantry, with great steadiness, had passed through the enemy's barrage, skirting the northern edges of Gomiecourt. Here, however, a galling machine-gun fire coming from the northern flank caused many casualties, but the battalion pressed on, and by noon had swung in a south-east direction and was advancing upon Behagnies according to orders. At 12.30 p.m. the battalion had reached A.30,d, central, but here unfortunately Lieut.-Colonel W. L. Brodie, V.C., M.C., was killed.[1] Point-blank artillery fire from Behagnies as well as direct machine-gun fire held up any further advance. The two leading companies (A and C) of the battalion had gained a footing on a ridge 500 yards north-west of Behagnies, but both company commanders had been killed, and the survivors were not in sufficient strength to go on. The reserve company (B) then came up, and with the survivors of A, C, and D Companies a position was taken up about 500 yards west-north-west of Behagnies.

The 24th Royal Fusiliers, also on a two-company frontage, who in the advance had remained 500 yards behind the Highland Light Infantry, on crossing the railway, pressed forward in line, and on the right of the latter battalion. The Fusiliers likewise came under machine-gun and artillery fire, but although the barrage was traversed with heavy casualties, "the advance pushed on in a determined manner, the drill-like precision, steady bearing, and unfaltering pace of the troops under the prolonged ordeal being wholly admirable."

The Fusiliers came upon the enemy moving back two of his field guns with feverish haste. But one of the leading companies pushed forward a Lewis-gun team; the German gunners were all shot down, and the two field guns captured. With the Highland Light Infantry the Fusiliers rushed the ridge north-west of Behagnies, and this position was consolidated and held.

---

[1] This very gallant officer had been with the 2nd Division and his battalion (2nd Highland Light Infantry) throughout the whole of the war. As a subaltern he gained his Victoria Cross at Ypres in 1914, and his death was a very great loss to the Division.

GAINS CONSOLIDATED.

Meanwhile the Oxford and Bucks had followed up the Highland Light Infantry and Fusiliers, and had reached the neighbourhood of an advanced enemy Aid Post in Triangle Copse, where a German medical officer and various other ranks, about fifty in all, with nine machine guns, were captured. About 1 p.m. Lieut.-Colonel R. B. Crosse, D.S.O., who with two other officers was in the dug-out, was wounded by a shell which burst in the entrance. A little later the battalion moved farther south in support of the Highland Light Infantry and the Fusiliers.

Thus ended the operations of the 5th Infantry Brigade on the 23rd August. Behagnies and Sapignies might both have been captured had the attacking battalions received the support of the tanks allotted to them, and in conjunction with which all their arrangements had been made. But that support could not be given; the tanks, having been subjected to very heavy fire, had been unable to carry out their *rôle*, though they did unquestionably give valuable assistance to the 37th Division.

The 99th Infantry Brigade, whose task was to form a defensive flank, had no sooner crossed the railway at about A.22,d, and A.28,b, than it was discovered that the enemy still clung to positions in the vicinity of A.28,d. From this area the brigade came under heavy machine-gun fire,[1] but the leading companies of the 1st King's Royal Rifle Corps wheeled to the right through A.29,a, and assisted by a tank took the enemy positions in rear, capturing 400 prisoners. The advance of the brigade then proceeded unchecked, and finally a defensive flank south of the 5th Infantry Brigade, in touch with the 63rd Brigade on the right, was formed. Here the Rifles and the remnants of the 23rd Royal Fusiliers dug in for the night.

Thus all three infantry brigades of the 2nd Division had progressed satisfactorily, but the enemy had put up a more determined resistance than he had offered on the 21st, and the casualties suffered by the Division were severe, the heaviest losses falling on the 5th Infantry Brigade.

Throughout the night 23rd–24th August, all troops in the front line re-organized and consolidated their positions. Active patrolling was maintained by the 5th and 99th Infantry Brigades,

---

[1] The words "heavy machine-gun fire" occur so frequently that some little explanation is necessary. There is no doubt that, from 8th August onwards until the Armistice, the bravest men in the enemy's ranks were the machine gunners. They fought their guns splendidly, and time after time died beside them. The guns were often placed in depth, and as the foremost gun was either captured or put out of action by the advance of the Allied troops, a retirement was made to the next gun, and so on.

but the villages of Behagnies and Sapignies, and the area just north of the former, were thick with machine guns and the enemy was in considerable strength.

North and south of the 2nd Division, all along the whole battle-front of thirty-three miles from just north of Lihons to Mercatel, the attack had gone well. South of the Somme, Herleville, Chuignolles, and Chuignes were captured. North of Albert the Vth Corps progressed along the left bank of the Ancre, north of Thiepval. The IVth Corps (as already stated) took Gomiecourt, Bihucourt, Ervillers, Boyelles, and Boiry Becquerelle. Thousands of prisoners and many guns and much war material were captured.

The Capture of Mory Copse, 24th August 1918.

At 8 p.m. on the 23rd August orders were issued by 2nd Divisional Headquarters to the 6th Infantry Brigade to push forward during the night 23rd–24th, and occupy the ridge about Mory Copse. The 1st Royal Berks (99th Infantry Brigade) were ordered to remain at the disposal of the 6th Infantry Brigade. The 5th and 99th Infantry Brigades were instructed to take every advantage of any signs of weakening on the part of the enemy.

The 1st King's were detailed for this operation, and on receipt of orders strong fighting patrols were organized and pushed out towards the Copse. But the enemy was too active; his machine guns swept the ground over which the troops were advancing and, assisted by the bright moonlight, he was able to hold up the advance in spite of very gallant efforts made by the King's to reach their objective.

24TH AUG.
MAP.

At 4.30 a.m. on the 24th small reconnoitring patrols, each consisting of from six to eight officers and men, went out along the whole front, but repeated efforts to advance only added further casualties to the heavy losses already incurred.

Between 8 and 9 a.m. a long skirmishing line of men of the Guards Division (on the left of the 6th Infantry Brigade) was seen advancing without opposition, through B.8, and B.14. The left flanking company of the King's (C) was immediately sent out, with the idea of prolonging the right of the Guards and pushing south-east towards B.29,b. This joint advance was, however, severely checked, heavy machine-gun fire being encountered from the western outskirts of Mory and from B.26,b, and B.27,a, and the troops retired to a sunken road, and a track.

THE CAPTURE OF MORY COPSE,
24th August 1918,
BY 99th INFANTRY BRIGADE.

(*Facing p. 622.*)

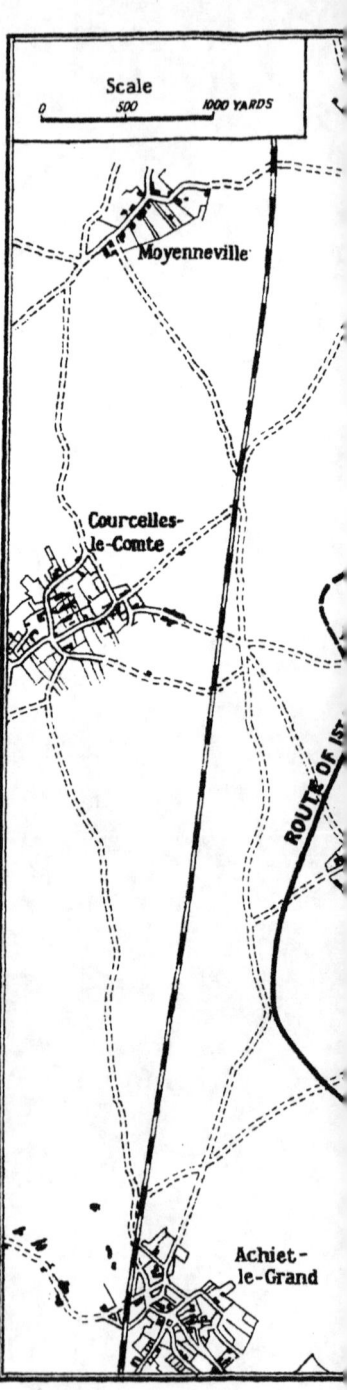

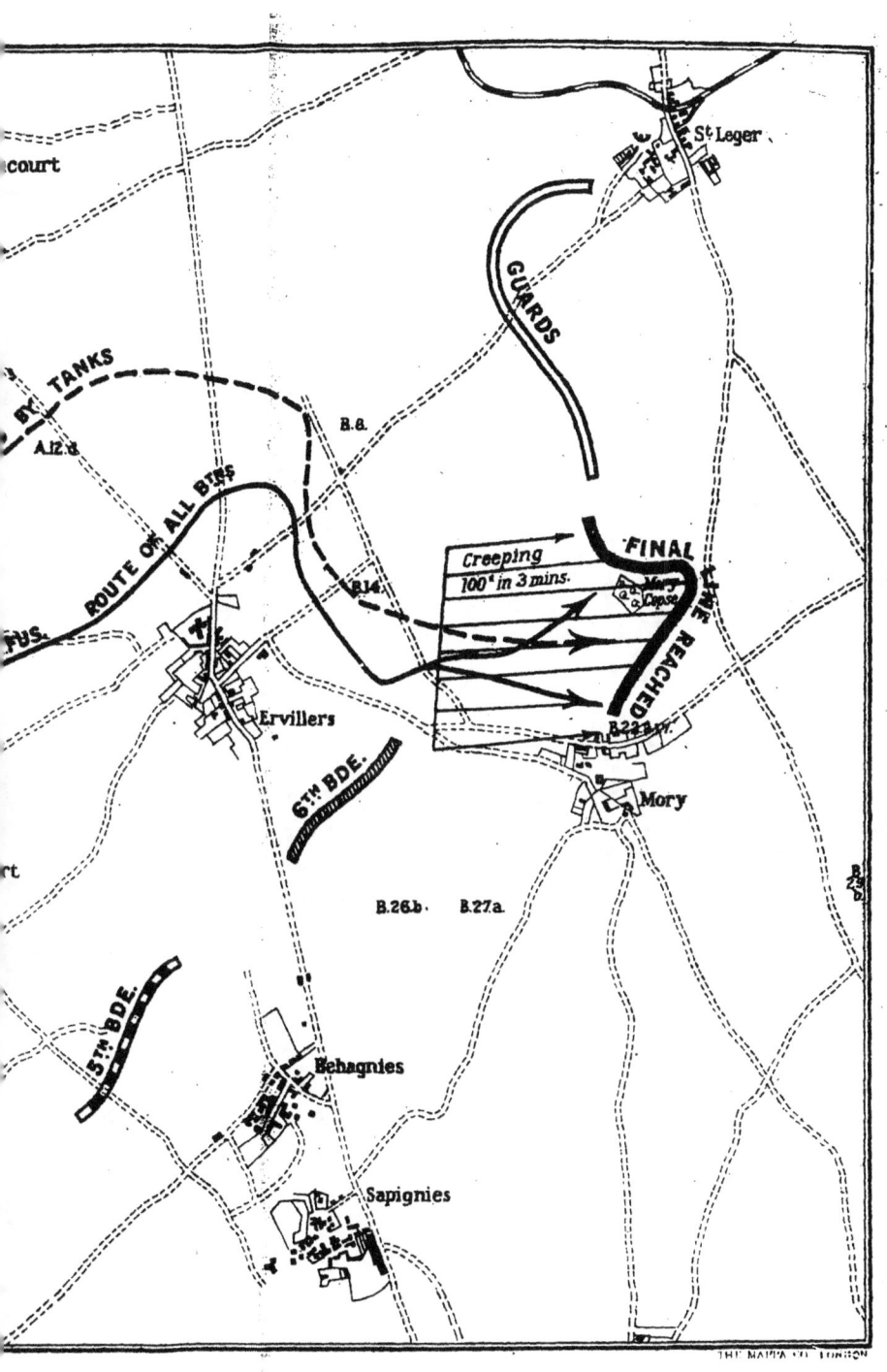

OBJECTIVES.

Still another attempt was made about 11.30 a.m. when B and D Companies of the King's, advancing with caution up the hill towards Mory Copse, and also south-south-east, had made a certain amount of progress. C Company had been withdrawn to rest and reorganize. The advance was proceeding when warning was received that the 99th Infantry Brigade was to launch an attack at 3.30 p.m. On receipt of this warning, seeing that his troops were worn out (they had been fighting and patrolling almost continuously for twenty-four hours), the Commanding Officer, 1st King's, checked the advance and ordered his men to lie down in observation facing east and south-east.

Orders for the attack had been issued by 99th Infantry Brigade Headquarters at 1.15 p.m., but they did not reach the King's until 2 p.m., and as the latter had been placed at the disposal of the 99th Infantry Brigade for the operation, and the Commanding Officer had been ordered to give support to the advance, there was no time to withdraw the two companies; they were therefore halted to wait until A and C Companies came up, and passed on behind the attack, when B and D would support them.

At the time of the conference when this attack was first planned (about 9.30 a.m.) the 99th Infantry Brigade still held the position it had occupied during the night 23rd–24th; the 5th Infantry Brigade also held the ground it had gained on the previous afternoon; the 6th Infantry Brigade (with the exception of the King's, who had taken part in the operations already described) was east and south-east of Ervillers.

The conference over, the 1st Royal Berks were ordered to concentrate in the low ground north of Gomiecourt; the 1st King's Royal Rifle Corps and the 23rd Royal Fusiliers were to withdraw from their positions, and move south and west of Gomiecourt to where the Berkshires were concentrating.

A creeping barrage was to begin at " zero," advancing from west of the line Mory Village–Mory Copse, at the rate of 100 yards every three minutes. Nine tanks were to move down the valley from A.17, central to A.12,d, three would enter the valley through B.8, and were to advance behind the barrage.

The objective of the 99th Infantry Brigade was the line B.22,a.1.7 and the northern outskirts of Mory Village to Camouflage Copse. The 1st Royal Berks were to lead, followed by the 1st King's Royal Rifle Corps, with the 23rd Royal Fusiliers, now reduced to one weak composite company.

At 3.30 p.m. the barrage descended, and gradually moved forward, behind which the tanks, followed by the Berkshires, advanced. Again the enemy's machine guns swept the ranks of the advancing troops, but although the left-flank company was held up, tanks and the remaining companies pressed on until the whole line was able to advance. The tanks lent great assistance, and finally the whole objective was captured and held, touch being obtained on the left with the Guards Division. About 100 prisoners were taken, representing five different regiments, and considerable casualties were inflicted on the enemy. Mory Copse was found to be strongly fortified. The Berkshires and the Rifles then consolidated the line won, though work was still much hampered by machine-gun fire, especially from the north-east corner of Behagnies. The Berkshires' casualties were from 60 to 80 other ranks; no officers were amongst them.

At 8 p.m. orders were received to hand over the position to the 187th Infantry Brigade (62nd Division), and by 1 o'clock on the morning of the 25th August the relief was complete; the 6th Infantry Brigade was also relieved by troops of the 62nd Division. The 5th Infantry Brigade, however, was ordered to remain in the line, as the brigade was to attack Behagnies and Sapignies before 5 a.m. on the 25th and capture it " at all costs," in order that the 62nd Division might pass through to further objectives.

The Capture of Behagnies and Sapignies by the 5th Infantry Brigade, 25th August 1918.

Warning of the attack had already been received by the 5th Infantry Brigade between 8 and 9 o'clock on the night of the 24th August. At 10 p.m. the General Officer Commanding Division arrived at 5th Infantry Brigade Headquarters, and there met the Brigadiers of the 5th and 6th Infantry Brigades and the Royal Artillery Group Commanders. Details of the attack were then decided upon. The first attack was to be frontal, the second in flank, in order to avoid the glacis slopes in front of Sapignies, which had already proved costly. The latter would also turn the defences of Sapignies and effect a surprise.

" Zero " hour was fixed for 3.30 a.m. for the attack on Behagnies, and at 4.30 a.m. for the attack on Sapignies. A preliminary bombardment, opening one hour before " zero " by all the available Heavy Artillery of the VIth and IVth Corps, was to take place. As the infantry approached Behagnies, the bombardment was to

THE CAPTURE OF BEHAGNIES
AND SAPIGNIES, 25th August 1918,
BY 5th INFANTRY BRIGADE.

(*Facing p. 624.*)

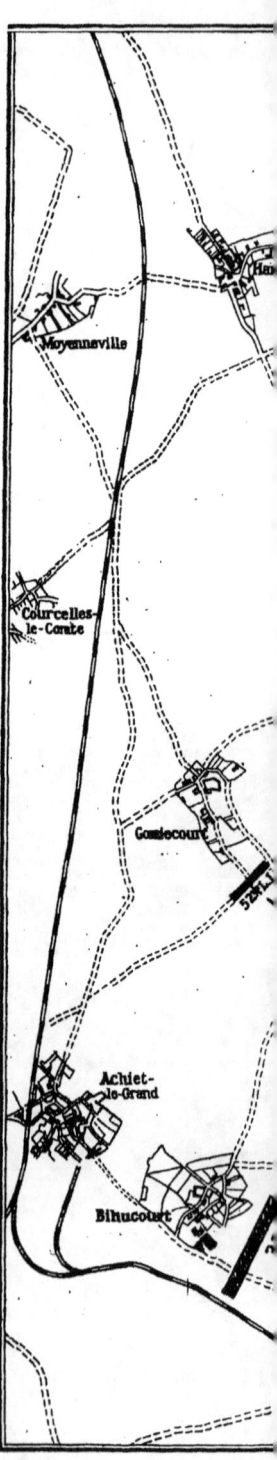

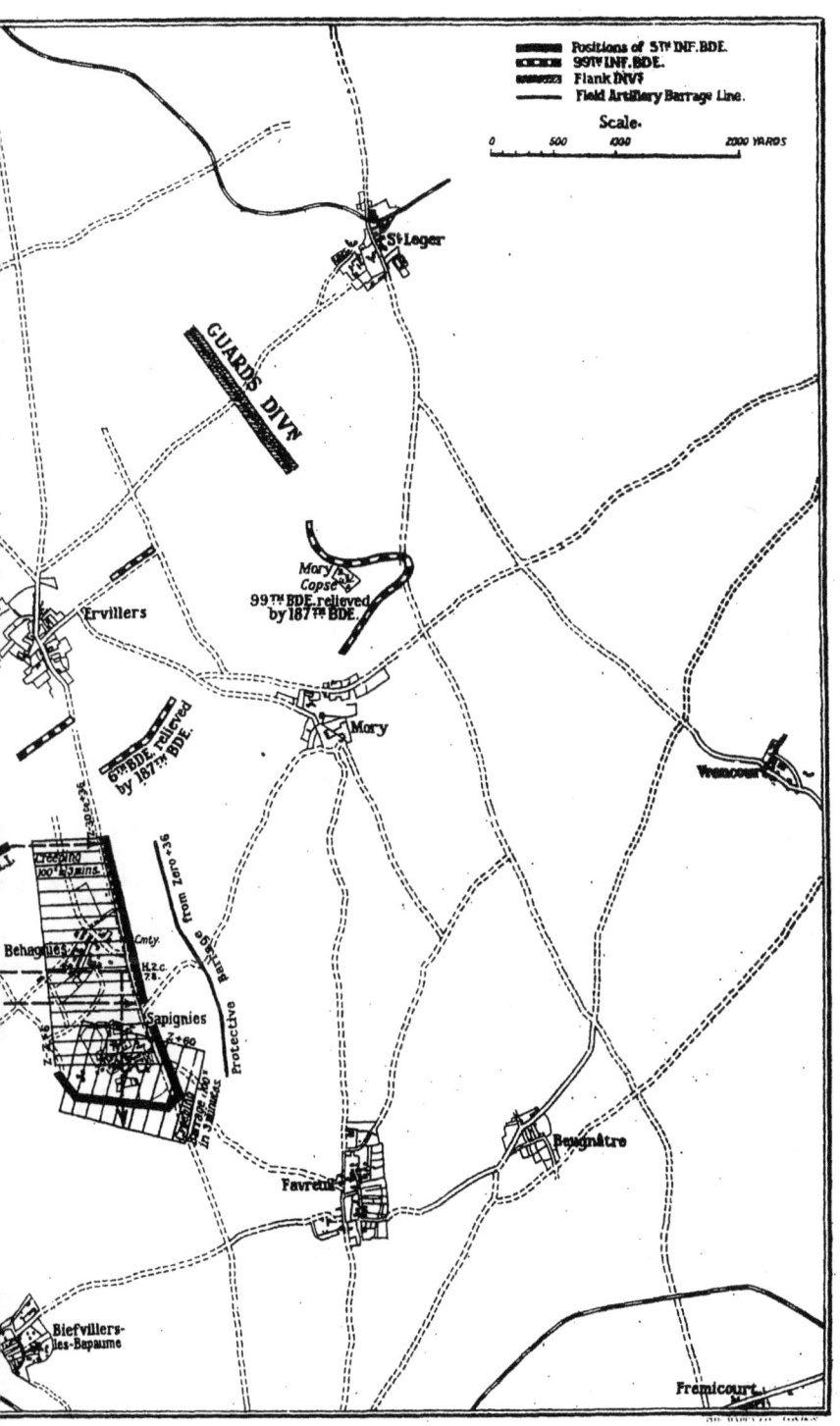

A COMPLETE SURPRISE.

lift off that place and concentrate on Sapignies until the latter village was attacked.

The 5th Infantry Brigade was to attack with the 24th Royal Fusiliers on the right and the 2nd Highland Light Infantry on the left, behind a creeping barrage moving at the rate of 100 yards in three minutes. These two battalions were to attack Behagnies.

The 2nd Oxford and Bucks were to follow the 24th Royal Fusiliers to the junction of the sunken road and the Arras–Bapaume road about H.2,c.7.8, and then change direction to the right, and attack Sapignies from the north, with the left of the battalion on the Arras–Bapaume road. The Oxfords were to advance behind a creeping barrage moving 100 yards in four minutes.

Fifteen Vickers guns of the 2nd Battalion Machine-Gun Corps were to support the attack. It was not until about 1.30 a.m. on the 25th that the three battalions received their written orders,[1] and some of the companies (especially of the Oxford and Bucks) were somewhat scattered. But just before "zero" hour the 24th Royal Fusiliers and the Highland Light Infantry were formed up ready for the attack. The guns had already opened on Behagnies, and were pounding the village with shell of all calibre. The enemy had also put down a barrage of high-explosive and gas shells, and through this the attacking troops had to pass.

But at 3.30 a.m. they went forward gallantly, each battalion disposing two companies in the front line, one in support to carry out the "mopping up" duties, and the remaining company in reserve.

The attack was a complete surprise. The Fusiliers, following close on the heels of the barrage, broke into the village, which was held by the enemy with large numbers of machine guns, estimated at 110. The gun teams were quickly overcome and either killed or made prisoners, and the guns captured. Many of the enemy's troops were discovered asleep in their dug-outs and surrendered without a struggle; those attempting to escape were shot down. The two attacking companies pushed on through the village to their objective—a ridge some 300 yards east of Behagnies, where the work of consolidation and reorganization was begun immediately. The support company "mopped up" the village in fine style, accounting for many enemy stragglers, and then swung round to protect the southern approaches to the village.

Meanwhile the 2nd Highland Light Infantry, on the left of the attack, despite a very heavy barrage of high-explosive and gas

25TH AUG. MAP.

[1] Verbal orders had been given between 8 and 9 p.m. on 24th.

shells, had advanced steadily towards their objective. In the sunken road, which ran north-west from the village, the enemy was encountered in great strength, and a grim bayonet fight ensued. But the Scotsmen were not to be denied, and the road was cleared, the two attacking companies passing on through to the eastern exits of the village, where detached posts were formed and consolidated. At 4.30 a.m. the " mopping up " company began to clear the northern part of the village of the remnants of the enemy's troops. A machine gun, mounted in the western corner of the cemetery, gave a great deal of trouble, but with the assistance of a tank the gun crew was killed and the gun captured.

By 6 a.m. the capture of Behagnies was complete.

The 2nd Oxford and Bucks had, on receipt of their orders, some difficulty in collecting their companies in their assembly positions, and the two attacking companies had to move off before the supporting company, leaving the latter to follow when it reached the line of assembly. The advance was begun at 3.50 a.m., the Oxfords following in rear of the 24th Royal Fusiliers. Soon after the advance had begun the support company came up, and was immediately sent after the two attacking companies. There was a slight loss of direction, but all three companies went through Behagnies, and finally, on the capture of the latter place, followed close on the barrage which fell at 4.30 a.m. on Sapignies. Here the enemy, finding himself attacked from the north and north-east, offered little resistance, and Sapignies, like Behagnies, fell to the victorious 5th Infantry Brigade.

The whole operation was brilliantly conceived and executed, and resulted in the capture of 300 Prussians, 150 machine guns, 3 field pieces, and some trench mortars; heavy casualties were also inflicted on the enemy. The success of the operation was due, not only to the fine dash of the infantry, but also to the splendid co-operation of the artillery, which numbered seven brigades of Field Artillery and three brigades of " Heavies."

At 8.10 a.m. the General Officer Commanding 62nd Division assumed command of the sector, and shortly afterwards advanced, leaving the 5th Infantry Brigade still dug in on the ground gained.

During the afternoon of the 25th arrangements were made to relieve the brigade, but a hostile counter-attack delivered at 5 p.m. delayed the relief. At 9 p.m., however, the situation had become normal, and by 11.30 p.m. the three tired but victorious battalions were on their way back to reserve positions along the Courcelles–Achiet-le-Petit road.

GAINS AND LOSSES.

Thus, after five days' strenuous fighting, the 2nd Division again passed into reserve, to reorganize and refit, and enjoy a well-earned rest. "The 24th Royal Fusiliers," said the General Officer Commanding 2nd Division, "had only 50 casualties; the Highland Light Infantry under 100 since the 21st, but they had lost Brodie; over 20 of their casualties are missing, but they are expected to have got mixed up with other units, and will rejoin. The King's have had the heaviest losses—11 officers and 322 other ranks, most of them in the attack on Ervillers, which they carried out with the utmost determination and which was strongly and stubbornly held. If we exclude our 500 gas casualties,[1] our prisoners exceed our killed and wounded, and a lot of Germans have been killed.[2] The ground we have captured was reached by the 2nd Division on March 28, 1917, when we were following up the enemy from Courcelette.[3] We have captured all our objectives and gone beyond those north of Mory. . . . The 6th and 99th Infantry Brigades are now bivouacked east of Ayette; the 5th Infantry Brigade came back there. . . . The VIth Corps now consists of the 2nd and 62nd Divisions on the right, Guards and 3rd Division on the left."

Finally, like good soldiers, having fought well and successfully, the Division settled down to rest for a few hours; the Divisional Troupe was hurried up from Pommier, and, on the ground captured on the 21st, entertained first the gallant 99th and later the other two brigades.

From 26th August to 1st September 1918.

For seven days, from the 26th August to the 1st September, the 2nd Division lay behind the front line in VIth Corps support; the 5th Infantry Brigade in the valley south and west of Courcelles; and the 6th and 99th Infantry Brigades in the valley east of Ayette. Divisional Headquarters remained south of Douchy. The private diary of the General Officer Commanding 2nd Division, during the period his Division was out of the line resting and training and reorganizing, is full of interest. In all

---

[1] The gas casualties were mainly amongst the 23rd Royal Fusiliers.

[2] On the 27th August, after sufficient time had elapsed in which to count up more closely gains and losses, the General Officer Commanding Division reported: "Our other rank casualties are 1,850, and include the 500 slight gas cases. Our prisoners are estimated at 1,500, and we have killed a good few Germans, and so the operations of the 21st to 25th are highly satisfactory."

[3] During the German retreat to the Hindenburg Line.

historical work the most valuable records are those which give a contemporary view of events. Beginning with the morning of Monday, August 26, 1918, the General said: " The general advance continued to-day. The most important event was the launching of the Canadian Corps. The XVIIth Corps is on our left, and the Canadians beyond them. They got right beyond Monchy-au-Preux, and were then to turn south-east so as to take the Hindenburg Line in flank. They are already on ground that we have not held before. . . . I rode round to all Commanding Officers of the 5th and 6th Infantry Brigades. All are in great form. All battalions are bivouacked in the open, and there is no comfort. There is a lot of material lying about, and a derelict aerodrome is providing corrugated iron for shelters. I am issuing orders that all Brigade and Battalion Headquarters must be clearly marked day and night by flag or lamp; communications are much delayed by want of proper signs that are visible from considerable distances, and I have often spent a long time wandering round quite close to a Headquarters without being able to find *the particular hole* that accommodated them. . . . S—— is drawing up artillery instructions to suit the latest conditions, so as to free the artillery from Divisional control and give the Brigadiers a free hand with their Group Commanders as advisers; Brigadiers are to allot some artillery to Battalion Commanders, even if it is only a battery, so that in the event of them being held up by local opposition they can get artillery support without delay. . . . The artillery officer in command will handle his own guns, but have close liaison, so that he can follow the course of the fight and send back to his guns any orders that are necessary.

"*Tuesday, 27th August.*—With D—— to see all Machine-Gun Companies. They have all got cover from the weather and are very cheery. . . . I instituted to-day as Salvage Day. All units are to sweep up the areas round their bivouacs, and a return of the results will be published.

" Resistance in front of the 62nd Division increased, and no great advance was made; elsewhere good advances are reported. Afternoon to 5th Infantry Brigade, and went round all battalions. The men are in good spirits and are looking well rested. . . . Brigadier-General —— came from advanced General Headquarters in Frevent. He is going to try and hurry up our reinforcements. He says that the Germans have 66 divisions in reserve; this, of course, includes all those out of the line, and of these only 17 divisions are fresh; 83 have been used in the present operations. . .

"*Friday, 30th August.*—The result of the Salvage Day was 80 wagon loads full—value, £15,000. We swamped the Corps Salvage Dump. Over 1,000 reinforcements have left the base for the Division. . . . There are on the Third Army front 15 German divisions in the line, and 3 possible reserve divisions; 12 divisions have been withdrawn. A most valuable bit of information has been established to-day, and that is that drafts are being taken from the withdrawn divisions for the divisions in the line." [1]

During the seven days the 2nd Division had been in Corps reserve, the Allies, south of Arras, had followed up their advantage and had continued to press the enemy, in spite of the increasing resistance of his rearguards. "The enemy," said the Official Dispatches, "clung to his positions in the later stages of this period with much tenacity. His infantry delivered many counter-attacks, and the progress of our troops was only won by hard and determined fighting." On the same night that the 5th Infantry Brigade won Behagnies and Sapignies, the 37th Division had cleared Favreuil, and the 62nd Division had driven the enemy from Mory Village. On the 27th the 18th Division captured Trônes Wood, beating off the repeated attacks of the German 2nd Guard Division fresh from reserve. The 28th witnessed the fall of Hardicourt and the spur south of it, to the 12th and 58th Divisions. The 38th Division on both these days (27th and 28th) had been engaged in bitter fighting about Longueval and that erstwhile abode of death—Delville Wood; and, in company with the 17th Division, attacking towards Flers, made progress. The enemy was driven out of Bapaume on the 29th by the New Zealand Division, and on the same day the 18th Division entered Combles. North of Bapaume a gallant thrust by the 56th and 57th Divisions penetrated the enemy's position as far as Riencourt, establishing their line subsequently on the western outskirts of Bullecourt and Hendecourt.

Thus by the night of the 30th August the line of the Fourth and Third Armies north of the Somme ran from Cléry-sur-Somme past the western edge of Marrières Wood to Combles, Lesbœufs, Ban-

---

[1] The losses of the Second German Army had been very heavy. Heavy demands had also been made on its reserves to fill up the gaps. "The infantry of some divisions had had to go into action straight off the lorries, whilst their artillery had been sent to some other part of the line. Units were badly mixed up. It could be foreseen that a number of additional divisions would become necessary, in order to strengthen the Second Army, even if the enemy continued the offensive, and that was not certain. Besides, our losses in prisoners had been so heavy that General Headquarters was again faced with the necessity of breaking up more divisions to form reserves. Our reserves dwindled."—LUDENDORFF.

court, Fremicourt, and Vraucourt, thence to the western outskirts of Écoust, Bullecourt, and Hendecourt.

On the French front Roye had been evacuated by the enemy on the 26th August, followed on the 27th by a general advance of the French and British armies between the Oise and the Somme. By the night of the 29th August Allied infantry had reached the left bank of the Somme on the whole front from the neighbourhood of Nesle (occupied by the French on the 28th August) northwards to Péronne.

On the night 30th–31st August, a brilliant attack on the Mont St. Quentin by the 2nd Australian Division was completely successful, and on the following morning, in support of this operation, the left of the Fourth Army, consisting of the 3rd Australian, 58th, 47th, and 18th Divisions, attacked towards Bouchavesnes, Rancourt, and Fregicourt, and by the 1st September had captured these villages. Along the Third Army front, also, heavy fighting had taken place on the 31st August and 1st September, and at the close of it Sailly Saillisel, Morval and Beaulencourt, and Rencourt-les-Bapaume were held, and also the ridge east of Bancourt, Fremicourt, Vaulx Vraucourt, and Longatte. The XVIIth Corps had also completed the capture of Bullecourt and Hendecourt, and finally Riencourt-les-Cagnicourt.

The operations of the Third and Fourth British Armies between 21st August and 1st September are (in the Official Dispatches) included under one title—the Battle of Bapaume.

North of the Third Army, the First Army east of Arras had attacked the German salient formed by the successful operations of the Third and Fourth Armies. This operation (the Battle of the Scarpe, 26th–30th August [1]) resulted in the retaking of Monchy-au-Preux by the Canadian Corps and the 51st Division. By the end of the month the First Army had gained the high ground east of Cherisy and Hancourt, had captured Eterpigny, and had cleared the area between the Sensée and the Scarpe rivers west of the Trinquis brook. Plouvain and Gavrelle, north of the Scarpe, were also taken and held by the victorious First Army.

The success of the Allies along the southern front had meanwhile opened a way for an offensive in the Lys salient. The

---

[1] The dates given in the report of the Battles Nomenclature Committee. In the Official Dispatches the dates are 26th August to 3rd September, but in the dispatches the Battle of the Drocourt–Quéant line, 2nd to 3rd September, is included. The Battles Nomenclature Committee give the Battle of the Drocourt–Quéant line as a separate operation.

THE LYS SALIENT.

exhaustion of the enemy's reserves, used up in defending himself against the British and French from, and south of, Arras, was followed by the inevitable necessity of shortening his front. He clung to the Lys salient as long as possible, but the terrible shell-fire to which his positions without cessation were subjected, had caused him such heavy losses that, early in August, he began to effect local withdrawals in the southern flank of the salient. Merville was the first to fall, British troops entering the ruined village on the 19th August. Various small gains of ground were made during the days following the capture of Merville, and finally, on the night of the 29th–30th August the enemy began an extensive withdrawal along the whole of the Lys salient. Early on the 30th Bailleul was occupied, and at evening on the next day British troops had reached Lacoutre, Lestrem, Noote Boon, east of Bailleul. By the evening of the 6th September the Lys salient had disappeared, and bloodstained Kemmel Hill had again passed into the hands of the British, whose front then ran along the general line Givenchy, Neuve Chapelle, Nieppe, Ploegsteert, Voormezelle.

THE BREAKING OF THE HINDENBURG LINE.

THE SECOND BATTLES OF ARRAS, 1918.
 The Battle of the Drocourt-Quéant Line, 2nd to 3rd September.
 Operations from the 4th to 8th September.

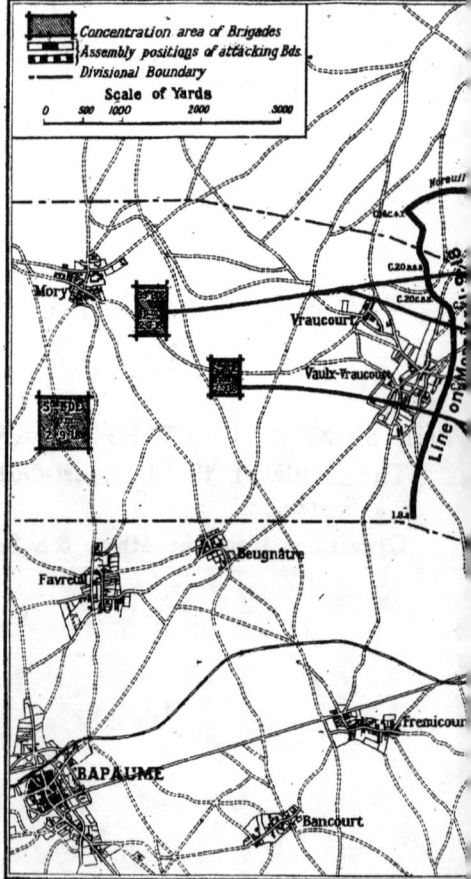

THE BATTLE OF THE DROCOURT-QUEANT LINE, 2nd-3rd September 1918: ACTION OF THE 2nd DIVISION ON THE RIGHT OF THE BATTLE LINE.

(*Facing p. 634.*)

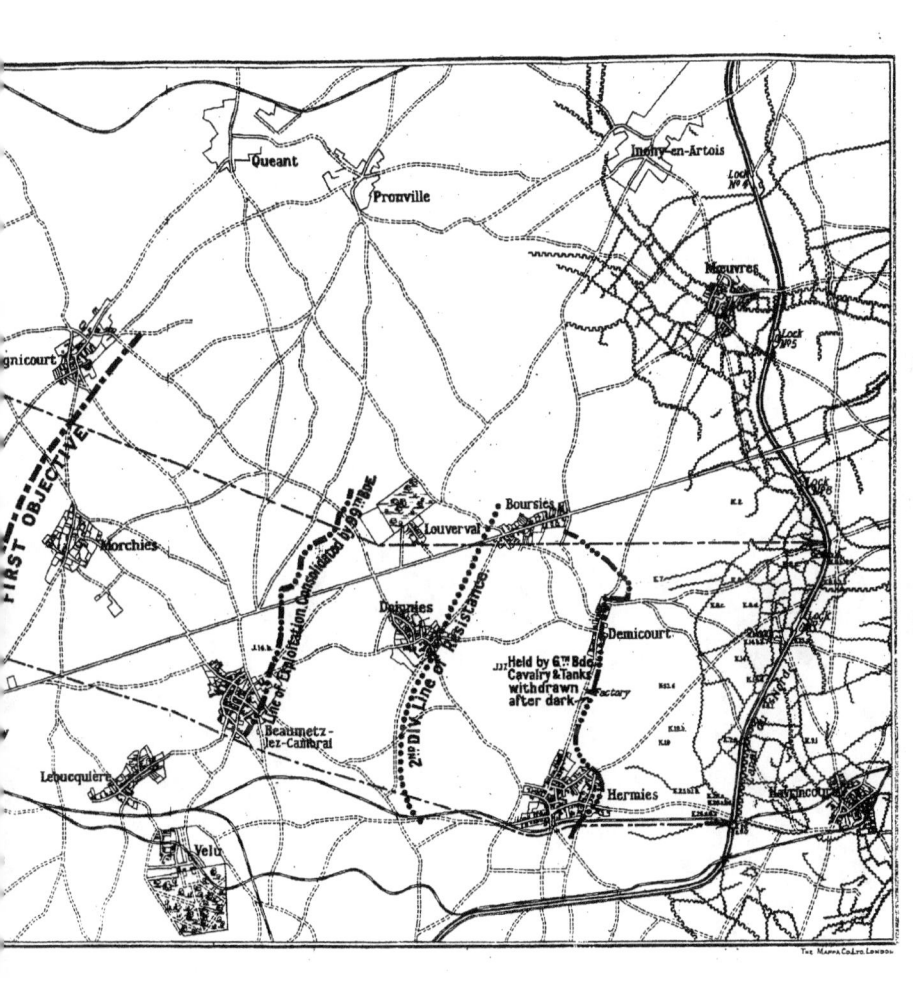

THE SECOND BATTLES OF ARRAS, 1918.

The Battle of the Drocourt-Quéant Line, 2nd to 3rd September.

THE result of the Battle of the Scarpe had been to bring the British troops to within assaulting distance of the powerful trench system running from the Hindenburg Line at Quéant to the Lens defences about Drocourt. The storming and breaking of this line would turn the whole of the enemy's organized positions on a wide front southwards. Accordingly, on the 1st September, orders were issued for an attack on the maze of trenches which formed the junction of the Drocourt-Quéant line and the northern flank of the Hindenburg Line. Both the First and the Third British Armies were to take part in the attack, the Canadian Corps of the former and the XVIIth Corps of the latter. But the line of attack of the Third Army was subsequently prolonged—the VIth Corps of the Third Army and the IVth Corps of the Fourth Army, and even troops as far south as Péronne, taking part in the attack.

Although the 2nd Division and the Guards Division, with the Corps Cavalry Regiment, were in reserve to the 62nd and 3rd Divisions, it is necessary to follow the advance of the first-named, whether it was actively engaged with the enemy or merely following him as he was being beaten back.

At 7.30 p.m. on the 1st September, 2nd Division Operation Order No. 352 was issued, the opening paragraph of which began: " The VIth Corps is attacking on the morning of the 2nd September in conjunction with XVIIth and IVth Corps on the left and right flanks respectively. The objectives of the VIth Corps include Morchies for the 62nd Division, Lagnicourt for the 3rd Division.

" The 2nd Division, with the Guards Division and the Corps Cavalry Regiment, are in Corps reserve."

Then follow instructions to the 6th Infantry Brigade and one Machine-Gun Company to move forward if required; the 5th and 99th Infantry Brigades were placed at "one hour's notice" from 6.30 a.m., 2nd September.

1ST SEPT. MAP.

636   THE HISTORY OF THE SECOND DIVISION.

On the morning of the 1st September the frontage of the VIth Corps extended from the high ground in I.8,a, through T.2,a, C.26,d.2.4, C.20,d.5.1, C.20,c.8.8, C.20,a.8.6, C.14,c.4.7, along Noreuil Switch, the sunken road in C.9,a and d, to Bullecourt Avenue. The 62nd Division on the right and the 3rd Division on the left.

2ND SEPT.   The general assault on the junction of the Drocourt–Quéant line and the Hindenburg system was launched on the morning of the 2nd September, the Canadians and the XVIIIth Corps, with great gallantry, attacking and breaking the enemy's front line, forcing him to make a precipitate retreat on the whole front and south of it.

The attack of the 62nd Division began favourably, but at 11 a.m. the 2nd Division received orders from VIth Corps Headquarters to move forward and support the attack of the West Riding Division. As a result of these orders the 6th Infantry Brigade moved to a position south-east of Mory; the 5th Infantry Brigade to east of Behagnies, and the 99th Infantry Brigade to the Old British Line between Mory and Vraucourt. About midday further information was received that the advance of the 62nd Division had been held up by counter-attack, and the situation was somewhat obscure. No instructions were, however, issued to the 2nd Division to make a move until 5 p.m., when VIth Corps orders arrived, containing the following instructions: The 2nd Division was to relieve the 62nd Division on the night 2nd–3rd September, and be prepared to continue the attack in the direction of Morchies, in conjunction with the 5th Division (IVth Corps) on the right and the Guards Division on the left, on the morning of the 3rd September.

At 8.30 p.m. orders for the following plan of attack were issued from 2nd Divisional Headquarters to all units of the Division: The 6th Infantry Brigade (right) and the 99th Infantry Brigade (left) each with one company of the 2nd Battalion Machine-Gun Corps, were to attack the Beugny–Lagnicourt Ridge (west of Morchies), and if possible a further advance was to be made to the Beaumetz–Louverval Ridge: the 5th Infantry Brigade was to be in Divisional reserve. Forming up on the jumping-off line, *i.e.*, the ridge east of Bois de Vaulx, was to be completed by 3 a.m. " Zero " hour was at 5.20 a.m. The attack would be made under a creeping barrage, the " Heavies " bombarding selected points from " zero " onwards. Only three Mark IV. tanks were available, and these were allocated to the 6th Infantry Brigade with the special object of dealing with Maricourt Wood, which sheltered numerous hostile machine-gun nests. A squadron of the Oxfordshire Hussars and six whippet tanks were in Corps reserve, ready to exploit any success.

During the evening news had arrived of the fine progress made by the Canadians and XVIIth Corps, on the left of the VIth Corps, and at 10 p.m. the 6th and 99th Infantry Brigades were warned that, owing to the success farther north, it was possible the enemy might withdraw his line, and the barrage would therefore lift when the final objective had been reached, in order that patrols might be pushed out immediately on to the Beaumetz–Louverval Ridge.

On the night 2nd–3rd September the enemy's artillery was active until about 11 p.m., after which hour it practically ceased, and the relief of the 62nd Division by the 2nd Division passed off without difficulty. At 5.20 a.m. ("zero" hour) on the morning of the 3rd September the General Officer Commanding 2nd Division assumed command of the line.

3RD SEPT.

Besides the XXXVIth and XLIst Brigades R.F.A., the C.R.A. 2nd Division had under his command the XVIIIth, LXXVIth, and XCIIIrd Brigades of Field Artillery. The last three were Army Artillery Brigades, and again included the XXXIVth Brigade—well-tried comrades of the 2nd Division.

The 6th Infantry Brigade (right) had disposed the 2nd South Staffords on the right and the 17th Royal Fusiliers on the left; the 1st King's were in Brigade reserve on the ridge immediately east of Vaulx Vraucourt; of the 99th Infantry Brigade (left) the 1st King's Royal Rifle Corps was on the left and the 23rd Royal Fusiliers on the right, with the 1st Royal Berks in Brigade reserve.

At "zero" the guns opened with a roar, all six brigades of artillery participating; the days of a shortage of shells had passed for ever, and the British gunners fed their guns without a fear of rebuke from "higher commands." North and south of the 2nd Divisional front the artillery of the flanking divisions also opened fire. But long before the attacking troops advanced on the heels of the barrage the impression had become general that the enemy had withdrawn during the night. And now as the battalions neared the hostile trenches it became clear, from the volume of fire which greeted them, that only rearguards had been left behind.

"At 5.20 a.m., under an excellent barrage," said the Commanding Officer of the 2nd South Staffords, "our troops went forward, and only encountered slight opposition. The objective was gained by 5.35 a.m., when patrols were sent out and consolidation commenced. Major B. C. Parr was killed by shell fire." Similarly, the 17th Royal Fusiliers gained their objective without difficulty, and " as soon as the barrage ceased the advance continued. Morchies and Beaumetz were taken (about 7 a.m.) without any serious opposition ; a few gas shells fell over the area east of Morchies and in the neighbourhood of Beaumetz." Thus the advance of the 6th Infantry Brigade.

" At ' zero ' hour, 5.20 a.m.," reported the 99th Infantry Brigade Diary, " the conditions were almost perfect—dry and cool, and just getting light. The barrage on our Divisional front opened punctually, and was all that could be desired. . . . It was soon found that the enemy had vacated the whole of the area under attack."

Both the 1st King's Royal Rifle Corps and the 23rd Royal Fusiliers reached the first objective about 6.30 a.m., and immediately pushed forward to the second objective, but halted on the latter, as the Guards Division on the left had received no orders to advance beyond Lagnicourt.

Six whippet tanks and a squadron of Oxfordshire Hussars accompanied the patrols as they pushed forward towards the Beaumetz-Louverval Ridge. A few of the enemy were killed and a small number of prisoners captured, but all along the front the enemy had vacated his positions, leaving only a few rearguards armed with machine guns, and even these were soon in rapid retirement. As touch on the right with the 5th Division had been lost, and the Guards were still at Lagnicourt, a halt was called. At 11.30 a.m. 2nd Divisional Headquarters received orders from the VIth Corps to push forward one infantry brigade, with an artillery brigade, six whippet tanks, and the Oxfordshire Hussars as an advanced guard. The advance was to begin at 1 p.m., the Hermies-Demicourt Ridge being the objective ; the cavalry and whippets were to seize the crossings over the Canal du Nord, if possible.

The 6th Infantry Brigade and the XLIst Brigade R.F.A. were detailed for this operation, the brigade to pass through the 99th Infantry Brigade, which had been ordered to consolidate the Beaumetz-Louverval Ridge. The 5th Infantry Brigade had moved forward at 8.45 a.m. to the area immediately east of Vaulx Vraucourt.

At 1 p.m., preceded by the vanguard (Oxfordshire Hussars and whippet tanks), the 6th Infantry Brigade advanced, with the 2nd South Staffords on the right and the 17th Royal Fusiliers on the left, and the 1st King's in support. The vanguard set out to

ALL OBJECTIVES REACHED.

clear the villages of Doignies, Boursies, Demicourt, and Hermies, while patrols of Hussars were detached to maintain touch with the flanking divisions. By 2.45 p.m. the whippets had reached the general line Demicourt–Hermies, but machine-gun fire was still giving trouble from Demicourt.

The South Staffords experienced little difficulty in advancing, though a few casualties were suffered from the enemy's shell fire and machine-gun fire. The 17th Royal Fusiliers, however, had a more difficult task : " Doignies was taken," said the Battalion Diary, " with very little opposition, but the advance was held up on the ridge running through J.17, central, by oblique and enfilade machine-gun fire from the vicinity of Boursies. On account of casualties sustained, B Company called for two platoons from the reserve company. Battalion Headquarters were established in trenches east of Doignies. At 5.30 p.m. our artillery brought fire to bear on the enemy's machine-gun positions, and at 6.20 p.m. the advance was continued on Demicourt. The village was taken, but considerable difficulty was experienced on account of very heavy shelling. Companies reported objective gained at 6.55 p.m. The companies reorganized and consolidated along Sturgeon Support, Grayling Trench, Trout Post, and the Demicourt–Hermies road, to just south of the Sugar Factory. Posts were thrown out 300 yards in front. . . . Touch was maintained with the South Staffords on the right, but was lost with the Guards on the left. B Company pushed north, took Boursies, thus regaining touch with the Guards."

But no further advance being contemplated that day, the 6th Infantry Brigade was ordered to hold the line Hermies–Demicourt as an outpost line. The cavalry, who had pushed east beyond Hermies and towards the Canal du Nord, had to retire under heavy machine-gun fire, having located considerable forces of the enemy along the western banks of the Canal. The cavalry and tanks were now withdrawn.

About 9 p.m. orders to continue the advance at 5.30 a.m. on the 4th September came to hand from VIth Corps Headquarters. The advanced guards were to locate the enemy's main line of resistance, but no attack on a large scale was to be undertaken. The advanced guards were, if possible, to establish themselves well east of the crossings over the Canal du Nord.

During the night of the 2nd–3rd September the enemy had fallen back rapidly along the whole front of the Third Army and the right of the First Army, and by nightfall on the 3rd he had taken up positions along the general line of the Canal du Nord from Péronne to Ytres, thence east of Hermies, Inchy-en-Artois, and Ecourt St. Quentin, to the Sensée, east of Lecluse.

Operations from 4th to 8th September 1918.

The line held by the 6th Infantry Brigade, when night fell on the 3rd September, extended approximately from the eastern outskirts of Hermies and Demicourt, the Hermies road, Trout Post, Grayling Trench to Sturgeon Support, with outposts thrown out in front. The 2nd South Staffords held the right of the line, the 17th Royal Fusiliers the left, and the 1st King's were in support.

At 11 o'clock on the night of the 3rd–4th September the General Officer Commanding 6th Infantry Brigade received the following order from 2nd Divisional Headquarters : " In order to discover the enemy's main line of resistance, the 6th Infantry Brigade will clear the ground to the west of the canal to-morrow, and will push forward patrols on the east of the canal to locate the enemy's main line. . . . The crossings over the canal believed to exist at K.9,b.3.3 to K.9,b.4.6 will be occupied. . . . " Zero " hour will be 5.30 a.m. . . . 99th Infantry Brigade will move up one battalion to about J.14,b. by 7 a.m. . . . C Company, Machine-Gun Battalion, is at disposal of 6th Infantry Brigade for this operation."

The 1st King's were detailed for the operation, the two remaining battalions of the 6th Infantry Brigade (the Staffords and Fusiliers) remaining in the positions occupied by them at nightfall on the 3rd. The King's were to advance through the Staffords and Fusiliers, who, throughout the night, had further consolidated their line from Hermies to Demicourt, thence to Boursies.

4TH SEPT.
MAP.

In the Battalion Diary of the 1st King's Regiment there is no narrative of this attempt to reach the canal, but the following from the Diary of the 6th Infantry Brigade summarizes briefly what happened during that early morning attempt on the 4th September to probe the enemy's positions : " At 5.30 a.m. two companies of the 1st King's Regiment pushed forward to endeavour to gain the line of the canal from K.26,a.6.2 to K.9,b.2.8, and, if no opposition was met with, they were ordered to send out patrols in the direction of Havrincourt and Flesquières." Everything seemed to promise well, for up to 8 a.m. all messages reported the situation quiet and the two companies well advanced towards their ob-

OPERATIONS OF THE 2nd DIVISION
from 4th–8th September 1918.

(*Facing p. 640.*)

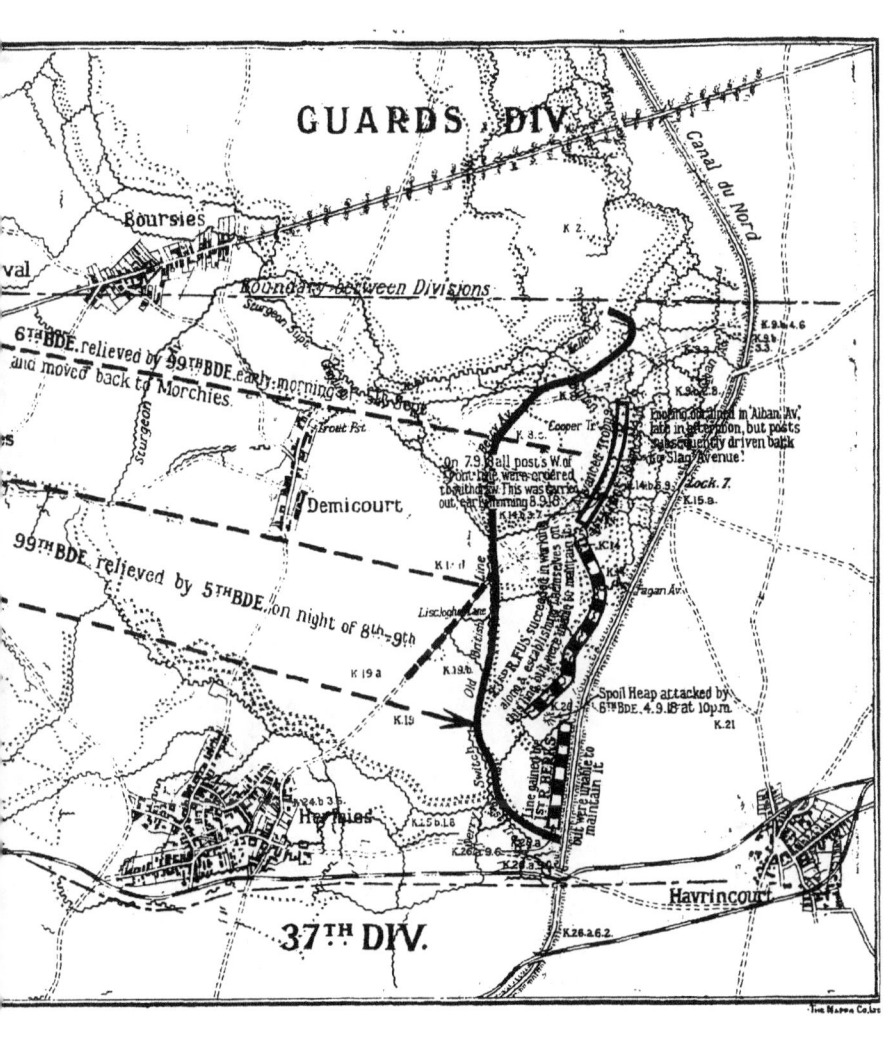

HARD FIGHTING BY THE KING'S.

jectives. But by 9.30 a.m. the situation had changed considerably, and the Commanding Officer, 1st King's, reported to 6th Infantry Brigade Headquarters: " My line is Cooper Trench, thence north along Alban Avenue (K.9,a. and c.). . . . We are up against heavy machine-gun and artillery fire. . . . C Company is on our right. . . . Troops are coming up on the left, though still some distance behind. . . . C Company is being worried by machine-gun fire."

To continue the account by 6th Infantry Brigade Headquarters: " At 10 a.m. news was received that these two companies had been held up on the line approximately—Slag Avenue in K.8,d. to K.14,b.3.7, thence along road through K.13,d. and K.19,b. and a. Enemy machine guns were very active, particularly from the Spoil Heap in K.20 central. One platoon, which had established itself in Cooper Trench, was counter-attacked by the enemy, but successfully drove them off, killing several and capturing one wounded man."

By this time any movement in the open drew heavy fire immediately from the enemy, and it was impossible for the attack to go forward.

At 12.30 p.m. orders were received at 6th Infantry Brigade Headquarters stating that the brigade would be relieved by the 99th Infantry Brigade on the night 4th–5th. But " before handing over, the Spoil Heap (in K.20 central) and the high ground in K.26,a. must be captured under cover of an artillery bombardment." The brigade was also ordered to establish a line of posts along the west bank of the canal from the junction of the railway in K.26,a. to Fagan Avenue. The XLIst Brigade R.F.A. was to barrage West Trench, the trenches immediately east of it on the Spoil Heap, the high ground west of Havrincourt, and the trench system in K.21.

" Zero " hour was to be 10 p.m.

Throughout the afternoon the enemy was particularly active. His bombing parties on the left of the brigade front succeeded in forcing back the left flank company of the 17th Royal Fusiliers, but the loss of ground was negligible. The King's still hung on to their gains of the early morning, but the position of the battalion was none too secure, as the following message sent by the Commanding Officer to 6th Infantry Brigade Headquarters at 3.56 p.m. shows : " Following from D Company timed 3.5 p.m. . . . The enemy is bombing very persistently; so much so that No. 13 platoon has been forced to retire with loss of officer, sergeant, and eight men from Alban Avenue . . . I have put the remnants into Betty Trench.[1] . . . No. 14 platoon in Cooper Trench are being bombed again, and have had to withdraw to Slag Avenue. . . . If things get too bad I shall have to withdraw to the Betty Trench line. . . . I hold at present Slag Avenue from K.14,b.6.9 to K.14,b.3.6, and Betty Avenue between two roads in K.8,c. . . . C Company's left is at Lisclogher Lane. . . . We have not been able to find the Guards (Division). . . . The enemy is on this side of the canal in force . . . enemy machine-gun and rifle fire comes from all round and from both sides of the canal . . . artillery cannot deal with the people who are giving us trouble—namely, bombers."

Ten minutes before "zero" the "Heavies" opened on the eastern edges of the Spoil Heap, and at "zero" hour the Field Artillery barrage fell on the objective. The King's pressed forward with great gallantry, but the Spoil Heap defied all attempts at capture, the enemy's machine guns, well placed, sweeping the ground in front of them. But the high ground in K.26,a. as far south as the railway was won, and, as it was impossible to achieve more, the relief of the 6th Infantry Brigade by the 99th Infantry Brigade was begun early in the evening of the 5th. On the right, the 1st Royal Berks relieved 2nd South Staffords and two companies 1st King's Regiment, while the 1st King's Royal Rifle Corps, on the left, relieved the remaining companies of the 1st King's and the 17th Royal Fusiliers; the 23rd Royal Fusiliers were in support. The King's and the 17th Royal Fusiliers were withdrawn to Beaumetz, and the South Staffords to just east of Morchies. The 37th Division was on the right flank of the 99th Infantry Brigade, and the Guards Division on the left.

The line taken over by the 99th Infantry Brigade extended from the canal bank at K.26,a.9.0 to K.26,a.9.6, thence along West Trench, Derry Switch, the Old British Line in K.19, K.20, and K.14, through Betty Avenue and Kellett Trench; Betty[2] and Bullen Posts were also held.

About 8 a.m. it was observed that the enemy was shelling the Spoil Heap, which pointed to the fact that he had withdrawn his troops from that position. The possession of the high ground in K.26,a. (gained by the 1st King's during the night 4th–5th) had caused the enemy to relinquish his hold on that dangerous spot. A patrol from C Company of the 1st Royal Berks went out and succeeded in establishing posts north and south of the Spoil Heap,

---

[1] Named after the C.R.E. of the 2nd Division.
[2] Given in the map as "Beatty Post."

AN AEROPLANE SHOT DOWN.

but they were withdrawn later, the ground being covered instead by Vickers and Lewis guns.

5TH, 6TH, AND 7TH SEPT.

The Division had, however, received orders not to initiate any serious attack, but rather to adopt a policy of persistent infiltration in order to gain possession of all trenches west of the canal. Thus, working up the very same trenches which were dug by the Division during the withdrawal from the Mœuvres–Bourlon Wood line in 1917, patrols from the Berkshires and Rifles pushed forward in order to gain the line of the canal. To this end constant efforts were made throughout the 5th, 6th,[1] and 7th of September. Twice the Berkshires established posts actually on the canal bank, but were heavily counter-attacked and had to retire. On the left flank the Rifles, in the face of very determined opposition, temporarily advanced their position, but were subsequently driven back again. On the night of the 6th–7th the 23rd Royal Fusiliers relieved the 1st King's Royal Rifle Corps, the relief being completed by 3.8 a.m.

During the morning of the 7th the 23rd Royal Fusiliers attacked the enemy and succeeded in establishing posts at the junction of Slag Avenue and Key Trench, but again the enemy launched heavy counter-attacks, and the Fusiliers were forced to withdraw, much as the Rifles and Berkshires had done. The enemy's machine guns and artillery were extremely active, and B Company of the Fusiliers sustained heavy casualties.[2] During the afternoon an enemy artillery aeroplane was shot down by rifle fire, the pilot was killed, and the observer captured. The wrecked machine was shelled and set on fire by the enemy.

The tenacity with which the 99th Infantry Brigade clung to their positions and endeavoured to advance them was fittingly observed by the General Officer Commanding Division, who sent his congratulations to both battalions. "The troops fought most gallantly," said the General Officer Commanding. During the night of the 7th a rain of heavy shells fell about 99th Infantry Brigade Headquarters, which were in a dug-out on the Doignies–Demicourt road. The brigade transport was passing at the time, and unfortunately Captain R. M. Vaisey, Adjutant of the XXXVIth Brigade R.F.A., and the brigade mess cook (Corporal N. G. Short,

---

[1] On the 6th September, to the general regret of the Division, Brigadier-General W. E. Ironside, C.M.G., D.S.O., handed over command of the 99th Infantry Brigade. He was succeeded by Brigadier-General A. E. M'Namara, C.M.G., D.S.O. General Ironside afterwards went to Russia on special duty.

[2] The battalion's casualties were 3 officers and 100 other ranks.

one of the original brigade when it landed in France in 1915) were killed.

By the 7th September it had become apparent that without considerable artillery preparation the policy of infiltration was not likely to produce the desired results. Accordingly, on the morning of the 8th, all advanced posts were withdrawn and the consolidation and improvement of the line from the Canal bank–West Trench–Old British Line Avenue–Betty Avenue–Kellett Avenue to Betty Post was begun, whilst the guns began their preliminary bombardment.

8TH SEPT.

On the 8th–9th the 5th Infantry Brigade relieved the 99th Infantry Brigade, the latter marching back to Beaumetz into Divisional reserve. The 5th Infantry Brigade disposed the 2nd Highland Light Infantry on the right, and the 2nd Oxford and Bucks, with one company of the 24th Royal Fusiliers, on the left ; the 24th Royal Fusiliers (less one company) were in reserve round Hermies.

THE BATTLES OF THE HINDENBURG LINE.

THE BATTLE OF HAVRINCOURT, 12th September 1918.
THE BATTLE OF THE CANAL DU NORD, 27th September to 1st October.
THE BATTLE OF CAMBRAI, 1918 (8th to 9th October).
  The Capture of Forenville by the Second Division.

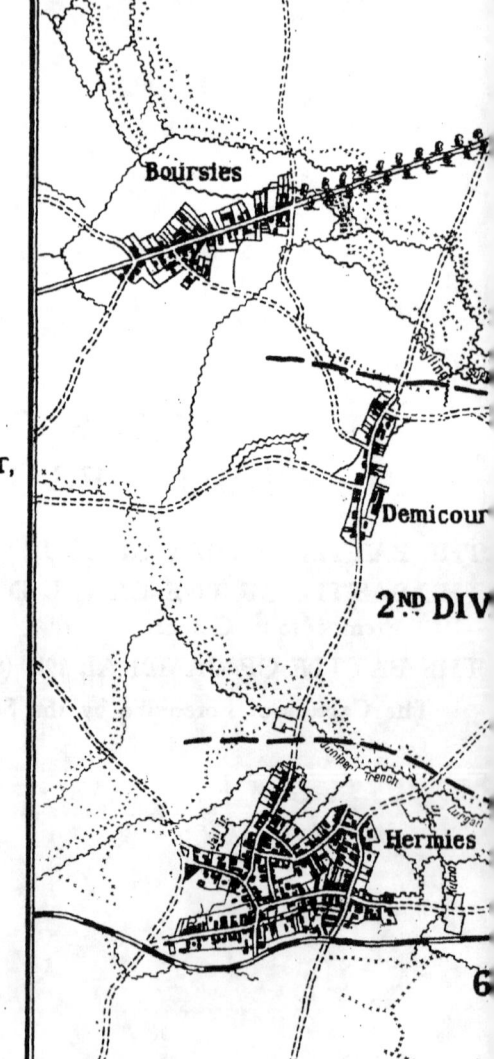

THE BATTLE OF HAVRINCOURT,
12th September 1918.

(Also to illustrate Preliminary Operations of the 2nd Division on night 11th September 1918).

(Facing p. 646.)

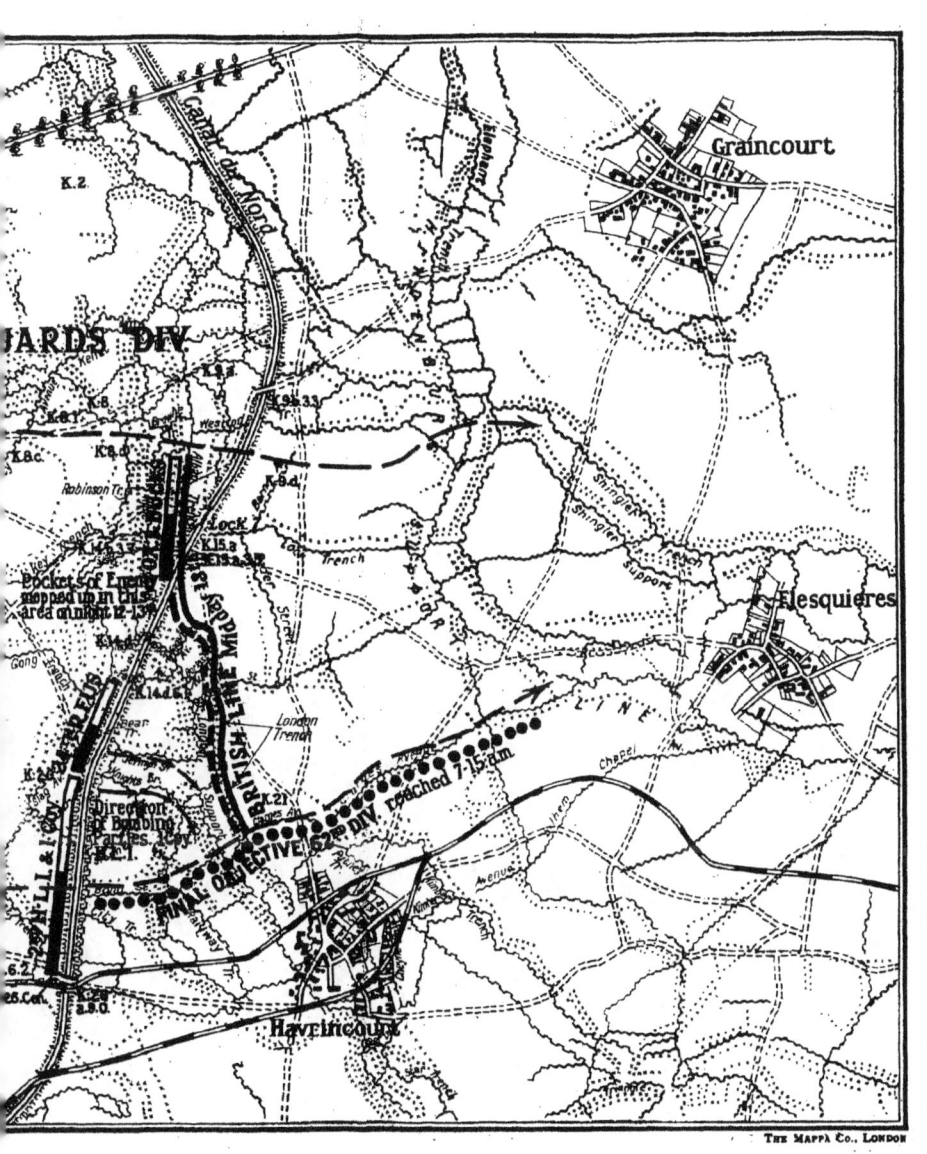

THE BATTLE OF HAVRINCOURT,
12th September 1918.[1]

ALTHOUGH the main operation—the Battle of Havrincourt—took place on the 12th September, preliminary operations against the Hindenburg front system west of the Canal du Nord, together with the canal crossings in K.15,a. and K.14,d., and the trenches east of the canal south of the Hindenburg front line, were carried out by the 2nd Division at 6.15 p.m. on the 11th September.

Under instructions from Third Army Commander (Sir Julian Byng), VIth Corps Headquarters had ordered these preliminary operations so that the 2nd Division should gain a footing in the Hindenburg front system east of the canal, in order to assist the main operations on the 12th :—

"Main operations (by 62nd and 2nd Divisions) : The capture of the Hindenburg front system east of the Canal du Nord, and Havrincourt village. . . . The IVth Corps is to co-operate in this operation, and will capture Trescault Spur."

These instructions reached 2nd Division Headquarters on the 8th September, and preparations were put in hand immediately. At 4.30 p.m. on the 10th the 5th Infantry Brigade, which had relieved the 99th Infantry Brigade in the line during the night 8th–9th, was duly notified, and plans for the attack were discussed. In view of the coming operations, selected targets were continually harassed by field and heavy artillery throughout the 9th and 10th. The enemy's guns were also active.

The terrain of the battlefield-to-be in the near future was thus described by the General Officer Commanding 2nd Division on the 9th September : " I took a stroll with —— to a high ridge to the west of our Headquarters. All the country now has a down-like appearance ; there is no vestige of cultivation, and no boundaries. There are the eternal belts of wire stretching away into the distance which belonged to former British and German back

[1] In the Official Dispatches this action is termed "The Battle of Havrincourt and Epéhy," and the date is given as 12th–18th September.

defence lines. There are shell-holes lightly scattered around, some fresh and some grass-grown. In one place there was a heap of German steel helmets. Evidently a batch of prisoners had been collected here, as they always cast their helmets at the first opportunity. Bourlon Wood stood up very distinctly, and the intervening country. We could see the flashes of our guns on the reverse slopes of the hills. To the north Vimy Ridge was very clear.

"Scattered all over the country there are smashed-up hutment camps. They were our old camps in the Cambrai salient; but since the retirement in March we have bombed or shelled them to smithereens. They are now invaluable in providing material for units bivouacked in the district. In an old trench with this material troops can make themselves quite comfortable. The enemy found these huts quite untenable, and they dug semicircular shelters into the banks of sunken roads, where they were extremely secure; but they must have suffered considerably from dust and constant traffic."

Then followed an instance of German treachery: "A man in one of our burial parties had a narrow escape; when he moved a German corpse a bomb exploded. A nice form of booby-trap, and in future I shall use German prisoners to bury the German dead if I hear of another case."

Well known to the 2nd Division was the ground over which the attack was to be found. Even the very trenches which sheltered the battalions of the 5th Infantry Brigade bore names intimately connected with the Division, for Bullen, Walsh, and Kellett Trenches were named nearly a year previously, after the brigadiers commanding the three infantry brigades at that period.

North of the Divisional front line, along the Canal du Nord, was Lock 5—famous in the history of the 2nd Division for the splendid fight put up by an isolated party of officers and men of the 13th Essex, with a few men of the King's, during the German counter-attack of November 1917. Away on the right, near the Sugar Factory, which stood just north of the Bapaume–Cambrai road, the 17th Fusiliers had fought their splendid action in the Rat's Tail—a small length of trench then surrounded on three sides by the enemy. South of the village of Mœuvres lay the very trenches in which Captain M'Ready Diarmid of the 17th Middlesex had himself killed over ninety of the enemy, driving the Germans back 300 yards, only to suffer death at the hands of a bomb-thrower when he had broken the counter-attack in that part of the line. And over all, that place of ill omen, Bourlon

THE ORDEAL OF WAITING.

Wood, looked down upon the comparatively silent yet living lines of trenches about the Canal du Nord, as if beckoning to those who had so often tried in vain to wrest its broken limbs and ruined beauty from the hands of the German invader.

The objectives of the 5th Infantry Brigade were more closely defined in 2nd Division Operation Order No. 355: "On 11th September the 5th Infantry Brigade will capture the enemy trench from Betty Post—canal crossing about K.15,a.3.5—Alban Avenue—Fagan Avenue on the east side of the canal—Canal crossing at K.14,d.6.1—thence along the west bank of the canal to the southern Divisional boundary. . . . Artillery arrangements are as follows: Creeping barrage on the front of attack at the rate of 100 yards in 4 minutes, opening with smoke at ' zero ' minus 2, and creeping forward at ' zero ' plus 4 (minutes) . . . a smoke barrage . . . a protective barrage beyond the final objective from ' zero ' plus 36 . . . machine-gun barrages."

Owing to the volume of the enemy's shell fire, and to the fact that every movement in the British positions was visible to the Germans from Bourlon Wood and Havrincourt, the forming-up operations had to be carried out during the night 10th–11th. So that all day long on the 11th the troops had to wait in their assembly positions until " zero " hour—6.15 p.m.

11TH SEPT.
MAP.

And how anxiously the men awaited the order to attack. For the enemy during the past few days had been using mustard gas, and already many casualties had resulted from that iniquitous invention.

The forming-up line ran from West Trench through Old British Line Avenue, Betty Avenue, and Kellett Trench. And on this line the 5th Infantry Brigade had disposed: " 2nd Highland Light Infantry—three companies in front line—namely, Western Canal bank from K.26 central, northwards to West Trench, along West Trench and Old British Line Avenue as far as K.14,a.1.0, and one company in close support in Juniper Trench and Kutno Trench. The 52nd Light Infantry (2nd Oxford and Bucks) on left—three companies in front line from K.14,a.1.0 along Betty Avenue and Kellett Trench to the grid line between K.2 and K.8.1, and one company in close support in trenches in K.7, with an additional supporting company of the 24th Royal Fusiliers south-east of Demicourt. The 24th Royal Fusiliers (less one company) in brigade reserve. Two companies about Beaumetz, the other north-west of Hermies about Jail Trench."[1]

[1] Report by 5th Infantry Brigade Headquarters.

The 2nd South Staffords (attached from the 6th Infantry Brigade) was also in brigade reserve to the 5th Infantry Brigade.

The 2nd Battalion Machine-Gun Corps had three batteries of A Company disposed in Old British Line Avenue and one in Jaffrey Alley, three batteries of B Company in Grayling Support, and three batteries of D Company in Kutno Trench and at K.25,b.1.8. The guns of C Company were in trenches near Beaumetz, having been withdrawn during the night 10th–11th after a tour in the line which began on 3rd September.

Parties of Pioneers (10th Duke of Cornwall's Light Infantry) had been ordered to form blocks in the trenches when captured.

A gas projector attack, ordered for the night 10th–11th, had to be cancelled owing to the supply tanks, which were carrying up the projectors, failing to reach their destination in time.

Punctually at 6.13 p.m. ("zero" minus 2 minutes) the guns of six brigades of Field Artillery fired smoke at rapid rate to cover the exit of the assaulting battalions. This barrage was extremely good, and formed a dense screen, through which it was impossible for the enemy to reply with aimed fire. From "zero" to "zero" plus 4 minutes the guns heavily bombarded the initial objective towards which the infantry were rapidly advancing. On the right of the attack the 2nd Highland Light Infantry soon overcame the enemy's resistance, which was of a feeble nature. The battalion Diary very briefly describes the action thus: "Little opposition was encountered, and D Company secured the crossings (over the canal) at Knight's Bridge and Jermyn Street. B Company, on the right, found no crossings opposite their front, and therefore crossed on the left front, and worked south to their objectives, which were gained. By 8 p.m. the situation was clear on our front. No touch, however, could be gained with the 52nd Light Infantry, who had attacked on our left."

In Knight's Bridge and Jermyn Street the battalion established posts, and scouts were then sent out to reconnoitre. At 10.25 p.m. the Highland Light Infantry sent back a message giving the battalion's situation: "West bank of canal from right divisional boundary, northwards to the Slag Heap, across the canal, Knight's Bridge, Jermyn Street, and Fagan Avenue, and in touch with the 52nd Light Infantry in the southern portion of Fagan Avenue, about 200 yards west of the canal." About 1 a.m. (on the 12th) the battalion again sent back a report: the forward companies had secured the canal crossings, and had pushed out posts in City Trench and Sloane Street, beyond the objective allotted them, but

THE GALLANT OXFORD AND BUCKS. 651

a withdrawal from the former post was ordered, as the retention of that post would interfere with the barrage which had been ordered for the 12th—*i.e.*, in the main operations.

Thus the right of the attack had gone extremely well, and the Highland Light Infantry had captured all its objectives with only a few casualties, and, so far as the battalion was concerned, no further preparation was necessary for the main attack by the 62nd and 2nd Divisions ordered for 5.25 on the morning of the 12th.

The Oxford and Bucks were, however, less fortunate. One company, D, had indeed advanced splendidly, and had crossed the canal without much difficulty, reaching its objective, as the Battalion Diary states, " fairly easily." It was this company with which the Highland Light Infantry gained touch. But the other three companies, A, B, and C, met with strong opposition. Heavy machine-gun fire coming from the front and left flank of the battalion drove the attack away from the right, and a gap of some 500 yards soon existed between the right flank company (D) and the remaining three companies. In this gap pockets of the enemy clung to their positions and prevented touch being obtained between the right flank of A and the left of D.

A map taken from a captured German officer showed the enemy's outpost line to be in Slag Avenue, some 500 yards west of the canal, and his main line of resistance along Bear Trench and Hunt Avenue (both west of the canal), thence across the canal, southwards along London Support. Thus, whilst the right of the attack had only to overcome an outpost line, the left was faced both by an outpost line and a main line of resistance.

With splendid gallantry the Oxford and Bucks worked slowly forward. The night was pitch black, the ground over which they advanced was thick with mud and slippery, and retarded progress; the enemy's guns had put down a terrific barrage, which included machine-gun fire, but yard by yard, using their bayonets and bombs freely, the devoted troops slowly pressed the enemy back. At ten minutes past eight a position near Browne Trench had been reached; but south of this machine-gun fire held up the advance. By this time all communication with Brigade and Divisional Headquarters had been cut. Visual communication was practically impossible, as it drew fire at once, and time after time runners had been sent back, only to become casualties on the way from the enemy's heavy artillery and machine-gun fire. By midnight it appeared that the most advanced troops had reached the line of Hunt Avenue, which, as the enemy's main line of resistance, was found to be held in great strength, with machine guns untouched by the barrage. The work of "mopping up" occasioned many miniature battles, and in the dark hours of the night British and Germans fought desperately.

About 10.40 p.m. the Officer Commanding Oxford and Bucks had called up the attached company of 24th Royal Fusiliers to help clear up the situation on his left flank. The Fusiliers had already formed a defensive flank on the left. Eventually practically the whole battalion had become involved in the attack, lending assistance both to the Oxford and Bucks and to the Highland Light Infantry.

Soon after midnight the 2nd Battalion Grenadier Guards took over the left flank of the Divisional front—Hunt Avenue down to Weston Trench—and afterwards advanced with the two left companies of the Oxford and Bucks, and secured Alban Trench as far south as Robinson Trench, whence the enemy held.

Just south of Lock No. 7 there was a crossing over the canal which formed also the apex of some four or five roads. In front of this crossing was a trench (a portion of Alban Avenue) protected by two belts of strong wire. From this trench two short communication trenches ran west to Hunt Avenue, the latter being protected by three more belts of wire. It was mainly this position which held up the advance, for it had been practically untouched by the barrage.

Throughout this action the guns of the 2nd Battalion Machine-Gun Corps were oftentimes in desperate straits. The guns of D Company assisted the 5th Infantry Brigade by firing a creeping enfilade barrage, but A and B Companies were "silent," three batteries of these companies having orders only to fire if S.O.S. signals went up from the front line. No enemy counter-attacks took place during the night, and in consequence the machine gunners were not called upon to open fire; but throughout the dark hours shells fell thick and fast about the gun positions. Men were constantly being buried, and in many places the trenches were blown in. A Company caught the full blast of the enemy's shell fire; but all ranks behaved splendidly, and although four men were killed, seven wounded, and seven more badly gassed, the guns were kept in action. An officer and one of his N.C.O's (Second-Lieut. R. C. Marsh and Sergeant J. O'Regan) were both badly gassed, but refused to leave their guns until ordered to the dressing station by their Commanding Officer. Both died later from the effects of gas poisoning.

THE LINE BEFORE THE BATTLE. 653

Before the beginning of the main operation at 5.25 a.m. on the 12th September the line gained by the 2nd Division ran from right to left as follows: The 2nd Highland Light Infantry held the line of the canal from the southern Divisional boundary to Fagan Avenue, with posts in Sloane Street, Knight's Bridge, and east of the canal in Fagan Avenue (the latter held jointly with the 2nd Oxford and Bucks). The left flank of the battalion was secured by the support company of the 24th Royal Fusiliers, which occupied Fagan Support, east of the canal.

12TH SEPT

The situation on the right of the 2nd Oxford and Bucks was obscure. The joint post in Fagan Avenue, held by D Company of the battalion with the left company of the Highland Light Infantry, was still not in touch with the remaining three companies of the Oxfords. Hunt Avenue and Alban Avenue as far north as Robinson Trench were in the hands of the British, but pockets of Germans still held out south of the latter trench. One company of the Oxfords (which had been relieved by the Guards) and one company of the 24th Royal Fusiliers were engaged in working their way northwards from Fagan Support.

At 5.25 a.m. the 62nd Division, under a creeping barrage, attacked Havrincourt and speedily cleared the village. The Division then pushed on northwards to Bond Street and Clarges Avenue, bombing its way up the trench until the final objectives (the two trenches already named) were reached by 7.15 a.m. Ten minutes earlier (after a two hours' preliminary bombardment of London Trench, London Support, Jermyn Street, and Knight's Bridge, followed by a creeping barrage) the 5th Infantry Brigade started to bomb down Jermyn Street, Knight's Bridge, London Trench, and London Support, with the object of gaining touch with the 62nd Division in Clarges Avenue. In this attack the 2nd Highland Light Infantry was assisted by the 24th Royal Fusiliers.

Touch with the 62nd Division at the junction of Bond Street and Railway Trenches by the party moving from Knight's Bridge was reported by the Highland Light Infantry at 10.40 a.m. But the party working along Jermyn Street on reaching London Support was held up by machine-gun fire. North of Jermyn Street the situation was obscure. But by the end of the morning touch had been gained with the 62nd Division in Clarges Avenue. London Trench was held thence to opposite Jermyn Street and London Support, to 100 yards north of Jermyn Street.

During the afternoon, as the Oxford and Bucks had not succeeded in bombing southwards down London Support and London

Trench, a fresh company of the 24th Royal Fusiliers was sent to bomb northwards from the portion of these two trenches held by the Highland Light Infantry. After a stiff fight both were cleared of the enemy as far as the canal, but pockets of the enemy still held out in the southern portion of Alban Avenue and Hunt Avenue.

From sheer exhaustion, rather than from the number of casualties sustained, little more could be done until fresh troops had been brought up and all ranks set to work to consolidate the positions won. With the Pioneers, who were of the greatest assistance in constructing blocks, the captured trenches were cleaned up and the defences improved.

During the night the 2nd South Staffords (6th Infantry Brigade) relieved the Oxford and Bucks.

As soon as the South Staffords had taken over the line " mopping up " was carried on, and by 2.50 on the morning of the 13th Hunt Avenue had been cleared of the enemy. It was not, however, until midday that all the trenches in the Divisional area had been cleared and the complete line—London Trench–Fagan Avenue–Alban Avenue—established, with no intervening pockets of the enemy.

Thus, as far as the 2nd Division was concerned, ended the Battle of Havrincourt.

After paying a well-earned tribute to the Tunnellers and Pioneers of the Division, and to the splendid co-operation of the Divisional Artillery, whose barrage "obliterated all German Observation Posts, even up to Bourlon Wood, and prevented attack from aimed fire," the report of the General Officer Commanding 5th Infantry Brigade concludes with several more points : " The number of prisoners captured is estimated at about 80 to 100 ; but owing to batches of them carrying wounded to advanced dressing stations, receipt for about 50 only were obtained. The German machine gunners put up a stout defence, but the infantrymen did not, as a rule, show much fight ; approximately, 60 machine guns were taken. In several cases Germans refused to quit their dug-outs, and much execution was done by bombing these. A captured German machine-gun team was recognized as the same that had previously been seen bombing our wounded. These prisoners were handed over to a party of Guardsmen to be suitably dealt with, which order was duly carried out. One of the above machine-gun team was found to be wearing a Red Cross brassard ; another German prisoner on being disarmed set about his captor with his fists. He also was suitably dealt with."

GENERAL SITUATION, 12TH SEPTEMBER.

The Official Dispatches summarize the general situation on the 12th September as follows: "On the 12th the IVth and VIth Corps of the Third Army attacked on a front of about five miles in the Havrincourt sector, employing troops of the New Zealand, 37th, 62nd, and 2nd Divisions. The villages of Trescault and Havrincourt were taken by the 37th and 62nd Divisions respectively, and positions were secured which were of considerable importance in view of future operations."

On the night of the 13th–14th September the 5th Infantry Brigade was relieved by the 6th Infantry Brigade.

13TH–14TH SEPT.

During the next few days patrols endeavoured to push forward to Ryder Street; but the trench was found to be strongly held, and no attack was made. On the nights of 15th–16th and 16th–17th the Guards Division and the 3rd Division took over the front held by the 2nd and 62nd Divisions respectively, the 2nd Division withdrawing into the Corps Left Support area on the night of 16th–17th; the Divisional Artillery alone remained in action. "Our unfortunate artillery," said the General Officer Commanding 2nd Division, "never get out."

On the morning of the 17th September 2nd Division Headquarters were established at L'Homme Mort; the 5th Infantry Brigade was in the Courcelles area; the 6th Infantry Brigade in and about Ervillers; and the 99th Infantry Brigade in Vaulx Vraucourt and vicinity.

17TH SEPT

After the Canal du Nord along the Divisional front, and Havrincourt, had been won, General Pereira, General Officer Commanding 2nd Division, sent the following message to the 5th Infantry Brigade: "I am gradually getting details of the magnificent work done by the battalions and other units of the 5th Infantry Brigade during the operations on the Canal du Nord on 11th and 12th September. In spite of the fatigue from the recent successful advance, weak battalions attacked a most formidable trench system on a wide front, and, in spite of very severe losses, carried on until all their objectives were secured. Will you kindly convey my very great appreciation to all ranks of the 5th Brigade for their splendid work." And to this message, as it was wired to all units of the 5th Infantry Brigade, the General Officer Commanding (Brigadier-General W. L. Osborn) added another: "I am proud to command men who have so worthily upheld the traditions of their distinguished regiments."

On the 18th September the Fourth and Third Armies attacked on a front of about 17 miles from Holon to Gouzeaucourt, the

18TH SEPT.

First French Army attacking south of the former village. Before nightfall Epéhy was captured ; and during the succeeding days positions required for an attack on the main Hindenburg Line were gained. At the close of these operations, in which fifteen British divisions had defeated twenty German divisions, the captures numbered nearly 12,000 prisoners and 100 guns.

THE BATTLE OF THE CANAL DU NORD,
27th September to 1st October 1918.[1]

From the 17th to the 27th September the 2nd Division occupied the left Divisional support area (VIth Corps), with Headquarters at L'Homme Mort, north-west of Vaulx Vraucourt. The 5th Infantry Brigade was in the neighbourhood of Courcelles, 6th Infantry Brigade near Ervillers, and the 99th Infantry Brigade about Mory and Vaulx.

All along the front preparations were being made for that great assault by the British, French, Belgian, and American armies which ended in the utter *débâcle* and defeat of the German armies in the West. On the very day upon which the Battle of Havrincourt was fought and won, the First American Army, assisted by certain French divisions, had attacked and driven the enemy from the St. Mihiel Salient, and had inflicted heavy losses upon him in prisoners and guns. On the success of these two battles, Marshal Foch decided to launch four convergent and simultaneous offensives which had been the subject of careful discussion between Sir Douglas Haig and himself.

These four offensives were :—

1. By the Americans west of the Meuse in the direction of Mezières.

2. By the French west of Argonne, in close co-operation with the American attack, and with the same general objective.

3. By the British on the St. Quentin–Cambrai front in the general direction of Maubeuge.

4. By Belgian and Allied forces in Flanders in the direction of Ghent.

" By these attacks it was expected . . . that the important German forces opposite the French and Americans would be pressed

---

[1] In the Official Dispatches this is termed " The Battle of Cambrai and the Hindenburg Line " (27th September to 5th October). The title and period adopted above are from the Report of the Battles Nomenclature Committee.

IMPORTANCE OF THE BRITISH ATTACK.

back upon the difficult country of the Ardennes, while the British threat struck at their principal line of communication. In Flanders it was intended to take advantage of the weakening of the German forces on this front to clear the Belgian coast by a surprise attack. Success in any one of these offensives might compel the enemy to withdraw to the line of the Meuse."[1]

There is no doubt whatever that the results to be obtained from these different offensives depended very largely upon the degree of success gained by the British attack in the centre. For in the centre the enemy's defences were most highly organized, and presented a very formidable obstacle. But apart from the very great effect upon the *moral* of the German army, the effect upon the German people by the smashing of the renowned Hindenburg Line would be tremendous. For they had been taught to believe that the Hindenburg Line was practically impregnable. Equally, of course, if failure resulted from the Allied attacks, the enemy's *moral* would receive a great fillip.

In spite, therefore, of the weakened state of his forces and the probable result of a costly failure, Sir Douglas Haig decided to attack the Hindenburg Line along the Cambrai–St. Quentin front as early as possible.

The attack was to begin on the 27th September with the Battle of the Canal du Nord. Three British armies—the Fourth, Third, and First, in the order given from right to left—held the line from the village of Selency (west of St. Quentin) to the Sensée River, at Ecourt St. Quentin. Approximately, the Fourth Army was disposed on a line from Selency to just west of Gouzeaucourt, the Third Army from Gouzeaucourt to the Bapaume–Cambrai road, and the First Army north of the latter.[2]

In order to deceive the enemy, the Third and First Armies were to open the battle; but the heaviest attack was to be made by the Fourth Army, when the two first-named armies had won nearer to their final objectives. The enemy's positions along the whole front of the three armies were to be subjected to a prolonged and heavy bombardment, beginning on the night 26th–27th Sep-

[1] Official Dispatches.
[2] From south to north, the Fourth, Third, and First British Armies were opposed by the right flank of the Eighteenth (von Hutier), the Second (von Marwitz), the Seventeenth (von Below), and the left flank of the Sixth (von Quast) German Armies. British divisions numbered 47 against 56 German divisions; 21 British and 1 American divisions were in the front line opposed by 28 German divisions. Prior to the Battle of the Canal du Nord, the Germans had massed by far the greater number of their divisions in France and Flanders opposite the Fourth, Third, and First British Armies.

tember. Before the British attack on the 27th, the Americans and French were to launch their offensives on the 26th.

All along the line in France and Flanders the tremendous stakes at issue were well known. From the front-line trenches to General Headquarters it was known also that the enemy was fighting with his back to the wall. Desperate fighting was ahead, but the *moral* of the Allied troops permitted no thought of failure. " To-morrow," said the General Officer Commanding 2nd Division in his Diary, dated September 25, 1918, " the biggest battle in the world's history begins. Twenty-four American divisions, equal numerically to fifty ordinary divisions at the present reduced scale, and sixteen French divisions open the ball, and then it will gradually extend until the whole front is moving."

As early as the 17th September, the day upon which the 2nd Division passed into Corps Reserve, VIth Corps Headquarters had issued a warning outlining operations to be carried out towards the end of the month.

The Corps plan of attack (framed, of course, in conjunction with the other corps of the Third and Fourth Armies) was as follows : The 3rd Division, on the right, and the Guards Division, on the left, were to attack under cover of a creeping barrage. When these two divisions had won as far as possible, the 2nd Division was to pass through the Guards Division, and the 62nd Division through the 3rd Division, drive the enemy across the Canal de L'Escaut, and capture Rumilly and the high ground south of the Faubourg St. Paris (south of Cambrai). Both the 2nd and 62nd Divisions were to assemble behind the Guards and 3rd Divisions (respectively) one day before " zero," and they were to move forward from their positions as the attack went forward, so as to be immediately available. Tanks were to support the attack of the leading divisions.

26TH SEPT. On the 26th September the 6th Infantry Brigade (leading brigade) moved up to between Demicourt and Doignies ; the 99th Infantry Brigade (support brigade) assembled east of Morchies and north of Beaumetz ; the 5th Infantry Brigade (reserve brigade) and the 2nd Battalion Machine-Gun Corps were concentrated about Morchies.

" Zero " hour on the 27th was fixed for 5.20 a.m.

" On our way up the roads were empty, but after dark they were stiff with troops and transport, moving up to the greatest battle of the war. What do the Germans expect or suspect at this moment ? I have a feeling that all must go with a swing

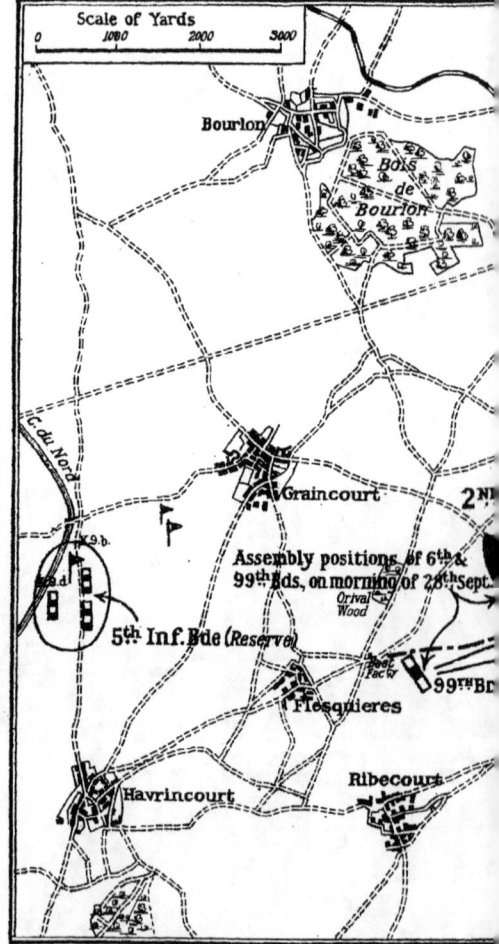

THE BATTLE OF THE CANAL DU NORD, 27th September-1st October 1918, AND THE CAPTURE OF MONT SUR L'ŒUVRES BY THE 2nd DIVISION.

(*Facing p. 658.*)

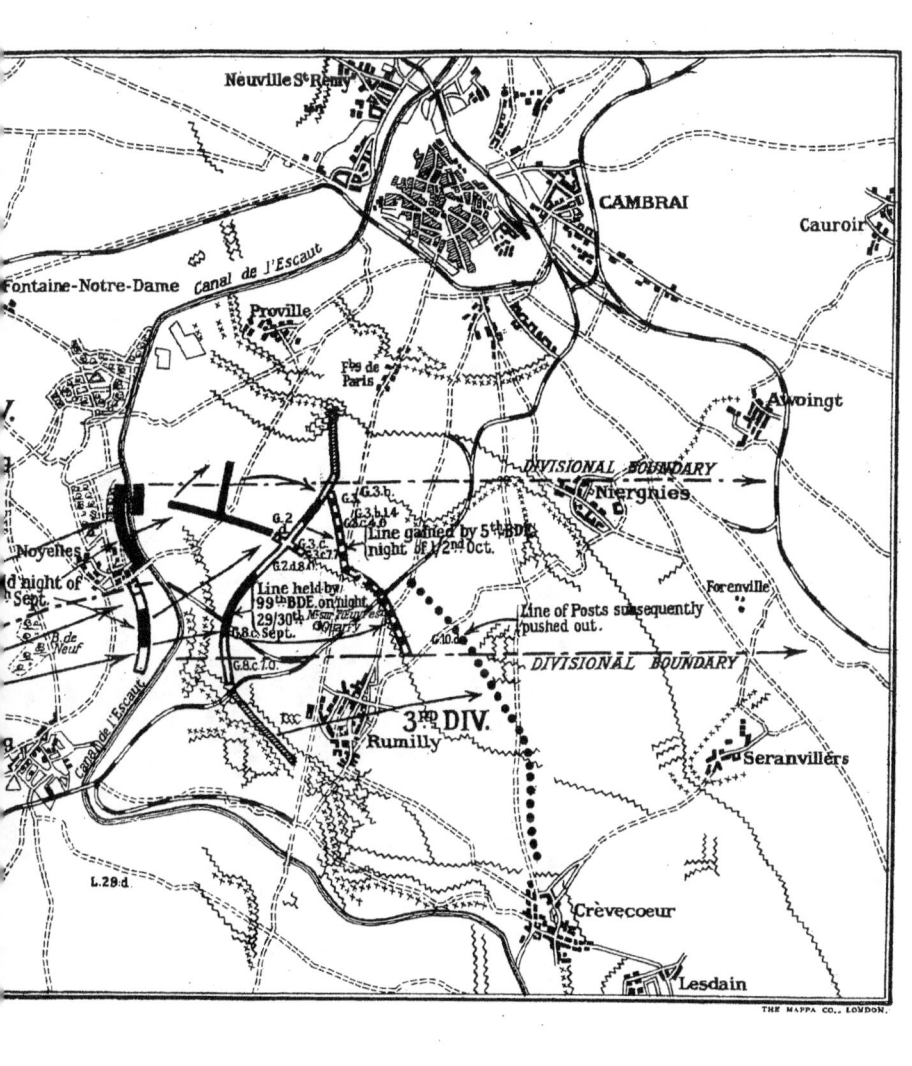

to-morrow. I have the greatest hopes and expectations, and with luck our Divisional Headquarters will be in Flesquières ere long."[1]

All night long the guns continued to roar and pour upon the enemy's positions a constant stream of shells—the like had never before been equalled in the war. So terrible, indeed, was the bombardment continued on the front of the Fourth Army throughout the 27th, that for two days the enemy's front systems were completely cut off, his ration parties could not reach their comrades in the front line, and in many instances the Germans betook themselves to their deepest dug-outs, there to await an uncertain end.

At "zero" on the 27th the IVth, VIth, and XVIIth and Canadian Corps of the Third and First Armies attacked along the whole front, and, assisted by some sixty-five tanks, broke deeply into the enemy's position. The 3rd Division moved forward with the Guards Division, and in face of heavy fire from machine guns and forward field guns, captured Ribécourt and Flesquières.

27TH SEPT. MAP.

At 6 a.m. the 6th Infantry Brigade advanced and formed up east of the Canal du Nord in K.9,b. and d. By 10.45 a.m. the 1st King's were assembled in K.9,b., the 2nd South Staffords just east of the Sunken Road in K.9,d., and the 17th Royal Fusiliers, 6th Trench Mortar Battery, and one section of the 5th Field Company R.E., in K.9,d., west of the Sunken Road. During the advance the enemy's machine guns posted on the high ground west of Graincourt opened fire, and on the troops reaching the canal a hostile aeroplane dropped bombs and obtained three direct hits. Unfortunately the 17th Royal Fusiliers, who were crossing at the moment, lost one officer (Second-Lieut. W. F. Harris) and three other ranks killed, whilst another officer was wounded.

About 11.40 a.m., acting on information received from the 3rd Guards Brigade, the General Officer Commanding 6th Infantry Brigade ordered the 2nd South Staffords to just north of the Beetroot Factory (east of Flesquières), the 1st King's to Orival Wood, and the 17th Royal Fusiliers and 6th Trench Mortar Battery to north of the village of Flesquières. But while the moves of these battalions were in progress further information came to hand that Orival Wood and the Graincourt line were still held by the enemy. The South Staffords came under heavy machine-gun fire from both these positions, and were forced to seek shelter in trenches and sunken roads north of Flesquières until an attack could be organized.

[1] Major-General C. E. Pereira, C.B., C.M.G.

During this advance the South Staffords and King's could see the Guards forming a defensive flank along Shingler Trench, north-west of Flesquières.

The XVIIth Corps, on the left of the Guards Division, having failed to take Graincourt, was hung up in front of that village; as a consequence, whilst the right of the Guards had advanced to the northern outskirts of Flesquières, the left was still west of Graincourt and had formed a defensive flank in order to keep touch with the right of the XVIIth Corps. South of the Guards Division, the 62nd Division was passing through the 3rd Division (which had captured Ribécourt) and was advancing on Marcoing. Such was the position about midday.

At 2 p.m. the XVIIth Corps renewed its attack upon Graincourt from the north, forcing the enemy to retire from the village.

About 3.30 p.m. the 1st King's and the South Staffords attacked Orival Wood, which was captured between 4 and 5 p.m. Meanwhile, at 4 p.m., the 6th Infantry Brigade was ordered to capture Cantaing Trench and Cantaing Support. At this period it was believed that the Guards held Premy Chapel. The 99th Infantry Brigade, which had been in support all day, was ordered forward to assist the 6th Infantry Brigade by exploiting any success gained; the 5th Infantry Brigade was also moved east of the Canal du Nord to the line taken up by the 6th Infantry Brigade at 6 o'clock in the morning.

The 2nd Divisional Artillery (XXXVIth and XLIst Brigades R.F.A.), to which had been affiliated two brigades of Guards Divisional Artillery, the XIVth (Army) Brigade R.H.A., a "Heavy" Brigade R.G.A., and one Brigade of R.F.A. from the 21st Division, were, with the exception of the latter, brought up east of the canal, and put down a heavy barrage. Smoke was also discharged, under cover of which the 6th Infantry Brigade attacked the enemy. The Graincourt line was captured, but it was found that the Guards did not hold Premy Chapel, and a further advance to the Cantaing Support was impossible without artillery preparation.

In this advance the 6th Infantry Brigade had passed through the 3rd Guards Brigade, and thus at 10.15 p.m. (on the night 27th–28th) command of the front line passed to the General Officer Commanding 2nd Division. The position of the 2nd Division was then as follows: 6th Infantry Brigade in the Graincourt line on the left of the Divisional front, with the 1st King's in Lathe Trench at about L.9,c., and the 2nd South Staffords in L.14,b. and d.; the 99th Infantry Brigade was in Beet Trench, and the 5th Infantry

AN INDIGNANT GERMAN.

Brigade just east of the canal; touch was maintained on the right with the 62nd Division, but both flanks of the 1st King's were in the air, the enemy being on both sides of the battalion.

Casualties throughout the day had been heavy; the 2nd South Staffords had five officers wounded and approximately 100 other ranks killed, wounded, and missing. One officer, Second-Lieut. F. H. Slingsby, was at one period captured by the enemy, but though wounded he succeeded in escaping. Two machine guns and several prisoners, one of whom was a German regimental commander, were captured by the South Staffords. The German commander was most indignant at being marched off to the cage by a South Staffords private; he demanded an officer's escort! Captain E. Beesley, M.C., of the King's, was killed by a machine-gun bullet just as the battalion had reached Lathe Trench, and a little later Second-Lieut. F. Cheetham was reported missing.

Elsewhere along the front, north and south of the VIth Corps, the enemy's positions, after the initial check in front of Graincourt, were everywhere carried, and the front of the Third and First Armies, on the night 27th–28th, extended from a mile west of Gouzeaucourt, thence to the western outskirts of Beaucamp, eastern exits of Ribécourt, to a mile west of Marcoing. At the latter point the line bent back slightly, running north-north-west to Anneux, west of Fontaine-Notre-Dame through Bourlon Wood, thence west of Baillescourt, east of Hagnicourt and Epinoy, to immediately north of Oisy-le-Verger. Bourlon Wood had been captured by the 4th Canadian Division, the Canadian troops fighting with great gallantry throughout the day.

Early on the morning of the 28th the advance was again continued; the 2nd Division had been ordered to attack Cantaing Support and Bois de Neuf (Nine Wood), and to exploit success in front of the former, seizing the crossings over the Escaut River and the Canal de l'Escaut. "Zero" hour was 5.15 a.m. The 62nd Division, on the right, was attacking Marcoing at 6.30 a.m., and arrangements were made for the 99th Infantry Brigade to form a defensive flank until the 62nd Division came up into line. The 57th Division was attacking on the left of the 2nd Division.

On the 2nd Division front, the 99th Infantry Brigade on the right and the 6th Infantry Brigade on the left, under cover of an artillery barrage creeping forward at the rate of 100 yards in five minutes, were to assault the enemy's positions; the 5th Infantry Brigade remaining in support just east of the Canal du Nord.

The barrage fell at 5.15 a.m. on Cantaing Trench and Cantaing

28TH SEPT.

Support, and was "devilish close to Lathe Trench," said the Commanding Officer of the King's, and for ten minutes remained stationary. "When it lifted we got every one out, and in four waves, with our right roughly on northern end of Nine Wood, we advanced towards the St. Quentin Canal.[1] No opposition . . . we halted temporarily in Cantaing Support. The Commanding Officer then ordered the whole battalion forward again, and, still distributed in depth, we swept on with the 2nd Battalion South Staffords and 99th Infantry Brigade towards the canal line, but managed to get a part of Battalion Headquarters across the canal by the lock-gate footbridge in L.29,d. We established Battalion Headquarters in the lock-keeper's house, and then had to sit down all day under a severe machine-gun fire at close range. The four companies remained west of the canal, and gradually reorganized and got some rest, which they badly needed. We were all rather dead beat now."[2]

The 2nd South Staffords, on the right of the King's, likewise made excellent progress, capturing, in their advance to the canal, 300 prisoners, a great number of machine guns and trench mortars, one 8-inch and one 4.2-inch howitzer, and four 77 mm. guns. But strong enemy machine-gun fire prevented the Staffords crossing the canal, and a line was established along the railway embankment, east of the village of Noyelles-sur-l'Escaut, which had also been captured.

A plucky incident in the day's fighting took place during an attempt by the 17th Royal Fusiliers to gain the high ground east of the canal. About 11 a.m. the General Officer Commanding 6th Infantry Brigade interviewed the Officer Commanding the Battalion on the subject of attacking Marcoing Trench and the high ground east of the canal along the brigade front. The Brigadier suggested that it might be possible to "get one company across the canal by using a raft and going down the river, and then getting under the arches of the canal and forming up on the eastern side of the canal," the attack to take place at dusk. D Company, with one platoon of B Company, was ordered to make the attempt. The difficulty was to get the raft (which was made by the Sappers) across. Second-Lieut. F. G. Waters then set out to reconnoitre the river. Holding a rope, this officer swam the river and attached one end on the eastern side. He then swam back to the western bank. But the raft was not a success, owing to the low clearance

[1] Or the Canal de L'Escaut.
[2] Battalion Diary, 1st King's Regiment.

THE RIFLES CAPTURE GUNS. 663

under the arches of the canal, and most of D Company filtered across the canal bridge. In spite of a shortage of bombs, and without the support of the Trench Mortar Batteries, the Fusiliers pluckily attacked Marcoing Trench, and succeeded in gaining a footing therein. But the position was too precarious, for the enemy's machine guns swept the trench, and reluctantly the Fusiliers fell back to a line just east of the canal and west of Marcoing Trench, where they remained for the night.

Meanwhile the 99th Infantry Brigade, with the 1st King's Royal Rifle Corps on the right and the 1st Royal Berks on the left, had also won through to its objective—the canal bank, south of the 6th Infantry Brigade. Both battalions attacked on a two-company frontage.

With but slight opposition the Rifles reached Premy Trench and passed on to the Graincourt line, where the supporting companies passed through and took up the advance, passing on towards Noyelles. One platoon had been detached to work through the northern exits of Marcoing. This platoon actually advanced through the village in front of the barrage put down by the 62nd Division; the latter was not to attack until 6.30 a.m. The platoon commander (Lieut. R. J. Anderson) surprised two German gun teams limbering up. One got away, but the second was captured. The teams were shot down, the German officer, his orderly, and the drivers were captured. A number of other guns were also taken in this area. Eventually, at 8.15 a.m., the Rifles reached Noyelles, where six prisoners were captured clad in pyjamas, and a number of others taken in various dug-outs in the village.

The Berkshires likewise had reached Noyelles, and when night fell the 6th Infantry Brigade was disposed along the canal bank, north of the road running through the centre of the village, and the 99th Infantry Brigade similarly south of the road. Two companies of the 17th Royal Fusiliers remained on the east bank of the canal. On the right of the 2nd Division the 62nd Division had captured Marcoing, crossed the canal, and had established a bridgehead. On the left, the 57th Division had advanced round Graincourt, forcing the enemy to retire and enabling the 63rd Division to gain the line of the canal.

The attack was resumed by the 99th and 6th Infantry Brigades at 5 a.m. on the 29th. The 1st Royal Berks (left) and the 1st King's Royal Rifle Corps (right) of the former brigade made a particularly successful attempt to cross the canal. Only one and a half platoons of the Berkshires got across, and then the bridge 29TH SEPT.

was destroyed by shell-fire, the enemy's shells falling thick and fast about the crossings. Nevertheless this small party established itself in Marcoing Switch. Of the Rifles, however, two companies succeeded in getting across the bridge, and, after making good the bridgehead, bombed northwards along Marcoing Switch and Support, gaining touch with the Berkshires. The latter and the Rifles eventually made good the whole of the trench system within the 99th Brigade boundaries, maintaining touch with the 62nd Division on the right and the 6th Infantry Brigade on the left.

Meanwhile the position of the 17th Royal Fusiliers was precarious. At 3 a.m. the enemy had counter-attacked the 57th Division on the left of the 6th Brigade, and the troops of the right battalion of that division had been forced back on to the Fusiliers. After considerable difficulty the situation was restored, though the enemy's machine-gun fire was very intense and the Fusiliers were losing heavily. A certain number of men had been carried back with troops of the 57th Division, but under orders of the General Officer Commanding 6th Infantry Brigade the Fusiliers maintained themselves on the eastern banks of the canal so as to advance with the 99th Infantry Brigade at 5 a.m. At 7 a.m., however, the Fusiliers were unable to do more than maintain their position, for at that period the Berkshires and the Rifles of the 99th Brigade had not worked northwards along Marcoing Switch, being still engaged on their front with the enemy.

At 10.50 a.m. a report reached the Officer Commanding 17th Royal Fusiliers that the enemy was retiring from opposite the canal. The bombing attack of the 99th Brigade had begun to tell, and very shortly afterwards the Fusiliers were able to push on and occupy Range Wood and a part of the Marcoing line, where touch was at last obtained with the Berkshires and Rifles. Between 200 and 300 prisoners had up to this time been captured.

It now became essential to get the remainder of the Berkshires across the canal. All the crossings and approaches were under intense shell and machine-gun fire, but, quite undaunted, Sappers from the three Field Companies R.E. set to work to construct bridges. If in the ranks of the 5th Field Company R.E. there were any survivors of the gallant old company which had so ably constructed bridges during the Battle of the Aisne in 1914, their present circumstances must have reminded them of that long-ago action. With the same old gallantry and intrepidity, the Sappers advanced under a galling fire, and in twenty minutes had con-

MONT-SUR-L'ŒUVRES.

structed an " infantry in single file " bridge across the canal. Over this bridge the Berkshires passed. A pontoon bridge was also constructed, the 226th Field Company leaving a maintenance party to guard it. Throughout the day all three companies (5th, 226th, and 483rd) most gallantly upheld the splendid reputation of the Royal Engineers.

During the afternoon an attempt was made to capture Mont-sur-l'Œuvres (99th Infantry Brigade) and Rumilly (62nd Division), but these two positions were regular hornet's nests of machine guns, and all attempts to advance were swept away by an extremely accurate and murderous fire.

At 9.45 p.m. the line of the 2nd Division ran from Flot Farm (inc.) through G.8,c.7.0–G.8,c. central–G.2,d.8.0–G.3,c.7.7 to G.3,b.1.4. During the night 29th–30th the 99th Infantry Brigade took over the whole of the Divisional front, the 23rd Royal Fusiliers having relieved the 1st King's Royal Rifles on the right and the 1st Royal Berks the 17th Royal Fusiliers on the left; both the Fusiliers and the Rifles went into billets in Noyelles.

In the meantime the 5th Infantry Brigade had received orders to be prepared to move up, pass through the 99th Infantry Brigade, and cross the line of the Masnières–Cambrai road at 6 a.m. on the 30th; this operation was dependent on the capture of Rumilly by the 62nd Division.

During the night the 99th Infantry Brigade was to move forward and clear up to the Masnières–Cambrai road. At 5 a.m. 30TH SEPT. on the 30th, therefore, the 23rd Royal Fusiliers again attacked the enemy, but he was too strongly posted on Mont-sur-l'Œuvres and the railway, from which positions his machine guns defied all attempts to advance. The 62nd Division also, although on the very outskirts of Rumilly, found the enemy's shell and machine-gun fire too heavy. The 23rd Royal Fusiliers therefore retired to their jumping-off line, and no appreciable advance during the 30th was made by the 2nd Division. For it had become evident that Rumilly and Mont-sur-l'Œuvres could only be captured by a combined attack by the 2nd and 62nd Divisions, supported by strong artillery fire.

At 4 p.m. the 5th Infantry Brigade was ordered to take over the front line as soon as possible after dark. The relief was completed at 1 a.m. on the 1st October, the 99th Infantry Brigade passing back into Divisional reserve in the Nine Wood–Flesquières area.

Again, throughout the 30th September the 5th, 226th, and 483rd Field Companies of the Royal Engineers were busily employed constructing footbridges and bridges to take the Field Artillery and 60-pounders whilst other bridges were repaired.

1st Oct. At dawn on the 1st October the 5th Infantry Brigade held the front line of the 2nd Division with the 24th Royal Fusiliers on the right and the 2nd Highland Light Infantry on the left ; the 2nd Oxford and Bucks in reserve in Noyelles. The 6th Infantry Brigade was in support, and the 99th Infantry Brigade in reserve ; 2nd Divisional Headquarters were at Flesquières. On the right of the 5th Infantry Brigade the 3rd Division had relieved the 62nd Division, and on the left the 52nd Division (XVIIth Corps) had come up into line.

In conjunction with the 3rd Division on the right, and under a slow creeping barrage preceded by a two-minute smoke barrage, the 5th Infantry Brigade attacked the enemy at 6 a.m. with the object of clearing up the ground between Marcoing Switch and the high ground in G.10,d. The attack, which was made by the Oxford and Bucks, who had been moved up from reserve for the purpose, progressed well in its initial stages, but was finally held up on the road running north and south-west of the Cambrai–Masnières road. German machine guns in Rumilly, in position along the Cambrai–Masnières road at the Halt, and at Mont-sur-l'Œuvres, put up a stout resistance and checked the Oxfords in their advance, the latter suffering heavy casualties. Touch was obtained with the 2nd Highland Light Infantry on the left by means of patrols.

Similarly at the outset the attack of the 3rd Division on Rumilly went well, and the south-west corner of the village was cleared, which ensured the right flank of the 2nd Division ; but here the 3rd Division was held up.

During the day, located enemy machine guns and occupied posts were severely harassed by the Divisional Artillery. At noon a gallant but unsuccessful minor operation by the 2nd Highland Light Infantry to clear out a machine-gun nest failed, owing to flanking machine-gun fire.

In the afternoon a further simultaneous attack by the 2nd and 3rd Divisions was arranged ; the objective of the 2nd Division was from G.3, central, to the Faubourg de Paris and Mont-sur-l'Œuvres. The objectives of the 3rd Division included Rumilly, which, with the exception of the southern and south-western exits, the enemy still held, also the general line of the Cambrai–Masnières road. The 52nd Division (on the left of the 2nd Division) was to assault the Faubourg de Paris.

At 5.45 p.m. the 52nd Division attacked the Faubourg de Paris, and at 6.30 p.m. the 2nd and 3rd Divisions simultaneously attacked Mont-sur-l'Œuvres and Rumilly. The attack was supported by an intense barrage of smoke, shrapnel, and high explosive, while trench mortars were used to smother and harass the enemy's machine guns in the quarry at Mont-sur-l'Œuvres and the road and trenches in G.3,c.4.o.

The 24th Royal Fusiliers on the right and the 2nd Highland Light Infantry on the left carried out the attack launched by the 2nd Division. The Fusiliers had an instant and striking success. B Company of the battalion made the attack proper, four platoons, keeping close up to the barrage, rushed the enemy's posts consisting of two quarries honeycombed with dug-outs and organized for a very determined defence. The garrisons of these quarries were considerable, but the splendid dash of the Fusiliers overcame all resistance, enabling the supporting company to push through and establish a new line east of the Cambrai railway. The strength of the leading company, which had captured the quarries, was only three officers and sixty-seven other ranks, but they captured over 200 prisoners and fifty machine guns. Little wonder that these quarries had defied all previous attempts to capture them.

Mont-sur-l'Œuvres thus passed into the possession of the 2nd Division.

On the left the attack had at first received a check. The 52nd Division, which had attacked three-quarters of an hour before the 2nd Division, was barraged, the barrage falling on the left of the 2nd Highland Light Infantry as that battalion, with C Company, half of A and half of B Companies, was forming up for the attack. Captain G. C. D. Spence was killed, Second-Lieut. Hamilton wounded, and the four section commanders either killed or wounded. The remaining half of A Company had therefore to be brought up. But on the forming-up operations being completed the battalion advanced steadily until a ridge north-west of the Cambrai road was reached. Here heavy machine-gun fire was encountered, but the enemy's positions were gallantly rushed by the Scotsmen, who soon put the deadly machine guns out of action. Many prisoners and machine guns were captured.

During the night both battalions (24th Royal Fusiliers and the 2nd Highland Light Infantry) organized and consolidated the position won.[1]

On the right the 3rd Division was successful, and at last Rumilly

[1] This action is known to the 2nd Division as "The Capture of Mont-sur-l'Œuvres."

fell; it was found to be a veritable mine of machine guns. Immediately south of the 3rd Division the New Zealand Division had captured Crèvecœur, whilst north of Cambrai the Canadian Corps cleared the ground west of Ramilies and entered Blécourt.

The Hindenburg Line had now been breached, and the threat to the enemy's communications was serious.

At nightfall on the 1st October—the date upon which the Battle of the Canal du Nord ended—the line of the First and Third British Armies between the river Sensée and the Banteaux–Gouzeaucourt road ran: First Army—Ecourt St. Quentin, thence eastwards along the southern banks of the Sensée to just west of Pressies, south-east to just west of Abancourt, eastern outskirts of Blécourt, thence bending back immediately west of Cambrai; Third Army—from just west of Cambrai, thence east of Rumilly to Crèvecœur, whence the line dropped almost direct south to Aubencheul, east of Epéhy.

The five days during which the Battle of the Canal du Nord had taken place (27th September to 1st October) were of vast importance to the Allies, and of dire consequence to the enemy. Not only were the enemy's positions in the Hindenburg Line (strong and powerful as they were) broken into deeply along the front of the First, Third, and Fourth British Armies, but south of the latter the French and American armies, continuing their attacks on both sides of the Argonne, between the Meuse and the Suippe Rivers, were threatening the enemy's communications.

At 5.30 a.m. on the 28th September, the Second British Army and the Belgian Army, to which had been added several French divisions, attacked on a front extending from some four and a half miles south of the Ypres–Zonnebeke road and northwards as far as Dixmude. The attack was everywhere successful, and by the evening of the 1st October the Second British Army (Sir H. Plumer) " had cleared the left bank of the Lys from Comines southwards, while north of that town they were close up to Wervicq, Gheluwe, and Ledeghem." [1]

On Sir H. Plumer's left the Belgian Army had passed the general line Moorslede–Staden–Dixmude.

Thousands of prisoners and a great number of guns had been captured, and the *moral* of the enemy, though not yet quite broken, had received a terrible shaking. Ever since the 3rd September, when Ludendorff had informed the German Chancellor that " there was . . . no longer any chance of the pendulum swinging in our

[1] Official Dispatches.

THE BATTLE OF CAMBRAI, 1918:
THE CAPTURE OF FORENVILLE
BY THE 2nd DIVISION.

(*Facing p. 668.*)

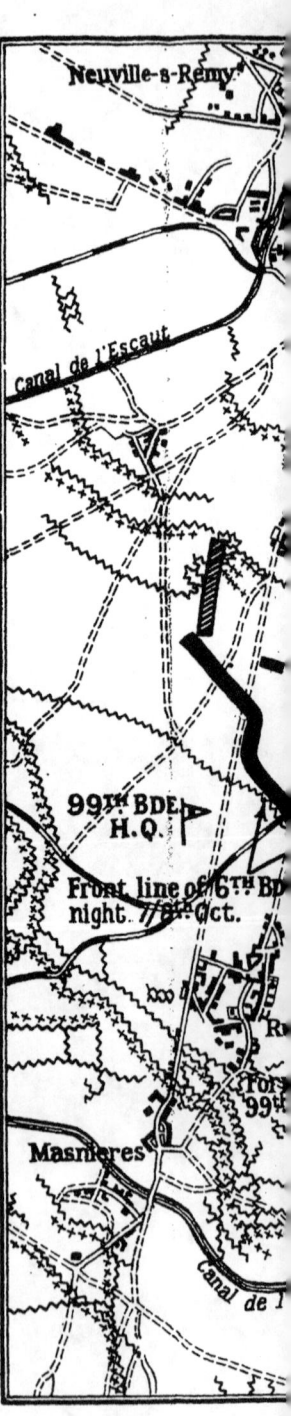

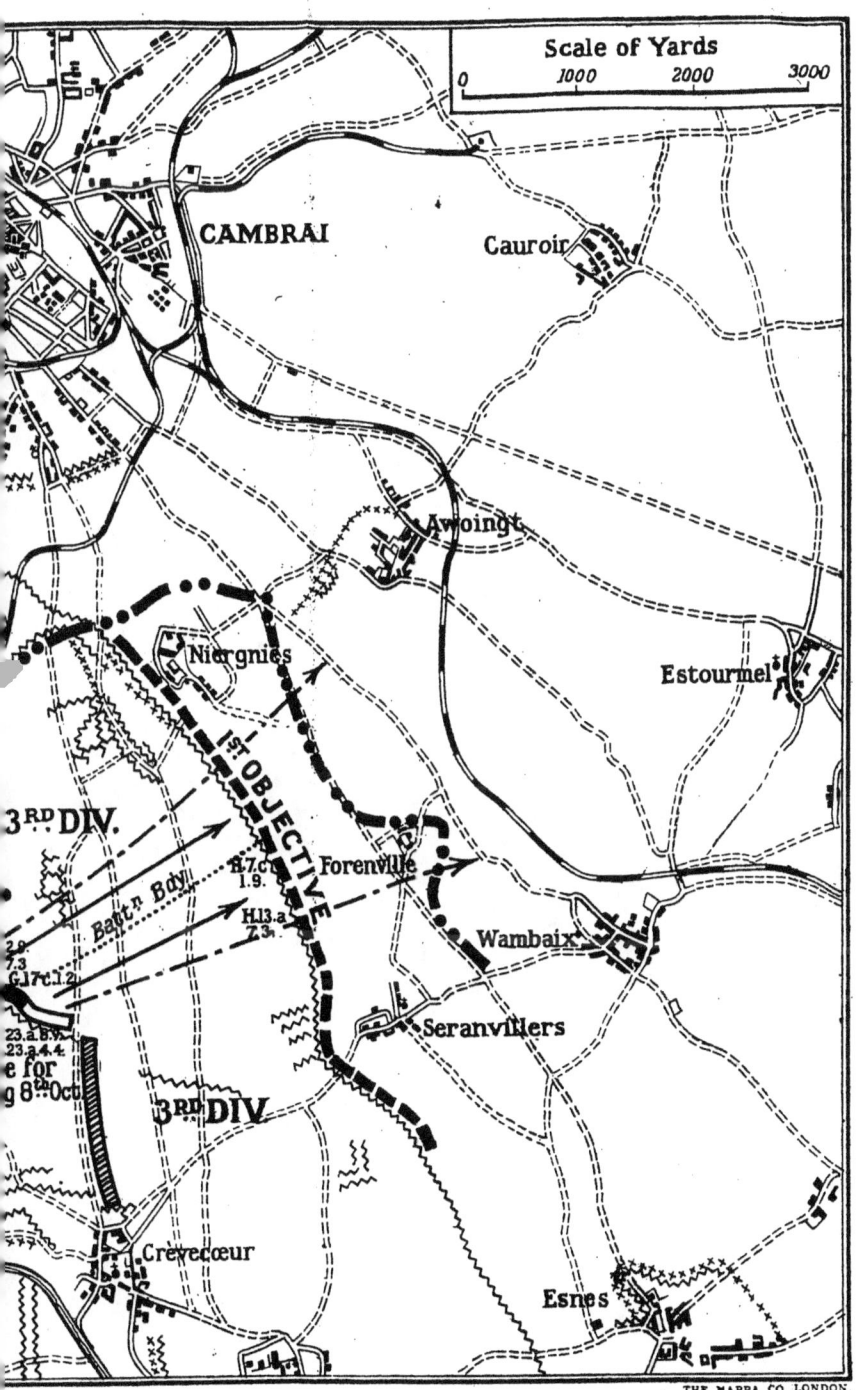

SITUATION EARLY IN OCTOBER 1918.

favour," the Central Powers, internally, were engaged in trying to avert the disaster which every day loomed larger in the distance. Before the Battle of the Canal du Nord opened, Bulgaria had collapsed, and the position of Turkey was parlous. " In Italy," said the Chief of the German General Staff, " an attack was sure to come, and it was quite uncertain how the Austro-Hungarian troops there would fight." When October dawned the words " Armistice " and " peace " were already being spoken at " O.H.L." (German General Headquarters) and in Berlin.[1]

During the first week of October the break in the Hindenburg Line was widened. On the 3rd the Fourth Army, attacking Sequehart and Le Catelet, captured those villages. On the 4th and 5th the villages of Montbrehain and Beaurevoir were captured, tanks co-operating.

The enemy was now compelled to evacuate the high ground about Le Terrière (in the bend of the Scheldt Canal, between Le Catelet and Crèvecœur), which enabled the right of the Third Army to cross the Scheldt Canal and occupy the Hindenburg Line, thus preparing the way for the next great attack.

During these days the 2nd Division made no move, but patrols were out constantly, and new posts were established along the front line.[2]

THE BATTLE OF CAMBRAI, 1918 (8th to 9th October).[3]
The Capture of Forenville by the Second Division.

The third phase of the great offensive launched by the Fourth, Third, and First British Armies on the 27th September against the Hindenburg Line and its rear defences opened at 4.30 a.m. and 5.10 a.m. on the 8th October, when the Third and Fourth

---

[1] On the 6th October VIth Corps Headquarters wired 2nd Division Headquarters that, " in view of a rumour that the Central Powers had asked for an Armistice, the enemy might attempt to fraternize with our troops under cover of a white flag. No notice to be taken of this except as laid down in F.S.R. (Field Service Regulations)."

[2] On the 5th October Brigadier-General W. L. Osborn, General Officer Commanding 5th Infantry Brigade, was wounded by a shell splinter, and handed over command of the brigade temporarily to Lieut.-Colonel R. H. Pipon.

During September, in spite of the important operations in which the 2nd Division took an active part, salvage valued at the enormous sum of £140,894, 3s. 6d. was collected.

[3] The Report of the Battles Nomenclature Committee divides the operations between the 8th and 12th October as follows : The Battle of Cambrai 1918, 8th–9th October ; the Pursuit to the Selle, 9th–12th October.

Armies respectively attacked on a front of over 17 miles from Sequehart to south of Cambrai; the First French Army south of the Fourth British Army continued the line of attack as far as St. Quentin. Still farther south French and American troops attacked the enemy east of the Meuse and in Champagne.

Information concerning these operations had been received at 2nd Division Headquarters on the 5th October, and on the 6th " zero " day was definitely fixed for the 8th. The objectives of the 2nd Division were the Seranvillers–Niergnies trench line, and Forenville, with exploitation farther east if the enemy's resistance weakened. The 3rd Division was to attack on the right of the 2nd Division, and the 63rd Division (XVIIth Corps) on the left. The 63rd Division was to pass through the 6th Infantry Brigade; a portion of the 57th Division, attacking on the left of the 63rd Division, was also to pass through the 6th Infantry Brigade. The 99th Infantry Brigade (2nd Division) was detailed to form up and attack through the 3rd Division. The attack was to be carried out under a creeping barrage; smoke was also to be fired and tanks were to co-operate.

Throughout the 7th preparations for the attack on the following day were pushed forward; the Sappers and Pioneers were hard at work on the bridges and a forward track. At 10.30 p.m. the 99th Infantry Brigade began to move forward to its assembly positions. The 23rd Royal Fusiliers were the first to march, followed by the 1st King's Royal Rifle Corps and then the 1st Royal Berks. The latter reported at 2.30 a.m. that all its companies were in position. At " zero " hour—4.30 a.m.—the 99th Infantry Brigade was disposed as follows: 23rd Royal Fusiliers (strength, 14 officers and 378 other ranks) on the right, with two companies disposed in depth on a line G.23,a.8.7–G.17,c.1.2, and the remaining companies close behind; 1st King's Royal Rifle Corps (strength, 16 officers and 385 other ranks) on the left, disposed similarly on a line G.16,d.7.3–G.16,d.2.9; 1st Royal Berks (strength, 19 officers and 444 other ranks), on a line G.23,a.4.4–G.16,d.2.1.

The first objective (Red Line) had been allotted to the 23rd Royal Fusiliers and 1st King's Royal Rifle Corps (less one company); the second objective, including the village of Forenville (Green Line), to the 1st Royal Berks and one company of the 1st King's Royal Rifle Corps. One section of the 2nd Battalion Machine-Gun Corps was attached to the Fusiliers and one to the Rifles for the first objective. A 3-inch Stokes mortar was also

ENEMY COUNTER-ATTACKS WITH TANKS.

to accompany each battalion. The primary *rôle* of the tanks (of which two had been allotted to the 99th Infantry Brigade) was to deal with any opposition met with in Forenville.

At 4.30 a.m. the barrage came down, and the troops followed quickly in its wake. The first objective—the trench line running between Seranvillers and Niergnies—was captured by 6 a.m., only slight resistance being experienced in the sunken roads between the jumping-off positions and the Red Line. The three companies of Rifles, with only a few casualties, had captured between them 200 prisoners, and, with the 23rd Royal Fusiliers on the right, set to work to consolidate their position.

8TH OCT MAP.

The 1st Royal Berks and D Company of the 1st King's Royal Rifle Corps then passed through the first objective towards the Green Line. In their advance behind the 23rd Royal Fusiliers the Berkshires had been fired on by enemy troops, who, having first surrendered to the Fusiliers, decided to fight again; these treacherous Germans were suitably dealt with.

At 8.15 a.m. the enemy counter-attacked, not with infantry, but with five tanks supported by heavy artillery and machine-gun fire. At this period the northern portion of the Green Line had been captured; but Forenville still held out, though the Berkshires had won through to the road in front of the village.

The hostile tanks were of British make (Mark IV.), having been captured by the enemy, and at first deceived the troops of the 63rd Division on the left flank of the 2nd Division, against whom the counter-attack was principally directed. One tank attacked the left of the 3rd Division. When, however, the Rifles and the Berkshires saw the troops on both flanks falling back from before these tanks, they realized the situation and opened a very heavy fire upon the "land-ships." With both their flanks entirely exposed, the Berkshires and Rifles withdrew to the Red Line.

Meanwhile the 99th Trench Mortar Battery, using a captured German light Minenwerfer, had also engaged the hostile tanks, and, assisted by the rifle fire of the infantry, caused them to divert from their original objectives. Only one of the tanks actually reached within 200 to 300 yards of the Red Line: one was driven off by fire from a Stokes mortar, and the crew of the other was compelled to leave its tank, and was eventually captured by the 23rd Royal Fusiliers.

By 10.30 a.m. the attacking troops of the 2nd, 3rd, and 63rd Divisions were back on the Red Line, where they had definitely established their positions, and had beaten off the enemy's counter-attacks. All attempts, however, to renew the advance were unsuccessful, as the troops came immediately under a very heavy and accurate machine-gun fire from both flanks.

During the morning, owing to the exhaustion of the attacking troops, the 17th Royal Fusiliers (6th Infantry Brigade) had been placed at the disposal of the General Officer Commanding 99th Infantry Brigade, with permission to use them, if necessary, for an attack on the Green Line.

At 3 p.m. another attack was launched, but was likewise unsuccessful.

"At 4 p.m. the General Officer Commanding, having heard that the 3 p.m. attack had failed, ordered the 17th Royal Fusiliers to attack Forenville at 6 p.m. The Commanding Officer ordered C and A Companies to move forward at once to the neighbourhood of the 23rd Royal Fusiliers Headquarters at G.16,d.7.3 (about 2,000 yards east of Rumilly). . . . The battalion was to form up just west of the Red Line, with the right resting at H.13,a.7.3, and the left at H.7,c.1.9; B Company attacking on the right, D on the left, A Company in support, and C Company in reserve. After the capture of the village touch was to be obtained as soon as possible with the 3rd Division on the right (the 3rd Division was attacking Seranvillers simultaneously) and the 23rd Royal Fusiliers on the left. . . . All the companies were in position at 5.15 p.m., and the creeping barrage opened 300 yards west of the Forenville–Cambrai road at 6 p.m. At 7.35 p.m. a message came in from Second-Lieut. Norrington, commanding B Company, timed 6.57 p.m., to say that the village had been captured and the final line was being consolidated, but that a certain number of the enemy were still in rear of the battalion in 'funk holes,' and that, owing to lack of bombs, he was unable to 'mop them up.' The Commanding Officer borrowed four pack animals from the 23rd Royal Fusiliers, and sent up one load of bombs, one of small-arms ammunition, and two of tools to the front line."[1] One company of the 23rd Royal Fusiliers was also detailed to assist the 17th Royal Fusiliers in "mopping up" the area, and finally 60 prisoners, 5 guns, and a large number of machine guns and Minenwerfer were captured. The casualties of the 17th Royal Fusiliers were slight. During the night the 1st King's Royal Rifle Corps pushed forward to the main road, and thus completed the capture of the final objective.

9TH OCT. Early on the morning of the 9th October the Guards Division

[1] Diary of the 17th Battalion Royal Fusiliers.

THE ENEMY DISORGANIZED. 673

passed through the 2nd Division, and took over the Green Line in order to continue the advance. The 2nd Division (less artillery) was then withdrawn into Corps Reserve, and at nightfall on the 9th was situated as follows : 2nd Division Headquarters—Doignies ; 5th Infantry Brigade—Demicourt area ; 6th Infantry Brigade—Canal du Nord area ; 99th Infantry Brigade—Flesquières–Orival Wood area.

The Divisional Artillery—XXXVIth and XLIst Brigades R.F.A.—were withdrawn from the line on the night 9th–10th October, and were billeted in the Noyelles–Marcoing–Rumilly area.[1] The Field Companies R.E. and the Pioneers (10th Duke of Cornwall's Light Infantry) were placed under the direct orders of the VIth Corps for work in the Canal de l'Escaut area.

The capture of Forenville was not a minor action, as might appear from the foregoing description, but a link in a connected chain of operations which began on the 8th October, with the object of breaking down the last resistance of the enemy in the rear positions of the now once-formidable Hindenburg Line. From south of Cambrai to Sequehart the enemy's positions had been penetrated to a depth of between three and four miles—Brancourt and Prémont, Serian, Villers Outreaux, Malincourt and Esmes, Seranvillers, Forenville and Niergnies fell to the Fourth and Third Armies, and the southern outskirts of Cambrai had been reached.

" As a result of this attack, the enemy's resistance temporarily gave way. His infantry became disorganized, and retired steadily eastwards, while our airmen reported that the roads converging on Le Cateau were blocked with troops and transport. Several thousand prisoners and many guns fell into our hands. During the following night (9th) the Canadian Corps captured Ramilies and crossed the Scheldt Canal at Pont a' Aire. Canadian patrols entered Cambrai from the north, and joined hands with patrols of the 57th Division working through the southern portions of the town. Next morning at 5.20 a.m., the Fourth and Third Armies renewed the attack on the whole front, cavalry assisting in the advance. By nightfall our troops were within two miles of Le Cateau, had captured Bohain, and were attacking Caudry from the south.

---

[1] On the previous day the gunners sustained a great loss. Amongst the officers casualties of the 8th October was Major G. Messervy, Commanding 16th Battery (" The Old Rooks ") of the XLIst Brigade R.F.A., who was killed. This officer joined the battery in 1913 on first appointment, and at the time of his death he had never served in any other unit. He was (with the exception of periodical leave) with his battery every day of the war. This, so far as the Royal Field Artillery is concerned, is a record of continuous service of an officer in one unit.

Cambrai was in our hands, and our troops were three miles to the east of the town."[1]

Back in Corps Reserve, the 2nd Division set to work to reorganize and train. For the Sappers and Pioneers of all divisions these were strenuous days, and to their splendid energies—fittingly recognized by congratulations from Corps and Divisional Commanders—was due the rapidity with which the divisions up and down the line were able to follow close on the heels of the retreating and by now almost demoralized enemy. But although the bridges and roads were repaired, it was extremely difficult to maintain the supply system upon which the rapid movement of troops entirely depended. Horse and motor transport, motor field ambulances, field guns and the " Heavies," all were continually on the move. The importance of the repair and upkeep of the roads and bridges, which the enemy did his best to destroy as he retired, will therefore be readily understood.

Before the 8th August—the day upon which the Allied attacks which led to the Advance to Victory began—those Divisional units which were ordinarily located behind the line had a comparatively peaceful existence. But now that the whole line was moving forward, such units as the Divisional train, " D.A.D.O.S." and his staff, the Mobile Veterinary Section, and the Divisional Ammunition Column, found life a much more strenuous business, and the areas behind the battle-front were full of movement. Yet no one complained; all ranks were on the very tiptoe of expectation. " Our men," said the General Officer Commanding 2nd Division, " are all in wonderful spirits."

The private Diary of the General Officer Commanding is extremely interesting at this period, for it gives a vivid picture of the battlefields across which the 2nd Division had fought its way. On the 11th October he said : " I motored to Forenville, and we crossed the Canal du Nord by the single span high level bridge which had been put up during the last few days. A large amount of labour is at work completing the roadway. We went through Rumilly, and walked along our first objective of the 8th October. The dead are still lying about, but the burial parties are at work. There were not many dead, and there were more Germans than British. There were a good many 77 mm. guns, heavy machine guns, and light trench mortars, the latter arranged to fire point-blank at tanks. There were quantities of rifles and equipment, and the trench was a very inadequate one, and not arranged with

[1] Official Dispatches.

the former cunning. I saw three of the five tanks that were used in the enemy's counter-attack.

"Forenville is a collection of large farm buildings, and is considerably knocked about. . . . We came home *via* Niergnies and Cambrai. The town is much knocked about, and the houses appear to be denuded of furniture except the humbler ones. There has been a certain amount of damage from shell fire. The main square is a typical piece of German 'frightfulness'; all the houses have been burnt and levelled to the ground, and were still smouldering. The Town Hall . . . is still standing, but burnt out and roofless. *The Mark of the Beast is upon the town.* There are many senseless and groundless accusations against the German, but there cannot be any justification for his criminal and spiteful destruction.

"We are now in a great salient, as the Guards Division is up against Solesmes, and the line to the south is well forward; but there has been no corresponding advance east of the Vimy Ridge, and our flank is along the Sensée River. We have no news of what is intended in that direction, but we can at times hear prodigious bombardments not very far to the north of us. The sound of our own battle has completely died down.

"Our casualties since the 27th September are 1,900, and since the 21st August, 3,900. A terrible figure, but nothing to compare with the losses in front trench attacks. The spirits of the men are marvellous, and they are full of dash."

The 2nd Divisional Artillery[1] was also out of the line for the first time since the terrible days of the March Retreat, enjoying a well-earned rest. For weeks and months on end the splendid gunners had covered the infantry in the front line trenches, and when their own comrades of the 2nd Division had been withdrawn into reserve, they still remained in their gun positions, covering the relieving division. Night and day, day and night, in fair weather and foul, the guns knew not silence!

On the 13th October 2nd Division Headquarters closed at Doignies, and moved forward to the château at Seranvillers; the 5th Infantry Brigade and the 2nd Battalion Machine-Gun Corps marched to Rumilly, the 6th Infantry Brigade to Niergnies, and the 99th Infantry Brigade to Wambaix.

The VIth Corps had received orders "to close up." The Guards Division held the corps front, and was disposed along the western banks of the Selle River, from opposite Solesmes to St. Python.

---

[1] The XXXVIth Brigade R.F.A. (Lieut.-Colonel A. A. Goschen) and XLIst Brigade R.F.A. (Lieut.-Colonel P. Barton).

The 62nd (West Riding) Division was supporting the Guards Division, and the 3rd Division was closing up behind the 2nd Division.

"Now for the first time," said the General Officer Commanding 2nd Division, "the Division is entirely on ground which had been in occupation of the Germans since 1914."

The end was very near!

THE BATTLE OF THE SELLE, 17th to 25th October 1918.

The events which led up to the Battle of the Selle are briefly as follows: As already stated, the VIth Corps of the Third Army had won forward to that river. At nightfall on the 13th October the western banks of the Selle south of Haspres were held by British troops, and at a number of places bridgeheads had been established. The First French Army, on the right of the Fourth British Army, had advanced its line east of St. Quentin, clearing the west bank of the Oise–Sambre Canal as far north as Bernot.

Meanwhile, owing to the blows he had sustained south of the Sensée River and the Scarpe, the enemy on the 7th October had begun to withdraw from Lens and his old line south of that place; and by the evening of the 13th October British troops had reached the western suburbs of Douai, and were close up to the western banks of the Sensée Deviation and Haute Deule Canals on the whole front from Arleux (south of Douai) to Vendin le Vieil. In the Argonne, French and Americans had pushed forward steadily, and, held by their attacks on his southern flanks, with his right being rapidly turned by the British, the enemy was forced to evacuate his positions in the Laon salient, which by the evening of the 13th October was in the hands of the French. On the 14th October, at 5.35 a.m., the British, French, and Belgian forces in Flanders, under the command of His Majesty the King of the Belgians, attacked the enemy's positions along the whole front between the Lys River at Comines and Dixmude. The attack was again a complete success. On the southern front of General Plumer's Second Army, in spite of heavy resistance, the troops reached the southern edge of the rising ground overlooking Wervicq, Menin, and Wevelghem. Along the northern front of the British line the enemy's positions to a depth of between three and four miles were penetrated. Moorseele was captured, and progress made beyond it to within a short distance of Gulleghem and Steenbeek. On the left, Belgian troops reached Iseghem, and French troops

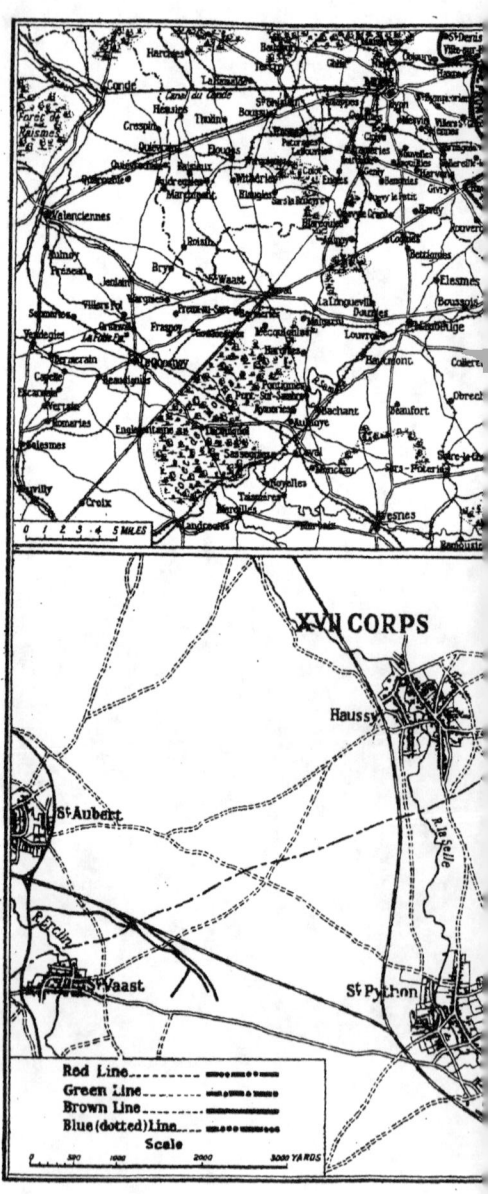

THE BATTLE OF THE SELLE,
17th–25th October 1918.

[Inset Map shows area (*vide* Map I., Vol. I.)
occupied by 2nd Division at the Battle of Mons,
23rd August 1914.]

(*Facing p. 676.*)

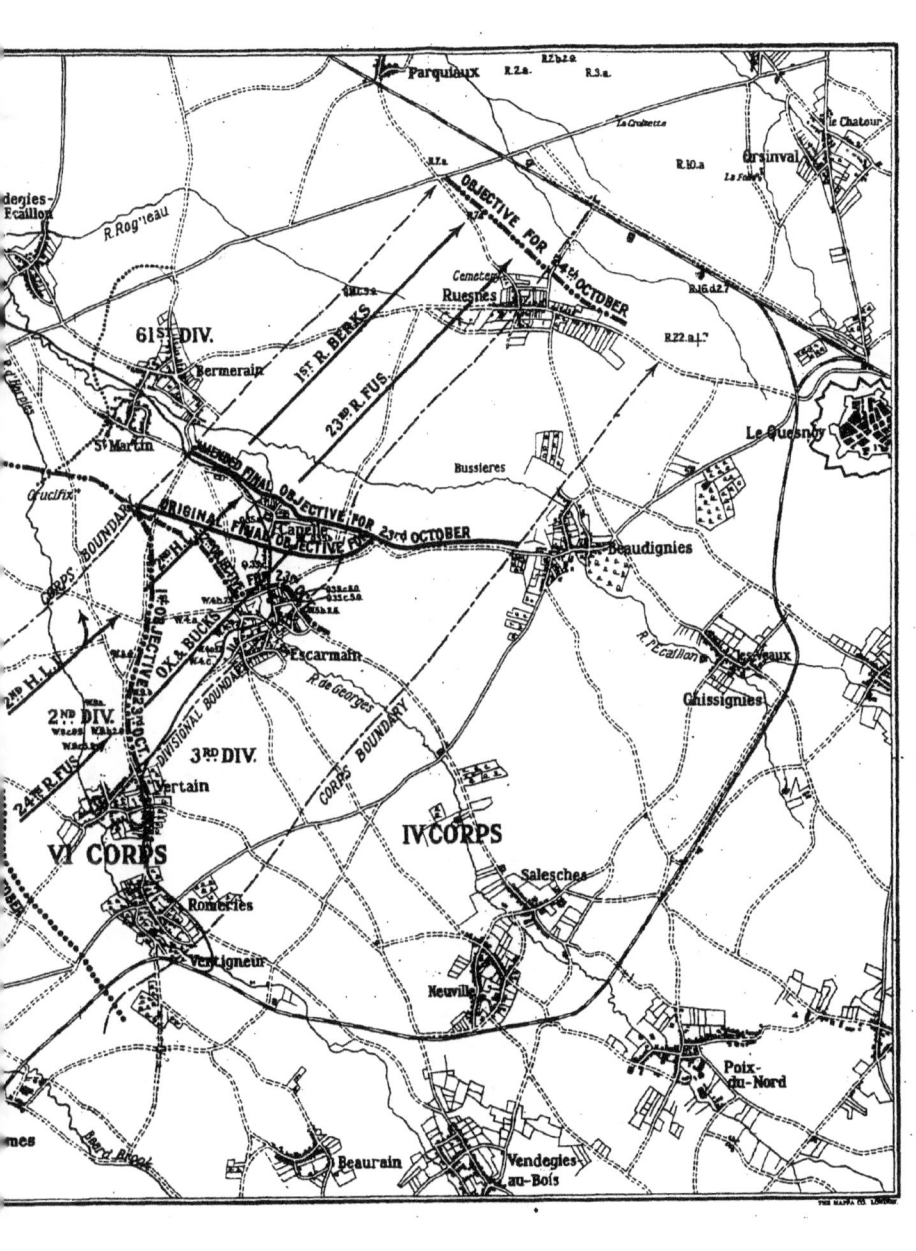

THE BATTLE OPENS.

surrounded Roulers; whilst farther north still the Belgians had also taken Cortemarck. By the afternoon of the 16th October General Plumer's troops held the northern bank of the Lys from Frelinghien to opposite Harlebeke, and had crossed the river at a number of points. Thourout had fallen to the Belgians on the 15th, the enemy retiring rapidly on the 16th. Ostend fell on the 17th, and three days later the northern flank of the Allied armies rested on the Dutch frontier.

But before the latter date the great enemy salient formed by the successful attacks of the Allies south and north, between the Sensée and the Lys, began to give way. This movement began on the 15th. By dawn on the 17th Douai had been entered and the XIth British Corps was on the outskirts of Lille. Everywhere along the front the enemy's rearguards were driven in, and many prisoners and guns and much war material were captured.

The moment had now arrived for a continuance of the attacks of the Fourth Army. "Communications on the Le Cateau front were improving," said the Official Dispatches, "and it was possible to recommence operations of a more than local character for the forcing of the Selle positions and the attainment of the general line Sambre et Oise Canal–west edge of the Forêt de Mormal–Valenciennes. This advance would bring the important railway junction at Aulnoye within effective range of our guns."

On the morning of the 17th October the Battle of the Selle opened with an attack by the Fourth Army on a front of about ten miles from Le Cateau southwards, in conjunction with the First French Army operating west of the Sambre et Oise Canal. The enemy, however, put up a very stout resistance. He was holding the difficult wooded country east of Bohain and the line of the Selle north of it, his infantry being well supported by artillery. For two days he clung obstinately to his positions, though fair progress was made both by British and American troops of the Fourth Army. Nevertheless, "by the evening of the 19th October, after much severe fighting, he had been driven across the Sambre et Oise Canal at practically all points south of Catillon, whence our line followed the valley of the Richemont east and north of Le Cateau."

The line of the Selle River, north of Le Cateau, was attacked on the morning of the 20th, at 2 a.m., by the 38th, 17th, 5th, 42nd, 62nd, Guards, and 19th Divisions of the Third Army, and the 4th Division on the right of the First Army, in the above order from right to left.

17TH OCT MAP.

On this occasion also the enemy's resistance was serious, but nothing could stay the advance of the British troops, who, assisted by tanks, gained all their objectives on the high ground east of the Selle, pushing out patrols as far as the River Harpies. North of Haspres the First British Army progressed on both sides of the Scheldt Canal, reaching the slopes overlooking the left bank of the Ecaillon River, and occupying Denain.

The Selle had been captured, but the operations had yet to be completed by the attainment of the required general line running from the Sambre Canal along the western edge of the Forêt de Mormal to the neighbourhood of Valenciennes.

This was the main operation. It was also the last set battle of the Great War in which the 2nd Division was destined to take part.

In the Operation Orders issued from VIth Corps Headquarters on the 18th October, the 3rd and 2nd Divisions were ordered to be prepared to pass through the 62nd and Guards Divisions respectively on the 22nd October, after the latter Divisions had captured their objectives.

On the 19th October the 2nd Division began to close up behind the Guards Division. The 5th Infantry Brigade group (consisting of 5th Infantry Brigade, 226th Field Company R.E., B Company 2nd Battalion Machine-Gun Corps, and the 5th Field Ambulance) marched during the afternoon from Rumilly to the Boussières–Carnières area. Further instructions from VIth Corps ordered the 2nd Division to be prepared to move its leading brigade (5th) to St. Hilaire, and the 99th Infantry Brigade from Wambaix to the Boussières–Carnières area " at two hours' notice " after 7 o'clock on the morning of the 20th. During the morning of the latter date the Pioneers marched from the Rumilly area to St. Hilaire, in readiness to work on the crossings over the River Selle if the attack succeeded. Final orders for the move forward of the 5th and 99th Infantry Brigades were received at 7.15 a.m., and a little later the necessary moves took place, on the completion of which the 2nd Division was disposed as follows :—

> 5th Infantry Brigade Group (the composition of which has already been given) : at St. Hilaire and St. Waast.
>
> 99th Infantry Brigade Group (consisting of 99th Infantry Brigade, 483rd Field Company R.E., 2nd Battalion Machine-Gun Corps (less B Company), and 100th Field Ambulance : at Boussières–Carnières.
>
> 6th Infantry Brigade Group (consisting of 6th Infantry

OBJECTIVES OF SECOND DIVISION.

Brigade, 5th Field Company R.E., and 6th Field Ambulance) : remaining in the Niergnies area.

The 10th Duke of Cornwall's Light Infantry were at St. Hilaire.

The XXXVIth Brigade R.F.A. occupied gun positions near Arbre de la Femme, whilst the batteries of the XLIst Brigade R.F.A. were between St. Waast and St. Python ; both brigades, with the LXXVIth Brigade R.F.A., formed the left group R.F.A., and were detailed to support the 3rd Guards Brigade (Guards Division) in the operations of the 20th.

The Trench Mortar Batteries—X/2 and Y/2—were at Estourmel. 2nd Division Headquarters were in the château at Seranvillers.

As already stated, the attacks of the Guards Division and the 62nd Division on the 20th were completely successful, but the situation of the 2nd Division throughout the day remained unchanged.

At a Corps Conference on the 21st objectives for the main operations on the 23rd were settled, and late at night—at 11.40 p.m.—orders for the attack were issued. " The VIth Corps is attacking on 23rd October, in conjunction with the IVth Corps on the right and the XVIIth Corps on the left.

" The 2nd Division (on the left) is advancing through the Guards Division. The 3rd Division, on the right, is advancing through the 62nd Division, with the 8th Infantry Brigade on the left, the 76th Infantry Brigade on the right, and 9th Infantry Brigade in reserve. The 57th Infantry Brigade, 19th Division, at present holding the line on the left, is advancing on the left of the 2nd Division.

" The objectives of the 2nd Division are shown on the map issued with this order : First objective—Red ; Second objective— Green ; Third objective—Brown ; Objective for the 24th October —Blue.

" The attack will be carried out by the 5th Infantry Brigade. The 99th Infantry Brigade will be in support with one battalion east of the River Selle before ' zero ' hour. The 9th Infantry Brigade will be in reserve.

" The troops detailed to attack Vertain and the Red Line from the right Divisional boundary to W.9,b.2.0 will form up about the road in W.19,a. and b. (the road running from north-west to southeast, cutting the Solesmes–Vendigies road just behind the Divisional front), and advance in touch with troops of the 3rd Division. The troops detailed to attack the Red objective from W.9,b.2.0 to the left Divisional boundary will cross the Harpies River at 'zero,' and, forming up on the east bank, will be ready to advance at 'zero' plus 20. The objective will be in the first instance the Red Line from the road junction in W.3,d. to the left Divisional boundary. After the troops detailed to capture Vertain have reached the Red objective, both detachments will work inwards, and effect a junction. The 99th Infantry Brigade will be prepared to go through to the Blue Line on 24th October.

"Five brigades of Field Artillery are available on the Divisional front for the attack on 23rd October. . . . For the troops attacking Vertain, a creeping barrage will come down at 3.30 a.m. . . . This barrage will dwell on the opening line for four minutes, and will then creep forward at 100 yards in six minutes. . . . For the attack on the remainder of the first objective from W.9,b.2.0 to the left Divisional boundary, the barrage will come down on a line 300 yards east of the Harpies River at 3.30 a.m. This barrage will creep forward at 100 yards in three minutes to the Red objective. From 'zero' onwards the roads forming the first objective will be bombarded in addition to other points." [1]

Barrages for the attacks on the second and final objectives for 23rd were also to be put down.

The 2nd Battalion Machine-Gun Corps was to support the attack by the 5th Infantry Brigade. A troop of Oxfordshire Hussars for communication purposes, and another troop of the same regiment, with a detachment of cyclists for tactical purposes, were to be attached to the 2nd Division. A detachment of Tunnellers to be employed in discovering and clearing "booby-traps" was also temporarily transferred to the 2nd Division.

"Zero" hour on the 23rd October was to be 3.20 a.m.

The front of the attack about to be launched by the Fourth, Third, and First British Armies (in the order given from right to left) stretched some fifteen miles from Mazinghien to Maison Bleu (along the Solesmes–Vendigies road), north-east of Haussy.[2]

22ND OCT On the 22nd the following moves preparatory to the attack took place: 2nd Divisional Headquarters from Seranvillers to St. Hilaire; 5th Infantry Brigade from St. Hilaire–St. Waast to St. Python area; 99th Infantry Brigade from Carnières–Boussières to St. Hilaire area, with one battalion (23rd Royal Fusiliers) in

---

[1] This Operation Order, No. 365, is of historical interest to the 2nd Division, the Battle of the Selle being the last main operation in which the Division was engaged before the Armistice.

[2] The Fourth Army employed the IXth and XIIIth Corps; the Third Army the Vth, IVth, VIth, and XVIIth Corps; the First Army the XXIInd Corps, from right to left in the order given.

THE DIVISION'S LAST BATTLE. 681

St. Python; 6th Infantry Brigade from Niergnies to St. Hilaire area.

During the evening the 5th Infantry Brigade (temporarily commanded by Lieut.-Colonel R. H. Pipon) relieved the 3rd Guards Brigade in the front line, and the command of the Divisional sector passed to the General Officer Commanding 2nd Division at 9.45 p.m. On completion of the relief of the Guards, the 24th Royal Fusiliers held the right sub-sector of the line, and the 2nd Highland Light Infantry the left. The 2nd Oxford and Bucks (the reserve battalion of the 5th Infantry Brigade) was in the open, north-east of St. Python.

The attack launched at 3.20 a.m. on the 23rd October was worthy of the best traditions of the 2nd Division, and as it was the Division's last battle, the battalions as far as possible shall tell their own story of the day's operations.

23RD OCT.

At 3.20 a.m. the barrage fell, under cover of which the 24th Royal Fusiliers, on the right, advanced on the Red Line and the village of Vertain: " The dispositions for the attack were D Company, on the right, attacking the village of Vertain; C Company, on the left, whose objective it was to push on and capture the line of the road east of Vertain. Two platoons of B Company were to 'mop up' for the attacking companies. A Company was in reserve. At 3.20 a.m. the attack was launched, and the right company attacked the village. To conform with the barrage arrangements, the left company did not attack until 4.20 a.m. From the outset the attack was a complete success. The men, splendidly led and full of fight, soon beat down all opposition, and by 5.15 a.m. the left company reported all objectives gained. Very soon after the right company, whose task was a more severe one, reported all their objectives gained. The 'mopping up' party met with some resistance, and took five machine guns in houses in Vertain; but so thoroughly did they do their work that 'all clear' was reported in time to allow the 52nd Light Infantry to pass through the battalion at 8.20 a.m. to carry on the tide of advance. Over 250 prisoners, 50 to 60 machine guns, one 77 mm. field gun, 4 trench mortars, and much other valuable booty were captured in this most successful operation by the battalion. That night, after a hard day, the battalion had the novel experience of being billeted in houses in the village of Vertain which they had so finely won in the morning."[1]

At "zero plus 20," the 2nd Highland Light Infantry on the

[1] Battalion Diary, 24th Royal Fusiliers.

left of the 24th Royal Fusiliers advanced behind the barrage, which had come down on the line of the river. The latter was crossed successfully by both the attacking companies (B on the right, D on the left) : " Right Company—No opposition was encountered until the line of the first objective was reached. It was here that a belt of wire still existed uncut in front of the line of the road (running from north-west to south-east). . . . The right platoon, under Second-Lieut. E. K. Humphries, penetrated through an existing gap and reached the Red Line up to time, capturing machine guns and about 40 prisoners. They were then able to give assistance by flanking fire to the left platoon, although they were troubled by enfilade machine-gun fire from the direction of Vertain until 5 a.m. The left platoon found the wire a greater obstacle," but " reached the Red Line some fifteen minutes later. Touch was obtained on the left with D Company. A line 100 yards in front of the road was then consolidated by B Company, and a Lewis-gun post established at the road junction. This post was taken over fifteen minutes later by the 24th Royal Fusiliers, and thus touch was established with the latter battalion.

" The Company (B) had a very long frontage, and at one point there was a very considerable gap which was filled by a pocket of the enemy. The Company Commander (Captain Gibbs) with Acting Company Sergeant-Major J. Smith rushed the enemy. They emptied their revolvers into the enemy, and the whole party surrendered. It was now 7 a.m., and so far 80 prisoners and 12 machine guns had been captured by this one company at a loss of 1 other rank killed and 8 wounded.

" In a similar manner the left company "—D—" pushed forward at ' zero,' but encountered opposition on the left from hostile machine guns at the cross roads, which were strongly protected by a belt of wire. This was dealt with by the left platoon, who captured it with 20 prisoners and two machine guns . . . the platoon succeeded in gaining their first objective and consolidated 200 yards beyond. Touch was gained with the 19th Division on the left, but not until after ' second zero ' with the right platoon. This platoon had, however, gained its objective and was in touch with the right company. It had also captured 50 prisoners, 3 heavy and 1 light machine guns. The gap between the two platoons had been filled up by sections of B Company of the 2nd Battalion Machine-Gun Corps." [1]

At 8.40 a.m. the attack on the second objective was launched.

[1] Battalion Diary, 2nd Highland Light Infantry.

The 2nd Oxford and Bucks passed through the 24th Royal Fusiliers, and the right and left support companies (C on the right and A on the left) of the 2nd Highland Light Infantry passed through the two front companies of that battalion. The second objective (Green Line) included the village of Escarmain.

With C Company on the right and B Company on the left, the Oxford and Bucks advanced to the attack on the Green Line. " A message from Lieut. Giles, Commanding B Company, timed 9 a.m., reported his Headquarters at W.4,c.7.5, with his line along hedge in W.4,a. and c. ; that he was held up by machine-gun fire from a strong point as yet not located, and that he was in touch on both flanks. Another message, timed 9.30 a.m., reported his company in the village of Escarmain with the enemy still in the strong point, and that he was still in touch on both flanks. About 11 a.m. Captain Anderson arrived with the following information : at 8.40 a.m., when formed up on the Red Line, Captain Bobby, Commanding C Company, was not sure of touch with the 3rd Division on the right, and that in consequence he had called on D Company (Captain Eagles) for support if necessary. Officer Commanding A Company had been warned to hold two platoons in readiness to cover the right flank of C Company ; and that at 8.15 a.m. A Company (Lieut. Whitehead) was established along the east banks of the Harpies River from W.9,c.o.9. He also brought a message from Officer Commanding C Company, timed 11 a.m., reporting the capture of all objectives and 50 prisoners, with little or no resistance, and slight casualties. The company held from W.5,b.2.6 to Q.35,c.5.0, at which point it was in touch with B Company but was not in touch with the 3rd Division. Company Headquarters at Q.35,c.8.0. At 11.30 a.m. Officer Commanding B Company reported (message timed 10.45 a.m.) capture of all objectives, consolidation proceeding, slight casualties, many prisoners and machine guns, and Company Headquarters in Sunken Road at W.4,b.7.9 ; also, touch obtained on both flanks." [1]

Meanwhile, at " zero "—8.40 a.m.—the two companies of Highland Light Infantry had passed through the Red Line (held by two other companies of the same battalion). As the right company (C) moved forward there was some resistance from enemy camouflaged posts in the turnip fields in W.4,a. central. " Numbers of the enemy were killed by our barrage fire in the Sunken Road in W.4, a. and b. (the road running almost direct west from the north-west exits of Escarmain). . . . The objective (Green Line) was captured

[1] Battalion Diary, 2nd Oxford and Bucks Light Infantry.

and consolidated by 9 a.m., touch being maintained with both flanks.

"As with the right support company (C), the left support company (A) moved to assembly positions on the first objective. When so doing the left platoon commander (Lieut. G. Lang) at 5 a.m. saw success signals from the front of the brigade on the left [1]—in Q.35, a. and b. Enemy lights, however, were put up from Ferme de Rieux . . . which had been reported in our hands. Officer Commanding A Company (Lieut. Thorburn) at once ordered Lieut. Lang to take his platoon and deal with the Ferme de Rieux. It was found strongly held by the enemy. The farm was surrounded by a high wall, which had two gaps in it. Lieut. Lang posted a Lewis gun at one gap, and under cover of bombs, which were flung by the Lewis gun section through the windows of the houses, and under the fire of the Lewis gun, Lieut. Lang and his rifle sections rushed the houses through the other gap, killing or capturing the garrison consisting of 1 officer and 25 other ranks, and two machine guns. The left platoon now returned and took up its assembly positions."

"At 'zero' A Company moved forward and gained and consolidated the second objective. The right platoon was hung up by our barrage, but by 9 a.m. the position was consolidated. The left platoon, in its advance to the Green Line, captured 1 officer, 22 other ranks, and 4 trench mortars; while the right platoon, under Lieut. M'Intosh, captured 20 prisoners and two 4.2 howitzers with sights complete.

"Major Thorburn, R.F.A., who kept in very close touch with these advancing companies, organized two teams, and the guns were fired at the retreating enemy." [2]

Thus both the first (Red Line) and second (Green Line) objectives had fallen to the attacks of the 2nd Division, and touch on both flanks—*i.e.*, with the 3rd Division on the right and the 19th Division on the left—had been maintained. The next objective (Brown Line) had, however, been amended and pushed forward, for owing to the energy and initiative shown both by the Highland Light Infantry and the Oxford and Bucks, both battalions in the third attack, which was launched at 2.26 p.m. under a barrage, had gone on beyond the original Brown Line, and by nightfall Capelle and the line of the railway running north-east of the village had passed into the possession of the 5th Infantry Brigade. But

---

[1] 57th Infantry Brigade, 19th Division.
[2] Battalion Diary, 2nd Highland Light Infantry.

THE ATTACK TO BE RESUMED.   685

the north bank of the Ecaillon and the villages of St. Martin and Bermerain were still held by the enemy, and any further advance of the 5th Infantry Brigade was held up until the left flanking division had captured these two places.

When darkness had fallen posts were pushed out towards the Ecaillon, and it was ascertained that all ground on the 2nd Divisional front south of the river was clear of the enemy.

As a result of the day's fighting, and up to 4 p.m., 9 officers and 434 other ranks had been taken prisoners and passed through the Divisional cages. The total casualties suffered by the 5th Infantry Brigade numbered only 134—killed and wounded.

The attack was to be resumed on the 24th, and for this purpose the 99th Infantry Brigade, which throughout the 23rd had closed up behind the 5th Infantry Brigade and at 5 p.m. was concentrated astride the western outskirts of Vertain, took over the Brown Line, the relief being completed at 11.30 p.m. The 5th Infantry Brigade then marched back to Vertain and billeted in the village, well pleased with the day's work—an advance of 3,000 yards. The 6th Infantry Brigade was now at St. Python.

Elsewhere along the front of the attack from east of Mazinghien to north-east of Haussy the IXth and XIIIth Corps of the Fourth Army, and the Vth, IVth, and XVIIth Corps of the Third Army had advanced on both flanks of the VIth Corps.

Owing to the successful operations of, and capture of Capelle by, the 5th Infantry Brigade, the 99th Infantry Brigade had a fine "jumping-off" line, and the original Blue Line was again put forward and ran from the north-east corner of Ruesnes to the apex of the four roads south-east of Parquiaux. This was the objective of the 99th Infantry Brigade, and if captured, posts were to be pushed forward to the line of the railway, in front of the Blue Dotted Line.

"Zero" was 4 a.m. on the 24th October, and at that hour the Divisional front line was disposed in the following order: The 23rd Royal Fusiliers were to attack on the right, the 1st Royal Berks on the left, and the 1st King's Royal Rifle Corps in reserve. On the right the 9th Infantry Brigade of the 3rd Division, and on the left the 183rd Infantry Brigade of the 61st Division, were to attack in conjunction with the 2nd Division.

The morning was fine and dry when, at 4 a.m., the artillery barrage opened on the line of the river Ecaillon, moving forward at "zero" plus 24.   24TH OCT.

Under cover of the barrage the 23rd Royal Fusiliers advanced to and crossed the Ecaillon without appreciable opposition. As the attack swept on over the ravine just north of the river, an enemy machine-gun nest, which had been "overrun" and unnoticed by the leading troops, attempted to come into action and engage the Fusiliers. The team of a Light Trench Mortar Battery, which had been detailed to accompany the Fusiliers, observing this attempt of the enemy, hastily put down its loads and advanced against the hostile machine-gun nest. Two Germans were killed, and the remainder of the gun team, with the machine gun, were captured. Meanwhile the Fusiliers had again been held up by heavy rifle and machine-gun fire coming from practice trenches in the line of the advance. "The officer in command proceeded forward personally and made a reconnaissance of the position whence this fire was coming from. Having located the enemy, he decided to envelop the practice trenches under cover of the fire of rifle grenades, rifles, Lewis guns, and smoke. This plan he put into execution with complete success, capturing 30 Germans and two machine guns which formed the enemy garrison of the post."[1]

While the 23rd Royal Fusiliers were thus dealing with the enemy on their front of attack, the 1st Royal Berks were advancing abreast of them on the left. "The Ecaillon River was found to be deeper than was expected, and most of the men went in up to their waists. On topping the rise (on the northern banks) heavy machine-gun fire was encountered from the direction of Parquaix, but the line continued to advance, and the objective was captured and consolidated, a total advance of 4,000 yards over two rivers and difficult country. On the final objective the battalion was in touch on the right with the 23rd Royal Fusiliers, but the 9th Northumberland Fusiliers on the left were driven back to the line La Folie–Larblin, leaving the left flank exposed for a depth of 2,500 yards. Accordingly, C and D Companies formed a defensive flank facing north-west from R.7,a.5.7 (the apex of the cross roads) to Q.18,c.5.9, with A and B Companies holding the road in R.7, a. and d. (the front line of the battalion just in front of the Blue Dotted Line). The 1st King's Royal Rifle Corps continued the defensive flank in a south-west direction to La Folie . . . about 300 prisoners and ten machine guns were captured during the advance. . . . At about 1.45 p.m. the enemy attempted to counter-attack, but the attack failed to make any progress, and the line remained intact."[2]

[1] Diary of the 99th Infantry Brigade Headquarters.
[2] Battalion Diary, 1st Royal Berkshire Regiment.

AT ST. PYTHON.

The 1st King's Royal Rifle Corps had little to do but, as already stated, continue the line of the defensive flank.

Orders were then issued to the Berkshires and the Fusiliers to organize their line in depth strongly consolidated. Arrangements were made for active patrolling to be carried out, and for the occupation of the railway at the first opportunity. During the night the 61st Division, on the left of the 2nd Division, advanced its right flank and effected a junction with the left flank of the Berkshires.

Headquarters of the 2nd Division were now at St. Python.

" The French inhabitants say that many Germans are getting into plain clothes and falling out of the fight. There are about 100 inhabitants in St. Python, men, women, and children; the latter are playing about happily in the streets, but they have had a dreadful time living cooped up in their cellars for about a fortnight whilst the village lay right in the middle of the fight. They told me the Germans fired machine guns at the windows so as to break all the panes rapidly. . . . I rode into Solesmes; it is only a mile away. There are quite a lot of inhabitants. All are smiling and bowing. . . . I got M——'s gleanings from the examination of prisoners during the last few days. We have captured men from the 21st Reserve, 9th Reserve, 4th, and 113th Divisions, and from eight different regiments of these divisions. We have got two battalion commanders. The 21st Reserve Division was completing a relief when we attacked, and one of their regiments—168th—had just been transferred to them from the 25th Division which had been broken up. The feeling of the prisoners is ' What is the good of going on, as we are beaten.' The officers say Germany has agreed to Wilson's fourteen points, but ' we must be allowed to evacuate occupied territory for the honour of Germany and the army.' Many prisoners still believe we shoot prisoners in cold blood, but the belief cannot be very strong, as they surrender so easily. The 2nd Division has met the 21st Reserve Division on more than one occasion when holding the line, and they used to be a fine division. Our total bag of prisoners through the cage for two days is 23 officers and 831 other ranks. We have captured ten guns. We have had another phenomenal advance to-day at a cost of 180 casualties. On the left, the 61st Division had very heavy fighting. . . . The results of our training in advancing covering great breadth and depth proved its value to-day; not only were our casualties very slight but, owing to the brigade being in depth, the troops on the left flank merely faced to their left and the whole flank was protected. . . . I received a deputation of the Mayor

688   THE HISTORY OF THE SECOND DIVISION.

and elders of the village, who came to render thanks to the British Army for relieving them from their four years of bondage." [1]

25TH OCT. The next morning, at about 9.30, reports reached 2nd Division Headquarters indicating the enemy's withdrawal from the line of the railway along the Divisional front. Both leading battalions of the 99th Infantry Brigade were therefore ordered to push forward strong patrols and occupy the railway. By 12 noon the Berkshires and the 23rd Royal Fusiliers had carried out these orders; the former had little difficulty, but the latter met with machine-gun fire. The enemy's resistance was, however, soon overcome, and five field guns and a machine gun were captured. On reaching the railway both battalions sent out patrols towards the Rhonelle River.

During the afternoon, in conjunction with the 3rd and 61st Divisions, an outpost line was established north of the railway. By 5 p.m. the 99th Infantry Brigade had placed outposts covering the 2nd Divisional front on the line La Croisette–R.2,b.2.9, in touch with both flanking divisions.

An hour later orders were received from VIth Corps Headquarters: The 3rd Division was to take over the duties of advanced guard on the whole Corps front on the morning of the 26th; the 99th Infantry Brigade was to remain responsible for defence and organization of the Corps Main Line of Resistance (the Blue Dotted Line) on the Divisional front, and later, when the 3rd Division had passed through the 2nd Division, was to become responsible for the main line of resistance on the whole Corps front.

The Battle of the Selle was over!

Once again the western outskirts of the Forêt de Mormal had been reached by some of those very troops who, in August 1914, had tramped the hot dusty roads between Le Quesnoy and Le Cateau.

"In the Selle battle twenty-four British and two American Divisions had captured a further 20,000 prisoners and 475 guns from thirty-one German divisions opposed to them." [2]

Everywhere the enemy was hard pressed, and Ludendorff was in despair. "On the evening of the 25th October," he said, "the Western front was enduring the greatest strain. There was fighting from the Dutch frontier to Verdun. No more help was coming from home. Not a word of encouragement was given. It was marvellous that the troops fought so heroically." [3]

[1] Diary of Major-General C. E. Pereira, C.B., C.M.G.
[2] Official Dispatches.
[3] *My War Memories, 1914-1918.* On October 26, 1918, Ludendorff resigned.

THE LAST PHASE. 689

The Return to Mons, the March into Germany, and the Break-up of the 2nd Division.

By 6 o'clock on the morning of the 26th October the 1st King's 26TH OCT.
Royal Rifle Corps had relieved the 23rd Royal Fusiliers and the
1st Royal Berks in the main line of resistance, and the 8th Infantry
Brigade of the 3rd Division had taken over the outpost line. The
2nd Division was then disposed as follows:

    2nd Divisional Headquarters at St. Python.

    99th Infantry Brigade: Headquarters at Capelle; 1st King's Royal Rifle Corps—holding the main line of resistance; the 1st Royal Berks in support at Bermerain; the 23rd Royal Fusiliers in Brigade reserve at Capelle.

    6th Infantry Brigade: Headquarters and 17th Royal Fusiliers—Vertain; 1st King's and 2nd South Staffords—Escarmin, but during the afternoon both battalions moved to Romeries.

    5th Infantry Brigade: Headquarters and 2nd Highland Light Infantry—Vertain; 2nd Oxford and Bucks and 24th Royal Fusiliers—St. Python.

All ranks at this period were much exhausted, for since the opening of the great Allied offensive, which had proved so wonderfully successful, constant action and long marches had tried the physical endurance of the troops to the very utmost. "It was evident," said one Battalion Diary on the 26th October, "that the men were much exhausted by the constant change of position and necessity for digging-in, usually with some attention from the enemy's 'heavies,' and severe doses of gas."

But if their physical powers were somewhat exhausted, their spirit was still that same grand old spirit which had brought the survivors through all the troublous years which had passed since the flower of the regular British army, in August 1914, had marched over those very same roads and through that very same area in which the units of the 2nd Division were now located.

On the night of the 27th–28th October the 3rd Division took over 27TH–28TH
responsibility for the main line of resistance along the whole of the OCT.
VIth Corps front, the 76th Infantry Brigade relieving the 99th
Infantry Brigade, which then marched back to Solesmes. On
completion of this relief, the 2nd Division became division in
support in the area Romeries–Vertain–St. Python–Solesmes. The
Division had, however, received warning that it would in all prob-

ability be called upon to relieve the 3rd Division as Advanced Guard on the night 29th–30th October.

29TH OCT. At 10.50 a.m. on the 29th, "2nd Division Order No. 367" was issued, giving details of the relief to take place during the coming night. The line to be taken over was: "The 3rd Division is at present in touch with the enemy holding the following line: Outpost line-R.16,d.2.7 (in touch with the New Zealand Division)-R.10,a. and c.-R.3,a. and c.-R.2,a. central (in touch with the 61st Division: Main Line of Resistance—R.22,a.1.7 to crossroads at R.7,a."[1]

The 6th Infantry Brigade was to relieve the 8th Infantry Brigade on the right, and the 5th Infantry Brigade the 76th Infantry Brigade on the left; the 99th Infantry Brigade to move from Solesmes to Escarmain in Divisional reserve, relieving the 9th Infantry Brigade (3rd Division).

The reliefs were carried out without incident, and on completion the 6th Infantry Brigade disposed the 17th Royal Fusiliers in the front line, the 2nd South Staffords in support, and the 1st King's in reserve; of the 5th Infantry Brigade, the 24th Royal Fusiliers held the front line, the 2nd Oxford and Bucks were in support, and the 2nd Highland Light Infantry in reserve.

30TH–31ST OCT. Throughout the 30th and the 31st little happened along the Divisional front. Desultory shelling with gas and high-explosive had little effect upon the spirits of the men, though several casualties were suffered. One man, a regimental cook of the 2nd Oxford and Bucks, was killed on the 30th by shell-fire; he had served throughout the whole war. One of the saddest things at this period was the loss of officers and men who had weathered the whole storm of the war, but were at last killed when almost within sight of peace and the goal they had striven so gallantly to reach.

At the end of October the last act of that great drama which had filled the world's stage for over four years, was on the point of beginning. "By this time the rapid succession of heavy blows dealt by the British forces had had a cumulative effect, both moral and material, upon the German armies. The difficulty of replacing the enemy's enormous losses in guns, machine guns, and ammunition had increased with every fresh attack, and his reserves of men were exhausted. . . . Though troops could still be found to offer resistance to our initial assault, the German infantry and machine gunners were no longer reliable. . . . The capitulation of Turkey and Bulgaria, and the imminent collapse of Austria consequent

[1] Sheet 51A, France: 1/40,000.

THE FUSILIERS MAKE FINAL RAIDS. 691

upon Allied success, which the desperate position of her own armies on the Western front had rendered her powerless to prevent, had made Germany's military situation ultimately impossible. If her armies were allowed to withdraw unmolested to shorter lines, the struggle might still be protracted over the winter. The British armies, however, were now in a position to prevent this by a direct attack upon a vital centre, which should anticipate the enemy's withdrawal and force an immediate conclusion." The Battle of Valenciennes, which included the capture of Mont Houx, was fought on the 1st and 2nd November, as a necessary preliminary operation to the greater and final battle. As a result of this operation, the enemy abandoned the Valenciennes–Le Quesnoy line, and fell back. On the morning of the 4th November, the Fourth, Third, and First British Armies launched an attack on a 30-mile front, extending from the Sambre, north of Oisy to Valenciennes. This was the Battle of the Sambre,[1] and included the passage of the Sambre–Oise Canal, and the capture of Le Quesnoy. The passage of the Grande Honelle was won on the 5th–7th November, and finally, early on the morning of the 11th November, Mons was captured.

In this final act of the great war-drama, however, the 2nd Division did not take part, for on the night of the 2nd–3rd November it was relieved by the Guards and 62nd Divisions. But before the reliefs were carried out the 17th and 24th Royal Fusiliers, holding the Divisional front line, carried out two successful raids on the enemy's posts—the last raids made by the Division.

The first raid took place at 2 a.m. on the 1st November, when 1ST NOV one officer and 25 other ranks of the 17th Royal Fusiliers attacked La Folie Farm. Two German officers and 7 other ranks were found in the cellars of the farm, and were captured without offering any resistance. In the second affair, the 24th Royal Fusiliers captured one German officer and 4 other ranks.

At 9.35 p.m. on the 2nd November, the 1st and 2nd Guards 2ND NOV. Brigades relieved the 5th Infantry Brigade, and the 187th Infantry Brigade of the 62nd (W.R.) Division relieved the 6th Infantry Brigade. On relief the 5th Infantry Brigade marched back to St. Python, and the 6th to Solesmes; the 99th Infantry Brigade was located at St. Hilaire and St. Vaast.

The attacks of the 4th and 5th November had broken the 4TH–5TH enemy's resistance, and from this date onwards to the signing of the NOV.

[1] In the Official Dispatches the whole operations between the 1st to 11th November are included under the heading of the Battle of the Sambre.

Armistice he was hurrying eastwards in disorder, stopping only occasionally in sheer desperation to dispute the passage of a river, or in a vain endeavour to stem the tide which pursued relentlessly. "The enemy was capable," said the Official Dispatches, "neither of accepting nor refusing battle."

Little remains to be written. As a division in reserve the 2nd Division moved forward as the front line progressed eastwards.

8TH NOV. On the 8th, the 6th Infantry Brigade had moved to Preux-au-Sart, the 5th Infantry Brigade to Villers Pol, and the 99th Infantry Brigade to Capelle and Escarmain.

9TH NOV. On the 9th November the General Officer Commanding 2nd Division (Major-General C. E. Pereira, C.B., C.M.G.) motored to La Longueville, and this is the entry in his diary: "This afternoon I motored to La Longueville. I was billeted there in the advance to and the retreat from Mons in 1914.[1] I recognized the church, but could not remember where I was billeted. The Guards Divisional Headquarters are there, and it was most fitting to find the village filled with Coldstreamers. Some spoons marked '2.C.G.' were produced by the inhabitants; they had treasured them up ever since our departure."

THE ARMISTICE, 11TH NOV. 1918. At 11 a.m. on the 11th November, in accordance with instructions received from Marshal Foch, hostilities in France and Belgium were suspended by the Allies. The enemy's surrender was complete—he had signed the terms of the Armistice.

None of the official war diaries express the slightest enthusiasm or anything comparable with that wild joy which at the "eleventh hour, of the eleventh day, of the eleventh month" turned men and women temporarily mad throughout the world, and produced in every city, town, and village in Great Britain scenes the like of which have never before been witnessed. All was quiet in France and Flanders; the silence of the battlefields was a thing almost too wonderful for belief.

Then came the advance into Germany. On the 15th all units were warned that the march would begin on the 17th, and for this purpose the 2nd Division "closed up" on the former date: the 6th Infantry Group moving to Bermeries–Mecquignies, the 5th Infantry Group to Preux-au-Sart–Wargnies, and the 99th Infantry Brigade Group to Villers Pol.[2]

[1] In August 1914, General Pereira commanded the 2nd Coldstream Guards.

[2] "Friday, 15th November: The Army Brigades, R.F.A., are being allotted, and we get back the old 2nd Division XXXIVth Brigade. All batteries are being reduced to four guns from six."—Private Diary of General Officer Commanding 2nd Division.

A MEMORY OF THE RETREAT, 1914.

On the 18th the 6th Infantry Brigade Group marched to Maubeuge, the 5th Infantry Group to Douzies (just west of Maubeuge), and the 99th Infantry Group to La Longueville.

The March to the Rhine had begun.

Thus, after four years and four months of terrible fighting, of experiences unequalled in the past, and hardly likely to be equalled in the future, the 2nd Division once again trod the ground over which it had advanced and retreated in August 1914. Yet how changed was the old Division. Take the battalions of infantry. Six only of the twelve which formed the original 2nd Division remained. Of the 5th Infantry Brigade, the 2nd Highland Light Infantry, and the 2nd Oxford and Bucks Light Infantry; of the 6th Infantry Brigade all four battalions remained; but the 1st King's Royal Rifle Corps and the 1st Royal Berks were with the 99th Infantry Brigade, leaving only the 2nd South Staffords and the 1st King's with their original Brigade. And even these six battalions had few officers and men who, on those hot and dusty days of August 1914, had first marched northwards through Malplaquet —of glorious fame to the British army—full of hope, and quite undaunted by rumours of the enemy's strength, and later trudged wearily back to the Marne, where the flood-tide of the enemy's advance was stayed. What said the General Officer Commanding on that day in November 1918, who knew so well what the original 2nd Division passed through during the first month of the war? —" During the afternoon I walked down the road we followed during the retreat, through Hargnies to the Forêt de Mormal, and the long, straight road to Pont sur Sambre. I had most vivid impressions of that road—the fearful block of traffic, and the enemy's forces always getting closer! There were the country carts filled with the household goods of the inhabitants, who were flying from their homes. I remember well how we had to side-track them so as to prevent further congestion."

Well indeed was all this area known to the Rifles, the South Staffords, the Oxfords and Bucks, the Berkshires, the Highland Light Infantry, and the King's Regiment. The Gunners[1] also were able to go over the ground where hastily improvised gun positions had been taken up to cover the retirement. Here was the very road down which the Sappers, the Field Ambulances, the Divisional Train, the Mobile Veterinary Section, the Divisional

---

[1] One battery of the 2nd Divisional Artillery—the 16th—on the day of the Armistice had still 23 horses with which it had left Bordon when the battery embarked for France in August 1914.

Mounted Troops and Cyclists had plodded on towards Noyelles, Maroilles, and Landrecies, the billeting area of the 2nd Division on the night of 25th August 1914.

South of La Longueville lay Hargnies,[1] and it was at the latter place that, as the British troops followed close on the track of the beaten enemy, a very touching incident happened.

On the night of 24th August 1914, two officers of the 2nd Division—one the late Prince Maurice of Battenberg, who then belonged to the 1st King's Royal Rifle Corps, and the other Major Knox Gore, also of the 1st King's Royal Rifle Corps—left their swords with an old farmer and his wife. For even at that early period of the retreat everything unnecessary was discarded. Prince Maurice of Battenberg was killed at Ypres in October of the same year, but his companion, who had come back to the 2nd Division in 1918 as an attached Staff Officer, with the help of the village curé, succeeded in finding the farm and the old couple with whom the swords had been left. On seeing Major Knox Gore the farmer's wife threw her arms around his neck and kissed him. The old couple then led the way upstairs to an attic, where they set to work and soon pulled up one of the floor boards. There beneath lay the two swords, which were handed back to Major Knox Gore.

In successive but painfully slow stages,[2] because of the enormous difficulty attending the transport of supplies and munitions of war, the 2nd Division in rear of the Guards Division and the 3rd Division in rear of the 62nd (W.R.) Division, moved forward towards the German frontier. The VIth Corps had been transferred to the Second Army on the reconstruction of the British force detailed for the Rhine.

It has been said that the Allies should have refused to treat with the enemy; that they should have forced him back upon his own

[1] See Map No. 3, Volume I.
[2] Owing to the untiring energies of Lieut.-Colonel Clayton, G.S.O.1, 2nd Division, the troops were comfortably billeted during the march into Germany. Colonel Clayton sent his reconnoitring billeting party of the Divisional Headquarters to areas forty-eight hours ahead, so that that evening distribution of billeting areas went out to the three Infantry Brigades, and they were able to issue their orders twenty-four hours in advance. Their billeting parties left the following morning and allotted billets, and the troops marched straight into them, battalions and companies having had time to allot. No hanging about for weary men not knowing which village, or part of a village, they would eventually get; no counter-marching. They marched straight into their billets. Major Tidbury (" Q " Staff), as head of the Divisional reconnoitring party, did wonders. This work necessitated rising and leaving at a very early hour, travelling a double march, and back one march, arriving in the evening; and then the orders had to be got out that night. The billeting arrangements were splendidly organized by the above officers.

frontiers and then advanced into Germany and dictated their own terms. Such a thing was not impossible, but impracticable. The supply question was so acute that during the advance into Germany many units went short of rations because of the sheer impossibility of keeping up a regular supply; the men's boots also were broken, and not a few tramped almost with bare feet; sufficient rations and stores could not be got forward. How then could the whole Allied forces in France and Flanders have marched immediately into Germany?

On the 9th December the 2nd Division marched through Spa, thus crossing the German frontier. The change in the attitude of the population now became most marked; it was now the enemy's turn to see conquering troops march through his country, and he did not appreciate it.

There is little need to follow the grand old Division through its last days. It had fought the good fight, covering itself with high honour and glory; no division amongst all the gallant divisions which fought in France and Flanders was more honoured.

On reaching the Rhine, the 2nd Division was allotted an area in the Army of Occupation, and its designation was changed: "Monday, February 17, 1919. The preliminary instructions for the formation of the Army of Occupation have now been received. Our six regular battalions are reduced to cadres, and go home; the 17th and 23rd Royal Fusiliers go to another division, and the 24th Royal Fusiliers and Cornwalls (10th Duke of Cornwall's Light Infantry) reduced to cadres. The three Brigades R.F.A., and the 5th Field Company R.E., are reduced to cadres and go home. The Division will be filled up by other units, and will be known as the 'Light Division.' I am glad that the name of the 2nd Division will come to an end out here when the units are all changed." [1]

Thus for the time being passed from the British army a Division whose officers, N.C.O's, and men had fought well and faithfully for over four years in the greatest war the world has ever known, deserving of all that noble epitaph:

"ALL THESE FOUGHT MOST VALIANTLY. THEIR NAMES ARE INSCRIBED IN THE ANNALS OF THE NATION."

[1] The General Officer Commanding 2nd Division.

APPENDICES.

Appendix XVIII.

ROLL OF HEADQUARTERS OF THE SECOND DIVISION.

Name.	Appointment.	Date of Joining.	Date of Leaving.	Remarks.
Maj.-Gen. C. C. MONRO, C.B.	G.O.C.	5.8.14.	26.12.14.	To Command 1st Corps.
Maj.-Gen. H. S. HORNE, C.B.	G.O.C.	1.1.15.	4.11.15.	To Chief Military Adviser, Near East.
Maj.-Gen. W. G. WALKER, V.C., C.B.	G.O.C.	5.11.15.	27.12.16.	To England, 27.12.16.
Maj.-Gen. C. E. PEREIRA, C.B., C.M.G.	G.O.C.	27.12.16.	17.3.19.	2nd Div. became Light Div., March 17, 1919.
Capt. Visct. GORT, M.V.O.	A.D.C.	5.8.14.	26.12.14.	To 1st Corps as A.D.C. to Lt.-Gen. MONRO.
Capt. W. E. ROTHWELL.	A.D.C.	5.8.14.	26.9.14.	Wounded.
Capt. R. G. CHERRY.	A.D.C.	7.10.14.	19.12.14.	To Royal Flying Corps.
Capt. E. A. B. ORR.	A.D.C.	26.9.14.	26.12.14.	To 1st Corps as A.D.C. to Lt.-Gen. MONRO.
Capt. J. A. DON.	A.D.C.	21.1.15.	22.8.15.	To R.A. 2nd Division.
Lieut. C. R. GERARD.	A.D.C.	17.1.15.	27.7.15.	Rejoined regiment.
Lieut. Hon. H. S. FEILDING.	A.D.C.	23.9.15.	30.12.15.	To Egypt.
2/Lieut. H. C. S. MUNRO.	A.D.C.	23.9.15.	30.12.15.	To Egypt.
Capt. Hon. H. W. GOUGH.	A.D.C.	28.1.16.	4.7.16.	To H.Q. Fifth Army.
2/Lieut. R. M. WATSON.	A.D.C.	21.2.16.	25.4.17.	To England.
2/Lieut. F. S. ARBUTHNOT.	A.D.C.	13.10.16.	1.1.17.	To H.Q. R.A. 2nd Division.
Lieut. C. D. W. PARISH.	A.D.C.	13.2.17.	19.7.17.	To H.Q. Guards Division.
2/Lieut. C. F. F. TWYNAM.	A.D.C.	8.6.17.	28.11.17.	Killed.
Capt. C. D. W. PARISH.	A.D.C.	29.10.17.	—.3.19.	
Capt. G. T. M. NEVILL.	A.D.C.	31.12.17.	—.5.18.	To England, sick.
Maj. C. R. STONE, D.S.O., M.C.	A.D.C.	18.5.18.	—.2.19.	
Col. Hon. F. GORDON, D.S.O.	G.S.O.1.	10.8.14.	5.9.14.	To Command 19th Inf. Bde.
Col. R. D. WHIGHAM, D.S.O.	G.S.O.1.	16.9.14.	26.12.14.	To 1st Corps as Brig.-Gen. G.S.
Lt.-Col. H. E. GOGARTY.	G.S.O.1.	4.1.15.	22.2.15.	To England.
Lt.-Col. L. R. VAUGHAN, D.S.O.	G.S.O.1.	22.2.15.	11.4.16.	To B.G.G.S. XVth Army Corps.
Lt.-Col. C. P. DEEDES, C.M.G., D.S.O.	G.S.O.1.	14.4.16.	7.5.17.	To War Office.
Lt.-Col. E. D. GILES, D.S.O.	G.S.O.1.	7.5.17.	4.1.18.	To Mission U.S.A.
Lt.-Col. E. R. CLAYTON, D.S.O.	G.S.O.1.	5.1.18.	26.3.19.	
Maj. A. J. B. PERCIVAL, D.S.O.	G.S.O.2.	5.8.14.	31.10.14.	Killed Ypres.

Name.	Appointment.	Date of Joining.	Date of Leaving.	Remarks.
Maj. L. R. VAUGHAN.	G.S.O.2.	7.11.14.	21.2.15.	To G.S.O. 1st Grade, 2nd Div.
Maj. F. A. BUZZARD.	G.S.O.2.	24.2.15.	23.7.15.	To 9th Division.
Maj. J. D. BELGRAVE, D.S.O.	G.S.O.2.	24.7.15.	12.9.16.	To Command a Battery, 33rd Division.
Maj. C. A. S. MAITLAND, D.S.O.	G.S.O.2.	13.9.16.	18.2.17.	To G.S.O.2 IInd Corps.
Maj. W. C. WILSON, D.S.O., M.C.	G.S.O.2.	19.2.17.	3.1.18.	To G.S.O.2. IInd Corps.
Capt. J. McD. LATHAM, M.C.	G.S.O.2.	6.3.18.	12.8.18.	To G.S.O.2. VIIIth Corps.
Maj. P. J. MACKESY, D.S.O., M.C.	G.S.O.2.	14.8.18.	22.10.18.	To G.H.Q. (G.S.)
Maj. R. C. W. G. FIREBRACE.	G.S.O.2.	23.10.18.	24.3.19.	To D.A.A. & Q.M.G., India.
Capt. L. A. E. PRICE-DAVIES, V.C., D.S.O.	G.S.O.3.	5.8.14.	24.9.14.	To G.H.Q.
Capt. W. W. E. SEGRAVE, D.S.O.	G.S.O.3.	5.8.14.	12.9.14.	To 17th Inf. Bde. as B.M.
Capt. R. OMMANEY.	G.S.O.3.	2.10.14	31.10.14.	Killed Ypres.
Bt.-Maj. C. F. WATSON, D.S.O.	G.S.O.3.	1.11.14.	23.2.15.	To England for New Army.
Capt. M. O. CLARKE.	G.S.O.3.	24.2.15.	10.6.15.	To VIth Corps as G.S.O.3.
Capt. E. H. DAVIDSON.	G.S.O.3.	11.6.15.	12.1.16.	To IVth Corps.
Capt. J. D. BOYD.	G.S.O.3.	12.1.16.	23.6.16.	To 5th Inf. Bde. as Bde.-Major.
Capt. C. K. STEWARD.	G.S.O.3.	25.6.16.	10.9.16.	To 143rd Infantry Brigade.
Capt. P. M. A. KERANS.	G.S.O.3.	11.9.16.	27.10.16.	To 9th Cav. Bde. as Bde.-Major.
T/Capt. G. M. GATHORNE HARDY, M.C.	G.S.O.3.	28.10.16.	27.12.16.	Rejoined Regiment.
Capt. W. J. JERVOIS, M.C.	G.S.O.3.	27.12.16.	10.8.17.	170th Inf. Bde. Bde.-Major.
T/Capt. F. M. HORNER.	G.S.O.3.	19.8.17.	22.7.18.	To England.
T/Capt. B. H. HARRISON, M.C.	G.S.O.3.	22.7.18.	—.1.19.	To England.
Lt. T/Capt. V. C. RUSSELL, D.S.O., M.C.	G.S.O.3.	3.2.19.	31.10.19.	To Regimental duty.
Lt.-Col. G. CONWAY-GORDON, D.S.O.	A.A. & Q.M.G.	5.8.14.	19.1.15.	To England.
Bt.-Lt.-Col. G. D. JEBB, D.S.O.	A.A. & Q.M.G.	7.2.15.	13.7.15.	To Xth Corps.
Lt.-Col. S. W. ROBINSON.	A.A. & Q.M.G.	15.7.15.	27.10.16.	To XIIIth Corps as D.A. & Q.M.G.
T/Lt.-Col. J. P. VILLIERS-STUART, D.S.O.	A.A. & Q.M.G.	28.10.16.	25.7.17.	To England to report to Indian Office.
Lt.-Col. E. ARMSTRONG, C.M.G., D.S.O.	A.A. & Q.M.G.	26.7.17.	17.7.19.	R.P. 18.7.19.
Bt.-Lt.-Col. W. A. WHITE.	D.A.A. & Q.M.G.	5.8.14.	18.8.14.	Invalided home.
Maj. F. F. READY, D.S.O.	D.A.A. & Q.M.G.	19.8.14.	1.6.15.	To 4th Div. as A.A & Q.M.G.
Maj. C. T. M. HARE.	D.A.A. & Q.M.G.	2.6.15.	12.2.16.	To England, sick.
Bt.-Maj. Visct. R. E. A. FEILDING, D.S.O.	D.A.A. & Q.M.G.	13.2.16.	24.2.17.	To 8th Division.
Maj. J. A. POLLOCK.	D.A.A. & Q.M.G.	11.3.17.	15.4.17.	To report to War Office.
Maj. G. H. BIRKETT, D.S.O.	D.A.A. & Q.M.G.	16.4.17.	17.8.18.	To G.H.Q., 1st Echelon.

Name.	Appointment.	Date of Joining.	Date of Leaving.	Remarks.
Bt.-Maj. O. H. TIDBURY, M.C.	D.A.A. & Q.M.G.	24.8.18.	23.2.19.	To Berlin.
T/Maj. C. G. LESLIE, M.C.	D.A.A. & Q.M.G.	24.2.19	—.4.19	
Maj. J. E. S. BRIND, D.S.O.	D.A.Q.M.G.	5.8.14.	13.7.15.	To Xth Corps.
T/Capt. Visct. R. E. A. FEILDING, D.S.O.	D.A.Q.M.G.	21.7.15.	12.2.16.	D.A.A. & Q.M.G. 2nd Div.
Capt. D. P. DICKINSON, D.S.O., M.C.	D.A.Q.M.G.	13.2.16.	6.11.17.	To Advanced G.H.Q. as D.A.Q.M.G.
T/Capt. T. D. STOWARD, M.C.	D.A.Q.M.G.	3.11.17.	—.2.19.	
Col. H. N. THOMPSON, D.S.O.	A.D.M.S.	5.8.14.	26.8.14.	Taken prisoner.
Lt.-Col. C. DALTON.	A.D.M.S.	27.8.14.	14.9.14.	Died of wounds 18.9.14.
Col. M. P. C. HOLT, C.B., D.S.O.	A.D.M.S.	16.9.14.	21.10.15.	To 22nd Division.
Col. W. L. GRAY.	A.D.M.S.	22.10.15.	5.1.17.	Home, sick.
T/Col. H. HERRICK, C.M.G., D.S.O.	A.D.M.S.	19.1.17.	13.10.19.	
Maj. F. S. IRVINE.	D.A.D.M.S.	1.6.14.	26.8.14.⎱	Taken prisoner.
Maj. P. DAVIDSON.	D.A.D.M.S.	17.8.14.	25.9.14.⎰	
Maj. F. S. IRVINE.	D.A.D.M.S.	25.9.14.	5.4.15.	Rejoined (Escaped).
Maj. O. IEVERS.	D.A.D.M.S.	11.5.15.	27.8.15.	To England.
Capt. W. B. PURDON.	D.A.D.M.S.	26.8.15.	25.3.16.	To Command 19th F.A.
Capt. E. SCOTT.	D.A.D.M.S.	22.3.16.	29.10.16.	Evac. sick to England.
Capt. K. W. MACKENZIE, D.S.O., M.C.	D.A.D.M.S.	30.10.16.	20.2.18.	To Command 9th F.A.
Capt. W. B. PURCHASE, M.C.	D.A.D.M.S.	2.2.18.	12.4.18.	To Command Hospitals, U.K.
Capt. E. B. MARSH, M.C.	D.A.D.M.S.	13.4.18.	—.5.19.	
Maj. J. BAKER.	D.A.D.O.S.	12.8.14.	29.1.15.	Left for New Army.
Major H. E. SMYTH.	D.A.D.O.S.	27.1.15.	10.1.16.	To Command H.Q. 1st Army.
Capt. H. J. L. PALMER.	D.A.D.O.S.	10.1.16.	12.2.18.	To A.D.O.S. XVth Corps.
Lieut. V. G. KNAPP.	D.A.D.O.S.	13.2.18.	2.12.19.	
Maj. F. C. STRATTON.	D.A.D.V.S.	4.8.14.	30.12.14.	To U.K.
Maj. D. BOLTON.	D.A.D.V.S.	1.1.15.	12.4.16.	
Capt. C. H. H. JOLLIFFE.	D.A.D.V.S.	9.5.16.	25.6.16.	To 3rd Cavalry Division.
Maj. A. N. N. SWANSTON.	D.A.D.V.S.	7.7.16.	23.2.17.	
Capt. L. L. DIXSON.	D.A.D.V.S.	3.3.17.	5.6.17.	To U.K., sick.
Capt. F. R. ROCHE-KELLY.	D.A.D.V.S.	22.6.17.	3.11.19.	
Capt. G. A. SULLIVAN.	D.A.P.M.	5.8.14.	9.2.15.	To H.Q. IInd Corps.
Capt. G. W. R. STACPOOLE, D.S.O.	D.A.P.M.	13.2.15.	15.12.15.	A.P.M. Vth Corps.
Capt. P. I. FOLEY.	D.A.P.M.	19.12.15.	30.1.16.	A.P.M. Adv. Base L. of C.
Capt. J. G. HALSTED.	D.A.P.M.	31.1.16.	20.1.17.	Evac. sick to U.K.
Capt. A. H. UPTON.	D.A.P.M.	20.1.17.	7.4.19.	

Name.	Appointment.	Date of Joining.	Date of Leaving.	Remarks.
S.S.M. ROWDEN, W.R.	A.S.C.	5.8.14.	21.3.15.	To England as Lieut. & Qr.Mr.
S.Q.M.S. HUMPHERSON, F.	A.S.C.	10.8.14.	12.8.15.	To H.Q. Vth Corps.
Sergt. BARRETT, F.E.	A.S.C.	5.8.14.	11.7.15.	To 4th Guards Brigade.
Corpl. ALLEN, S.	A.S.C.	5.8.14.		
Corpl. EVENS, R.C.	A.S.C.	5.8.14.	12.4.15.	To 2nd Division Train.
Corpl. SOLLETT, W.	A.S.C.	5.8.14.	5.10.15.	To A.M.S. G.H.Q.
Sergt. FRESHWATER, C.	R.E.	5.8.14.	13.12.15.	
S.S.M. HARRISON, G.	A.S.C.	19.3.15.		To H.Q. Fifth Army.
Sergt. CONNALLY, J.M.	A.S.C.	11.8.15.	9.8.15.	To Guards Division.
Sergt. GILLETT, J.F.	Queen's Regt.	11.8.15.	17.1.16.	To Base.
Corpl. SPENCER, B.C.	Royal Berks.	16.8.15.	2.6.16.	Returned to Unit.
Corpl. WHITLEY, C.	Herts Regt.	9.8.15.		To Fifth Army.
Corpl. TURNER, W.	A.S.C.	24.7.15.	15.12.15.	To Base.
Sergt. SMITH, G.	A.S.C.	11.9.15.	2.1.16.	To 55th Division.
Sergt. MARSH.	A.S.C.	13.12.15.	8.4.16.	To Base.
Corpl. ECCLES, R.	A.S.C.	28.12.15.	14.6.16.	To 12th Division.
Sergt. PRICE, R.	A.S.C.	12.4.16.		Killed in Action.
S.S. DUNLOP, H.A.S.	A.S.C.	7.10.15.		
S.Q.M.S. ALLEN, S.	A.S.C.	5.8.14.		
Sergt. WHITTAKER, A.	A.S.C.	11.6.16.	5.8.16.	To 1st Corps.
S.S. FIRTH.	A.S.C.	19.9.16.	1.2.17.	
S.S. SPENCE, N.	A.S.C.	10.9.16.	21.9.16.	To Base.
S.S. LOOMBE, R.M.	A.S.C.	3.6.17.		
S.S.M. BIRMINGHAM.	A.S.C.	21.9.18.		
S.Q.M.S. MAIN .	A.S.C.	8.11.18.		

Appendix XIX.

OFFICERS KILLED, OR DIED OF WOUNDS RECEIVED IN ACTION.

In Trench Warfare, 13th January to 16th February 1917.

17th January.
2nd Oxford and Bucks Light Infantry : Lieut. N. W. Hill.

19th January.
17th Royal Fusiliers : Lieut. W. W. Edwards (died of wounds, 22nd January 1917).

4th February.
22nd Royal Fusiliers : Captain R. L. Roscoe.

16th February.
1st Royal Berks Regiment : Captain N. West.

In the Actions of Miraumont, 17th and 18th February, 1917.

17th February.

1st King's Regiment : Second-Lieut. R. C. E. S. de Segund. 2nd South Staffords Regiment : Captain S. W. H. S. Douglas-Willan, Captain H. G. Tate, Lieut. J. D. Chipman, Second-Lieuts. F. Cave, W. Wright. 22nd Royal Fusiliers : Major J. Walsh (died of wounds, 19th February 1917), Captain L. Simons, Second-Lieuts. W. H. Payne, E. A. Burgess, S. F. Boulter (died of wounds, 18th February 1917). 23rd Royal Fusiliers : Captain D. L. Rattray, Second-Lieuts. C. Carpenter, E. N. Kentfield, A. Symons, R. H. Wiggen, T. Chubb, R. M. Morris. 1st King's Royal Rifle Corps : Second-Lieuts. J. J. Cragg, C. V. Erwood, P. Mason, Hon. G. Rowley, W. A. D. Eley. 99th Machine-Gun Company : Second-Lieut. A. E. Thomas.

18th February.

13th Essex Regiment : Second-Lieut. C. Stokes. 23rd Royal Fusiliers : Second-Lieut. G. C. de Beck.

APPENDIX. 703

In Trench Warfare, 19th February to 9th March 1917.

23rd February.

13th Essex Regiment: Second-Lieut. E. G. Munday.

6th March.

10th Duke of Cornwall's Light Infantry: Second-Lieut. M. A. Bucknall.

In the Capture of Irles (Grevillers Trench), 10th March 1917.

10th March.

13th Essex Regiment: Second-Lieut. V. A. Lavers (died of wounds, 22nd April 1917). 22nd Royal Fusiliers: Second-Lieut. N. S. Done. 1st Royal Berks Regiment: Second-Lieut. A. D. C. Brazies. 1st King's Royal Rifle Corps: Second-Lieut. R. W. B. Levett.

In the German Retreat to the Hindenburg Line, March–April, 1917.

12th March.

13th Essex Regiment: Captain C. W. Dunscombe (died of wounds, 13th March 1917).

14th March.

1st King's Regiment: Second-Lieut. H. Crowder.

In the Battle of Vimy Ridge, 9th–14th April 1917.

13th April.

24th Royal Fusiliers: Second-Lieuts. H. Daft, C. F. Stafford (died of wounds, 14th April 1917), Lieut. A. J. Lissaman. 1st King's Royal Rifle Corps: Second-Lieut. J. C. Blyth.

14th April.

17th Royal Fusiliers: Second-Lieut. R. A. Fergusson.

In Trench Warfare, 15th–27th April 1917.

17th April.

23rd Royal Fusiliers: Lieut. T. A. Aris. 17th Royal Fusiliers: Second-Lieut. S. W. Brodie.

21st April.

Royal Army Medical Corps: Captain R. H. Wilson, attached XXXIVth (Army) Brigade R.F.A. (died of wounds, 15th May 1917).

23rd April.

24th Royal Fusiliers: Second-Lieut. D. M. Allman. 1st King's Regiment: Second-Lieut. W. F. Bennett. 17th Middlesex Regiment: Second-Lieut. B. H. Last.

24th April.

1st Royal Berks Regiment: Lieut. A. R. D. Bacon.

26th April.

XXXVIth Brigade R.F.A.: Major V. Walrond, Major P. G. Bailey, Second-Lieuts. W. H. Manifold, H. T. Ball.

27th April.

2nd Highland Light Infantry: Captain R. A. F. Whistler (died of wounds, 27th April 1917). 2nd Oxford and Bucks Light Infantry: Second-Lieuts. G. C. Galloway.

In the Battle of Arleux, 28th and 29th April 1917.

28th April.

5th Field Ambulance: Captain P. E. Lones, R.A.M.C. 17th Royal Fusiliers: Second-Lieut. E. F. Beale. 2nd Oxford and Bucks Light Infantry: Second-Lieut. G. S. La W. Lyle (died of wounds, 29th April 1917), Second-Lieut. A. E. Walter (died of wounds, 13th May 1917). 2nd Highland Light Infantry: Captain W. A. Grieve. Second-Lieuts. G. D. Maclellan, A. B. Watson, G. B. Miller, J. M. Maclean, E. G. Taylor (died of wounds, 23rd May 1917). 5th Machine-Gun Company: Lieut. F. J. Hepple, Second-Lieut. J. F. Beck. 1st King's Regiment: Second-Lieut. R. P. Whiteside. 2nd South Staffords Regiment: Captain W. A. Simmons, Second-Lieuts. H. Johnson, J. J. Smith, R. S. O'Connor. 13th Essex Regiment: Second-Lieuts. C. W. Ritson, W. Brown-Paterson, D. H. Mason, J. A. Barrett, S. F. Vowles, R. Ibbotson. 17th Middlesex Regiment: Captain S. Read, Captain E. Parfit (died while prisoner of war), Second-Lieuts. A. White, J. S. Abercromby, F. S. Bonathan, A. R. Henderson, N. B. Dick, A. G. Secrett. 6th Machine-Gun Company: Second-Lieut. H. M'Cormick, 5th East Lancashire Regiment attached (died of wounds in German hands, 8th May 1917). 6th Trench Mortar Battery: Captain C. Wilkes, Lieut. A. L. Wade.

29th April.

22nd Royal Fusiliers: Second-Lieuts. S. F. Jeffcoat, E. C. Hodson, D. N. de Wet, R. Sanford, F. Stevenson, F. M. Perraton, E. M. Wardley. 1st Royal Berks Regiment: Second-Lieuts. M. A. Simon, G. M. Archdale (died of wounds, 30th April 1917), H. A. Gibbs, E. C. Ready. 2nd Highland Light Infantry: 2nd Lieut. D. M'Ara. 1st King's Royal Rifle Corps: Second-Lieuts. T. M. Hext, A. C. Graham-Roe. 5th Machine-Gun Company: Second-Lieut. G. H. Powell. 24th Royal Fusiliers: Second-Lieuts. V. K. Barnes, G. D. Griffiths (attached 5th Trench Mortar Battery). 1st King's Regiment: Captain P. R. Bland.

APPENDIX. 705

In the Third Battle of the Scarpe (Capture of Fresnoy), 3rd-4th May 1917.

3rd May.

1st King's Regiment; Captain P. R. Bland. 23rd Royal Fusiliers: Captain M. L. Hilder, Second-Lieut. R. C. Burgess. 1st Royal Berks Regiment: Captain O. J. Dowson, Lieut. H. F. R. Merrick, Second-Lieut. F. C. James (died of wounds while prisoner of war).

In Trench Warfare, 5th May to 4th October 1917.

5th May.

XXVIIIth (Army) Brigade R.F.A.: Major A. J. Bolster.

8th May.

17th Middlesex Regiment: Second-Lieut. S. A. Kempster.

26th June.

1st King's Regiment: Captain F. F. Ryan.

3rd July.

1st King's Royal Rifle Corps: Second-Lieut. M. G. Roberts.

16th July.

2nd Highland Light Infantry: Second-Lieut. J. B. R. Gemmell.

22nd July.

251st Field Company R.E.: Captain R. W. Hislop.

29th July.

17th Royal Fusiliers: Second-Lieut. S. F. Drummond.

17th August.

2nd Highland Light Infantry: Second-Lieut. D. Reid. 226th Field Company R.E.: Second-Lieut. W. W. Houston.

19th August.

24th Royal Fusiliers: Captain W. H. Bambridge.

20th August.

1st Royal Berks Regiment: Lieut. R. C. S. Baker.

27th September.

23rd Royal Fusiliers: Second-Lieut. H. P. G. Cornes.

28th September.

23rd Royal Fusiliers: Second-Lieut. W. G. J. Pratt.

APPENDIX.

28th November.

17th Royal Fusiliers : Second-Lieut. C. W. Sherwood. 1st King's Royal Rifle Corps : Second-Lieut. G. Goodwin.

In the German Counter-attack, 30th November to 3rd December 1917.

30th November.

1st Royal Berks Regiment : Captain E. P. Jackson. 17th Royal Fusiliers : Captain W. H. Stone, Lieut. S. Benzecry, Second Lieuts. C. F. Yellen, R. W. K. Cocker, J. Lucas (died of wounds, 28th December 1917). XCIIIrd Army Brigade R.F.A. : Second-Lieut. H. Payne, attached 2nd Division. 1st King's Regiment : Second-Lieuts. F. Hampson, C. H. Broadhurst (died of wounds, 1st December 1917). Royal Army Medical Corps : Captain J. M'D. Matheson, attached 17th Middlesex Regiment. 13th Essex Regiment : Second Lieut. E. C. Hall.

1st December.

2nd South Staffords Regiment : Second-Lieut. J. A. M'Kee. 17th Middlesex Regiment : Captain A. M. C. M'Ready-Diarmid, Second-Lieut. P. R. Hislop (died of wounds, 7th December 1917). CLXXIIIrd Brigade R.F.A. : Major R. L. Thompson, attached 2nd Division.

2nd December.

23rd Royal Fusiliers : Captain W. A. Fugeman. 6th Machine-Gun Company : Second-Lieut. A. R. Chapman. CLIIIrd Brigade R.F.A. : Second-Lieut. G. S. Whitehead. 17th Middlesex Regiment : Captain F. N. Stansfield.

In Trench Warfare, 7th December 1917 to 20th March 1918.

30th December 1917.

1st King's Royal Rifle Corps : Second-Lieut. W. R. C. Ffolkes.

27th January 1918.

2nd Oxford and Bucks : Second-Lieut. C. W. N. Barclay.

28th January.

10th Duke of Cornwall's Light Infantry, attached : Lieut. T. S. Reay (died of wounds, 1st March 1918).

1st March.

XXXVIth Brigade, R.F.A. : Second-Lieut. H. G. Shapland (died of wounds, 2nd March 1918).

7th March.

1st Royal Berks Regiment : Second-Lieut. J. A. G. Rimes.

9th March.

2nd Oxford and Bucks Light Infantry, attached 5th Trench Mortar

APPENDIX.

Battery: Captain E. J. Osborn (died of wounds, 13th April), Second-Lieut. W. H. Seale (died of wounds, 14th March).

In the Battle of St. Quentin, 21st–23rd March 1918.

21st March.

2nd Battalion Machine-Gun Corps: Second-Lieut. E. G. Meggit.

22nd March.

2nd Highland Light Infantry: Lieut. J. M. Mitchell.

23rd March.

10th Duke of Cornwall's Light Infantry: Lieut. F. B. Crouch. 24th Royal Fusiliers: Second-Lieuts. W. J. Coppard, D. R. Nyren, W. Remington. 2nd Oxford and Bucks Light Infantry: Captain W. J. Littledale. 1st King's Royal Rifle Corps: Second-Lieuts. P. Hambro, H. M. Barnet (died of wounds in German hands).

In the First Battle of Bapaume, 24th–25th March 1918.

24th March.

Brigadier-General R. Barnett Barker, General Officer Commanding 99th Infantry Brigade; Captain E. I. Bell, Staff Captain, 99th Infantry Brigade. 10th Duke of Cornwall's Light Infantry: Lieut. J. E. M. Wilkins, Lieut. S. C. McIntyre (died of wounds, 25th March). 2nd Oxford and Bucks Light Infantry: Captain C. H. B. Slocock (died of wounds, 3rd May), Second-Lieut. W. A. F. Bailey. 2nd Highland Light Infantry: Lieut. J. F. Tomlinson, Second-Lieut. D. B. Howell, Lieut. C. D. Mitchell (died of wounds, 26th March), Second-Lieut. D. Sheridan. 17th Royal Fusiliers: Major H. Pretty, Second-Lieut. F. C. Campbell. 1st King's Regiment: Captain E. R. Last, Second-Lieuts. G. E. Crawley, R. S. Tarran. 2nd South Staffords Regiment: Lieut. R. H. Poynder, Second-Lieut. J. Atkinson. 22nd Royal Fusiliers, attached 24th Royal Fusiliers: Second-Lieut. C. R. S. Coppack. 24th Royal Fusiliers: Second-Lieut. W. Neate.

25th March.

23rd Royal Fusiliers: Second-Lieut. H. D. Bird, Second-Lieut. C. A. E. Freston (died of wounds). 2nd South Staffords Regiment: Second-Lieut. J. Miller. 1st King's Royal Rifle Corps: Second-Lieut. H. D. West.

After the Withdrawal to the Old British Line on 26th March 1918.

31st March.

XLIst Brigade R.F.A.: Lieut. T. H. Fox, Second-Lieut. G. H. Perry.

APPENDIX.

In Trench Warfare from the Beginning of April to 20th August 1918.

14th April.
2nd Highland Light Infantry : Second-Lieut. T. H. Oldershaw.

15th April.
23rd Royal Fusiliers : Second-Lieut. D. F. Davies.

16th April.
2nd Highland Light Infantry : Lieut. C. F. F. Twynham. 1st King's Regiment : Second-Lieut. G. P. Williams.

24th April.
2nd Battalion Machine-Gun Corps : Second-Lieut. A. T. Birdseye (died of wounds, 25th April 1918.)

4th May.
17th Royal Fusiliers : Lieut. A. F. Menzies.

7th May.
23rd Royal Fusiliers : Second-Lieut. A. E. L. Dixon.

9th May.
24th Royal Fusiliers : Second-Lieut. A. Mackay (died of wounds, 10th May).

12th May.
6th Infantry Brigade Headquarters : Captain E. L. Wright, Brigade Major.

22nd May.
10th Duke of Cornwall's Light Infantry : Second-Lieut. W. C. Heath.

1st June.
1st Royal Berks Regiment : Captain E. D. D'O. Astley.

5th June.
1st Royal Berks Regiment : Captain J. H. Spencer (died of wounds, 5th June 1918), Second-Lieuts. S. C. Beresford, H. N. Avery, A. L. Row.

6th June.
17th Royal Fusiliers : Second-Lieut. G. H. Spicer.

7th June.
XLIst Brigade R.F.A. : Major J. E. M. Bromley.

2nd July.
1st King's Regiment : Second-Lieut. G. P. Wright.

APPENDIX. 709

5th July.
2nd Highland Light Infantry: Second-Lieut. W. A. Blair (died of wounds, 8th December 1918).

7th July.
2nd Oxford and Bucks Light Infantry: Captain G. H. Fuller.

23rd July.
1st Royal Berks: Second-Lieut. F. S. Boshell. 2nd Battalion Machine-Gun Corps: Lieut. M. W. Burgess.

27th July.
1st King's Regiment: Second-Lieut. W. Ellis.

14th August.
1st King's Royal Rifle Corps: Lieut. S. Barrand.

20th August.
2nd Oxford and Bucks Light Infantry: Second-Lieut. J. P. Sears.

In the Battle of Albert, 21st–23rd August 1918.

21st August.
XLIst Brigade R.F.A.: Lieut. E. A. W. Cruickshank.

23rd August.
1st Royal Berks: Lieut. W. L. Humbly, Rev. C. H. Bell, C.F. (attached 1st Royal Berks). 2nd Highland Light Infantry: Lieut.-Colonel W. L. Brodie, V.C., Lieut. T. Catto, Lieut. A. Bryan. 24th Royal Fusiliers: Lieut. F. L. Stocker. 1st King's Regiment: Captain R. E. Head (died 24th November 1918), Lieut. W. J. A. Pratt, Lieut. R. T. Reese, Lieut. G. V. Harrison (died of wounds, 26th August 1918), Second-Lieut. N. Erskine. 2nd South Staffords: Captain H. W. S. Hatton, Lieut. E. D. Rawson, Second-Lieut. E. R. Shakespear. 2nd Oxford and Bucks Light Infantry: Second-Lieut. E. A. Brown.

In Operations from 26th August to 1st September.

27th August.
XXXVIth Brigade R.F.A.: Lieut. A. M. Coate.

In the Battle of the Drocourt–Quéant Line, 2nd–3rd September 1918.

3rd September.
1st King's Royal Rifle Corps: Lieut. H. W. F. Ponter. 2nd South Staffords Regiment: Major B. C. Parr.

APPENDIX.

In Operations from 4th to 8th September 1918.
6th September.

1st King's Regiment : Major H. J. Duff, Second-Lieut. E. A. Wilson.

7th September.

XXXVIth Brigade R.F.A. : Captain R. M. Vaisey.   17th Royal Fusiliers : Second-Lieut. W. F. Hughes.

In the Battle of the Canal du Nord, 27th September to 1st October 1918.
27th September.

17th Royal Fusiliers : Second-Lieut. W. F. Williams. 1st King's Regiment : Captain E. Beesley, Second-Lieut. J. Shoreman, Second-Lieut. F. G. Cowman.

30th September.

2nd Highland Light Infantry : Captain E. L. Jones, R.A.M.C. (attached 2nd Highland Light Infantry).   17th Royal Fusiliers : Lieut. J. M'D. Bradley, Second-Lieut. H. D. Etheridge (died of wounds, 2nd October 1918).   23rd Royal Fusiliers : Lieut. F. Coull.

1st October.

2nd Battalion Machine-Gun Corps : Lieut. A. Adam.   2nd Highland Light Infantry : Captain G. C. D. Spence.   2nd Oxford and Bucks Light Infantry : Lieut. L. Bartlett, Second-Lieut. H. A. I. B. Stokes (died of wounds, 28th November 1918).

In the Battle of Cambrai, 8th–9th October 1918 : the Capture of Forenville.
8th October.

1st King's Regiment : Lieut. D. McCarthy.   1st Royal Berks Regiment : Lieut. C. C. Hedges, Second-Lieut. L. E. Savile, Second-Lieut. W. Tomey (died of wounds, 9th October 1918), Second-Lieut. H. Street (died of wounds, 24th November 1918).   XLIst Brigade R.F.A. : Major G. Messervy.

In Operations from 10th–16th October 1918.
10th October.

17th Royal Fusiliers : Second-Lieut. A. A. Gault.

Appendix XX.

APPROXIMATE TABULATED CASUALTIES OF THE SECOND DIVISION DURING THE YEARS 1917 AND 1918.

	Killed.		Wounded.		Missing.		Total.	Operations.
	Officers.	Other Ranks.	Officers.	Other Ranks.	Officers.	Other Ranks.		
1917.								
Jan.	1	27	3	143	1	3	178	Trench Warfare
Feb.	17	196	37	820	11	317	1,398	Miraumont, Grevillers, and German Retreat to Hindenburg Line.
March	4	64	17	372	1	30	488	
April	37	356	71	1,527	30	1,043	3,064	Trench Warfare & Battle of Arleux.
May and June	1	44	7	254	1	2	309	Third Battle of the Scarpe and Trench Warfare.
July	4	59	18	309	..	9	399	
Aug.	4	37	10	178	..	2	231	
Sept.	2	25	11	105	..	1	144	Trench Warfare.
Oct. and part Nov.	..	1	2	36	..	..	39	
Nov. 30–Dec. 6	12	264	49	1,165	14	622	2,126	Cambrai Operations.
Dec. 8–31	1	66	13	297	..	17	394	Trench Warfare.
	83	1,139	238	5,206	58	2,046	8,770	
1918.								
Jan.	1	27	3	170	..	16	217	Trench Warfare.
Feb.	..	41	6	231	..	3	281	
March	21	161	70	841	38	1,462	2,593	German Offensive & Trench Warfare.
April	4	81	14	351	1	30	481	
May	4	55	6	253	..	..	318	Trench Warfare.
June	5	51	18	288	..	3	365	
July	5	32	14	264	..	2	317	
Aug. 21–Sept. 15	26	255	107	2,546	1	216	3,151	
Sept. 27–Oct. 11	13	288	73	1,588	3	128	2,093	The Advance to Victory.
Oct. 22–Nov. 3	2	48	18	305	..	12	385	
	81	1,039	329	6,837	43	1,872	10,201	

Appendix XXI.

ADDENDA.

Page xii, line 17 : the date should be " 1815," not " 1814."
Page 38. For " Britton," read " Button."
Page 48. For " 10 p.m.," read " 10 a.m."
Page 112-13. Major-General H. R. Davies, C.B. (who commanded the 2nd Oxford and Bucks Light Infantry in 1914), writes : " The 5th Brigade formed up for attack along the Zonnebeke–Langemarck road from about Sheet 28, C.6.,d.2.1 to Sheet 20, U.29.,d.7.2, the 3rd Brigade of the 1st Division joining up with our left. The 5th Brigade advanced to a position extending from about Sheet 28, D.1.,a.5.8 to Sheet 20, U.30.,b.5.0 along the Stroombeek and Haanixbeek (Lekkerboterbeek in later maps). Here, owing to the 1st Division not coming up, we had to stop. . . . The story about 10 officers and 200 men being hit in a quarter of an hour is incorrect. . . . The Haanebeek of the 1914 maps is called the Steenbeek in later maps."

Page 143. For " 71st Battery (XXXIVth Brigade R.F.A.)," read 71st Battery (XXXVIth Brigade R.F.A.)."

Page 169. For " Lieut.-Colonel W. G. Fleming," read " Lieut.-Colonel C. C. Murray."

Page 257. The 1st King's Royal Rifles belonged to the 99th Infantry Brigade, not the 5th Infantry Brigade.

Page 304, line 10. For " 6th Infantry Brigade," read " 5th Infantry Brigade."

Casualty Omissions.

15th September 1914. 2nd Worcester Regiment: Captain G. R. Lea, wounded, and died of wounds ; Captain J. P. L. Stoney, wounded.

Add to page 472.

Staff changes had taken place as follows : Second-Lieut. C. F. F. Twynham joined the Division as A.D.C., and Lieut. C. D. W. Parish, A.D.C., left on 19th July to join Headquarters Guards Division. A new G.S.O.3—Captain F. M. Horner—joined on the 19th July, *vice* Captain W. J. Jervois, posted to 170th Infantry Brigade as Brigade-Major. The A.A. and Q.M.G., Lieut.-Colonel J. P. Villiers Steuart, left on 25th July for England, and was succeeded on 26th by Lieut.-Colonel E. Armstrong.

APPENDIX. 713

Add to page 531.

Between July 1917 and March 21, 1918, the following Staff changes had taken place : On October 29, 1917, Captain C. D. W. Parish returned to the Division as A.D.C., Captain G. T. M. Nevill joining on 31st December in a similar capacity. Captain T. D. Stoward assumed the duties of D.A.Q.M.G. on November 3, 1917, *vice* Captain D. P. Dickinson. On January 4, 1918, Lieut.-Colonel E. D. Giles, G.S.O.1, left the Division to proceed to the U.S.A., and was succeeded by Lieut.-Colonel E. R. Clayton. On February 2, 1918, Captain W. B. Purchase took over the duties of D.A.D.M.S. from Captain K. W. Mackenzie ; while on the 13th of the same month Lieut. V. G. Knapp became D.A.D.O.S., *vice* Captain H. J. L. Palmer. Captain J. M'D. Latham joined as G.S.O.2 on 6th March, *vice* Major W. C. Wilson, who went to IInd Corps.

Add to page 631.

Staff changes in the 2nd Division since March were as follows : Captain E. B. Marsh assumed the duties of D.A.D.M.S. on 13th April, *vice* Captain W. B. Purchase, transferred to England in command of a hospital. On 18th May Major C. R. Stone became A.D.C. to the G.O.C. 2nd Division. Captain B. H. Harrison assumed the duties of G.S.O.3 on 22nd July, *vice* Captain F. M. Horner ; while on 14th August Major P. J. Mackesy arrived as G.S.O. in succession to Captain J. M'D. Latham, who had been posted to VIIIth Corps. On 24th August Brevet-Major O. H. Tidbury succeeded Major G. H. Birkett[1] as D.A.A. and Q.M.G.

[1] Joined the 2nd Division Staff on April 16, 1917.

As footnote to page 681.

On 23rd October Major R. C. W. G. Firebrace succeeded Major P. J. Mackesy as G.S.O.2.

INDEX

INDEX

ABERCROMBIE, Lieut.-Col. A. W., 39, 40.
Aisne, Battle of the, 74 ; dispositions of opposing forces, 74–75 ; advance to the river, 76–77 ; 5th Infantry Brigade cross the river, 77 ; the Guards cross, but are withdrawn south of the river, 78 ; situation, night 13th September, 79 ; good work by the Sappers, 79 ; advance resumed, 80 ; artillery positions, 80 ; Private G. Wilson, 2nd H.L.I., wins the V.C., 82 ; the fighting at La Cœur de Soupir Farm, 83 ; position of 1st Corps at nightfall on the 14th Sept., 84 ; German guns outrange British artillery, 84–85 ; death of Lieut.-Col. Dalton, A.D.M.S., 85 ; casualties of 2nd Division at Battle of the Aisne, 86.
Aisne Heights, Actions on the, 86 ; relative positions of opposing forces on, 87 ; Divisional Artillery unable to come into action, 87 ; work of the Royal Engineers, 88 ; trenches, description of, 89 ; Brigadier-General Haking wounded, 89 ; " Black Marias," 89 ; position of 2nd Division on 19th September, 90 ; action of 20th September, 91 ; 15th Battery (XXXVIth Brigade R.F.A.) commended, 92 ; the 6-inch howitzers arrive, 93 ; good work of the Divisional Artillery, 94 ; stagnation sets in, 95 ; gallantry of the doctors, 96 ; the " Race to the Coast " begins, 97 ; casualties of 2nd Division on the Aisne Heights, 97.
Alban, Lieut.-Col., 567.
Albert, Battle of, 615 ; the 23rd Royal Fusiliers badly gassed in their assembly positions, 615 ; the attack goes like clockwork, 615 ; the 2nd Division gains and consolidates all its objectives, 616 ; success of the IVth, VIth, and Vth Corps, 616 ; orders for the attack on 23rd issued, 617 ; the three infantry brigades of the Division in their assembly positions, 618 ; the 6th Infantry Brigade attack and capture Ervillers, 618–19 ; action of the 5th Infantry Brigade, 619–20 ; death of Lieut.-Col. W. L. Brodie, V.C., 2nd H.L.I., 620 ; action of the 99th Infantry Brigade, 621 ; general situation north and south of 2nd Division, 622.
Ancre, 1916, Battle of the, 305 ; Allied scheme of operations, 305 ; objectives of Vth Corps, 306 ; front of attack allotted to 2nd Division, 306–7 ; bar-

rage table, 307; preliminary bombardment begins, 308; attacking battalions, 309; dispositions of battalions, 309–10; the attack, 311; the 6th Infantry Brigade in difficulties, 312; attack on the Quadrilateral by 13th Essex Regiment, 313; the 5th Infantry Brigade gains all its objectives, 314–15; good work by the Pioneers and Sappers, 316; the fighting about Lager Alley and Munich Trench, 316; the spirit of the troops, 317; general situation along the whole line about noon, 317; orders for the attack to be continued on the 14th, 318; attacking battalions, 318; attacks on Leave Avenue and New Trench, 319; the Berkshires attack Munich Trench, 321; fine work by the 99th M.G.C., 322; dispositions of 2nd Division on the night 14th November, 322; gallant conduct of the R.A.M.C., 323; attack on the Quadrilateral on the 15th, 323; an appreciation of the Gunners, 324; the 2nd Division is relieved by the 32nd Division, 324; losses of 2nd Division, from 13th to 16th November, 324; official summary of the results of the Somme battles, 1916, 325; a new Howitzer Battery (521st) joins the 2nd Division, 326; order of battle of 2nd Divisional Artillery at the end of November 1916, 326; Major-General C. E. Pereira assumes command of the 2nd Division, 326.

Ardee, Lieut.-Col. Lord, 89, 162.

Arleux, Battle of, 418; orders for the assault on Oppy issued, 418; dispositions of 5th and 6th Infantry Brigades, and of attacking battalions, 418; artillery arrangements, 419; the assault begins, 420; action of the 5th Infantry Brigade, 420–421; action of 6th Infantry Brigade, 421–5; general situation at 9 a.m., 425; the enemy's new system of holding his front lines a cause of failure of the attack of 6th Infantry Brigade, 426; position at 3.30 p.m., 427; the 99th Infantry Brigade takes over the line held by the 6th Infantry Brigade, 427; the attack to be resumed on the 29th, 427; objectives and attacking battalions of the 99th Infantry Brigade, 427; the attack opens, 428; the gallantry of Lieut. Jeffcoat and Acting Company-Sergt. Hogan, 428–9; gallant fighting by the Berkshires, 430; Lance-Corpl. J. Welch, 1st Royal Berks Regiment, wins the V.C., 431; the enemy fights well, 433; action of the 5th Infantry Brigade, 433; splendid work by the machine gunners, 434; the gallantry of the Sappers and Pioneers, 435; strenuous work for the artillery, and heavy losses during the operations, 436; official summary of the operations of April 28–29, 1917, 437; losses of the 2nd Division during the battle, 437.

Armitage, Lieut.-Col. G. A., 246.

Armstrong, Lieut.-Col. E., 712.

INDEX. 719

BAILEY, Major P. G., 436.
Baker, Major J., 187.
Bannatyne, Lieut.-Col. W. S., 124.
Bapaume, 1918, First Battle of, 560; situation of 5th Infantry Brigade on the night 23rd March, 561; position at midnight on left of 2nd Division front, 562; the battle opens, 563; the Bertincourt salient evacuated, 564-5; the 6th Infantry Brigade in a desperate situation, 565; gallantry of the machine gunners, 566; fine stand by the 2nd South Staffords, 567; tenacity of the 2nd H.L.I., 567; the 2nd Batt. M.G.C.'s splendid fight, 568 – 70; the Red Line reached, 570; retirement continued to the Bapaume–Péronne road, 570; the work of two gallant padres, 571; orders to retire to the Thilloy–Ligny-Thilloy line, 571; action of the 99th Infantry Brigade, 571-3; intrepidity of the Gunners, 573; situation of the 2nd Division on the night of March 24, 1918, 574; the 5th and 6th Infantry Brigades continue the retirement on the morning of the 25th, 575; a gallant exploit by the Pioneers, 576; rearguard action fought by the 99th Infantry Brigade, 576-7; orders issued for the formation of a defensive line east of Beaumont Hamel, 578; a great fight by the 17th Royal Fusiliers, 579-80; dispositions on the night of 25th March, 581; the battle ended —general results, 582.
Barnett-Barker, Lieut.-Col. R., 246, 286, 432, 433; Brigadier-General, 522, 548, 556. 573 (*death of*)
Barton, Lieut.-Col. P., 597, 675.
Battenberg, H.H. Prince Maurice, 130.
Beaumont Hamel, Capture of, 305. See under *Ancre, Battle of the*.
Behagnies and Sapignies, Capture of, 624; scheme of operations, 624-5; attacking battalions, 625; the attack on Behagnies a complete surprise and successful, 625; the capture of both places complete, 626; gains and losses of the 2nd Division from 21st to 25th August, 627.
Belgrave, Major J. D., 216, 304.
Bird, Major L. W., 236.
Birkett, Major G. H., 713.
Bolton, Major D., 248.
Bond, Major, 62.
Bonnyman, Lieut.-Col. F. J. C., 246.
Bourlon salient, Withdrawal from the, 508; the decision to withdraw, 508; results of the battle, 509; 2nd Division order for the withdrawal, 509-510; the 186th Infantry Brigade of the 62nd (W.R.) Division lend valuable assistance to the 2nd Division, 510; preparations made for the withdrawal, 510-11; withdrawal takes place unperceived by the enemy, 511; the enemy having discovered the withdrawal, advances, but is held up by the covering troops of the Division, 511; the withdrawal from the covering line, 512; the new line, 513; gallant actions by Gunners and infantrymen, 514-15.

Bourlon Wood, Capture of. See under *Cambrai, Battle of*, 475.
Boys, Lieut.-Col. R. H. H., xiii., 136.
Brady, Major, 555.
Brind, Major J. E. S., 216.
Brodie, V.C., Lieut. W. L., 150.
Buchanan - Dunlop, Lieut.-Col. H. D., 526, 568.
Bullen-Smith, Brigadier-General G. M., 248, 398.
Burt, V.C., Corporal A. A., 235.
Buzzard, Major F. A., 187, 216.

CAMBRAI, 1917, Battle of, 475; 2nd Division ordered to relieve the 36th Division southwest of Bourlon village, 476; why the Battle of Cambrai was fought, 477–8; the enemy's defences, 479; battle opens, action of the Tanks and situation until 26th November, 480; the 2nd Division relieves the 36th Division, 480; dispositions of the three infantry brigades, 480–481; general situation in the front line, 481; the Division lends assistance to the 62nd Division, 482; situation down to the evening of 29th November, and general results of the battle, 483.
Cambrai, 1918, Battle of, 669; the third phase of the great offensive opens, 669; objectives of 2nd Division and attacking battalions, 670; the first objective captured, 671; the enemy counter-attacks, using British Tanks, 671; the attack on Forenville successful, 673; the enemy disorganized, 673; the 2nd Division in Corps Reserve, 674; ruined Cambrai, 675; casualties of the 2nd Division since 27th September, 675; the end approaching, 676.
Canal du Nord, Battle of the, 656; the four offensives, 656; scheme of the battle, 657; plan of the VIth Corps, 658; the 2nd Division moves forward, 659; the King's and South Staffords attack Orival Wood, 660; 2nd Division takes over the front line from the Guards Division, 660; the advance continued and Cantaing Support and Nine Wood attacked, 661; both places captured, 662; the Rifles capture guns, 663; dispositions of 6th and 99th Infantry Brigades at night, 28th September, 663; attack again resumed on the 29th, 663–664; disposition of 2nd Division at 9.45 p.m., 665; the attack on Mont-sur-l'Œuvres, 666–7; general situation, 668–9.
Carrington, Major C. R. B., 361.
Carter, Lieut.-Col. B. C. M., 194, 231, 236, 237, 313.
Cavan, Brigadier-General the Earl of, 69, 108, 110, 114, 132, 143, 147, 150, 151, 158, 159, 160, 161, 162, 164, 175, 180, 181.
Cavan's Force, October 30–November 17, 1914; the operations of Lord, 160; formation of the Force, 160; the line taken up by the Force, 160; holding attacks by the enemy on 31st October, 161; trenches of the Irish Guards blown in, 161; position of the Force on the night of 1st November, 161; casualties sustained, 162; gallantry of Lieuts. Pepys and Pendavis

INDEX. 721

and Privates Merry and Hall, 162; the Force again heavily attacked on 6th November, 162; a new line formed, 163; terrible losses of the Irish Guards, 163; the Grenadiers heavily shelled on 10th November, 163; the achievements of Lord Cavan's Force, 164.

Chichester, Brigadier-General A. A., 174, 216.

Clayton, Lieut.-Colonel E. R., 694, 713.

Collingwood, Major P. H., 35, 36.

Connaught, H.R.H. the Duke of, 459.

Connaught Rangers, 2nd, at the Battle of the Aisne, Appendix V. (Vol. I.).

Conway-Gordon, Lieut.-Col. G., 187.

Copeland, Lieut.-Col., 42.

Corkran, Brigadier-General, 216, 246, 248.

Cotton, Major, 108.

Counter, V.C., Private J. T., 592.

Counter-attacks, November 30–December 3, 1917, The German, 484.

I. 30th November, 484; dispositions of units of the 2nd Division at dawn, 484–5; the enemy advances to the attack, 485; the storm breaks on the junction between the 2nd and 47th Divisions, 486; four posts of the Berkshires overwhelmed, 486; the splendid gallantry of the 17th Royal Fusiliers, 486; Capt. N. Stone of the 17th Royal Fusiliers wins the V.C., 486–7; the King's Royal Rifles hotly engaged, 487; the enemy mown down, 487; terrible casualties inflicted on the Germans, 488; the final attack on the Rat's Tail fails, 489; fine targets for the 18-pounders, 489; the attack on the Mœuvres sector held by the 6th Infantry Brigade, 489–90; dispositions of battalions of the 6th Infantry Brigade, 490; the attack on Lock 5, 490; heavy attacks on the gallant King's Regiment, 491; the 17th Middlesex rout the enemy, 493; splendid conduct of officers of the Essex and South Stafford Regiments, 494; the H.L.I. and 24th Royal Fusiliers moved up, 495; what happened at Lock 5, 495–6; artillery action, 497; fine work by the Lewis gunners and M.G. Companies, 498; the gallant Pioneers, 498–9; devotion of the R.A.M.C. 499; work of the Sappers, 499; results of the German counter-attack on November 30, 500.

II. 1st to 3rd December, 500; dispositions of units along the Divisional front on the morning of 1st, 501; the enemy attacks the King's and the 17th Middlesex, but is beaten off, 502; fine bombing by Capt. M'Ready Diarmid, 17th Middlesex Regiment, who wins the V.C., 502–3; the 6th Trench Mortar Battery makes good shooting, 503; dispositions later on in the morning, 504; dispositions on the morning of 2nd December, 504–5; the enemy's attacks continue, 505; action of the H.L.I., 505; the 22nd Royal Fusiliers also attacked, 506; the 23rd Royal Fusiliers attack

the enemy and capture a machine gun, 506; the enemy again attacks the H.L.I., but is beaten back, 506–7; the spirit of the troops, 507–8; position at midnight, December 3, 508.
Croft, Lieut.-Col. H. P., 246.
Crosse, Lieut.-Col. R. B., 621.
Cuinchy, Affairs of, 177; operations of 29th January, 177; the 4th (Guards') Brigade takes over the Cuinchy sector, 178; description of the trenches, 178–9; attack on the 2nd Coldstream on 1st February, 179; counter-attack, 179; good shooting by the guns, 180; a new counter-attack organized, 180; Lance-Corpl. O'Leary, 1st Irish Guards, wins the V.C., 181; all lost ground recovered and more gained, 181; plans for an attack on the Brickstacks, 182; attacking battalions and objectives, 183; the Brickstacks won in four minutes, 183; fine wiring work by the Sappers, 184; losses in the attack, 184; the 9.2-inch Howitzer ("Mother") used, 184.

DALTON, Lieut.-Col. C., 85, 89.
Daly, Brigadier-General A. C., 213, 246, 282, 292, 360.
Davidson, Lieut.-Col., 117, 174.
Davidson, Major, 89.
Davies, Brigadier-General R. H., xii., 22, 23, 68, 72, 93.
Davies, Col., 155, 156.
Deedes, Lieut.-Col. C. P., 247, 454.
Delville Wood, Battle of, 270; the 2nd Division joins the Fourth Army on the Somme, 271; orders for the relief of the 3rd Division in Delville Wood, 271; the 5th Infantry Brigade relieves the 8th Infantry Brigade in Waterlot Farm, 272; orders for the attack on Delville Wood, 272; dispositions of the 99th Infantry Brigade prior to the attack, 273; artillery arrangements, 273; the assault, 275; Delville Wood captured, 276; attack of the 23rd Royal Fusiliers, 276; the Rifles counter-attacked, 277; fine bombing by Lance-Corpl. Bell of the 23rd Royal Fusiliers, 277; Sergt. A. Gill, 1st K.R.R.C., wins the V.C., 278; gallant fighting by the 99th M.G. Company, 279; the position at night, 27th July; work of the Sappers, 280; effectiveness of the artillery bombardment, 280; casualties of the 2nd Division in the battle, 280; a German's opinion of the British barrage, 281; the 99th Infantry Brigade relieved by the 6th Infantry Brigade, 281; the South Staffords heavily counter-attacked, 282; casualties of the British army on the Somme from July 1 to 28, 1916, 283.
Denison, Col., 277.
Dobson, V.C., Private F. W., 96, 97.
Dooner, Lieut.-Col. J. G., 287, 361.
Drocourt–Quéant Line, Battle of the, 635; results of the Battle of the Scarpe, 635; scheme of the attack on the Drocourt–Quéant line, 635; orders for the attack issued by VIth Corps, 635; the 2nd

INDEX. 723

Division moves up to support the 62nd Division, 636; the 2nd Division to continue the attack, 636; scheme of the attack, 636; dispositions of the attacking battalions of the 6th Infantry Brigade, 637; the attack launched, 637; all objectives gained by the 6th Infantry Brigade, 637–8; action of the 99th Infantry Brigade, 638; the advance continued, 638–639; orders issued to continue the advance on the 4th September, 639.

Durand, Major A. A. M., 361.

EDEN, Lieut.-Col. A. J. F., 246.
Evans, Major P. M. A., 304.

FALKNER, Major, 36.
Fanshawe, Brigadier-General R., 93, 117, 132, 133, 142, 174, 175, 207, 213.
Feilding, Brevet-Major Viscount R., 248, 399.
Feilding, Lieut.-Col. G., 30, 35, 59, 89, 111, 112.
Fenwick, Lieut.-Col. H. F., 246, 255, 314.
Festubert, Battle of, 198; general situation, 199; orders for the attack, 199; attack by 1st Division fails, 200; the 6th Infantry Brigade moved up to attack through 1st Division, 200; the 2nd Division relieves the 1st Division in the line, and is ordered to continue the attack, 201; operation orders for the battle, 202; the objectives of the 2nd Division, 202; objectives of the 6th and 5th Infantry Brigades, 203; calibre of the guns employed, 203; assaulting battalions, 294; the attack begins, 294; two lines of trenches captured, 205; the 5th Brigade held up, 205; position of 2nd Division at 2 a.m., 16th May, 206; the Guards move up, 206; the attack on the 16th, 206; the position at 2 p.m., 207; how Lance-Corpl. J. Tombs, 1st King's Regiment, won the V.C., 207; the fatal policy of trying to squeeze out the enemy, 208; orders for the attack on 17th May, 208; the objectives, 208; disposition of the 5th Infantry Brigade at 9.30 a.m., 209; the death of Lieut.-Col. P. C. L. Routledge, 2nd South Staffords, 210; the 5th and 6th Infantry Brigades again attack at 3 p.m., 210; the Guards attack, 211; operation orders for the attack on 18th May, 211; the 2nd Division relieved, 212; casualties of the 2nd Division at Festubert, 213.

Fighting from November 1 to 10, 1914, 139; the work of the artillery under difficult conditions, 139; work of the Sappers, 139–40; Lieut. Martin Leake, R.A.M.C., gains a bar to his V.C., 140; work of the R.A.M.C., and Divisional troops, 140; the 2nd Division much scattered, 141; position of the 1st Corps at 3 p.m. on 1st November, 142; abortive attack by the French on 2nd November, 143; no brigade of the 2nd Division intact, 244; the Rifles lose three companies, 144; the German counter-attack of 2nd November, 145; summary of fighting on 2nd November, 146; the construction of " small closed works" begun, 147; German use of British uniform, 147; the Berkshires and Connaughts attacked on 5th November, 148; terrible plight of the 1st Coldstream, who were attached to the 4th (Guards) Brigade, 148; the H.L.I. attacked on 7th November, but cause the Germans heavy losses, 149; the 5th Field Company R.E. sent up as infantry supports, 150; Staff changes, 150; Lieut. W. L. Brodie, 2nd H.L.I., gains his V.C., 150.

Finch, Major, 146.
Firebrace, Major R. C. W. G., 713.
FitzClarence, V.C., Brigadier-General, 138, 155.
Forenville, Capture of. See under *Cambrai, Battle of*, 1918, 669.
Forsett, Major I. W., 136.
Foulkes, Major, 184.

GARFORTH, V.C., Corporal C. E., 23.
Gaunt, Major, 558.
Germany, The march into, 689; dispositions of the 2nd Division on the morning of 26th October, 689; the Division is relieved and becomes Division in support, 689; the Division relieves the 3rd Division, 690; the broken German army, 690-1; last raids by the 2nd Division, 691; La Longueville once more, 692; the Armistice, 692; the 2nd Division closes up for the march into Germany, 692; the march begun, 693; the 2nd Division on the old ground of 1914, 693; the story of the two swords, 694; the Division marches through Spa, 695; orders for the break-up of the 2nd Division, 695.

Gheluvelt, Battle of, 131; enemy reported massing near the cross-roads south-east of Gheluvelt, 131; junction of the 1st and 7th Divisions broken, 132; 2nd Divisional Reserve formed to meet possible events, 132; 1st Irish Guards sent to assist 1st Brigade, 132; position on 29th October, 133; the 6th Infantry Brigade attacked on 30th October, 133; the 2nd Grenadiers, 1st Irish Guards, and 2nd Oxford and Bucks L.I. sent off to Zillebeke under Lord Cavan, 134; signs of a big attack on the morning of the 31st October, 135; splendid tenacity of the 5th and 6th Infantry Brigades, 135; fine shooting by the 70th Battery, 135; high-explosive first issued to the 2nd Division, 135; attack against Gheluvelt develops, 136; Generals Monro and Lomax wounded, and other Staff officers of the 1st and 2nd Divisions killed and wounded by enemy H.E. shells, 136; the most critical stage of the battle, 136-7; the British troops vastly outnumbered by the enemy, 137; the charge of the 2nd Worcesters, 137-8; Worcesters' casualties, 139.

Gibson, Padre, 571.
Giles, Lieut.-Col. E. D., 454, 531.

INDEX.   725

Gill, V.C., Sergt. A., 278.
Givenchy, The 2nd Division delivers a " holding attack " at, 191 ; terrible condition of the trenches in March 1915, 191–192 ; why the Allies made attacks in 1915, 192 ; the Battle of Neuve Chapelle the first vigorous offensive of the year, 193 ; the 2nd Division ordered to make a " holding attack" from Givenchy, 193 ; the points of attack, 193 ; the assaulting parties, 193–4 ; the attack begins at 7.30 a.m. on the 10th March, 194 ; the South Staffords, 194 ; the King's Royal Rifles, 195 ; the King's, 194–5 ; results of the attack, 195.
Goff, Lieut.-Col., 291.
Gogarty, Lieut.-Col. H. E., 187.
Gordon, Colonel the Hon. F., 89.
Gordon-Lennox, Major Lord B. C., 163.
Goschen, Major A. A., 287 ; Lieut.-Col., 361, 584, 675.
Graham, Colonel, 141.
Gray, Col. W. L., 248, 398.
Gregg, Major R. H., 428.
Grevillers Trench, Capture of. See under *Irles, Capture of,* 377.
Guillemont, Battle of, 283 ; Sir Douglas Haig and Marshal Foch discuss the situation north and south of the Somme, 283 ; the Battle of Guillemont decided upon, 283; 2nd Division operation orders for the attack, 283 ; 5th Infantry Brigade's attack, 284 ; results of the first attack, 284 ; the position of the 6th Infantry Brigade in Delville Wood, 285 ; the losses of the Division in five days, 285 ; huge losses of the Fourth Army from July 1 to 31, 1916, 285 ; dispositions of 2nd Division on August 1, 1916, 285–6 ; orders for a second attack on Guillemont issued on 2nd August, 286 ; terrible artillery fire, 287 ; attack fixed for 8th August, 287 ; orders and objectives, 288–9 ; the 6th Infantry Brigade make the attack, 289 ; the attacking battalions, 290 ; how three companies of the gallant King's Regiment were lost, 291–2 ; the attack broken off, 293 ; the results of the 2nd Division's operations on the Somme up to August 14, 1916, 294.
Gwynn, Father, 184.

HAKING, Brigadier-General R. C. B., xii., 22, 23, 38, 72, 73, 89, 175.
Hale, Major, 468.
Hall, Col., 80.
Hankey, Major E. B., 138, 175.
Hare, Major C. T. M., 213, 248.
Harman, Major C. C., 271.
Harris, Lieut.-Col., 362.
Havrincourt, 1918, Battle of, 647 ; preliminary operations by the 2nd Division ordered, 647 ; orders for the main operation, 647 ; a picture of the battlefield-to-be, 647–8 ; the terrain well known to the 2nd Division, 648 ; objectives and attacking battalions for the preliminary operations, 649 ; the preliminary operation begins at 6.13 p.m. on the night 11th September, 650 ; fine fighting by the Oxford and Bucks L.I., 651 ; the H.L.I. gain their objectives, 651 ;

the line before the main operation on 12th September, 653; the main attack launched—result, 653; report of the operation by G.O.C. 5th Infantry Brigade, 654; the Guards Division relieves the 2nd Division, 655; general results of the battle, 655–6.
Herrick, Col. H., 398.
Hewett, Major W. G., 434.
Higgins, Major C. G., 246.
Hindenburg Line, German retreat to the, 390; the retreat began earlier than the official dates state, 390; hard work by the Field Companies R.E., 391; enemy "booby-traps," 391; the Bihucourt Line, 392; cavalry attached to the Division for purposes of the pursuit, 392; the red flares—enemy signals for withdrawal, 393; the Bihucourt Line and Biefvillers evacuated, 393; the 2nd Division Advanced Guard formed, 394; Sapignies occupied, 395; general situation at 11 a.m. on 18th March, 395; dispositions of 2nd Division at nightfall, 18th March, 396; the 2nd Division relieved on 19th March, 396; general situation along the whole front of the retreat, and the devastation spread by the enemy, 397; good salvage work done by the 2nd Division whilst in the line, 397; formation of the 2nd Division at the end of March 1917, 398.
Hohenzollern Redoubt, Actions of the, 241; general attacks of October 13, 1915, 241; the 5th Infantry Brigade only of the 2nd Division engaged, 241; line held by the Brigade, 241; the task given the Brigade, 242; gallantry of Lieut. Abercrombie, 243; results of the attack, 242–3; general results of the operations since 25th September (the Battle of Loos), 243; the 2nd Division has a new C.R.A., 243.
Holt, Colonel M. P. C., 89, 248.
Horne, General H. S., 27, 42, 175, 217, 247.
Hunt, Lieut.-Col. G. P., 553.

Ievers, Major O., 218.
Irles, Capture of, 377; preliminary operations by the 2nd Australian and 18th Divisions, 377; general situation after the Somme, 378; German plans for the retreat to the Hindenburg Line, 379; the enemy forced to retreat before the date projected, 380; orders for the attack on Irles and Grevillers Trench issued, 380; the 99th Infantry Brigade detailed to attack Grevillers Trench and the Lady's Leg Ravine, 380–1; how the Hun heartened his troops, 381; objectives and the attacking battalions, 382–383; the attack begins, 383; Grevillers Trench captured, 384; Lady's Leg Ravine also captured, 384–5; casualties of the 2nd Division, and captures, 385; splendid work of the 5th Field Company R.E., 386; results of the general attack, 386; terrible difficulties experienced by the Artillery, 387; the 6th Infantry Brigade relieves the

INDEX. 727

99th Infantry Brigade, 387; the advance continued, 388–389–90.
Ironside, Brigadier-General E., 588, 643.
Irvine, Major F. S., 36, 90.

JEBB, Lieut.-Col. C. D., 187, 216.
Jeffreys, Major-General G. D., 83.
Jones, Major W. H. F., 287.

KELLET, Brigadier-General R. O., 246, 280, 386, 398, 439, 440, 443, 522.
Kilby, V.C., Capt. A. F. G., 227.
King George, H.M., 170.
Knox Gore, Major, 694.

LA BASSÉE CANAL, 2nd Division moves back to the, 448; the state of the 2nd Division at the beginning of May 1917, 448; the Riflemen's School formed, 448; the Division moves back to the Oppy sector, 450; adventures in No Man's Land, 451; patrol work, 452; the 2nd Division relieved by the 5th Division, 453; and begins to move back to the La Bassée sector, 453.
Lambton, Lieut.-Col., 237.
Landrecies, Affair of, 33; dispositions of the 3rd Coldstream in the village, 33; a German cavalry patrol appears, 33; the enemy's attack, 34; dispositions of the 4th (Guards) Brigade in Landrecies, 34; Private G. Wyatt, 3rd Coldstream Guards, wins his V.C., 34–5; losses of the 3rd Coldstream, 35; the loss of the 4th Field Ambulance, 35–6; situation east and west of the

2nd Division on the night August 25–26, 1914, 36–7.
Langemarck, Battle of, 110; orders and dispositions of the 1st Corps, 110; 2nd Division operation orders issued, 110; Zonnebeke–Langemarck road reached, 111; action of 4th Guards Brigade, 111–12; action of 5th Infantry Brigade, 112–13; the 9th Battery heavily engaged, 114; the 1st Corps unable to reach its objective, 115; a defensive rôle taken up, 115; casualties of 2nd Division, 115; Zonnebeke evacuated, 116; abandonment of the original plan to turn the right flank of the enemy, 116; the enemy attacks the Oxford and Bucks L.I., 118; a counter-attack launched which captures 500 prisoners, 118; heavy attacks on the 5th Infantry Brigade on 23rd October, 119; orders for the relief of the 2nd Division by the 17th French Division, 120; the enemy admits failure, 121; the arrival of the Ninth French Army, 122; the 2nd Division takes over the line held by the 7th Division, 122–123; the Polygon Wood taken by the Division, 123; orders and objectives for the attack of 25th October, 124; the advance towards Becelaere, 125; action of the 4th Guards Brigade, 126; fine fighting by the 1st King's and 1st K.R.R.C., 127–8; the gallantry of the 6th Infantry Brigade, 129; dispositions of the 1st Corps, 130–1; information received of an impend-

ing heavy attack on Gheluvelt, 131.
Leake, V.C., Lieut. A. Martin, 140.
Loos, Battle of, 218; position at the end of summer, 1915, 218; decision of the Allies to use gas, 218; intentions of the Allied commanders, 218-19; dispositions of the British Armies, 219; extracts from Ist Corps and 2nd Division operation orders, 219-21; the preliminary bombardment begins, 221; dispositions of the 2nd Division for the battle, 222-3; the attack begins, but the gas is a failure, 223; attack of the 5th Infantry Brigade north of the La Bassée Canal, 224-5; attack of the 6th Infantry Brigade, 225-7; Capt. A. F. G. Kilby, 2nd South Staffords, wins the first V.C. at Loos, 227; attack of the 19th Infantry Brigade, 228-9; summary of the general attack, 229-30; casualties of the 2nd Division on the 25th September, the first day of the battle, 230; general situation of Ist and IVth Corps, 230; the formation of Carter's Brigade, 231; orders issued to Carter's Brigade, 231; results of the attack by Carter's, 232-3; general situation on the Ist and IVth Corps fronts at nightfall, 26th September, 234; no change on the 2nd Division front, during the 27th, 234; Corporal A. A. Burt, of the 1st Herts, wins his V.C., 235; Carter's Brigade ordered to attack at 2.30 a.m. on the 28th, 235; Sec.-Lieut. A. B. Turner, 1st Royal Berks Regiment, wins the V.C., 236; a bombing feat, 232; the break-up of Carter's Brigade, 238; the enemy's counter-attacks, 239-240.
Lushington, Lieut.-Col., 62.

M'NAMARA, Brigadier-General A. E., 643.
M'Ready - Diarmid, V.C., Capt. A. M. C., 502-3.
Mackesy, Major P. J., 713.
Maitland, Col. Viscount, 246.
Maitland, Major C. A. S., 304, 454.
March 1918, The last days of, 587; the three infantry Brigades of the Division bivouac behind Mailly Maillet on the night 26th March, 587; the 5th and 6th Infantry Brigades relieve brigades of the 63rd Division, 588; dispositions of the Brigades, 588; the Composite Battalion, 589; the weakened state of the 2nd Division after the March retreat, 589; the Division relieved, 590; the Division relieves the Guards Division in the Bertrancourt sector, south of Arras, 590; the King's heavily raided, 591-2; Private J. T. Counter, 1st King's Regiment, wins the V.C., 592; Brigadier-General A. H. Hart Synnot wounded, 593; Lieut.-Col. Brett, 1st Royal Berks, wounded, 594; the Division takes over the Bazeque Wood sector, 594; strength of the Division on June 8, 1918, 594; raids and counter-raids, 595-7; the Advance to Victory begins, 598.
Markham, Major R. A., 119.
Marne, Battle of the, 55; von

INDEX.

Kluck's tactical blunder, 55; operation orders, 56; the advance begins, 56; movements of 2nd Division on 6th September, 56–7; dispositions at nightfall of the British, French, and German armies, 59; advance continued on 7th September, 59; 1st Corps orders, 60; billets and bivouacs of the 2nd Division at night, 7th September; 1st Corps operation orders for 8th September, and summary of the operations of 7th, 61–2.

Marne, Passage of the, 65; position of the British Expeditionary Force on the night of September 8, 1914, 65–6; the Marne crossed, 67; lack of discipline of the enemy's troops, 67; the enemy encountered just south of Hautevesnes and attacked by the Berkshires and Rifles, 68–9; the South Staffords and Artillery also engaged, 69; the enemy beaten, and surrenders, 69; summary of the general situation on the night September 10, 1914, 70–1; the 2nd Division again moves forward on the 11th, 72; the march on the 12th, 73; the 2nd Division reaches positions south of the Aisne, 74.

Martin, Lieut.-Col., 424.
Matheson, Major T. H., 34, 62, 112.
Matheson, Lieut.-Col., 216.
May, Lieut.-Col. J. C., 246.
Messervy, Major G., 361, 673.
Mills, Major F. L. V., 361.
Miraumont, Actions of, 365; operation orders issued, 365; intentions of the Commander-in-Chief, 365; objectives of the 2nd Division, 366; 99th and 6th Infantry Brigades to carry out the attack, 366; the assault begins, 367–8; Sergt. F. W. Palmer, 22nd Royal Fusiliers, wins the V.C., 369; subsidiary attack by the 6th Infantry Brigade, 370; heavy losses sustained by the 99th and 6th Infantry Brigades, 370–1; devotion of the R.A.M.C., 371; horrible conditions in the line, 373; orders to gain ground wherever possible issued, 373; the advance continues, 374–5; future operations of the 2nd Division outlined, 376.

Monro, Major-General C. C., xiii., 23, 41, 108, 136, 172, 174, 175; Monro, Lieut.-General Sir C., 214.

Mons, Battle of, 19; concentration of the British Expeditionary Force complete, 19; dispositions of the French and German armies, 20; the British Force on the line Conde–Mons–Binche, 21; dispositions of the corps and divisions of the British Expeditionary Force, 22; orders to the 2nd Division, 22; the 2nd Division in its battle positions, 23; the Divisional cavalry engaged with the enemy, 23; Corpl. C. E. Garforth, 15th Hussars, wins his V.C., 23; the Guards in action, 24; dispositions and action of the 5th and 6th Infantry Brigades, 25; the artillery in action, and suffer casualties, 25; general situation at nightfall on August 23, 1914, 26; Sir John French receives information which compels him to retire, 26–7.

Mons, Retreat from, 27 ; the retreat begins, 27 ; the 2nd Division makes a demonstration, 27 ; the H.L.I., Oxford and Bucks, and the Worcesters at Frameries and Paturages, 27 ; position of the 2nd Division on the night 24th August, 28 ; the retreat continues to Noyelles, Maroilles, and Landrecies, 29–31 ; the Berkshires and Rifles engaged at Maroilles, 32 ; the Affair of Landrecies, 33–7 ; the retreat resumed, 37 ; the rearguard action of Le Grand Fayt, 39–40 ; why the Ist Corps could not have taken part in the Battle of Le Cateau, 40 ; billeting areas of the 2nd Division at night, 27th, 41 ; an enemy aeroplane shot down during the day, 41 ; the march to La Fère and billeting and bivouac areas on the night 28th, 42 ; the exhaustion of the troops, 43 ; position of the British Expeditionary Force at nightfall, 28th, 43 ; the 29th—a rest day, 43 ; casualties of the 2nd Division, 43 ; a further retirement made to the line Compiègne–Soissons, on the 30th, 44 ; billeting and bivouac areas of the 2nd Division at night, 30th, 45 ; the British line at night on 31st August, 45 ; the Rearguard Actions of Villers-Cotterets, 46–9 ; the position of the British Expeditionary Force at night, 1st September, 49 ; bivouac areas of the 2nd Division at night, 2nd September, 50 ; intense sufferings of the troops during the 3rd, 4th, and 5th September, 50 ; bivouac areas of the 2nd Division, 50–51 ; the retreat at an end, 51 ; the mileage covered by the troops in the retreat from Mons, 51 ; General Joffre informs Sir John French that he intends taking the offensive, 52.

Mons, Return to, 689.

Morgan, Lieut.-Col. R. W., 246.

Mory Copse, Capture of, 622 ; the 6th Infantry Brigade ordered to occupy Mory Copse, 622 ; the 1st King's detailed to carry out the operation, 622 ; the attack launched, 622 ; the attack of the King's checked, 623 ; the 99th Infantry ordered to relieve the 6th Infantry Brigade, and complete the capture of Mory Copse, 623 ; the Copse taken, 623–4 ; the 6th and 99th Infantry Brigades relieved by the 62nd Division, 624.

Murray, Padre, 571.

Murray-Lyon, Lieut.-Col., 574, 589.

NEUVE CHAPELLE, Battle of, 191 ; the 2nd Division delivers a holding attack at Givenchy as a secondary operation, 191.

Newcome, Major H. W., 94, 139 ; Lieut.-Col., 419.

Nonne Bosschen, Battle of, 151 ; enemy preparations for the battle, 152 ; the forces employed by the Germans, 152 ; the formation of the Prussian Guards Division, 152 ; the guns open, 153 ; the attack launched, 153 ; the line of the 1st Infantry Brigade

INDEX. 731

broken, 153; the enemy reaches the Nonne Bosschen Wood, 153; he is counter-attacked by the Oxford and Bucks L.I., and driven back, 153; the 5th Field Company R.E. as infantrymen, 153; the enemy fails to penetrate the Polygon Wood, 154; a small stretch of ground the only advantage won by the Prussian Guard, 154; the Gunners use their rifles, 155; a counter-attack organized under Brigadier-General Fitz-Clarence, V.C., 155; General FitzClarence killed, 155; general situation along the whole front, 156; the 1st Corps ordered to be relieved, 157; the enemy's belief that the British front line at Ypres was merely an outpost line, 158; conditions in the trenches at Ypres, 158; the 2nd Division relieved, 159; the 2nd Division resting and training, 159–60.

Norris, Lieut.-Col. S. E., 314, 388, 394, 395, 439, 441.

North, Major C. N., 141.

OLD BRITISH FRONT LINE, March 26, 1918; withdrawal of the 2nd Division to the, 583; the main line of resistance allotted to the 2nd Division, 583; dispositions of the 2nd Division at 8.30 a.m. on the 26th March, 583; the enemy follows the withdrawal, 584; the Divisional Artillery save the situation, 584; the New Zealanders arrive to take over from the 2nd Division, 584; the 10th Duke of Cornwall's L.I. in the trenches have

good "sport," 585; the 2nd Division withdrawn from the front line, 585; review of the operations of the 2nd Division from 21st March, 585–587.

O'Leary, V.C., Lance-Corpl. M., 181.

Onslow, Brigadier-General W. H., 177, 243.

Operations from August 26 to September 1, 1918, 627; the 2nd Division in VIth Corps reserve, 627; summary of events which were happening during the period the Division was out of the line in reserve, 628–31.

Operations from September 4 to 8, 1918, 680; the line held by the 6th Infantry Brigade on the night of September 3, 1918, 640; the Brigade ordered to clear the ground west of the Canal du Nord, 640; the King's detailed for the operation, and make the attack, 640–1; the terrible Spoil Heap, 641; a second attack to be made at 10 p.m. on 4th September, 641; the attack launched, but the Spoil Heap still defies capture, 642; the enemy withdraws, 642; the 99th Infantry Brigade relieves the 6th Infantry Brigade, 642; efforts made during the 5th, 6th, and 7th September to gain the line of the Canal, 643; the 5th Infantry Brigade relieves the 99th Infantry Brigade on the night 8th–9th September, 644.

Order of Battle of 2nd Division at Mons, 1914, Appendix I. (Vol. I.).

INDEX.

Osborn, Brigadier-General W. L., 655, 669.
Owen, Major L. M., 287.
PALMER, V.C., Lance-Sergt. F. W., 369.
Papillon, Lieut.-Col. P. R., 246, 259, 285.
Parr, Major B. C., 638.
Parry, Lieut.-Col. C. F., 361, 545.
Perceval, Brigadier-General E. M., xiii., 81, 83, 92, 175, 177.
Percival, Lieut.-Col. A. J., 136.
Pereira, Lieut.-Col. C. E., 97, 112, 132, 133, 141, 147, 148, 179, 180, 213; Major-General C. E., 320, 359, 437, 467, 495, 542, 574, 582, 655, 659, 688, 692.
Petit-Morin, Passage of the, 62; the Guards set out from Voigny, 62; Rebais found blocked, 62; the advanced guard approaches Le Tretoire, 62; the enemy opens fire with his artillery, 62; the Petit Morin crossed, 63; the capture of Boitron, 64; also of a complete German machine-gun company, with six guns, 64; bivouac areas of the three infantry brigades on the night 8th September, 65; the 47th Battery's little adventure, 65; casualties of the 2nd Division during the action, 65.
Phythian-Adams, Major, 318.
Pipon, Colonel R. H., 562, 574, 669, 681.
Pollock, Major J. A., 399.
Potter, Lieut.-Col. H. C., 246.
Prentice, Lieut.-Col. R. E. S., 246.
Pretty, Major, 572, 580.
QUÉANT LINE, Battle of the Drocourt-. See under Drocourt, 635.

Quiller-Couch, Major B. B., 361.
RANKEN, V.C., R.A.M.C., Capt. H. S., 96.
Ready, Major F. F., 213.
Robertson, Brigadier-General P. R., 216, 304.
Robinson, Lieut.-Col. S. W., 216.
Robinson, Major, 383, 386.
Routledge, Lieut.-Col. P. C. L., 212.
SANDERS, Brigadier-General S. H., 243, 361.
Sapignies, Capture of Behagnies and. See under *Behagnies*, 624.
Scarpe, Third Battle of the, 437; the operations undertaken solely to assist the French offensive of 5th May, 438; the scope of the British attack, 438; the 2nd Division, though exhausted, ordered to co-operate in the attack, 438; the formation of the Composite Brigade, 438-9; objectives of the Composite Brigade, 439-40; General Kellet's difficult task, 440; C Battalion gains its objectives, 441; B Battalion less successful, 441-2; action of D Battalion, 442; gallant work by the Pioneers, 442; situation at 11.30 a.m., 443; the Brigade relieved, 444; casualties and captures, 444; the general results of the Third Battle of the Scarpe, 444; the strength of the 2nd Division after the battle, 444; general results of the Allied offensives of April and May 1917, 445.
Scholfield, Lieut.-Col. H. P., 136 175.

Scott-Kerr, Brigadier-General R., xii., 22, 23, 46, 49.
Selle, Battle of the, 676; events which led up to the battle, 676; the battle opens, 677; the 2nd Division begins to close up behind the Guards Division, 678; the 5th and 99th Infantry Brigades receive orders to move forward, 678; dispositions of the 2nd Division at 7.15 a.m., 20th October, 678; position of the guns, 679; VIth Corps orders for the attack, 679; artillery arrangements, 680; preparatory moves of 2nd Division, 680; the attack launched by the 5th Infantry Brigade, 681–4; results of the attack, 684; the 5th Infantry Brigade relieved by the 99th Infantry Brigade, 685; the attack to be resumed, 685; dispositions of the 99th Infantry Brigade for the attack, 685; the attack, 686–7; at St. Python, 687; general summary of the Battle of the Selle, 688.
Shakerley, Major G. C., 194.
Shute, Major J. J., 246.
Situation in the spring of 1917, A Note on the general, 445.
Situation in March 1918, A Note on the general, 537.
Situation between March 21 and August 8, 1918, A Note on the general, 598.
Situation up to " zero " hour on 21st August, The, 607.
Sloan, Major A. T., 361.
Smith, Col., 156.
Smith, Major, 583.
Smythe, Major H. E., 187, 248.
Somme, 1916, Battles of the, 265; situation on the Western front which led up to the Somme battles of 1916, 265; three offensives decided upon, 265; preparing for the battle, 266; the enemy's defences, 267; the offensive launched, 268; number of rounds fired in the preliminary bombardment, 268; the enemy prepares to counter-attack, 269; the situation when the 2nd Division was ordered up into the line, 269–270.
Somme, 1918, First Battles of the, 537; the relative strengths and the general situation of the Allies and the enemy in March 1918, 537; signs of the enemy's intended offensive in March, 538; the German orders for the offensive, 539; strength of the British and the German forces engaged, 540; the 2nd Division relieved in the line on the night 20th–21st March.
Somme, 1918, Second Battles of the, 607; collapse of the enemy's offensive of 15th July, 607; the Allies' forces increasing, 607; plans and objectives for the Advance to Victory, 608; Germany's Black Day, 609; the results of the Battle of Amiens, 8th August, 609; the 2nd Division receives orders to capture Moyblain Trench, 610; preliminary instructions for the operations of 21st August, 610–11; preparations for the attack, 611; artillery arrangements, 611; the 99th Infantry Brigade to make the attack, 612; dispositions

of the attacking battalions, 612; good work by the Divisional Ammunition Column, 613; orders to the Pioneers, and the 2nd Battalion M.G.C., 614; German forces opposing the VIth Corps, 615.
Stafford, Major R. S., 439, 442; Lieut.-Col., 554, 555, 561, 573, 574, 576.
Stepney, Major H. A. H., 130, 163.
Steuart, Lieut.-Col. J. P. Villiers, 304, 712.
Stevenson, Major, 91.
Steward, Major C. K., 304.
Stewart, Rev. R. J., 233.
Stone, V.C., Capt. N., 486, 487.
Stone, Major C. R., 713.
Stormonth-Darling, Major J. C., 246.
Stott, Lieut.-Col., 196.
Stratton, Major G. B., 290.
Suttie, Major H. F. Grant, 361.
Swanston, Major A. N. N., 248, 398.
Sweetman, Major, 122.
Synnot, Brigadier-General A. H. Hart, 593.

Taylor, Lieut.-Col. St. L. L. H. du Plat, 361.
Thompson, Colonel H. H., 36.
Thorburn, Major, 684.
Tidbury, Major O. H., 694, 713.
Todd, Major W. M., 434, 526.
Tombs, V.C., Lance-Corpl. J., 207.
Trench, Capt. F. M. Chevenix, 136.
Trench Warfare, Beginning of, 86; the erection of barbed wire entanglements and trip wire, 88; kind of trenches first used, 89; conditions in the trenches in September 1914, 93; sapping begins, 95; hand-grenades of "hairbrush" pattern first used by the Germans, 96; the coming of the trench mortar, 96.
Trench Warfare, November 21, 1914–January 28, 1915, 169; H.R.H. the Prince of Wales attached to the 2nd Division, 170; sand-bags used as footmuffs, 170; the 2nd Division relieves the right of the Lahore Division, 171; the 2nd Division in the Festubert and Givenchy sectors, 171-2; hand grenades and rifle grenades used by the 2nd Division, 172; instructions for the co-ordination of bomb-throwing and bayonet attacks on the enemy's trenches first issued, 172; terrible conditions in the trenches at the end of December 1914, 173; sniping, bombing, and shelling the principal features of warfare during January 1915, 174; reorganization of the British Expeditionary Force, the Indian Corps, and the 27th Division, into the First and Second Armies, 174; General Monro appointed to command the Ist Corps, and hands over command of the 2nd Division to Major-General H. S. Horne, 175; the construction of redoubts and strong posts, 176; flares and Véry lights and searchlights in use, 176; the "gas-pipe" gun, 176; a "curtain of fire" first mentioned, 176; Givenchy lost and re-captured, 176; the enemy obtains a footing in the Triangle, south of the La Bassée Canal, 177.
Trench Warfare, February 20–March 9, 1915, 185; the 6th

Infantry Brigade attacks the Duck's Bill (Givenchy sector) on the 20th February, 185; formation of the attacking parties, 185; the attack launched, 185–6; results and casualties of the attack, 186; H.R.H. the Prince of Wales again attached to the 2nd Division as extra G.S.O. 3, 186; the 5th King's join the 2nd Division, 186; the 22nd Battery of the XXXIVth Brigade R.F.A. leaves the 2nd Division, 186; at the end of February the 4th (Guards) Brigade holds the Cuinchy sector, and the 6th Infantry Brigade the Givenchy sector, 187; Staff changes in the Division during January and February 1915, 187.

Trench Warfare, March 14–April 30, 1915, 196; the 35th (Heavy) Battery leaves the Division, 196; the 7th King's join the 2nd Division, 196; British trench mortars silence the enemy's mortars, 197; the catapult bomb-thrower issued, 197; the first appearance of "whizz-bangs," 197; Bangalore torpedoes first mentioned, 197; improvised gas-masks issued, 197; B Squadron 15th Hussars leave the 2nd Division and replaced by the Irish Horse, 198; a new type of minenwerfer shell used by the enemy, 198; mining and counter-mining active on both sides, 198.

Trench Warfare, May 21–September 24, 1915, 213; changes in the 2nd Division, 213; the 2nd Division marches south of the La Bassée Canal, and takes over a portion of the French front on the right of the 47th Division, 213; the First Army temporarily reorganized, 213–14; the Howitzer Brigades broken up which involves the XLIVth (Howitzer) Brigade R.F.A. of the 2nd Division, 214; liquid fire first used by the enemy, 214; Mills and "T. and P." grenades in use, 215; the West bomb thrower, 215; Battye bombs mentioned, 215; mining operations, 215; the 2nd Royal Inniskilling Fusiliers leave the 2nd Division, and are replaced by the 1st Queen's Royal West Surrey Regiment, 216; Staff changes in July, 216; the 4th (Guards) Brigade leaves the 2nd Division on the formation of the Guards Division, 216; the 19th Infantry Brigade joins the Division in place of the Guards, 216; the mining work and crater fighting of the 2nd Division praised by the Commander-in-Chief, 217; aerial torpedoes first used by the enemy against the 2nd Division, 217; retaliatory measures adopted, 217.

Trench Warfare, November 1915–July 1916, 244; trench fighting, bombing, raiding, mining, and counter-mining features of the fighting in November and December 1915, 244; description of raiding or "cutting out" parties, 245; the old divisions of the Regular Army losing their original character by the influx of New Army troops, 245; the 19th Infantry Brigade transferred from the 2nd Division to the 33rd Division, and the 99th Infantry Brigade joins the 2nd Division, 245; the 11th Field Company R.E., the 2nd Battalion Worcester, and 1st Queen's Regiment leave the 2nd Division, 245; the 13th Essex and 17th Middlesex Regiment join the Division, 245; the order of battle of the three infantry brigades of the 2nd Division on December 15, 1915, 246; the 5th King's and the 9th H.L.I. leave the 2nd Division, 246; the 1st Herts also leave the Division, bringing the infantry brigades back to a four-battalion formation, 247; Major-General H. S. Horne leaves the 2nd Division, and hands over command to Major-General H. S. Walker, V.C., 247; Staff changes, 247-8; Gibson's Crater, 249; bad condition of the trenches, 250; a retaliatory bombardment, 251; Field-Marshal Sir J. D. P. French, G.C.B., O.M., G.C.V.O., K.C.M.G., relinquishes his command, and returns to England, 252; General Sir Douglas Haig, G.C.B., K.C.I.E., K.C.V.O., assumes command of the British Army in the field, 252; the 2nd Division in the Angres–Calonne sector, 252; artillery changes, 252; the 2nd Division in the Souchez–Angres area, 253; the Berkshires and the 22nd Royal Fusiliers lose heavily in an enemy attack, 253-4; the 17th Middlesex make their first attack, 255-7; the 13th Essex make a fine raid, 258-9.

Trench Warfare, August 19–October 31, 1916, 294; the 2nd Division just south of Hebuterne, 294-5; patrol work by the H.L.I., 295; work on the trenches, 296; general situation on the Somme at the close of August 1916, 296-7; three raids made on the enemy on the night 14th–15th September, 297-9; the 1st King's raid the enemy, 300; the South Staffords lose heavily in an enemy bombardment to which the guns of the 2nd Division are unable to reply owing to the restriction of ammunition, 301; the King's Royal Rifles raid the enemy, 301-2; a period of training in preparation for the Battle of the Ancre, 302-3; the Divisional Artillery remains in the line, and subjects the enemy to heavy bombardments, cutting his wire, and smashing his trenches, 303; Staff changes, 304.

Trench Warfare, January 13–February 16, 1917, 357; the 2nd Division relieves the 51st Division in the Courcelette sector, 357; the situation as described in the official dispatches, after the Battle of the Ancre, 357; description of the Courcelette sector, 359; the 5th Infantry Brigade takes over the front line, 359; hard conditions in the line, 360; Brigadier-General A. C.

INDEX. 737

Daly invalided home, and is succeeded in command of the 6th Infantry Brigade by Brigadier-General R. K. Walsh, 360; the Divisional Artillery again reorganized, 361; the Berkshires ordered to raid the enemy, 361-2; the raid begins, 362; the raid a great success, 363; the 17th Royal Fusiliers raid the enemy and take more prisoners, 364; the enemy raids the 17th Royal Fusiliers, 364.

Trench Warfare, June 20–October 4, 1917, 454; after nearly two years the 2nd Division is back again in the Givenchy sector, 454; the 6th Infantry Brigade takes over the front line, 454; the Duck's Bill again, 454; the 99th Infantry Brigade takes over the Cambrin sector, and the 5th Infantry Brigade the Cuinchy sector, 455; each brigade ordered to prepare to raid the enemy, 456; the enemy raids the 1st King's Regiment, 456-8; he raids the 23rd Royal Fusiliers, but is unsuccessful, 458; H.R.H. the Duke of Connaught inspects the 2nd H.L.I., 459; a smart patrol of the 13th Essex Regiment enters the enemy's trenches, 459; description of front line held by the 99th Infantry Brigade, 459; Death or Glory Sap attacked by an enemy patrol, but attackers repulsed, 460; Tino, Ferdy, and Karl —trench mortars, 461; the Portuguese are raided by the enemy, 461; the 24th Royal Fusiliers raided, 461; various raids made by the enemy, 462; why the 2nd Division did not raid the enemy's trenches more often, 463; a big raid by the 23rd Royal Fusiliers on the enemy, preceded by an oil projection—the first used by the 2nd Division, 464; results of the raid, 465; the corporal's pants, 465; the enemy raids the 17th Royal Fusiliers, 466; raids by the 1st King's and 2nd H.L.I., 466-7; " Murray's Light Infantry "—a deception practised on the enemy, 466; the 242nd M.G. Company joins the 2nd Division, 467; the Division gradually gains strength after its terrible exhaustion following the operations in the Oppy sector, 468; lethal gas and phosphorus bombs, 469; general situation in September 1917, 470; the enemy heavily " gassed," 471.

Trench Warfare, December 7, 1917–March 20, 1918, 515; the 2nd Division settles down to trench warfare after the Bourlon Wood – Mœuvres operations, 516; conditions in the line, 516; improving the line, 517; the enemy attacks with flammenwerfer, 518; the enemy raids the 22nd Royal Fusiliers, but fails, 519; he again fails in an attempt to raid the 17th Royal Fusiliers, 520; hard work by the Sappers, 520; splendid salvage work by the 2nd Division, 521; the Division relieved, 521; three weeks' rest, and then the Division moves into the La

Vacquerie sector, 521; description of the front line, 522; three gallant battalions disbanded, 523; organization of the three infantry brigades on the disbandment of three battalions, 523–4; the Vth Corps front reorganized, 524; first rumours of the great German offensive of March 1918, 525; the formation of the 2nd Battalion M.G.C., 525–6; on the eve of great events, 527; the 17th Royal Fusiliers raid the enemy, 528–9; the Divisional area heavily shelled by " rum jars," 529; mustard gas poured on to the Divisional area, 529; terrible effect of the gas on the troops, 530; the 2nd Division is relieved on the eve of the great German offensive, 531.
Truman, Major A. J., 32.
Turner, V.C., Sec.-Lieut. A. B., 236.
Tyler, Major A. H., 154.

VAUGHAN, Major L. R., 150; Lieut.-Col. L. R., 187, 247.
Vernon, Lieut.-Col. H. A., 439, 441.
Victoria Cross, Recipients of:—
 Brodie, W. L., Lieut., 2nd H.L.I., 150.
 Burt, A. A., 1,665, Corpl., 1st Batt. Herts Regt. (T.F.), 235.
 Counter, J. T., Pte., 1st Batt. King's Liverpool Regt., 592.
 Dobson, F. W., L.-Corpl., 2nd Batt. Coldstream Guards, 96–7.
 Garforth, C. E., Corpl., 15th Hussars, 23.
 Gill, A., Sergt., 1st Batt. King's Royal Rifle Corps, 278.
 Kilby, A. F. G., Capt., 2nd Batt. South Staffordshire Regt., 227.
 Martin - Leake, A., Lieut., R.A.M.C., 140.
 M'Ready-Diarmid, A. M. C., Capt., 17th (S.) Batt. Middlesex Regt., 502–3.
 O'Leary, M., L.-Corpl., 1st Batt. Irish Guards, 181.
 Palmer, F. W., L.-Sergt. (afterwards Second - Lieut.), 22nd Royal Fusiliers, 369.
 Ranken, H. S., Capt., R.A.M.C., 96.
 Stone, W. N., Capt., 17th (S.) Batt. Royal Fusiliers, 486–7.
 Tombs, J., L.-Corpl., 1st Batt. King's Liverpool Regt., 207.
 Turner, A. B., Sec.-Lieut., 1st Royal Berkshire Regt., 236.
 Welch, J., L.-Corpl., 1st Batt. Royal Berkshire Regt., 431.
 Wilson, G., Pte., 2nd Batt. H.L.I., 82.
 Wyatt, G. H., L.-Corpl., 3rd Batt. Coldstream Guards, 34–5.
Villers-Cotterets, Rearguard Actions of, 46; dispositions and moves of the 2nd Division on the morning of September 1, 1914, 46; the Guards Brigade passes through the 6th Infantry Brigade in order to take up a position from which to cover the retirement of the 6th and 5th Infantry Brigades, 47; dispositions of the four Guards battalions when attacked by the enemy, 47; the action begun, 48; the Guards fall back through the 6th Infantry Brigade, south of Villers-Cotterets, 48; casualties of the Guards Brigade, which included Brigadier-General Scott Kerr, wounded, 49; billeting areas of the Guards on the night 1st–2nd September, 49.

INDEX. 739

Vimy Ridge, Battle of, 405; dispositions of the 2nd Division on March 30, 1917, 405; the Allied scheme of operations in the spring of 1917, 405–7; the corps scheme of operations, 407–8; the enemy's lines heavily bombarded, and a gunner's description of the effect, 408; the offensive opens, 409; orders received by the 2nd Division to relieve the 51st Division in the line on the night 11th–12th April, 409; description of the Divisional front, 410; the enemy withdraws, 411; the Divisional front gradually extended, 412; the Divisional front on the night 14th April, 413; results of the British offensive, and the enemy's disappointment, 413.

Vitre, Major P. Denis de, 128.

WALES, H.R.H. the Prince of, 170, 186.
Walker, V.C., Major-General H. S., 247, 270, 320.
Walrond, Major Victor, 282, 308, 361, 436.
Walsh, Brigadier-General R. K., 360, 396, 398, 593.
Walsh, Major R., 368, 371.
Warner, Major Lee, 287.
Watson, Brevet-Major C., 150.
Webber, Major, 156.
Welch, V.C., Lance-Corpl. J., 431.
Westmacott, Lieut.-Col. C. B., 89, 108, 109, 141, 143.

Weston, Lieut.-Col. S. V. P., 439, 443, 578, 579, 580.
Whigham, Col. R. D., 89, 136, 174, 187.
Whiteman, Major H., 559.
Wilding, Lieut.-Col. C. A., 176.
Wilkinson, Major A. C., 95.
Willan, Brigadier-General F. G., 594.
Wilson, Major W. C., 454, 713.
Wilson, V.C., Private G., 82.
Winter, Major E. A., 440; Lieut.-Col., 572, 573.
Wood, Major G. F., 597.
Wyatt, V.C., Private G., 34, 35.

YPRES, 1914, Battles of, 101; stagnation on the Aisne and life in the trenches during September 1914, 101; reasons for the withdrawal of the British Force from the Aisne, 101; the "race to the coast," 102; outline of operations of the British Force on leaving the Aisne, 102–3; the formation of the new Fourth German Army in Belgium, 103; relief and entrainment of the 2nd Division for St. Omer, 104–6; scheme of operations in the Ypres area, 107; the 2nd Division ordered to advance, 108; at nightfall on 20th October the 2nd Division reaches all its objectives ready for the battle to open, 109.

www.ingramcontent.com/pod-product-compliance
Lightning Source LLC
Chambersburg PA
CBHW061924220426
43662CB00012B/1797